The Outdoor Athlete

Courtenay Schurman
Doug Schurman

Human Kinetics

Library of Congress Cataloging-in-Publication Data

Schurman, Courtenay, 1966-
The outdoor athlete / Courtenay Schurman, Doug Schurman.
p. cm.
Includes bibliographical references.
ISBN-13: 978-0-7360-7611-1 (soft cover)
ISBN-10: 0-7360-7611-5 (soft cover)
1. Outdoor recreation. 2. Physical education and training.
I. Schurman, Doug, 1968- II. Title.
GV191.6.S38 2009
796.5--dc22

2008027380

ISBN-10: 0-7360-7611-5 (Print)
ISBN-13: 978-0-7360-7611-1 (Print)
ISBN-10: 0-7360-8168-2 (Adobe PDF)
ISBN-13: 978-0-7360-8168-9 (Adobe PDF)

This publication is written and published to provide accurate and authoritative information relevant to the subject matter presented. It is published and sold with the understanding that the author and publisher are not engaged in rendering legal, medical, or other professional services by reason of their authorship or publication of this work. If medical or other expert assistance is required, the services of a competent professional person should be sought.

The Web addresses cited in this text were current as of August 2008, unless otherwise noted.

Acquisitions Editor: Laurel Plotzke; **Developmental Editor:** Amanda Eastin-Allen; **Assistant Editor:** Laura Podeschi; **Copyeditor:** Jocelyn Engman; **Proofreader:** Darlene Rake; **Graphic Designer:** Nancy Rasmus; **Graphic Artist:** Francine Hamerski; **Cover Designer:** Keith Blomberg; **Photographers (cover):** main © Brand X Pictures, lower left/right © PhotoDisc, lower center © EyeWire; **Photographer (interior):** Neil Bernstein, unless otherwise noted; **Photo Asset Manager:** Laura Fitch; **Visual Production Assistant:** Joyce Brumfield; **Photo Office Assistant:** Jason Allen; **Art Manager:** Kelly Hendren; **Associate Art Manager:** Alan L. Wilborn; **Illustrator:** Mic Greenberg; **Printer:** Sheridan Books

Human Kinetics books are available at special discounts for bulk purchase. Special editions or book excerpts can also be created to specification. For details, contact the Special Sales Manager at Human Kinetics.

Printed in the United States of America 10 9 8 7 6 5 4 3 2 1

Human Kinetics
Web site: www.HumanKinetics.com

United States: Human Kinetics
P.O. Box 5076
Champaign, IL 61825-5076
800-747-4457
e-mail: humank@hkusa.com

Canada: Human Kinetics
475 Devonshire Road Unit 100
Windsor, ON N8Y 2L5
800-465-7301 (in Canada only)
e-mail: info@hkcanada.com

Europe: Human Kinetics
107 Bradford Road
Stanningley
Leeds LS28 6AT, United Kingdom
+44 (0) 113 255 5665
e-mail: hk@hkeurope.com

Australia: Human Kinetics
57A Price Avenue
Lower Mitcham, South Australia 5062
08 8372 0999
e-mail: info@hkaustralia.com

New Zealand: Human Kinetics
Division of Sports Distributors NZ Ltd.
P.O. Box 300 226 Albany
North Shore City
Auckland
0064 9 448 1207
e-mail: info@humankinetics.co.nz

For Brooke, who inspires us daily to match her courage, curiosity, creativity, and compassion and constantly reminds us of our family and business motto: Don't just dream it, live it.

Contents

Guide to Muscles vi
Acknowledgments viii

PART I Foundation for Outdoor Fitness

1 **Principles of Training** **2**
2 **Fitness Assessment and Adaptation** **18**
3 **Increasing Endurance** **36**
4 **Maximizing Strength** **47**
5 **Fueling for Outdoor Pursuits** **66**
6 **Overcoming Environmental Challenges** **78**

PART II Conditioning for Specific Activities

7 **Hiking, Trekking, and Backpacking** **88**
8 **Alpine Scrambling and Mountaineering** **104**
9 **Rock and Ice Climbing** **120**
10 **Trail Running** **144**
11 **Off-Road Biking** **158**
12 **Canoeing, Kayaking, and Rafting** **170**
13 **Snowshoeing, Cross-Country Skiing, and Backcountry Skiing** **186**

PART III Exercises for Peak Performance

Exercise Finder 206

14 **Flexibility and Mobility** **212**

15 **Body Stabilization and Support** **220**

16 **Strength** **241**

Appendix: Test Results Tracking Forms 279
References 284
Suggested Readings 286
About the Authors 288

Guide to Muscles

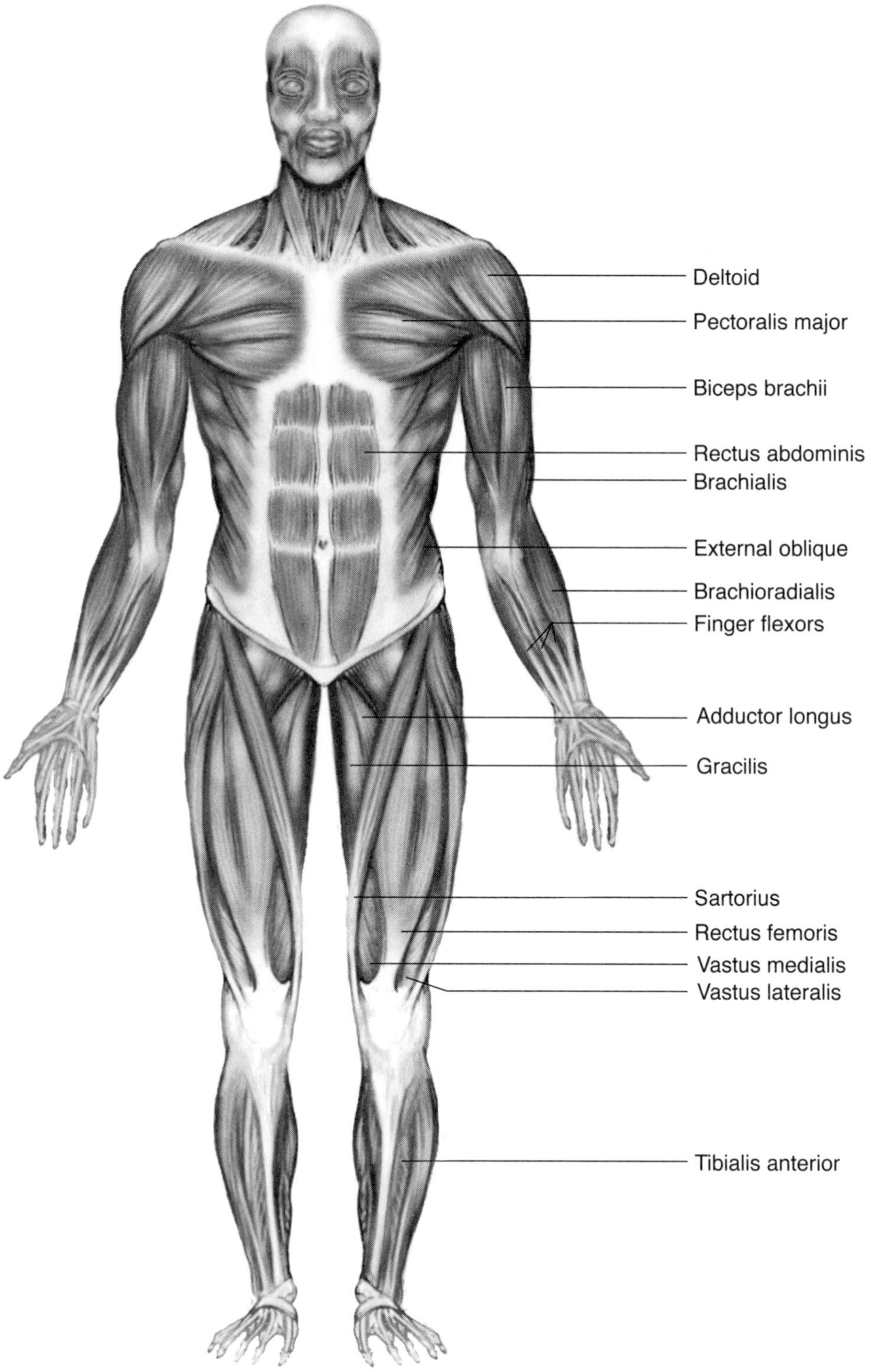
Deltoid
Pectoralis major
Biceps brachii
Rectus abdominis
Brachialis
External oblique
Brachioradialis
Finger flexors
Adductor longus
Gracilis
Sartorius
Rectus femoris
Vastus medialis
Vastus lateralis
Tibialis anterior

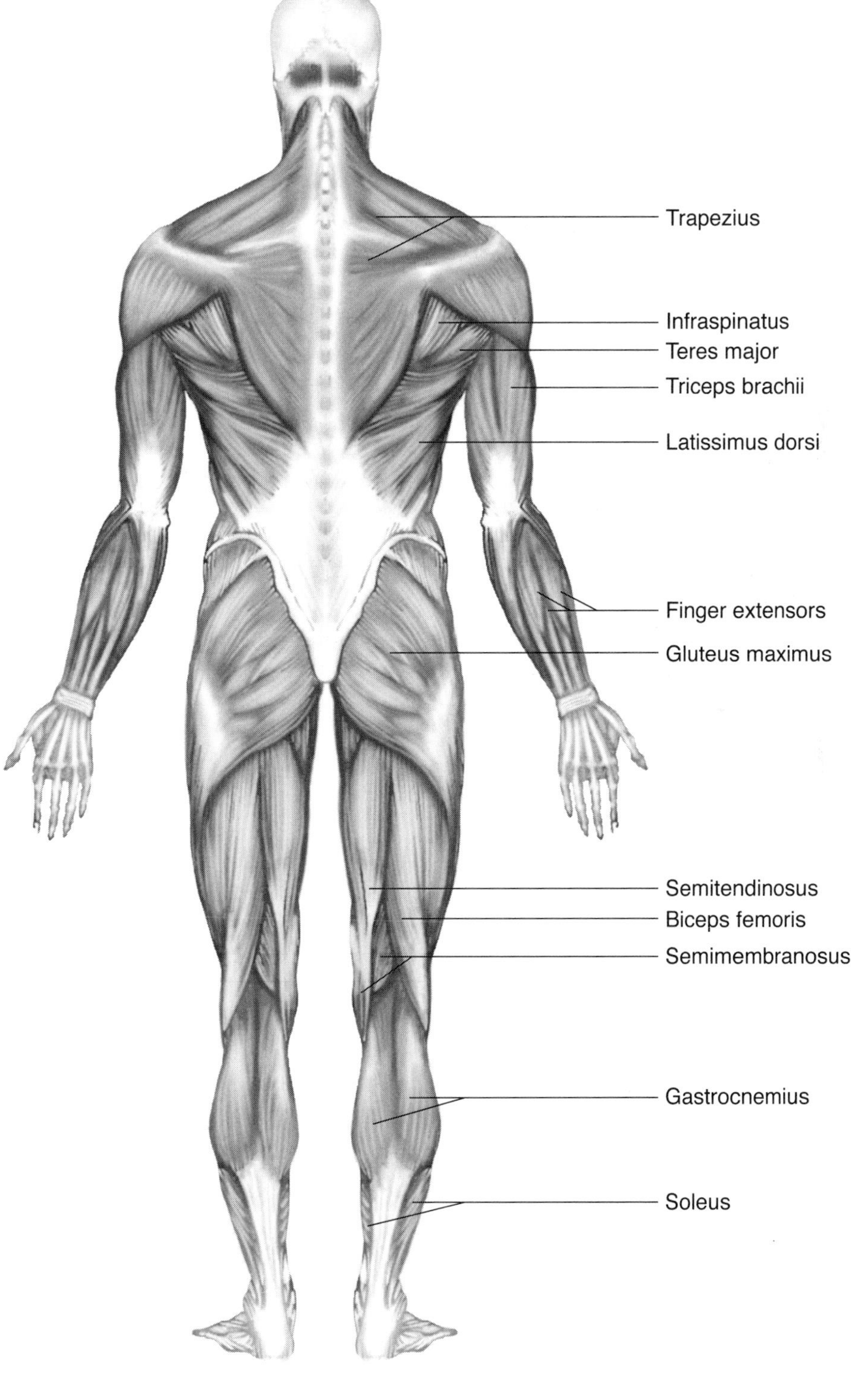

Trapezius
Infraspinatus
Teres major
Triceps brachii
Latissimus dorsi
Finger extensors
Gluteus maximus
Semitendinosus
Biceps femoris
Semimembranosus
Gastrocnemius
Soleus

Acknowledgments

First and foremost, we recognize and thank all our in-person and online Web-Trainer clients from the past 10 years, who have taught, inspired, and challenged us to grow with them as they prepare and continue to train for each new outdoor adventure and strive toward various fitness goals. We thank our expanding newsletter readers, who have brought numerous topics of interest to our attention and challenged us in ways we never could have imagined. This book would not have been possible without the climbing partners, mentor group members, instructors, and volunteers of the Seattle Mountaineers, its climbing program, the Climbing Committee, and the participants in workshops and classes we have attended and taught since 1999.

Thanks to Jeff Bowman, Debbie Wick, Brach Poston, Christa Michel, Marc Van Hoek, and Marci Farrell for reviewing and offering insights into various chapters. The late Mel C. Siff was an initial source of inspiration for the organizational concepts behind our work. Thanks to editors Laurel Plotzke and Amanda Eastin-Allen and to the rest of Human Kinetics for making this book a reality. We also wish to acknowledge Jana Hunter for initially approaching us with the idea for the book. Thanks to our families and friends who believed in us and supported our efforts throughout the project. Courtenay extends special thanks to three particular mom friends who made this book possible by offering valuable moral support and help with child care: Florence Deleranko, Joanne Haberman, and Laura Koch.

Foundation for Outdoor Fitness

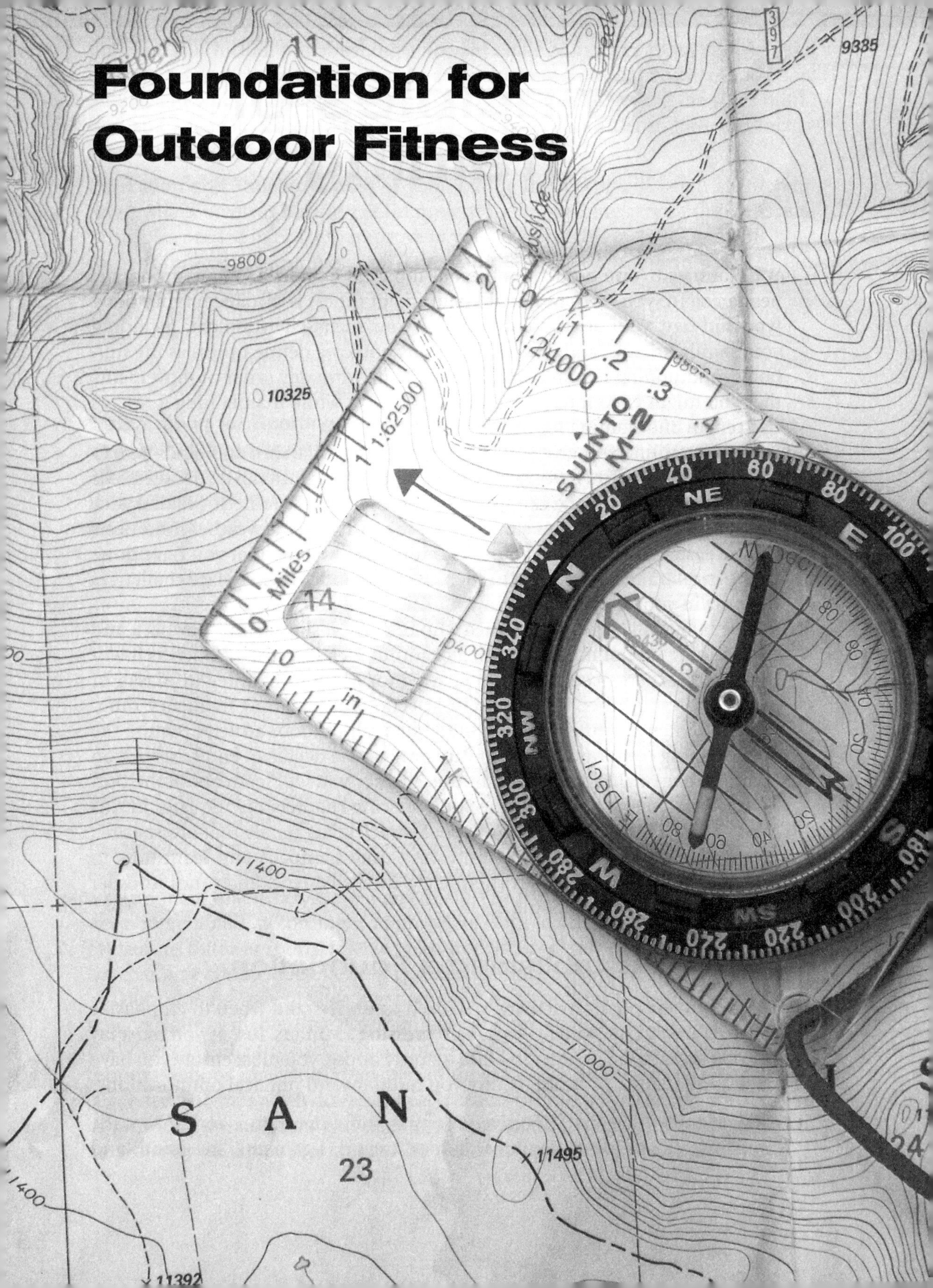

Table 1.1 Components of Sport-Specific Fitness

	Chapter 7	Chapter 8	Chapter 9	Chapter 10	Chapter 11	Chapter 12	Chapter 13
Sport needs	Hiking, trekking, back-packing	Scram-bling, moun-taineer-ing	Climbing	Trail running	Off-road biking	Canoeing, kayaking, rafting	Snow-shoeing, cross-country skiing, backcoun-try skiing
Aerobic conditioning	3	3	3	5	4	3	4
Anaerobic conditioning	1	3	5	2	4	3	2
Upper-body strength	1	3	5	1	3	4	3
Lower-body strength	3	4	3	2	5	1	4
Flexibility	2	4	5	1	2	3	3
Skill	1	3	5	2	4	3	4
Cross-training	2	1	4	4	1	5	3

1 = lowest priority; 5 = highest priority; i.e., upper-body strength is a lower priority in a hiking or trail running program but the highest priority in a climbing program.

Cardiovascular Training

Cardiovascular endurance, or stamina, is the body's ability to perform any repetitive activity for an extended length of time. During cardiovascular work, the body uses large muscle groups simultaneously, either aerobically or anaerobically. A strong cardiovascular base is a prerequisite for all outdoor sports. In simplest terms, *cardio* refers to the heart and *vascular* refers to the lungs; hence cardiovascular activities require the heart and lungs to pump blood and oxygen to the muscles for as long as the body is being overloaded with work.

Aerobic Exercise

Aerobic exercise is any cardiovascular activity that requires a significant amount of oxygen for sustained effort. These products are removed by sweating and exhalation. Aerobic endurance can be categorized as being short (2-8 minutes), medium (8-30 minutes), or long (30+ minutes). When compared with anaerobic activities, aerobic activities are performed for longer durations and at lower intensities. All sports featured in this book rank 3 or higher in priority for aerobic conditioning.

Maximal aerobic capacity ($\dot{V}O_2max$) refers to the greatest amount of oxygen a person can use while performing repetitive movements. The average value for a sedentary American is about 35 milliliters per kilogram per minute; elite endurance athletes average more than 70 milliliters per kilogram per minute (Hampson 2002). As you perform aerobic exercise, your respiration rate increases in order to get more oxygen into the blood that is racing through the arteries to supply the working muscles.

Even if you are training for activities that are not considered to be cardiovascular activities, you will benefit from having a solid endurance base. If you spend a day in the mountains while lacking an aerobic foundation, you might get tired simply from being at an altitude where the reduced atmospheric pressure makes the air feel thin. Likewise, if you are a downhill skier who lacks aerobic fitness, after one or two downhill runs, your legs may burn or feel starved for oxygen. This condition will not happen as quickly if you have established a foundation of endurance training for your sport. Suitable aerobic activities vary widely depending on the sport, but all involve large muscle groups working at submaximal levels. Options include cycling, running, rowing, cross-country skiing, hiking, power walking (with or without a pack), stepping, Spinning, aerobics, water aerobics, swimming, and training on cardiovascular exercise equipment.

Anaerobic Exercise

Anaerobic exercise, or near-maximal cardiovascular training, takes you to the upper levels of your aerobic training zone and beyond. During anaerobic work the body lacks sufficient oxygen to support aerobic metabolism; energy is gained through glycolysis or the breakdown of creatine phosphate. Such exercise is performed at far higher intensities than aerobic activity requires and can be sustained for only a short time. As soon as you cross the anaerobic threshold, aerobic activity is compromised and rest is required to return to optimum performance. The trained human body can sustain work in the anaerobic zone for about 2 minutes before it shifts into using oxygen as its primary fuel source (i.e., aerobic activity). Interval training involves repeatedly alternating times of higher intensity (and higher heart rates) with recovery times of lower intensity. Anaerobic intensity varies from person to person and workout to workout.

Anaerobic training involves working at heart rates that are higher than those you are able to sustain during aerobic sessions. It helps you when you need a sudden burst of adrenaline to respond to emergencies in the mountains, a surge of energy to motor up the next slope on your mountain bike, or an extra kick to pass a slower trail runner in front of you. Anaerobic training helps hikers and trekkers increase their leg turnover rate so they can build speed. It boosts your entire aerobic zone so that activities that once made you breathless feel easier and more comfortable.

Anaerobic training prepares you for the challenge of working at your anaerobic threshold (AT). During high-intensity training, the body uses stored muscle glycogen for energy. A by-product of this process is lactic acid, and the point at which your body can no longer remove the lactic acid quickly enough to sustain anaerobic metabolism is your AT. Through proper training, you can increase your AT by improving your ability to handle the lactic acid. Without anaerobic training, you will not be able to sustain high heart rates for any substantial length of time.

Also, when you are at high altitudes, you may struggle to catch your breath unless you slow down. This is because at high altitudes, the density of air decreases, and the hemoglobin in your blood is unable to carry as much oxygen to the working muscles. If you have trained your body to deal with a lack of oxygen and to recover quickly from this situation at lower elevations, you will be more comfortable dealing with similar stresses up high.

Suitable anaerobic activities vary widely depending on your sport, but all options should involve large muscle groups working at maximal levels. Choose from rowing, cross-country skiing, racewalking (especially with a pack and trekking poles), Versa-Climbers, Jacob's Ladders, and other cardiovascular exercise equipment involving both the upper and lower body.

Strength Training

Maximum strength is the greatest force that is possible in a single maximal contraction, whereas strength endurance measures the length of time your musculoskeletal system can perform. You will feel the benefits of strength training whenever you add pack weight to your body, paddle against the wind to get to shore, or bike over rocky ground. High-altitude expedition climbing and backpacking require more strength endurance in the legs and core than day hiking, trail running, and paddling require. Trail runners and mountain bikers, however, need more strength to handle varied terrain than flatland runners and cyclists need.

Strength training is crucial to success in outdoor pursuits, as it gives you the power and force to withstand both predictable and unforeseen challenges in the mountains and elsewhere. As an outdoor athlete, you should strive to be stronger than you think will be necessary. When you factor in the endurance aspect of outdoor sport, the conflicting demands on your body will result in a loss of strength, and thus the extra training will put you exactly where you need to be. Strength training also prevents injuries by helping your body to adapt to overloading, provides muscle balance, improves performance, and enhances body composition.

Adapt to Loading Strength training challenges muscles gradually in order to help them adapt to increasing loads so that they can handle greater stresses than they could prior to training. The muscles need to be loaded often so that the accumulated adaptations result in measurable change over a month or more. Strength training prepares the outdoor athlete to portage a canoe, carry a heavy pack, heft a mountain bike over an obstacle, or tolerate the eccentric forces of downhill travel. If you start an outdoor sport without taking enough time to adapt to strenuous loading, you may injure yourself.

Provide Muscle Balance Strength training helps keep your joints healthy by making sure you work your opposing muscle groups in direct proportion to the primary movers of your outdoor sport. If your muscles are imbalanced you may do fine for a while, but if you continue to use one group of muscles to the exclusion of others, over time your body will stray from its ideal posture. For example, climbers who hang on straight arms need to include overhead pushing movements (the movements opposite of vertical pulling) and horizontal pulling exercises such as a seated row in their training in order to avoid imbalances. They also need to stretch the pectorals to prevent the shoulders from rounding forward and the torso from slouching.

Improve Performance In addition to preventing injury and keeping the muscles in balance, strength training can significantly improve performance during both outdoor sport and indoor everyday activities. An aerobically fit trail runner with superior cardiovascular endurance may struggle on short but weighted hikes that include several thousand feet of elevation gain. By including preseason leg exercises and gradually increasing the pack weight, this person will feel more comfortable tackling progressively harder hikes.

Enhance Body Composition Strength training helps men and women increase bone density and ward off osteoporosis. It increases lean muscle mass and improves calorie-burning metabolic functions. For sports such as mountain biking and technical climbing, lighter gear and lower body mass can mean the difference between successfully completing a route and ending early. Expedition high-altitude mountaineers and paddlers, on the other hand, may find that supreme strength endurance in conjunction with additional body fat is beneficial for insulation against extreme cold or immersion in water.

Training options that increase strength and strength endurance include training with free weights, uphill training, sled dragging, weighted pack work, training with body resistance and bands, bouldering and campus board training, and power yoga.

Flexibility Training

Flexibility refers to the active range of motion about a particular joint. Stretching can help prevent discomfort after strenuous workouts. It can also help with changes in body alignment that occur during pregnancy, with injury recovery, and with correcting faulty biomechanics. Targeted stretching can increase the space between nerves and structures and thus reduce pain from impingements. Stretching the shoulder, hip, or lower back can relieve tension on a nerve enough to diminish pain (i.e., sciatica, iliotibial band syndrome, tensor fasciae latae discomfort, or piriformis pain) both temporarily and over the long term.

While experiencing minor stiffness when starting a new training routine is normal and expected, you can prevent delayed-onset muscle soreness (DOMS) to some degree by stretching. DOMS occurs most often after workouts that stress the body with the eccentric, or lowering, phase of an exercise, such as extended downward travel with a heavy pack, downhill trail running, or bouldering, which requires you to drop repeatedly onto your feet. Whenever you start exercising or return to training following time off, you may experience mild pain, soreness, stiffness, and joint aches unless you ease back into your routine by using lower intensity, weight, duration, and volume. Training options that help increase flexibility include yoga, Pilates, martial arts, and dynamic, active, and static stretching.

Measurable (M) Make sure your goals are measurable so that you know when you have reached them and can move on to others. If your goal is to increase strength, it will be difficult to gauge when you have succeeded, as any given workout can momentarily increase your strength. The point of setting measurable goals is to make sure that you can regularly assess whether you are making forward progress. If your goal is to hike the Grand Canyon in Arizona (United States) rim to rim to rim, which means hiking 46 miles (74 km) with a gain and loss of 9,000 feet (2,740 m) in 24 hours while carrying limited supplies of water and food and having support friends along the route, you have a very measurable goal and you can design a suitable program to attain it. As you train for your measurable goal, record in a training journal your sets, repetitions, changes in heart rate, and workout durations so you can learn how your body responds to training and quantify what is too much or too little.

Action Oriented (A) Create an action-oriented plan that will ensure your goals become reality. A goal of shaving off 20 seconds per mile (1.6 km) on 10K trail runs is both specific and measurable, but how do you plan to accomplish it? What actions will help you reach your goal? What cardiovascular workouts do you need to do? What variables might you need to adjust in your diet? What strength exercises can you use to develop speed? As you design your plan, enlist the help of an expert, a training book such as this one, or a trusted buddy who has achieved the same goal to provide advice that will motivate and educate you.

Realistic (R) Keep your goals realistic so that you do not get discouraged and lose your motivation. Keep your goals within the realm of what is possible. Competing in the Olympics in white-water kayaking without planning for the necessary technical training, skill development, or experience is both dangerous and unrealistic. Smaller goals such as participating in local paddling contests or attending national clinics with the best kayakers in the region are much more realistic and can be intermediate steps to bigger goals. While a goal of losing 10 pounds (4.5 kg) in two weeks so you can be more competitive in a mountain bike race may be attainable, it is potentially dangerous and could spell disaster come race day. Losing any more than 2 pounds (1 kg) a week can result in dehydration, destruction of lean muscle mass, reduced energy levels and training performance, and a slowed metabolism. Talk with others who have attained the same goal you are trying to reach so that you can learn what is reasonable and realistic.

Time Stamped (T) Finally, commit to action and follow through so you can complete your goal by a certain deadline. Signing up, buying airline tickets, and paying a deposit for a climb up Mount McKinley in Alaska means you will have to either get in condition by the time the climb commences in 5 months or not go and lose money. Write your deadline on paper next to your goal. Put your goals on your calendar and remind yourself daily of your commitment and your actions. The success rate of those who write down their goals is many times higher than the rate of those who do not. Select a long-term goal and break it down into the steps you need to take between now and your deadline. For each step, decide on something that you can do this week to get closer to reaching that goal. Put the steps on your calendar, complete them, and cross them off your checklist. Without action, goals are only wishes. Set SMART goals and start working toward them today.

FITT Parameters

The FITT parameters are the training variables you should manipulate in order to get the most from your program. They include frequency (how often you exercise), intensity (how hard you exercise), time (how long you exercise), and type (what exercise modes you do). Together these four parameters constitute your training load, or stress. A person who trains for a short weekend canoe trip has a low workload (low intensity, low frequency, low duration); the trail runner who prepares for a series of endurance footraces has a very high workload (low to high intensity, high frequency, low to high duration). Each sport-specific chapter in part II manipulates the FITT parameters according to a periodized program that results in balanced, varied, results-oriented training.

Frequency (F) How often you should train depends on your current fitness level and your desired level of achievement. A person who aspires to climb high-altitude peaks needs to train more frequently than a person who wishes to run a few trails throughout the summer. If you plan to do a lot of hikes, climbs, races, or paddling trips, pay close attention to how your body feels so you can adjust your weekday workouts to prevent overtraining. Sometimes novice outdoor athletes become so enthusiastic about training for their growing hobby that they experience mental burnout, strain from overuse, or even injury due to training too much too quickly, with too little recovery time.

For most outdoor sports, a good starting program for establishing basic health includes two 30-minute full-body strength training workouts and three 20- to 30-minute cardiovascular workouts per week, or 2 to 2.5 hours of accumulated weekly exercise. As you progress to more demanding goals, the frequency of your cardiovascular, sport-specific, and strength training workouts will increase, and your workouts will vary in intensity and duration. Each sport-specific chapter in part II includes a frequency recommendation as well as summarizes the elements and weekly exercise time required for beginner, intermediate, and advanced programs.

Intensity (I) The intensity parameter indicates how hard your workouts are. The optimum cardiovascular intensity for fitness improvement is 65 to 95 percent of your maximum heart rate (MHR; see chapter 3). You should keep most of your early-season workouts at a low intensity and then gradually build your cardiovascular endurance before adding high-intensity workouts. Exercising too hard too soon can tap into anaerobic systems rather than build aerobic systems and may result in overuse or injury.

Strength training should also start with low-intensity workouts. You should work with lighter weights for a moderate number of repetitions (complete sets of 8-10 repetitions) and keep 3 or 4 repetitions in reserve for motor learning (see chapter 4).

This is most important for people new to strength training or to particular exercises. Next, you should progress to a phase where you emphasize gaining strength by performing more sets with fewer reps. Finally, as you peak for your goal, your focus will be on strength endurance using lighter weights than the strength phase but completing more repetitions. Chapter 2 provides suggestions for assessing and applying intensity for strength, aerobic, and anaerobic workouts.

Time (T) Aerobic and strength workouts range in length according to the end goals, training cycle, and exercise type. You need to do aerobic exercise in your training zone for at least 15 to 20 minutes in order to see improvements. A strength workout as short as 8 to 10 minutes can provide some benefits, although a typical strength workout ranges from 20 to 60 minutes, depending on the frequency of the strength training. Chapter 3 addresses strategies for increasing endurance, while chapter 4 concentrates on maximizing strength.

Type (T) Aerobic and strength workouts vary according to the specific cardiovascular exercises and strength exercises they encompass. Exercise selection depends on individual preference, location (climate and terrain), season, and chosen sport. Supplemental cross-training outside of the chosen sport provides rest and recovery as well as an additional training stimulus for the cardiovascular system. Chapters 15 and 16 describe sport-specific strength exercises that include unilateral (involving one limb) and bilateral (involving both limbs simultaneously) movements that you can do with free weights and, in some cases, bands, packs, or body weight.

Training Guidelines

Following are general guidelines for a wholesome, well-balanced, safe, and complete training program. They incorporate FITT parameters in conjunction with SMART goal setting and provide a framework you can use to develop your personalized plan. These guidelines are also interwoven into each of the sport-specific programs outlined in part II.

Train Specifically The cardiovascular and strength exercises you select for your workouts need to be the right types for your sport, a concept known as *specificity of training*. You should match your cardiovascular modes as closely as possible to the primary movements of your sport. You should also train at the intensities you will encounter in your sport. Running long and steady on flat roads while training for a hilly trail run is just as ineffective as spending your days climbing indoors when preparing for a multiday high-altitude expedition. The best training for trail running is running on comparable terrain; the best training for kayaking is to get out on the water and paddle.

Sometimes it is difficult to train by practicing your sport—preseason skiing is challenging in a low snow year, canoeing can be difficult when there are no lakes or rivers nearby, and high-altitude trekking may be hard to do regularly when you live at sea level. Sometimes it is also beneficial to include cross-training for rehabilitation or injury prevention. For most of your training, however, choose comparable activities that work the muscle groups in the same ways your sport works them. Rowing on an ergometer may be a good substitute for paddling, and Spinning classes may replace mountain biking in inclement weather. However, because neither rowing nor Spinning loads the spine and legs the way that trail running, stair-climbing, and hill walking do, they are secondary options for sports such as hiking, scrambling, and technical climbing.

Train Functionally You should keep your exercise selection functional, choosing exercises that integrate as many muscle groups as possible rather than train the body in isolation. Working with free weights provides far greater benefits compared with training on weight machines. Training with free weights requires you to balance weight and to coordinate in all three dimensions; such training loads the spine in the same way you load it when on a trail, bike, boat, pair of skis, slope, or rock ledge. When you are participating in outdoor sport, you rarely lift heavy weight while you are sitting, leaning, or lying down. However, you can take the concept of functionality too far and try to exactly replicate your sport movements in the gym. The best way to train for rowing is to sit down and row; creating a simulated movement that requires setup time, complicated equipment, or gear that is not readily available can interfere with motor learning.

Overload Gradually To make progress in training, you need to add stress gradually and incrementally so that the body has time to adapt to the increasing loads. Sufficient recovery is also required to avoid overtraining and injury. With enough rest, the body overcompensates and becomes more fit. Athletes who increase volume, frequency, or intensity without sufficient rest may regress in their training. Taking several days off when you are low in energy, prone to illness, or not making suitable progress may be what you need to regain your health and make a breakthrough in subsequent workouts.

Program Development Guidelines

The exercise program that you build for yourself will be based on your goals, exercise history, age, health, diet, sleep habits, time availability, job, and family. All these factors affect how you react to stress, training, and workload. A program that works for someone else may not fit your unique needs. The following guidelines will help you figure out what and how much you should include in the different phases of your training.

Prioritize Your Training Your priorities will shift depending on your training background and whether you are in-season or in your off-season, preseason, or postseason. Your priorities will also shift whenever you begin a new sport. Priorities relate directly to how you perform in your particular sport. A runner who begins mountaineering training will need to shift emphasis from aerobic conditioning to lower-body strength training and pack-loaded uphill training for handling extra weight beyond body weight. Conversely, the paddler who takes up trail running will need to transfer focus from upper-body training to core and lower-body endurance training. In general, anaerobic training will remain a lower priority until you establish a good base of endurance and strength; flexibility may increase in priority any time your body alignment changes. While the programs developed in the chapters of part II outline the training frequency and intensity considered optimal for reaching a given goal in a given sport, the outdoor athlete always has to balance what is optimal with what is realistic. In order to see how to evaluate training priorities, let's contrast the priorities of a high-altitude mountaineer who is in the late stages of training for an intermediate level 4-day outing at a 15,000-foot (4,572 m) elevation with those of a trail runner preparing for a beginner 8K race with a 400-foot (122 m) elevation gain.

Priority 1: The closer you get to your goal, the more important sport-specific training becomes. For the mountaineer, weighted hikes are the top priority. By including hikes every other weekend, he can select nicer weekends and not get stuck doing an outing during the rare mosquito week or highly unusual flash flood of the century. For the trail runner, distance runs with elevation changes comparable to those of the 8K event are the highest priority.

Priority 2: High-intensity anaerobic training is the second highest priority as your goal nears. Anaerobic training is relatively easy to do when time is tight, especially since it requires less time than distance workouts require. This far into a training program, it would hurt to miss a weekly anaerobic workout, as this workout is scheduled less frequently than other training components are scheduled. For the mountaineer, anaerobic training that targets altitude preparation is crucial to physiological adaptation and success in scrambling and trekking. Likewise, the trail runner who wants to place high in a race should emphasize sprint training in the form of uphills or repeats (see chapter 3).

Priority 3: For the mountaineer, improving leg and core strength is the next highest priority, especially if strength training was added recently to the program. Several months of solid strength training can make a huge difference in the mountains. The trail runner who scored low in core strength and flexibility may feel that yoga is crucial for maintaining muscle balance and range of motion in the legs and put that as her third priority.

Priority 4: Distance endurance training forms a baseline for everything else and pays off in terms of getting the body prepared for sustained and repeated effort. While endurance training requires a large time investment, skimping on it may mean the difference between enjoyment and survival. While the alpinist might put such training as his fourth priority, the trail runner may put an additional recovery run or upper-body strength workout as her fourth priority.

Other Priorities: If you are close to your goal and pressed for time, the first things to drop from your program are non-sport-specific conditioning, any components that you are naturally strong in (see chapter 2), and any components that are not crucial to achieving your goal. While cross-training can help you maintain muscle balance and preserve your sanity, if you have to shave an hour from your week, you should forego these non-sport-specific workouts before eliminating workouts that are more specific to your goal. For the high-altitude mountaineer who has excellent flexibility and upper-body strength, yoga and upper-body training may take a backseat for several busy weeks until he finishes his goal of a 4-day outing at 15,000 feet (4,572 m).

Periodize Your Program A periodized program is broken into periods of time such as macrocycles, mesocycles, and microcycles and varies according to how far out you are from your goal event. Macrocycles are long-term plans on the scale of a year or more. Mesocycles are intermediate-term programs on the scale of 1 to 6 months. Microcycles are on the scale of days to weeks. If you are a year-round athlete involved in multiple sports, the training cycles can get quite intricate. Part II outlines periodized sport-specific programs that incorporate mesocycles and microcycles, while part III discusses the specific strength, balance, and flexibility exercises that are included during the different cycles of the programs.

Establish Training Blocks Once you know how much time you need to train for your goal, you can break the time between your end goal and your starting point into five distinct training blocks, each of which has a different objective: (1) to establish a solid foundation on which the rest of the training builds (this will be referred to as establishing a *baseline)*, (2) to increase cardiovascular endurance, (3) to build strength, (4) to enhance mental toughness and stamina, and (5) to peak and taper for your event. If you are training for a beginner event, the early phases of your program may last only 1 to 2 weeks; if you are working toward challenging goals that require more than 6 months of training, you may spend 2 months in blocks 2, 3, and 4 or do several short cycles that last a month each and are separated by an active recovery week. Table 1.2 illustrates how a year may be divided into training blocks. Your in-season encompasses a series of sporting events that you participate in for your primary sport, while your postseason lasts the 2 to 4 weeks immediately following the completion of these in-season events. Depending on the length of your primary season and your level of participation, preseason can last from 1 to 6 months (see Part II), and off-season is the time that remains between postseason and preseason, generally several months unless you participate in multiple sports.

Table 1.2 Training Blocks and Goals

PRESEASON			IN-SEASON	POSTSEASON	OFF-SEASON
Early	Middle	Late			
Establish baseline	Increase cardiovascular endurance and build strength	Enhance mental toughness and stamina; peak and taper	Maintain performance level	Focus on imbalances developed from sport-specific activities	Prioritize training of weak points

After you create a program overview, figure out how many workouts per week you will include during each block of your program. When you are working on beginner goals or the preseason phase of longer programs, 3 to 4 workouts per week may suffice. When you are preparing for an intermediate goal, you should build to at least 5 weekly workouts by the time you are 2 weeks away from your goal. Advanced goals may require 6 or more weekly workouts that include a day of rest after long or high-intensity workouts. Look at your current program in terms of the FITT parameters. Then study the sport-specific workloads in the sample programs of part II that are suited to your goal. If your program matches the sample program in frequency, you can manipulate the time and intensity variables. If the programs do not match in frequency, add short, low-intensity workouts to build volume and recovery ability. Once the frequencies of the two programs match, build endurance in your long cardiovascular workouts until your endurance conditioning meets the sample program recommendations. Once you have achieved the frequency and endurance recommendations of the sample programs, increase intensity to build speed specific to your sport.

Adhere to the 5 to 15 Percent Rule Increase training volume by 5 to 15 percent at a time. For example, if you start with 20-minute workouts, you can add 2 minutes (10 percent) to subsequent cardiovascular sessions. This suggested progression is based on the amount of musculature used, impact on joints, and relative support provided for the body. Activities that rely heavily on smaller upper-body musculature or rigorous full-body movements (i.e., cross-country skiing or technical climbing) should increase by no more than 5 percent at a time; high-impact activities that use large muscles (i.e., trail running or telemark skiing) should increase by no more than 10 percent at a time; and low-impact activities (i.e., hiking or scrambling) or seated, supported activities (i.e., biking) should stay under 15 percent.

Include Adequate Recovery Time High-intensity workouts need more recovery time. Endurance days may be done at low intensities, but if you add pack resistance or hilly terrain, you should follow them with a recovery day. Low-intensity (<65 percent MHR) recovery cross-training exercises can include walking, swimming, dancing, easy flat biking, yoga, or yard work. Such light days help you avoid overtraining by allowing tired muscles to rest before they perform again. As you grow older, you may need to add additional recovery time as well as training time to goals.

Keep at least 48 hours between strength workouts, and limit strength training sessions to 1 hour from the first to last set. Put a day of rest or active recovery between strength workouts and endurance workouts with packs or hikes. Modify your day's workout plan if your resting heart rate is abnormally high or low (plus or minus 5 beats or more), your basal temperature is plus or minus .5 degrees Fahrenheit (.28 C) from your normal temperature, or you feel sluggish, are extremely sore, or experience pain.

Recognize Overtraining Symptoms Signs of overtraining include slowed performance times and recovery times, altered sleep patterns, weakness, extreme muscle soreness, sluggishness, or lack of enthusiasm for training (see chapter 2). Keep in mind that delayed onset muscle soreness (DOMS) is normal and is to be expected following changes in routine, but extreme soreness or stiffness may mean that you may have worked too hard, or you may have neglected your warm-up or stretching. If it persists over prolonged periods of time, it can lead to overtraining. If you experience several symptoms of overtraining, add more recovery or rest days; reduce your training frequency, intensity, or time; or choose a different type of movement (adjusting FITT parameters) as needed.

Putting It All Together

The following sample annual training program is one you can use for any goal. Start with the end objective and work backward to optimize the training time you have available. The template included here details training for a primary summer sport and secondary winter sport.

Macrocycles

Postseason summer (preseason winter): October to November

In-season winter: December to February

Preseason summer: March to April

In-season summer: May to September

Mesocycles

Preseason winter: After an intense summer, the body needs a break. The postseason includes shorter aerobic workouts, reduced pack weights, and cross-training workouts related to your winter sport. The postseason strength sessions should address any muscle imbalances developed over the summer. Late in the cycle, you can add winter sport-specific training.

In-season winter: Add weekly plyometric or anaerobic workouts as needed for altitude preparation, allowing sufficient recovery following outdoor events. Include cardiovascular workouts for your summer sport in the 75 to 85 percent (tempo) range.

Preseason summer: Include unilateral strength exercises for balance and agility to address any problems detected in your winter sport; introduce pack carrying (where appropriate) and other sport-specific training for your summer sport at somewhat reduced intensities from those of the previous fall and build back up to goal weight and distance. Increase training volume by 5 to 15 percent per week.

In-season summer: Participate in as many trips or events as desired and schedule suitable recovery time following outings. Shift your training focus to maintenance. Do full-body strength training twice a week and weekly anaerobic training when appropriate.

Microcycles

These day-to-day workouts specify intensity, frequency, exercise type, and time spent on each exercise. The programs included in part II make recommendations at this level, and part III addresses sport-specific stretches and strength exercises.

Fitness Assessment and Adaptation

Understanding how to evaluate effort and performance will help you maximize your gains in training. In this chapter we discuss ways of assessing each fitness component identified in chapter 1. We focus on tests that can be done easily and without professional evaluation. You will learn how to conduct self-assessments and gauge your improvement in aerobic and anaerobic fitness, functional upper-body and lower-body strength, and sport-specific flexibility without having to undergo clinical testing. You will understand how to use your test results to create your training program and refine your workouts as your fitness increases. You will learn about overtraining and how to avoid it through proper program development. Sample recording charts are available in the appendix on page 279.

Assessing Cardiovascular Fitness

In order to apply the FITT training parameters of frequency, intensity, type of exercise, and time (see chapter 1) and develop a cardiovascular program specific to your sport, you need to learn how to gauge your intensity, assess your cardiovascular fitness, and reevaluate your aerobic and anaerobic capacity. By learning to do these things, you can progress your training at the appropriate times and reduce your risk of overuse or injury. Chapter 3 includes additional specifics on how to properly load the body during cardiovascular workouts. Using the principles outlined in chapters 1 and 3 and the tests described in this chapter, you will be able to design, use, and modify an appropriate, goal-specific cardiovascular training program. The sport-specific programs in part II build from the fundamentals covered in part I to help you reach your training goals.

Establishing Starting Levels

We assume that you are starting from a fitness foundation of basic health (chapter 1) that allows you to perform continuous movement for at least 20 minutes, whether that movement is doing one of the sport activities discussed in this book or at the bare minimum walking briskly. If you are starting with a higher baseline, your first step is to assess where that baseline is. Some exercise physiologists feel that the best indicator of cardiovascular fitness is $\dot{V}O_2max$, which is defined as the maximum volume (V) of oxygen (O_2) in milliliters that you can use per minute per kilogram of body weight while breathing at sea level. Others, however, dismiss $\dot{V}O_2max$ as something that cannot be changed to a great extent.

The $\dot{V}O_2$max of a single individual can vary depending on the mode of exercise and the amount of muscle mass used in a particular test. You may feel compelled to compare your score to those of others in your sport who are similar to you in age and gender. However, regardless of $\dot{V}O_2$max test scores, a 60-year-old woman and a 25-year-old man need comparable strength and endurance to reach the summit of a high-altitude mountain or compete over a challenging mountain bike course. In this chapter, instead of concentrating on $\dot{V}O_2$max, we focus on relative self-improvement and how you rate against best-fit tests in your sport.

Evaluating Aerobic Progress

To reach your goal, you need to know where you are starting from, where you need to be, and how to make steady progress toward your goal. You need tools that assess the effectiveness of your training so that you do not waste valuable time. These tools include an inexpensive, sport-specific 13-minute ramp test or 30-minute field test that you can duplicate monthly in order to gauge how you are doing.

The ramp test is based on the idea that as you increase your aerobic fitness, your heart rate will decrease for a specific workload. Conversely, when you are working at a standard heart rate, you will be able to do more work (increase your output) as your fitness level rises. Because the ramp test is relatively short, it is one that athletes of all levels can do to get baseline fitness information. The longer field test is higher in intensity and becomes applicable once you have developed baseline endurance and started to increase the intensity of your workouts. For both the ramp test and the field test, you will need to measure distance or workload (provided by your cardiovascular machine) and heart rate (provided by a heart rate monitor). Calibrations can differ from one machine to another, and these variations may affect your test results. If you choose to do the testing outside, note the humidity, wind, temperature, and other factors beyond your control so you can make future test conditions as similar as possible. Assessing the effectiveness of your training program may be done more easily on cardiovascular machines that are in more controlled environments and that provide visual output of workload.

When you are ready to assess your aerobic fitness level, determine your starting resting heart rate (RHR), which is the number of times your heart beats per minute while you are resting. For greatest accuracy, measure your RHR after you have been lying flat in a comfortable position for at least 3 to 5 minutes. To establish your RHR norm, test yourself when you are healthy, have emptied your bladder, and are at least an hour from any meal or exercise. Your RHR will be roughly 15 to 20 beats lower than what it is when you are sitting in the middle of the day. Check it first thing in the morning and check it again at night before you go to bed; the lowest number you see is your RHR. Fit athletes may see numbers as low as 30 to 50 beats per minute; 55 to 80 beats per minute is common for adults. Track your RHR for 3 days and record the numbers in a training log. As your cardiovascular fitness improves, your RHR will gradually decrease. Knowing your typical RHR can help you identify the onset of illness or overtraining in the future.

13-Minute Aerobic Graded Ramp Test You should complete a suitable sport-specific ramp test every month; to track your results, you can use the testing form provided in the appendix. The goal of this test is threefold: (1) to provide you with heart rate numbers that reflect various levels of exertion on readily available equipment, (2) to provide you with baseline measurements against which you can compare subsequent efforts in order to gauge your improvements, and (3) to help you define your gasping zone, or anaerobic threshold (AT).

Ramp tests that are done without weight and on flat terrain assess cardiovascular endurance, whereas ramp tests that include pack weight, resistance, or elevation gain gauge strength endurance as well as cardiovascular endurance. Sometimes when you combine elements in a test it can be challenging to determine which element needs improvement. For example, if you get tired on a 45-minute hilly bike ride, you may be weak in the core and legs, you may be low on endurance, or you may be both. If you become winded before your legs fatigue, you should focus on building endurance; if your legs give out before your heart rate increases, you need to build leg strength. If biking feels difficult in both respects, you need both strength and endurance training. As another example, if you hike for an hour without any pack and feel breathless going uphill, you need to increase your endurance; if your legs have no pop as soon as you add a pack, you need more strength. If both hiking uphill and carrying a pack feel challenging, you should build both cardiovascular endurance and strength.

Assessing your fitness and planning your training accordingly will help you overcome any obstacle on your way to meeting your goals.

The best-fit goal tests described in part II simultaneously assess all areas specific to your sport. Tips on how to separate elements so you can identify what you need to work on are included in each chapter in part II. If you wish to gauge only your cardiovascular endurance, you should increase speed instead of resistance or incline. Since machines with vertical strength components such as a VersaClimber or Jacob's Ladder are excellent full-body cardiovascular training options, we include them in the following test options. It may be a bit harder for you to identify which fitness component needs more work whenever you add a vertical or strength component in ramp testing.

The ramp test described here is modeled after submaximal graded exercise tests used with specially calibrated cycle ergometers. To perform your test, choose a cardiovascular machine that closely replicates your sport's primary movements. Suitable equipment options for the ramp test include an upright bike or a cycle ergometer for mountain biking; a treadmill for trail running; a rowing ergometer for paddling; a NordicTrack for cross-country skiing; an elliptical trainer or a treadmill for hiking; a StepMill, Jacob's Ladder, or stair-climber for scrambling; and a VersaClimber for climbing. While working on varied terrain outdoors is preferable when conducting best-fit tests and distance training, machines provide direct information about completed workloads that allows for easier comparison among tests. If you have limited access to cardiovascular machines and cannot use the one recommended for your sport, you can substitute it with any of the other machines listed. Simply recognize that you may not gauge your improvement in your sport as accurately when you use equipment that requires movements different from those used in your sport. The steps of the ramp test are as follows:

1. *Warm up.* Before starting your test, spend 5 to 10 minutes warming up to a perceived exertion (PE) of 5 (see chapter 3 for a complete explanation of PE). You can complete your warm-up on the same equipment you will use for your test or you can warm up on something else. Measure your heart rate with a heart rate monitor, and use paper and pen, a voice recorder, or a training partner to record your test data. Before you start, carefully note all variables (time, starting speed, stride rate or cadence, resistance) so that you can duplicate the test setup in subsequent tests. After your warm-up, begin the ramp test with 3 minutes at a workload that elevates your heart rate to at least 65 percent of your MHR, which for most people will be above 120 beats per minute (PE 6). At any two half-minute readings (i.e., taken at 2, 2:30, or 3 minutes), your measured heart rate should be within 2 to 3 beats of the previous measured heart rate, indicating that your heart rate is steady at this workload.

2. *Perform increments.* After the first 3 minutes have passed, record your heart rate and work output or distance traveled. Immediately increase the resistance, incline, or speed so that you move to the next workload. (Later, when you move to subsequent workloads, be sure to increase the resistance, incline, or speed by the same increments.) For example, if you start the ramp test at level 5 on an elliptical trainer, increase to level 6 when your first 3 minutes are finished. On a treadmill, if you start walking at a 5 percent incline at 3.5 miles per hour (5.6 kph), you can

either increase ramp height to 6 percent *or* increase speed to 3.6 miles per hour (5.8 kph)—do not do both! On a bike, you may switch to a larger gear and maintain cadence. On a Jacob's Ladder, you can increase stepping rate by 3 to 5 steps per minute. On a VersaClimber, you can increase vertical feet by 5 to 10 per minute. Then, at minute 6, record your heart rate and resistance level and increase your workload by the same increment you used before. At minute 9, again record your heart rate and other specifics and increase your workload once more. If you start gasping for air or feel like your PE is 9 or 10, note the speed, ramp height, resistance, output, and heart rate, as you have reached your AT. If at any point the test becomes too challenging, simply drop to below your warm-up level and begin a cool-down. Use the testing form provided in the appendix to record your test results.

3. *Find your recovery heart rate.* After completing the 12 minutes of work (and four levels of workload), drop the intensity, cadence, ramp height, and speed so you are barely moving for a full minute. Move only enough to return blood from the hard-working muscles to the heart so that you do not get light-headed. The goal in the final minute is to gauge your recovery heart rate, which indicates how fast your cardiovascular system recovers from hard exertion. The larger the difference between your heart rates at minutes 12 and 13, the faster your rate of recovery and the greater your fitness (assuming you selected a hard enough starting point). Heart rates can drop anywhere from 20 to 50 beats in a minute. As your fitness level increases, you will be able to recover more quickly from workouts of comparable intensity.

At the end of minute 13, record your heart rate and complete an easy cool-down for 3 to 5 minutes. Your ramp test score is the sum of your heart rates at minutes 3, 6, 9, 12, and 13. Record all your test data on the form provided in the appendix. Keep your testing workloads (i.e., speeds, ramp heights, resistances) the same for at least one subsequent test so that you duplicate your initial ramp test as closely as possible. As your fitness increases and you become more aerobically efficient, your final ramp test score will decrease for identical workloads. When you can no longer get your heart rate above 65 percent MHR or 120 beats per minute at your first workload, move up to your second workload. Use this workload as your new starting point and establish a new baseline. Every increase means you have improved your fitness and need to reset the ramp test parameters (see Friel 2006). Repeat the ramp test in 4 to 6 weeks.

Because the ramp test is short (13 minutes), everyone, even people in the initial stages of training, should be able to complete it. Since the test is graded (it incrementally tests different levels of work), it provides immediate feedback on where you should start training at different intensity levels. For example, if when you set an elliptical trainer to level 8 and the highest possible ramp height, you start to gasp when your heart rate reaches 148 beats per minute, then your current AT is roughly 148 beats per minute. If you go above that rate, you will be anaerobic. Your goal is to increase your fitness level so that the next time you reach level 8 at the highest possible ramp height, your heart rate stays lower *or* you do not struggle as hard to catch your breath. A lower heart rate or breathing more easily means your AT is increasing, and this is a positive sign of improved fitness. You can use your current AT to determine your anaerobic training zone; in this example, you know that work sessions performed on the elliptical trainer over the next month need to be completed at level 8 or greater. A lower resistance level or lower ramp height can be used for recovery and distance cardiovascular training (see chapter 3). If on subsequent tests your heart rate is higher at the first two workloads (which will increase the total ramp score) but lower on the last two, your heart is becoming more efficient at getting blood and oxygen to the working muscles; a lower final heart rate and RHR indicate improved fitness given the same test parameters.

30-Minute Aerobic Steady Field Test Once you have completed a solid month of baseline cardiovascular training and have seen improvements on your ramp tests, you will have built your endurance significantly. If you did not reach your AT on either test and if you can sustain 45 minutes of steady movement, you are ready to do a 30-minute sport-specific field test (described here) or best-fit test (see part II). Field tests are designed to help you use a heart rate monitor to determine your AT more solidly without clinical testing. For field tests, a stair-stepper, Jacob's Ladder, or set of stairs (at least five stories) is the most applicable to hiking, scrambling, and climbing. Biking is the most applicable to mountain biking, and treadmill running is best to approximate trail running. The NordicTrack is good for cross-country skiing, and still-water paddling or a rowing ergometer is best for paddling. When you do your field test, you can use the form provided in the appendix to record your test results.

As you did for the ramp test, warm up for 5 to 10 minutes before beginning and continue straight into the time trial. For this test, you will work as hard as you possibly can (80-85 percent MHR; see chapter 3) while maintaining a constant level of exertion for the entire 30-minute test. If you do the test indoors on a machine, use a metronome to set a constant cadence. Avoid starting out too hard; you want to be able to complete the test at the desired intensity level. At 10, 15, 20, 25, and 30 minutes, record your heart rate on the sheet provided. When you have finished the test, cool down for 3 to 5 minutes. Average your heart rates from minutes 10 through 30 (add the five numbers together and divide by 5) for a rough assessment of your AT. If you worked out at a sufficiently high intensity (80-85 percent MHR), the average over the last 20 minutes of your test provides you with a good estimate of your AT (Friel, 2006).

Review table 1.1, which summarizes how important the different fitness components are to success in various outdoor sports. If your sport requires a level of 4 or 5 in aerobic training (i.e., trail running, biking, or snow sports) and you struggled with either the 30-minute field test or the 13-minute ramp test performed at low workloads or your RHR failed to drop 20 beats or more during minute 13 of the ramp test, you should put cardiovascular endurance training as the highest priority in your conditioning program. For climbing, in which anaerobic capacity, strength, and flexibility rank higher in importance, you may still benefit from boosting a low aerobic capacity if you already score high in the other areas. If you did your ramp test at a mid-resistance level on your machine, then you have sufficient cardiovascular training for sports requiring a level 3 in aerobic endurance, and you should maintain your stamina or increase it once your other scores match your sport's needs. Trail runners, cross-country skiers, and mountain bikers require superior aerobic conditioning, so in most cases, aerobic training forms the main component of the program and secondary emphasis is placed on any low results in the other fitness components.

The necessary sport-specific aerobic parameters are identified in part II. In general, though, the outdoor athlete who struggles to run a 10-minute mile on level terrain, who cannot bike 12 miles per hour on rolling terrain, or finds it difficult to sustain a 2.5 miles per hour hiking pace with a suitable pack for several hours needs to improve cardiovascular endurance. Performing below these values would result in an aerobic endurance rating below 3. While it does not mean you cannot participate in trail running, off-road biking, or hiking if your pace is below these parameters, it means the additional terrain challenges and elevation gain and loss would reduce your speed even more. The same running, biking, or hiking performance, however, may be quite suitable for someone whose sport is kayaking or climbing (rated level 3 for aerobic endurance).

In addition to using your test results to improve your sport, you can conversely use the information to choose your sport. If you are interested in multiple sports and wish to assess what fits you best given your current level of conditioning, you can try to match your test scores to the requirements of the various sports. If you score high in aerobic performance but low in strength and flexibility, you can look for activities that require a 4 or more in aerobic capacity and a 2 or less elsewhere. Trail running or hiking would be your natural fit. If you score a 2 in aerobic performance but a 4 and 5 in strength and anaerobic conditioning, climbing or paddling fits you best, especially if you allow sufficient time to improve aerobic endurance.

The strength parameters for each of the tests suggested below and in part II provide you with suitable gauges and ranges for strength levels for the outdoor athlete. If, for example, you are unable to perform at least 5 repetitions of the flat dumbbell bench press with at least 40 percent of your bodyweight (the weight of both dumbbells), then your rating for that particular strength exercise would be 1. If you can press 100 percent (with both dumbbells), then your rating would be 5. If you find that your anaerobic heart rate is not noticeably higher than your end ramp or field test numbers, anaerobic performance would rank as a 1; conversely, if you can push quite hard and match repeat efforts with short recovery times, you would rank 5.

Remember that both the ramp test and the field test are relative tests that help you gauge your personal improvement in cardiovascular capacity. Because of the large number of complex variables that factor into success in a sport, it is impossible to specify an exact level of cardiovascular capacity needed for that sport. Someone with lower cardiovascular capacity and higher strength may perform just as well as someone with higher cardiovascular capacity and lower strength, based on experience, skill, age, and so forth. The tests in this chapter are designed to give you ways to assess areas that you feel you may need improvement and to give you tools to gauge whether program changes are effective.

Evaluating Anaerobic Progress

Since anaerobic effort can be maintained for only a very brief time, most often the gauge of anaerobic capacity is not heart rate. Instead, PE, speed, or power is used to assess anaerobic performance. The quickest way for you to determine your anaerobic progress is to sprint as hard as you can—in any mode of cardiovascular exercise—for 1 full minute (following a thorough warm-up) and then repeat the test every 3 to 4 weeks. Another way to gauge your progress in high-intensity anaerobic training is to follow the Tabata protocol (see chapter 3). Wear a heart rate monitor and warm up for 5 to 10 minutes on the same machine you will use for your test, and then reset your machine to 0. Go as hard as you can for 20 seconds, and then stop or move very easily for 10 seconds. Repeat this cycle seven more times until you complete 8 cycles, which together equal 4 minutes of intense work. Record your highest heart rate, maximum power, and total distance for the 4 minutes on the test form provided in the appendix. Treadmills do not work for the Tabata protocol due to the time they require to make ramp or speed adjustments. If you wish to run when performing Tabata intervals, run on a track and record the total distance covered in the 4 minutes. Each time you repeat the protocol, try to improve on your previous results. Though this test is not a purely anaerobic assessment due to its built-in rest intervals (even as short as they are), it provides useful information for gauging anaerobic improvement for endurance outdoor sports.

Again review the sport-specific requirements summarized in table 1.1 on page 4. If your sport requires a 3 or greater for anaerobic fitness (as is the case for mountaineering, climbing, paddling, and off-road biking) and you struggle with the Tabata protocol or sprint training, make anaerobic training a high priority in your conditioning program. Because all cardiovascular settings and machines differ, it is impossible to set standard goal numbers for the Tabata protocol. However, you can use the Tabata protocol to gauge relative improvement. You can also use PE and heart rate to assess whether workouts at comparable loads are getting easier to perform over time or to determine whether you are able to cover more ground. For the beginner participating in sports requiring a level 2 or lower in anaerobic fitness, such training is a lower priority; you may only need to include anaerobic workouts once or twice a month until you progress to higher levels in your sport.

Assessing Strength Fitness

To apply the FITT parameters of frequency, intensity, type of exercise, and time to your sport-specific strength training program, you need to learn how to gauge strength intensity for outdoor sports via your 5- and 10-repetition maximum (5RM and 10RM) for various movements. Chapter 4 details how to overload the musculoskeletal system during strength workouts. Using the principles from chapters 1 and 4 and the test results from this chapter, you will be able to design, use, and modify a goal-specific strength training program such as those provided in chapter 4. Sample recording charts are available with sport ratings in the appendix on page 279.

If you are just beginning an exercise program that includes free weights, err on the side of caution and start with weights you know you can handle for at least the first 5 repetitions. You should start light, because any time you perform unfamiliar movements, you are risking strain or even injury. If you are newer to free weights (have been training with them for less than 2 years) or are new to a particular movement, follow the 10RM protocol and progress to 5RM loads as you master form and motor learning and can handle higher intensities. If you have more than 2 years experience with free weights, start with 5RM loads for those movements that are already familiar to you. Avoid high-intensity (less than 5RM) testing or training within a month of your goal objective so that you get plenty of recovery time and reduce the risk of experiencing strain from working at high intensities when you are so close to your goal.

You can estimate the maximum weight you can lift by doing lighter lifts that take you to failure in 5 repetitions (by performing a 5RM test). Allow 10 to 15 minutes per exercise to determine a true 5RM. You can test your 5RM for a given lift as frequently as every 4 weeks. However, the central nervous system may require 3 or more days to recover from such a high-intensity test. Rather than testing the whole body for 5RMs in a single workout, select 1 to 2 test exercises per workout and then supplement them with several support exercises. To perform a 5RM test, complete the following steps:

1. Select a test exercise and complete your normal warm-up.
2. Begin your warm-up for the test by choosing a weight that is 50 percent of what you can lift for 10 to 12 repetitions. Do 5 repetitions at this weight and then rest 1 minute.
3. Use a weight that is 75 percent of what you can do for 10 to 12 repetitions but do only 4 repetitions and then rest 1 minute.
4. For your final warm-up set, use the weight you can do for 10 to 12 repetitions but do only 3 repetitions and rest 2 minutes.
5. For your first test lift, increase the weight used in step 4 by 10 percent and do 5 repetitions. Rest 2 minutes. You will likely be within 5 to 20 percent of your 5RM.
6. If you feel you were close to your 5RM (i.e., the sixth repetition would be a struggle), increase the weight by 5 percent for the next set; otherwise, increase by 10 percent and try for 5 repetitions. If you feel you can lift more, rest 3 minutes and repeat step 6.
7. When you can lift a weight no more than 5 repetitions, record your result as your 5RM on the test form available in the appendix.
8. Repeat this test for each major strength exercise you wish to assess.

Following are eight tests that assess your strength. For each test, complete the protocol just described. If you anticipate that you cannot do more than 5 full-range pull-ups, do your warm-up sets on the lat pull-down or weight-assisted pull-up machine. Record your results for each of the eight tests along with the date and time you performed the test. To get the best gauge of your strength improvement, perform retests at similar times during the day. Since the body is usually stiffer in the morning, wait several hours after waking to complete heavily loaded lower-body exercises involving spinal flexion.

Remember that the following strength tests are relative indicators of areas you may want to focus on in your training program. A low, average, or high score on any particular test does not by itself indicate whether you will succeed in your chosen sport—it simply tells you where you should focus your training. Adding the proper strength training to address weak areas may dramatically improve your sport performance. Instead of being discouraged by a low test score, embrace that score as a learning opportunity and a source of positive feedback that will help you make educated decisions about program development and will help you attain the next level of performance.

Assessing Upper-Body Strength

The following four exercises measure strength in the vertical pull, horizontal pull, vertical push, and horizontal push movements. Complete the upper-body assessment at least once every 4 to 6 weeks, preferably after a few weeks of cardiovascular baseline training, so that you can assess your starting point and monitor strength progress. You may want to do the vertical pull and push tests in one session and the horizontal pull and push tests in another session a few days later.

Vertical Pull: Pull-Up The pull-up (page 242) tests the latissimus dorsi, biceps, and abdominals. For this test, you should perform as many pull-ups in a row as possible. If you have never tried a pull-up before, or if you already know that you cannot do 5 in a row, do your warm-up sets on the lat pull-down machine (page 243) using the above protocol. For pull-ups, grasp the bar with your palms forward and shoulder-width apart and hoist your body from a straight-arm hang until your chin is above the bar. Keep tension in your arms and through your shoulder blades so that your muscles are contracted throughout. Recommendations for the number of pull-ups you should be able to complete vary widely from sport to sport and differ from males to females; however, a reasonable goal for outdoor athletes is to be able to do *at least* 2 (below that rates you at 1) and to target about 20 (above that rates you at 5), with 8 to 12 rating you as 3. The vertical pull is especially important for technical climbers.

Vertical Push: Dumbbell Overhead Press The dumbbell overhead press (page 251) tests the deltoids, triceps, abdominals, and spinal erectors. Determine your 5RM for the standing overhead dumbbell press. You should be able to complete 5 repetitions while pressing at least 25 percent of your body weight (weight of both dumbbells; below that rates you as 1), and you may be able to press up to 70 percent of your body weight (above that rates you as 5), with 40 to 50 percent rating you as 3. Be sure to maintain strict form. If the suggested minimum weight is too heavy, record the weight you can do for 5 repetitions and work up to the optimal range. The vertical push is especially important for mountaineers, snow sport athletes, and climbers.

Horizontal Pull: One-Arm Dumbbell Row The one-arm dumbbell row (page 246) tests the latissimus dorsi, rhomboids, and biceps. You should be able to perform 5 repetitions with at least 25 percent of your body weight (weight of one dumbbell; below that rates you as 1); you can work up to lifting 60 percent of your body weight while maintaining strict form (above that rates you as 5), with 35 to 45 percent rating you as 3. If the suggested minimum weight is too heavy, record the weight you can do for 5 repetitions and work up to the optimal range. The horizontal pull is especially important for climbers, snow sport athletes, and paddlers.

Horizontal Push: Dumbbell Bench Press The dumbbell bench press (page 253) tests the pectorals, triceps, and deltoids. You should be able to perform 5 repetitions of the flat dumbbell bench press with at least 40 percent of your body weight (weight of both dumbbells; below that rates you as 1). You may work up to pressing 100 percent of your body weight while maintaining strict form (above that rates you as 5), with 60 to 70 percent rating you as 3. If the suggested minimum weight is too heavy, record the weight you can do for 5 repetitions and work up to the optimal range. The horizontal push is especially important for paddlers, snow sport athletes, and climbers.

Once again refer to the sport-specific fitness recommendations presented in table 1.1 on page 4. If your sport ranks a 3 or higher for upper-body strength (as do climbing, paddling, and cross-country skiing) and you struggle to perform at the lowest level in any of these upper-body strength tests, a focus on increasing upper-body strength, at least initially, may greatly enhance your performance, especially if you are already strong in the other fitness components your sport requires. Place the highest priority on the movements directly involved in your sport and put secondary emphasis on those movements involved in muscle balance. If you score within the suggested range and your sport requires less emphasis on upper-body strength, simply include a maintenance strength program to keep your body balanced and prevent injury.

Assessing Lower-Body Strength

The following four exercises measure movements dominated by the quadriceps, hamstrings, abdominals, and lower back. Complete the lower-body and core assessment every 4 to 6 weeks, preferably after a few weeks of cardiovascular baseline training, so that you can assess your starting point and monitor strength progress. You may want to test the quadriceps and hamstrings in one session and the abdominals and lower back in another session a few days later.

Quadriceps: Step-Up The step-up (page 275) tests the gluteals, hamstrings, and quadriceps as well as assesses ankle stability. You should be able to do 5 repetitions using 100 percent of your body weight. The movement should be fully under your control and the leg that is up on the step should do all of the lifting (no rebounding off the floor). You should be able to use a step height that is at least 50 percent of your inseam (measurement from floor to groin; below that rates as 1), and you can work up to a step height that is 80 percent of your inseam (above that rates as 5), with 65 percent rating you as 3. If you are unable to use target step height or keep the movement under control, do this exercise with reduced height and added weight as part of your training program. If the step height is too high, record the step height you can use for 5 repetitions and build to the desired range of motion. Note any discrepancies between legs. The quadriceps-dominated movement is particularly important for hikers, scramblers, climbers, and mountain bikers.

Hamstrings: Barbell Deadlift The barbell deadlift (page 261) tests the quadriceps, hamstrings, gluteals, spinal erectors, and muscles of the forearm. You should be able to do 5 repetitions with at least 50 percent of your body weight (below that rates as 1); you can work up to doing 150 percent of your body weight (above that rates as 5), with 90 to 110 percent rating you as 3. If you are unable to lift the target weight from the floor to a straight vertical end position (from midshins to thighs) without experiencing discomfort, record the amount of weight you can lift for 5 repetitions and build to the desired range of motion before adding any more weight. This movement is particularly important for runners, hikers, scramblers, climbers, and (for balance and flexibility) paddlers.

Abdominals: Medicine Ball Twist The medicine ball twist (page 224) works the rectus abdominis and obliques. You should be able to do 5 rotating repetitions (touching the floor on each side) for a total of 10 repetitions while leaning back at least 15 degrees and holding at least 15 percent of your body weight (rating of 3). If you are unable to perform the movement with any weight, rate yourself as 1. If you are unable to move the target weight from side to side, record what you can use for 5 repetitions and build to the desired range of motion before adding any more weight. Note any weakness you experience as you move to either side, as your flexibility may hamper your strength and prevent successful performance of the exercise. This movement is particularly important in paddling, climbing, and cross-country skiing.

Lower Back: Back Extension The back extension (page 233) tests the spinal erectors, gluteals, and hamstrings. You should be able to do 5 back extensions, finishing with your legs in line with your spine, with at least 20 percent of your body weight (below that rates as 1). You may work up to performing 5 extensions (without experiencing discomfort) while holding 60 percent of your body weight at the chest (above that rates as 5), with 35 to 45 percent rating you as 3. If you are unable to use the targeted weight, record what you can use to complete 5 repetitions and build to the desired range of motion before adding any more weight. This exercise is especially important for promoting good back health for paddling, trail running, and mountain biking.

If you performed in the low range and your sport is trail running or paddling, include maintenance lower-body strength training to keep the body in balance and prevent injury. If you participate in any of the other outdoor sports, you should strive to achieve midrange or greater values in order to improve your sport performance.

Assessing Flexibility

The following five stretches provide initial data points for your sport-specific flexibility program. Include these tests with either a cardiovascular or a strength assessment and note what day you complete the tests. These stretches provide an estimate of which areas of the body need early-season priority and in-season focus in your flexibility training. If any stretch is especially challenging, include it or a variation of it (see chapter 14) to increase your flexibility. Refer to page 283 of the appendix for more information.

Frog Stretch To assess flexibility in your shoulders, torso, hips, and calves, do the frog stretch (page 217) while holding a dowel, solid broomstick, or ski pole directly overhead. In your final position, your heels should be flat, your feet should be shoulder-width apart or up to 6 inches (15 cm) wider, your buttocks should be close to or touching your heels, and your arms should be straight and wide (the space between your hands should equal half your height) so you can keep the dowel directly overhead. If you cannot keep your heels flat on the floor (rating of 1), your program should include the stair calf stretch (page 217) and downward dog (page 215) to stretch the calves; if you cannot get your arms straight overhead (rating of 1), your program should include arm circles (page 214) to increase the range of motion in your shoulders; and if you have trouble keeping your torso upright (rating of 1), you should add upper-back and core strengthening exercises as well as the piriformis stretch (page 216), leg swings (page 213), and triangle pose (page 216) to stretch your hips. If you shift noticeably over to one side or the other, rate yourself as 1 and include this stretch daily.

Hamstring Range of Motion To assess the flexibility in your hamstrings, lie on your back on the floor with one leg extended straight along the floor and the other leg bent at your hip so that it is lifted into the air (keep the leg itself straight). Bring the lifted leg as close to your head as you can when applying light pressure with your hands. If you have normal range of motion in the hamstrings, you should be able to get the lifted leg at a right angle to your prone body without the other leg bending or other hip rising off the floor. If you fall short of that goal (rating of 1), include the bench hamstring stretch (page 218), straddle hamstring stretch (page 217), or triangle pose (page 216) in your program. This test is especially important for paddlers who sit for hours with their legs out in front of them. If you have really flexible hamstrings (i.e., beyond 90 degrees comfortably, rating of 5), include strengthening exercises such as the machine leg curl (page 266), ball leg curl (page 267), or Romanian deadlift (page 262) in your program to protect your joints.

Butt Kicker To assess unilateral flexibility in your quadriceps, march in place, swinging your heels back behind you as though to kick yourself in the butt. After 5 marches, grab one leg with the same-side hand and bring the flexed heel to your butt. You should be able to engage the hamstrings without cramping and touch your calf to the back of your thigh. Repeat 5 marches and test the other side. If your legs cramp or for whatever reason you are unable to do this (rating of 1), add the

90-90 quadriceps psoas stretch (page 219) to your program. Butt kickers are an important test for trail runners, bikers, and anyone with tight quadriceps.

Lying Trunk Rotation To assess rotational flexibility in your lower back, hips, and torso, perform the lying trunk rotation (page 215). If you have a normal range of motion, you should be able to keep the top thigh on either side parallel to the floor while the top arm and shoulder rotate open to touch the floor on the opposite side (rating of 3). Note whether you are tighter on one side than you are on the other and, if so, include this stretch or the standing dowel torso rotation (page 214) in your program. Trunk rotation is important for snow sport athletes, trail runners, climbers, and paddlers.

Reach Behind Back To assess flexibility in your shoulders and triceps, bend your right arm at the elbow and raise it up overhead. Dangle your hand behind your head and between the shoulder blades. Bring your left hand behind your back and see if you can touch your hands behind your back. Repeat the stretch, switching hands. If you have a normal range of motion, you should be able to overlap at least one fingertip regardless of which hand is up and which is down (rating of 3). If you are unable to touch your fingertips behind your back (rating of 1), grasp a towel or rope in both hands and gently pull to increase the stretch. Add arm circles (page 214), the tree hug stretch (page 219), the triangle pose (page 216), and the trapezius stretch (page 219) to your routine if you are tight in this stretch, which is an important one for climbers, cross-country skiers, and paddlers.

If you struggle with these stretches and your sport ranks a 3 or higher in flexibility, you should include flexibility training as a high priority in your program. Hikers, trail runners, and mountain bikers should add lower-body flexibility training to help prevent injury and muscle imbalance. Climbers, cross-country skiers, and paddlers should focus on results from the overhead squat, trunk rotation, and behind-the-back stretches to assess torso range of motion.

Determining Training Levels

Armed with your initial test results, you can combine the fitness components into a suitable training program. Your program will depend on many factors, including your experience in a particular sport, skill level, lifting experience, training age, previous cardiovascular training, workout consistency, and previous intensity of effort. If you have had less than a year of sport-specific training, classify yourself as a beginner until reassessment suggests otherwise. If you have additional skill but have been inconsistent in your training for several years, start at the beginner level until the second assessment. If you have been training in your sport for 1 to 5 years, try training at the intermediate level and add a best-fit or field test to gauge whether you are at the appropriate level. If you have been training consistently for more than 5 years and you can complete the intermediate objectives with relative ease, consider yourself advanced. Specific guidelines for determining appropriate training levels are included for each sport in part II.

Successful Program Adaptation

Armed with the test results from this chapter, the training principles from chapter 1, and the additional information from chapters 3 and 4, you can add stretching, strength, aerobic training, and anaerobic training specifics to your program. In the following sections you will learn how to monitor your progress, determine when you have adapted to your program, identify overtraining, and get proper rest and recovery.

Gauging Progress

Once you identify your training level, select an appropriate goal to tackle and plan for short-term goals (see chapter 1) along the way. For help, you can refer to the examples in part II. Include a ramp test, field test, or sport-specific best-fit test (part II) to gauge cardiovascular progress every 4 to 6 weeks. Keep your tests as specific to your sport and goal as possible so that they reflect the changes your training is bringing about in your particular activity. Assess flexibility daily by including the appropriate stretches in your program. Gauge your strength every 4 to 6 weeks. Strength improvements will be fairly easy to spot, particularly if you include some test exercises in your program.

To design your program, compare the results of each test described in this chapter against the summarized sport-specific guidelines presented in chapter 1 (table 1.1 on page 4). If your sport ranks 4 or 5 in a fitness component in which you struggled, make that component a high priority in your training. If you need to increase aerobic or anaerobic capacity, turn to chapter 3. If you need to increase strength, turn to chapter 4. To increase flexibility, turn to chapter 14.

If your sport has recommended levels of 1s or 2s in a fitness component in which you scored a 3 or higher, you can spend the minimum time needed to maintain that component and focus your training on areas in which you are weaker (unless you are involved in multiple sports that require greater levels). If your testing identifies several areas needing improvement, include a few workouts or days each week that will develop those areas. If you match your sport's profile in all fitness components, develop a program that emphasizes the components equally so that you stay in balance and continue to improve gradually in each area. If you excel in all areas, jump to an advanced objective for a suitable challenge.

Tracking Progress

The more involved you become with your sport, the greater the chance that you may experience an acute or a chronic injury. Excellent year-round conditioning and proper technical training will reduce your chance of injury. As you begin to train, watch for clues that tell you to back off. By keeping detailed training records, you can find out how much stress you can handle when you have sufficient recovery before you train, race, or exercise at high intensity again. You should keep a journal containing your test results as well as other noteworthy training information. Small spiral notebooks work fine for journaling, but you may prefer the commercial training journals available for your sport. Whether you record your training on paper or online, keep track of the details you feel are most pertinent. Following are suggestions of what to include in your journal.

Daily Conditions

- Date and time of workout
- Amount and quality of undisturbed sleep
- Waking basal temperature and RHR
- Any aches, pains, discomforts, or injuries (onset, duration, cause)

Strength Workouts

- Exercises, repetitions, sets, loads, rests
- PE and how you feel before, during, and after workouts
- Personal records
- Any discomfort

Cardiovascular Workouts

- Type of exercise, duration, intensity
- Average, maximum, and recovery heart rates during workout
- PE and how you feel before, during, and after workouts
- Any discomfort or personal records

Flexibility Workouts

- Exercise, time, sets
- Discomfort or stiffness

You may also find it useful to track what and when you eat and drink and any altitude variations or adaptation methods you incorporate in your program (such as AltoLab or hypoxia chambers). If applicable, you can note any work with lessons, partners, classes, or groups. Finally, you can record your body weight and body fat percentage (if known) at the same time of day on the same day each week.

Adaptation Cues

With continued exercise, your performance should improve weekly. While it is normal to have down days when your energy lags, your times are slower, and you feel weaker, you will see a gradual trend toward increased fitness as your body adapts to overload. Your RHR will drop. Your working heart rate for a given amount of effort will decrease. Your endurance will increase and you will have more energy after previously draining workouts. You will travel more distance over a given length of time. The more time you put into practicing your sport, the greater your skill will grow, assuming you do not experience illness or injury. You may lose weight, notice your clothes fit differently, and observe increased muscle definition, all signs that your body is adapting to your training. You will feel stronger, as indicated by being able to lift more weight or shorten the recovery interval.

If you plateau or reach a sticking point at which you stop making gains, if you grow bored with your routine, or if you make excuses not to exercise, your body and mind may have adapted to your routine and you may need to change your program. Adaptation to a given workload takes anywhere from 3 to 6 weeks, depending on how experienced you are with the selected exercise components. By adhering to the FITT parameters and gradually increasing your workload according to principles in chapter 1, you will know you have avoided undertraining. If your progress stalls, you start to feel run down, or you start to regress, you may be overtraining.

Overtraining

In *Supertraining,* Siff (1999) states, "Exhaustion is the systemic result of short-term imbalance, whereas overtraining is the result of imbalance accumulated over a prolonged period" (p. 429). The overtrained athlete is a step beyond exhaustion. Overtraining results from repetitive training beyond recovery capabilities (i.e., always training at your highest intensity, training when injured, or training the same body parts or repeating the same movements day after day week in and week out). Any time you experience whole-body stagnation or decreased performance over several successive workouts, take several days off to allow your body to recover and to regain your enthusiasm for training.

Following are the general indicators of overtraining most common to outdoor sports. They are your body's natural way of preventing you from increasing your stress levels any further. Experiencing any one indicator by itself does not necessarily mean you are overdoing your training. You may experience a combination of symptoms. Keep an eye open for clues that might tell you that you are not getting enough rest. If you experience several of these indicators at the same time, reduce exercise frequency, intensity, time, or workload to see if symptoms diminish. Once they disappear and you are well rested, you should feel a desire to train again and see an increase in your overall performance.

Behavioral Indicators

Mood changes, including apathy, anxiety, depression, lethargy, irritability, nervousness, lack of motivation

Altered brain function, including loss of ability to concentrate, sluggishness

Unusual habits, including new sleep patterns, increased thirst, sugar cravings, reduced appetite

Physical Indicators

Reduced performance, including slower performance times, weakness, muscle soreness beyond the typical 1 to 2 days of DOMS, injury, increased recovery time

Altered scientific measurements, including weight fluctuation, increased RHR of 10 or more beats per minute, waking body temperature that has changed by .5 to 1 degree Fahrenheit (.28-.55 C), increased blood pressure

Poorer health, including slow-healing cuts or bruises, headaches, colds, prolonged illness

Recovery and Restoration

A correctly designed program includes sufficient time for active rest and recovery. If you are strength training 4 days a week, with 2 days of gym training and 2 days of sport-specific training, adjust the volume on all 4 days so that you do not overwork targeted muscle groups. After a high-intensity race or long-distance session, take a day or two off to allow for recovery. Experienced outdoor athletes can benefit from 1 to 2 weekly recovery workouts performed at less than 65 percent MHR. For example, a trekker might add a very light bike ride or brief walk lasting 15 to 30 minutes to allow the body to work through any residual soreness. An alpinist might add some light reverse wrist curls for the forearms or endurance core training involving high repetitions and low weight. The climber might do a short wall session focused on climbing with arms at or below shoulder level (i.e., mantel and stem positions), footwork, or rest-position traversing. The cyclist or runner may cross-train by adding in-line skating, rowing, or swimming in order to use muscles in different patterns from those used in the sport.

A professional massage can help your muscles recover completely in just a few short days following your adventure. Self-massage on the elbow tendons, feet, and knees or use of a tennis ball for hard-to-reach trigger points in the upper back and shoulder blades can be invaluable in maintenance. The combination of heat and gentle rhythmic pressure from hot tub jets can help speed recovery in sore, tired, or painful spots. You may find that you enjoy a hot shower, soak in a whirlpool, or sauna after a challenging workout. If so, drink plenty of fluids to help with recovery. Try alternating several cycles of heat and cold—spend a few minutes in the hot tub followed by a few minutes in a pool. Proper rest and recovery prepare you for the next stage: increasing your cardiovascular endurance.

Increasing Endurance

Cardiovascular training improves aerobic function; increases stamina in the mountains; creates a strong base on which subsequent anaerobic, strength, and sport-specific training can be added; combats stress; and helps with weight management. Once you have assessed your aerobic capacity, strength, and flexibility, you are ready to develop a training program to help you reach your sport-specific goals.

How hard should each cardiovascular workout be? Is it okay to do intervals on consecutive days? What is the best type of workout to do following loaded distance training? How do you make consistent progress toward specific goals? Can you exercise safely if you are feeling a little tired? When should you redo assessment tests? What level of training should you incorporate in your workouts? Such questions are addressed in this chapter, and sport-specific recommendations for cardiovascular training can be found in part II.

FITT Components Applied to Cardiovascular Training

The FITT parameters form the framework for incorporating cardiovascular training into your program. They provide you with a clear sense of how (what activities to include), how often, how hard, and how long. We begin this chapter by discussing endurance training for basic health (the minimum requirements for training with this book), and then we explain how to build toward optimal aerobic conditioning.

Frequency of Training Frequency is how many cardiovascular sessions you include in a week. According to recent recommendations from the American College of Sports Medicine (ACSM) and American Heart Association (AHA), healthy adults should participate in aerobic activity for 20 or more minutes 3 to 5 days per week. Outdoor endurance athletes need a higher frequency, greater intensity, and longer duration of aerobic activity. Frequency can vary seasonally; during the off-season, when your focus is on improving weaknesses and increasing strength, you may include fewer aerobic sessions than you include during in-season training, when you might have six aerobic workouts a week. If you are satisfied with your aerobic conditioning, several weekly cardiovascular workouts of varied intensities and lengths may suffice.

Intensity of Training To translate the training ranges suggested here and throughout the book into heart rate numbers that will keep you at the appropriate intensities, you must first find your heart rate reserve (HRR) by using the Karvonen formula. Take your RHR (see page 19) for 3 consecutive days. Average the results and record the average as your RHR. The formula 208 – .7(age) gives you your theoretical MHR, and MHR – RHR = HRR. Multiply your HRR by .65 (65 percent) and .75 (75 percent) and add each of these numbers to your RHR to get your target training zone for cardiovascular training.

For example, imagine you are a 40-year-old with an RHR of 60 beats per minute. This means you have an MHR of 180 beats per minute, because 208 – .7(40) = 180, and so your HRR is 120 beats per minute. Your training zone percentages are .65 × 120 = 78 and .75 × 120 = 90. Adding each of these numbers to your RHR gives you 138 to 150 beats per minute as your target training zone for distance workouts. If you wanted to find the target training zone for anaerobic training, you would multiply your HRR by .85 and .95 to get 162 to 174 beats per minute.

The cardiovascular workouts discussed in this book are categorized into four zones: recovery sessions (<65 percent MHR), distance aerobic sessions (65-75 percent MHR, or long, sustained low-intensity training), tempo aerobic sessions (75-85 percent MHR, or medium-intensity training that can be sustained for less than 45 minutes), and anaerobic sessions (85-95 percent MHR) consisting of hard intervals that last up to 2 minutes alternating with recovery intervals. Methods for gauging intensity, including perceived exertion (PE), the talk test, the use of heart rate monitors, and instinctual training, are discussed later in this chapter.

Time (Duration) of Training How long you perform each cardiovascular training session varies according to the current stage of your training cycle, the length and difficulty of your training goal, and the intensity of each workout. The higher the intensity, the shorter your session will be. If you have only a short amount of time to train on a specific day, include a short, high-intensity workout there. The more endurance that is required for your end objective, the more time you will need to spend training in a single session in order to be comfortable with the distance. Cardiovascular workouts range from short 20-minute recovery or high-intensity anaerobic workouts to long endurance-building distance sessions. To succeed at your goal without spending countless hours training, you should include the proper amount of each zone of cardiovascular training (recovery, distance aerobic, tempo aerobic, and anaerobic training) in your program.

Type of Training The modes you include in your program will vary according to your goal, personal preference, available equipment, days allotted to cross-training, and time available for each workout. Aerobic training can be performed in the wilderness, around town, on flat or variable terrain, on cardiovascular machines, or in classes. The more advanced you become in your training, the more important it becomes to select activities that support your sport. If you are doing four weekly cardiovascular workouts, you may be able to do your target activity in all four sessions with sufficient recovery time between workouts.

Table 3.1 Cross-Training Chart

Training activity	High overlap	Moderate overlap	Low overlap
		WILDERNESS TRAINING	
Climbing	Climbing, scrambling	Cross-country skiing, paddling, hiking, snowshoeing	AT skiing, trail running, cycling
Cross-country skiing	Cross-country skiing and snowshoeing	Trail running, hiking, scrambling, climbing, paddling, AT skiing	Cycling
Cycling	Cycling	Trail running, hiking, AT skiing	Scrambling, climbing, paddling, cross-country skiing, snowshoeing
AT skiing	Skiing, cross-country skiing	Trail running, hiking, scrambling, cycling, snowshoeing	Paddling, climbing
Hiking	Hiking, scrambling, snowshoeing	Climbing, trail running, cross-country skiing, AT skiing	Cycling, paddling
Paddling	Paddling	Climbing, cross-country skiing, scrambling	Cycling, AT skiing, trail running, hiking, snowshoeing
Scrambling	Hiking, scrambling, climbing, snowshoeing	Trail running, cross-country skiing, AT skiing	Cycling, paddling
Snowshoeing	Snowshoeing, hiking, scrambling, cross-country skiing	Climbing, AT skiing, trail running	Cycling, paddling
Trail running	Trail running, hiking, scrambling	Climbing, cross-country skiing, AT skiing, snowshoeing	Paddling, cycling
		OUTSIDE IN-TOWN TRAINING*	
Biking	Cycling, AT skiing	Hiking, scrambling, climbing, trail running, cross-country skiing, snowshoeing	Paddling
Hill walking	Hiking, scrambling, climbing, trail running, snowshoeing	Cycling, AT skiing, cross-country skiing	Paddling
In-line skating	Cross-country skiing, trail running, hiking	Scrambling, climbing, snowshoeing	Cycling, paddling, AT skiing
Speed walking	Trail running, hiking, cross-country skiing	Scrambling, climbing, snowshoeing	Cycling, paddling, AT skiing
Stair-climbing	Hiking, scrambling, climbing, trail running, snowshoeing	Cross-country skiing, cycling, AT skiing	Paddling
		INSIDE TRAINING WITH MACHINES**	
Cross-country skiing	Cross-country skiing, trail running	Scrambling, climbing, paddling, AT skiing, snowshoeing	Cycling, hiking
Cycling, recumbent	Cycling	Trail running, hiking	Scrambling, climbing, cross-country skiing, AT skiing, paddling, snowshoeing

Training activity	High overlap	Moderate overlap	Low overlap
		INSIDE TRAINING WITH MACHINES *(continued)***	
Cycling, wind training, Spinning or upright biking	Cycling	Trail running, hiking, AT skiing	Scrambling, climbing, paddling, cross-country skiing, snowshoeing
Elliptical cross-training	Hiking, scrambling, trail running, snowshoeing	Cycling, climbing, paddling, cross-country skiing	AT skiing
Ergometer training	Paddling	Cross-country skiing, climbing	Hiking, scrambling, AT skiing, trail running, cycling, snowshoeing
Jacob's Ladder training	Scrambling, climbing, paddling, cross-country skiing	Trail running, hiking, snowshoeing	Cycling, AT skiing
StairMaster	Hiking, scrambling, trail running, cycling, snowshoeing	AT skiing, climbing, cross-country skiing	Paddling
StepMill training	Scrambling, trail running	Hiking, climbing, cycling, AT skiing, snowshoeing	Cross-country skiing, paddling
VersaClimber training	Paddling, cross-country skiing, climbing, scrambling	Hiking, AT skiing	Trail running, cycling, snowshoeing
		INSIDE TRAINING WITH CLASSES***	
Aerobics, high impact	Trail running, cross-country skiing	Scrambling, climbing, paddling, AT skiing	Cycling, hiking, snowshoeing
Aerobics, step	Scrambling, climbing, hiking, snowshoeing	Cross-country skiing, AT skiing, trail running, cycling	Paddling
Kickboxing	Paddling, AT skiing	Cross-country skiing, climbing, trail running, cycling	Hiking, scrambling, snowshoeing
Lap swimming	Paddling, climbing	Cross-country skiing	Hiking, scrambling, cycling, AT skiing, trail running, snowshoeing
Ski conditioning	AT skiing, cross-country skiing, scrambling	Cycling, climbing, trail running, snowshoeing	Paddling, hiking
Spinning	Cycling	Trail running, hiking, AT skiing	Scrambling, climbing, paddling, cross-country skiing, snowshoeing
Yoga		Climbing, cross-country skiing, trail running, paddling	AT skiing, cycling, hiking, scrambling, snowshoeing

* Backward walking is an excellent choice for rehabilitation and muscle balance for sports involving the legs.

** The treadmill lends itself to so many uses—whether the ramp is high or low, the speed is fast or slow, the movement is forward or backward—that it is universally beneficial for all sports.

*** Circuit strength training and boot camp can apply to all sports. Aquatics classes can be used at the *education and training* level (see chapter 1) as a supplemental activity in off-season or rehabilitation training, as can Pilates as a supplemental activity.

Once you reach high-volume training in which you are doing six or more weekly workouts, you should include at least one cross-training session in your week. Table 3.1 on pages 38 and 39 lists the training activities discussed in this book and how much they overlap (high, moderate, or low overlap) with various outdoor sports. Activities that share high overlap with your sport (meaning muscle recruitment is fairly similar) should form the bulk of your training, while low-overlap options are best as occasional cross-training workouts. Some low-overlap activities may complement your sport nicely and be suitable recovery options; others may be off-season activities to give your body and mind a break from an intense season of training. For example, the hiker looking for suitable indoor machine options with high overlap to her sport might choose elliptical training or stair climbing; the same athlete wanting to include a low-overlap wilderness option with cross-training benefits may select paddling. Note that in table 3.1, the term *hiking* encompasses hiking, trekking, and backpacking; *scrambling* includes scrambling and mountaineering; *AT skiing* encompasses telemark skiing, and *climbing* includes all forms of technical climbing.

Gauging Intensity

To gauge the intensity of your cardiovascular workouts, you can use several methods that do not require number manipulations. If you have difficulty taking your pulse at either the carotid (neck) or the radial (wrist) artery, you can use the talk test, PE, a heart rate monitor, or instinctual training.

The talk test is a simple way to tell whether you are working aerobically. If you can link 6 to 8 words together or chat briefly with your training partner, you are solidly in your aerobic zone. If your intensity jumps to the point where you begin to gasp for air, you are no longer at a sustainable aerobic pace. Unless you are aiming for that level, you need to lower the intensity. Conversely, if you can utter several phrases in one breath, you may be working at too low an intensity to receive much cardiovascular benefit.

Perceived exertion (PE) can be measured on a scale from 1 to 10, 1 being very little exertion (lying down) and 10 being your hardest possible workout. Recovery workouts should rate a 5 to 6 (<65 percent MHR), distance workouts should rate between 6 and 8 (65-75 percent MHR), tempo workouts should be between 8 and 9 (75-85 percent MHR), and anaerobic training should hit 9 and 10 (greater than 85 percent MHR). A PE system for gauging strength is provided in chapter 4. Keep in mind that perceived intensity levels vary from person to person and sport to sport. What might be intense exercise for one athlete may be moderate for another. For example, the off-road cyclist who is fit for her sport may have a much higher perceived exertion performing a cross-training activity such as the VersaClimber or Jacob's Ladder simply because the movements in the supplemental activity are less familiar and involve different muscles than cycling uses.

Heart rate monitors are valuable tools for measuring cardiovascular intensity and work well for anyone wanting precise, measurable feedback. They range from basic models that simply read your heart rate to more complicated models that you can synchronize to your computer for tracking and analysis. Depending on the features you want, many models are inexpensive, easy to use, and accurate. GPS and altimetry data are available on some models. Heart rate monitors can provide the following benefits:

- You can approach your workouts systematically and see improvement over time. As your fitness increases, you will see a decrease in your working and recovery heart rates during workouts of comparable effort. You will also find that you can sustain higher heart rates for longer durations.
- You will be able to gauge the intensity of your cardiovascular workouts and eliminate guesswork. If your training plan suggests you should work at 65 to 75 percent of your MHR, which for you works out to about 140 beats per minute, you have a direct way of knowing whether you are meeting your goal.
- You can maximize the benefits of your workouts by detecting whether you are overdoing things or not training hard enough.
- You can use a monitor during interval training to get a feeling for what it is like to work at your AT. As you participate in other activities, you will have a better feel for your energy reserves, even if you are not wearing your heart rate monitor.

Instinctual training, or training by feel, is suitable for intermediate to advanced exercisers who are in tune with their bodies. It involves paying close attention to your body and doing what you feel your body needs. If you are a multisport athlete with a program that calls for an intense anaerobic ergometer workout, but you prefer to be outside, you may decide to run or bike hill repeats instead (do a different workout of comparable intensity). If your feet are tired, you may do a long mountain bike ride instead of a long trail run (do a different workout of comparable duration). Such substitutions are perfectly fine. They allow for comparable cross-training and are fun and psychologically beneficial. While it may seem like athletes who train instinctually are diverging from their programs, these advanced exercisers are in fact finding a way to keep training while preventing overuse and burnout.

Building Tolerance

Once you have completed a fitness assessment and have learned how to apply FITT parameters to cardiovascular training and how to gauge intensity, you need to understand why you should vary the intensity and duration of your workouts for outdoor sport training. In simplest terms, variation allows you to train all of your energy systems. Activities that last less than 15 seconds (i.e., completing a demanding rock climbing move or carrying your bike over a log) tap into the immediate energy systems, activities lasting 15 to 60 seconds (i.e., passing a ski competitor on a short, steep hill or helping a fallen companion over the lip of a crevasse) tap into the short-term lactate energy system, and activities lasting longer than 1 minute tap into the long-term aerobic energy system. While all three systems are involved in outdoor sports, the dominant energy systems deserving the greatest focus are your aerobic and anaerobic systems.

Aerobic Tolerance

Aerobic tolerance involves preparing your body for sustained effort over long durations. All sports discussed in part II involve aerobic conditioning, whether that means two short weekly sessions for preseason paddling or six weekly cardiovascular sessions for ultradistance trail running. The early stages of any conditioning program consist primarily of distance sessions preceded by a short 5- to 10-minute warm-up that increases blood flow and prepares the body for more rigorous activity.

You should gradually increase your endurance in the lower end of your training zone until you can comfortably sustain constant exertion for 30 minutes or more. Following the 5 to 15 percent rule, you can then extend the longer endurance workouts by 3 to 5 minutes each session until you reach 45 to 60 minutes, depending on your target goal. In the early season, building duration takes priority over adding intensity because it prevents overtraining and injury. In most programs lasting longer than 3 months, you will increase the intensity of several weekly workouts while keeping the duration the same or slightly shorter.

No matter what your activity, if you have to reduce your pace to a walk, slow ride, easy paddle, or flat glide ski, you are spending increased time on the activity and, by definition, building aerobic tolerance. As your fitness increases, you will find you can sustain your pace longer and at higher heart rates. The three types of aerobic tolerance workouts discussed here and throughout part II are recovery workouts (lowest intensity), distance workouts, and tempo training (highest intensity).

©Woods Wheatcroft/Aurora Photos

To build aerobic tolerance, be sure to include weekly sport-specific distance workouts on terrain similar to your end goal.

Recovery Workouts These easy-distance workouts are not geared toward increasing aerobic capacity per se. Rather, their aim is recuperation. They add to the total volume of distance training and should be very light in intensity, less than 65 percent of your MHR. They follow high-intensity anaerobic, hard strength, or long, weighted distance workouts. If you experience extreme DOMS after a hard workout, go for a short flat walk or bike ride the next day and follow with stretching. Such active recovery helps stiff muscles become more limber and allows you to return to activity more quickly. Waiting several days until all soreness is gone before returning to training can set you back by a whole week. If you wait too long between workouts, you may keep experiencing soreness. By resuming training more quickly, you will be able to tolerate increased workloads with less recovery time, improving your overall fitness. Recovery workouts can also include supplemental cross-training that complements your primary sport (see table 3.1 on pages 38 to 39). At beginner levels of training, a recovery workout may be a short walk, a yoga class, or gardening; at advanced levels, recovery may include easy hiking, swimming, or flat biking.

Distance Workouts Distance workouts help you develop your base pace, or the speed and heart rate that you can sustain indefinitely. They are geared toward increasing baseline cardiovascular stamina and are the longest workouts in your program. Your training effort should be at 65 to 75 percent MHR. You should increase the duration of these workouts by 5 to 15 percent over the previous week. Once you reach your target distance, you can add intensity by increasing speed, introducing challenging terrain, or adding resistance via pack weight or machine adjustments. If you introduce new terrain or resistance, you may need to reduce your pace to remain at 65 to 75 percent MHR until your body adjusts to the added difficulty. For advanced goals such as climbing Mount Everest or biking the entire Pacific Coast Trail (United States), see advanced considerations in chapters 7 and 8.

Tempo Training Tempo workouts differ from distance and recovery workouts in that the work segments are shorter and the intensity ranges from 75 to 85 percent MHR. The 30-minute monthly field test is an example of such training. Tempo workouts help you complete shorter portions of races or endurance workouts at a higher effort by helping you increase speed and stroke or leg turnover rate. While tempo training does not play as large a role as the other two endurance components play, it should be included weekly when you get near your goal event.

Anaerobic Tolerance

In a book about outdoor endurance sports for experienced exercisers, it makes sense to discuss how to raise the higher end of your training zone so that your baseline aerobic fitness grows at the same time. During anaerobic training, waste products in the muscles, including lactic acid, build up faster than the heart and lungs can remove them. The body enters a state known as *oxygen debt,* in which the muscles are literally starved of oxygen. If you train to the point that you start gasping for air, you have entered oxygen debt and are training at your AT. You cannot sustain your AT pace for long. By including anaerobic training in your program, you build your tolerance for short-term work such as you might experience at the end of a race, during a sprint, or at high altitude.

Once your muscles run out of stored fuel (20 seconds to 2 minutes), you must reduce your intensity to allow your body to replenish its energy stores. As soon as the working muscles receive oxygen and enough lactic acid has been removed, you can usually resume anaerobic activity; such practice is known as interval training. To build tolerance for anaerobic training, repeatedly alternate intervals of high-intensity work with intervals of low-intensity recovery. As your fitness increases, your recovery time will decrease until you can eliminate rest intervals—an improvement in aerobic and anaerobic capacity.

After spending at least a month building a solid foundation of cardiovascular endurance and strength, you can add weekly anaerobic workouts—add two for advanced goals. Pay close attention to your exertion levels and recovery time to avoid overtraining. Activities in part II programs that develop anaerobic tolerance include fartlek (lowest intensity), uphill, pyramid, and Tabata (highest intensity) training.

Fartlek Training This type of interval workout involves bursts of speed and recovery lasting random durations. Let yourself play in the natural environment, sprinting to the big tree, dashing to the top of the hill, or passing the athlete in front of you. Make some intervals shorter and harder than others and take as much recovery time as you need between each. Throw in different movements: sidestepping to emphasize the abductor and adductor muscles, walking or jogging backward to target the quadriceps, or cycling with one leg or paddling with one arm to get in unilateral work. High stepping recruits the psoas, kicking your butt while running engages the hamstrings, and high-knee bounding develops the calves.

Vary the number, duration, and frequency of your bursts according to how you feel on a given day. Modified fartlek training can also add variety to your distance workouts: Simply vary your speed and effort, doing intervals of slightly higher intensities during the endurance session.

Uphill Training Especially beneficial for sports that involve vertical travel (trail running, hiking, mountaineering, climbing, snowshoeing, skiing, and mountain biking), uphill training involves walking, jogging, running, or biking up roads, hills, or stairs as hard as possible for a specific time interval (elevating the heart rate to 85-95 percent MHR) and then recovering before repeating the work. The first time you try an uphill workout, warm up at least 5 to 10 minutes on flat ground. Then spend 2 minutes or less walking with a pack, jogging without a pack, or biking up a fairly steep hill so that you elevate your heart rate 20 to 30 beats per minute higher than your normal aerobic rate. As you return to your starting point, your heart rate will return to base level; repeat the trip uphill 5 to 6 times. Aim for feeling winded when you hit the top and feeling ready to go again by the time you reach the bottom. Suggestions for uphill training specific to each sport are provided in part II.

Pyramid Training Pyramid training begins with short intervals that gradually lengthen and then shorten again toward the end of the workout. For example, if you are exercising on a Jacob's Ladder, a VersaClimber, or another machine working multiple muscle groups, follow a suitable warm-up, sprint for 10 seconds, and recover for 50 seconds to complete the minute. Next, sprint for 15 seconds and recover for 45 seconds, then sprint for 20 seconds and recover for 40 seconds, and so on. Continue adding 5 seconds of work while shortening the rest interval until you are up to 40 seconds of high effort with 20 seconds of rest. As the work interval increases and the rest decreases, your intensity may decline slightly. Shorten the intervals the same way you lengthened them, returning down the other leg of the pyramid to 10 seconds on, 50 seconds off. Cool down afterward for at least 5 to 10 minutes.

Repeats Repeats can be done for set time, set distance, or set power output (i.e., wattage). For example, on a rowing ergometer you can do 10 to 15 sets of 10 hard strokes followed by 10 easy strokes, powering through the work strokes with leg drive and arm pull and then resting on the recovery strokes. Try sprinting on the spinner or elliptical machine, powering the stride rate into the 175 to 225 range for 15 seconds and recovering for 45 seconds before repeating. As your anaerobic tolerance increases and rate of recovery improves, lengthen the work intervals and shorten the recovery times. To develop a good sense of pacing, try to complete the same or a slightly greater amount of work during each interval. Add an interval to each anaerobic workout as both your strength and your speed increase.

Tabata Intervals The most intense form of interval training, Tabata intervals, maximizes oxygen consumption with very short bouts of focused exercise. The Tabata protocol works best on training modes that incorporate as much muscle mass as possible, such as rowing ergometers, Jacob's Ladders, VersaClimbers, elliptical machines that work the arms, or calisthenic movements such as burpees or squat thrust jumps. Dr. Izumi Tabata at the National Institute of Fitness and Sports in Tokyo, Japan, determined that his high-intensity protocol improves aerobic *and* anaerobic capacity in as little as 4 minutes per session by maximally taxing both systems (Tabata et al. 1996). The protocol involves eight 20-second sets of all-out effort alternated with 10 seconds of recovery time. On a VersaClimber, the short recovery time may mean you stand still for 10 seconds between efforts. On an ergometer it may mean doing 2 to 3 slow-motion strokes before resuming with all your might. Before dismissing the Tabata protocol as not providing enough training time, add an anaerobic Tabata workout once or twice a week and watch your aerobic power *and* anaerobic capacity increase in all your other training sessions.

Anaerobic workouts can be done 1 to 2 times a week for several months leading up to your goal event. Your anaerobic workouts should last no longer than half the time of your endurance workouts. If your longest weekday workout is 45 minutes, a 20- to 25-minute anaerobic workout will suffice; if you enjoy 2-hour trail runs on Saturdays, a single 45-minute midweek hills workout may be the appropriate length, frequency, and intensity for you. If your time is limited during a particular day each week, put your anaerobic workout on that day. You may want to combine leg-dominant anaerobic training (i.e., running, cycling) with an upper-body strength workout. If you incorporate anaerobic and strength training into the same session, start with a low-intensity warm-up, complete your strength exercises, and then do the anaerobic training. If you put the intervals first, you may be so tired that you cannot complete your strength workout at the desired intensity.

Each time you do an anaerobic session, try to increase your performance. Heart rate monitors are helpful for gauging your intensity during your work and rest phases. Raise your heart rate to 85 to 95 percent of your MHR during the work phase and let it fall to below 65 percent MHR before repeating. Your initial work-to-rest ratio may be 1 to 4 (i.e., 15-second sprint, 1-minute recovery), but over time you can shoot for 1 to 2 (30-second sprint, 1-minute recovery). If you do your anaerobic training on machines, be aware that some, such as treadmills, take considerable time to change speed and height settings. For work intervals lasting less than 30 seconds, select machines that adjust quickly if you wish to experience the full benefits of the workout.

If you sense you are approaching burnout, tiring earlier than usual in the intervals, or feeling discomfort beyond normal muscle fatigue, back off the intensity and duration for a few days and allow yourself more recovery time between anaerobic sessions. Over time, your anaerobic tolerance will increase, your endurance will improve, and your working heart rate will drop on other cardiovascular workouts so that you can increase the pace, difficulty, resistance, or ramp height as you get stronger.

Developing Your Own Cardiovascular Program

You are now ready to put together your cardiovascular training program to help you meet your sport-specific goal. Compare your results from the cardiovascular fitness assessment from chapter 2 with the sport-specific recommendations in table 1.1 on page 4 so that you can determine whether you need to focus on aerobic or anaerobic training. Then integrate your test results with the FITT parameters and the chapter 1 principles for creating a training program.

First, determine how many weeks you have for training, and then break your program into five relatively even training blocks. Using the 5 to 15 percent rule, determine what your weekly distance training workouts need to be so that you reach your goal. Follow your distance workouts with recovery workouts. Determine what training modes you want to include in your program. Using the template programs in part II, work backward from your goal event to the present and fill in the necessary recovery, distance, tempo, and anaerobic workouts. Test your cardiovascular conditioning at least once every 4 weeks.

Remember that the sample programs developed in part II are ideal, best-case scenarios that cannot possibly factor in all work, family, and travel disruptions that inevitably occur. Instead of cramming missed workouts together in late stages of training, remember your priorities. Ninety percent adherence with adequate rest and recovery will be your recipe for success. With a suitable cardiovascular template in hand, your next step is to continue to chapter 4 and refine your program with strength training.

Maximizing Strength

Do you need to train to failure to get strength results? How many strength workouts should you do each week? How much weight should you use for each exercise? How do you know when to work harder and when to back off? What exercises should you do? Some of you may be thinking that strength training sounds too complex to include in your program. Consider, however, that travel in the wilderness is much more strenuous than urban exercise such as running and cycling. Imagine carrying a pack full of food, water, and overnight gear while ascending 3,000 vertical feet (915 m), wading though strong river currents en route to a camping spot 30 miles (50 km) away, or traversing up and down steep grades, crossing streams, and navigating tree roots while riding a mountain bike. Such tasks require much greater strength than moving over level terrain in the city requires.

By following the straightforward guidelines in this chapter, you will be able to develop speed, power, control, balance, and muscular endurance; reduce the risk of injury by preparing the muscles, joints, and ligaments for added stresses involved in outdoor sports; enhance joint integrity and durability of tendons and ligaments to prevent strains; and increase your self-confidence when facing difficult and unexpected challenges in the wilderness. More specifically, increased lower-body strength will allow you to react appropriately to added stimuli such as biking through water or sand, running uphill, balancing and carrying a pack for hours, or navigating challenging downhill slopes on skis. Increased core strength will provide a strong base of support that allows transfer of power between the lower and upper body, which is crucial for paddling, technical climbing, and cross-country skiing. Having a strong upper body makes all activities easier, such as pulling upward on handle bars, swinging arms freely in uphill propulsion on trail runs or cross-country ski paths, successfully reaching shore against a strong current and headwind, or using trekking poles or an ice axe effectively and efficiently.

Age and Sex Variables in Strength Training

Strength training can level the playing field in terms of the effects of age on performance. Without strength training, most people achieve their maximal strength in their 20s and then gradually lose strength each year thereafter. However, with strength training you can increase your strength beyond any level you have achieved before, through your 60s and sometimes beyond that (though you may need to include more recovery time if you are older than 50). It is never too late to start strength training. People can begin lifting weights for the first time in their 50s, 60s, and beyond. Through proper and consistent training, many of these people will be able to achieve greater strength levels than those they experienced in their 20s. In this chapter we do not delineate among age groups or between sexes; male or female, young or old, if you cannot carry a weighted pack while gaining 9,000 to 10,000 feet (2,743-3,048 m) of elevation on Mount Rainier, Washington, in 2 to 3 days, you will not reach the summit.

Strength training is essential for optimal sport performance. Untrained women typically possess 40 to 60 percent of the upper-body strength and 70 to 75 percent of the lower-body strength of men. Their wider pelvises require appropriate exercise selection for muscle balance, particularly when it comes to exercises affecting the quadriceps angle, or Q angle, in the legs. Women also carry additional fat stores to help with childbearing. However, when lean body mass is factored in, the relative strength difference between men and women decreases. If strength is calculated per cross-sectional area of muscle, there is essentially no difference between men and women (Ebben and Jensen 1998). Through appropriate training, women can surpass their untrained male counterparts in strength. They can use conventional resistance training to gain strength and size that on a percentage basis is similar to that in men without developing overly large muscles (McArdle, Katch, and Katch 2000). Women and men should train similarly in terms of workout constructs and FITT parameters.

FITT Parameters Applied to Strength Training

Every athlete's body reacts differently to strength training. Your program should be based on your immediate goals and your unique strength and flexibility needs. Thus, your program may look entirely different from anyone else's program. How often, how hard, and how long you strength train during a given week should depend on the goals you identified in chapter 1 and on your test results from chapter 2. Armed with this information, you can then apply the FITT parameters to create an appropriate sport-specific strength program.

Frequency of Training

Frequency is how many strength sessions you do each week and depends on your training priorities, available time and equipment, and training age, among other variables. If you prefer to do more frequent and shorter strength workouts throughout the week, you can split your sessions to focus on different parts of the body or different movement patterns. The most recent position paper released conjointly by the American College of Sports Medicine and American Heart Association (Haskell et al. 2007) states that every adult should perform activities that maintain or increase muscular strength and endurance a minimum of 2 nonconsecutive days a week. These workouts should include 8 to 10 full-body, multiple-muscle group exercises for 8 to 12 repetitions each so that the targeted muscles are sufficiently fatigued by the end of each set of repetitions (Haskell et al. 2007). This recommendation is the bare minimum for outdoor athletes, as most outdoor athletes strive for performance results well beyond the requirements for general health.

Frequency varies seasonally. During the midseason, you may prefer 1 to 2 short traditional weight training sessions along with sport-specific loading; during the preseason, you may require 3 to 4 traditional strength sessions per week; and during the postseason, you may want to focus on weaknesses or imbalances in addition to targeting the major muscle groups several times a week. Sport-specific activities such as carrying a pack, bouldering, cycling in high gear at a low cadence, and performing plyometric drills can all provide strength training benefits. The more frequently you schedule your sessions, the shorter and more concentrated each workout can be, targeting fewer movements.

If you are satisfied with the results from your strength assessments (chapter 2), you may embark on a maintenance program of twice weekly full-body strength training that lasts 20 to 30 minutes per session. If you wish to increase your strength gradually, you may engage in 45 to 60 minutes of full-body strength training 2 to 3 times a week. To cause more dramatic hypertrophy, you may include as many as six short strength workouts per week, rotating among upper-body pushing, upper-body pulling, and lower-body workouts (performing each twice a week). Some people see more progress with short and frequent weekly sessions rather than longer and fewer weekly sessions. While the possibilities for split workouts are endless, following are three common ways of dividing weekly strength exercises that apply well to training for outdoor sports.

- Full body: Because outdoor athletes have so many training components to include in their program, 2 to 3 full-body sessions a week will be optimal and allow for sufficient recovery. The full-body strength training should include several exercises targeting upper body, lower body, and core. Choose free-weight exercises that work multiple muscle groups simultaneously. Change variables every 3 to 6 weeks as the body adapts.

- Upper body and lower body: By splitting the body into upper and lower halves, you can strength train three times a week (alternating upper, lower, upper on three different days of week 1 and then doing lower, upper, lower the following week). On those weekends that your cardiovascular program calls for long endurance runs, bike rides, cross-country ski trips, or heavy pack workouts, you may do a single leg workout and two upper-body workouts during that week to allow for optimal lower-body recovery before your long-distance session. This training split also works nicely if you lift 4 days a week; you can then perform each workout twice a week.

- Thirds: Such a hypertrophy-focused split might incorporate an upper-body push routine (i.e., push-up, dumbbell overhead press, lying dumbbell triceps extension), an upper-body pull routine (i.e., pull-up, dumbbell shrug, biceps curl), and a lower-body and core routine (i.e., barbell back squat, barbell deadlift, dumbbell lunge, and exercises for the lower back, obliques, and abdominals). By selecting different exercises for each workout, you can allow for sufficient recovery, keep your sessions effective and interesting, and perform each strength workout once a week.

Intensity of Training

The intensity of your strength training is determined by how much weight you use in a particular exercise. The intensity is often described as a percentage of the heaviest weight you can lift with good form for a single repetition. This heaviest weight is called a *1-repetition maximum,* or *1RM.* Intensity is a relative term since it is directly related to an athlete's 1RM. A person who can complete only one pull-up with good form is working out at a higher intensity (100 percent of his 1RM) compared to the person who can do six pull-ups (usually 80-85 percent of his 1RM), even though they may weigh the same amount.

Another way to refer to intensities is to state a weight in terms of the maximum number of repetitions you could do for a particular exercise. For example, if you could do 10 reps with 100 pounds on the bench press but could not get 11 reps, 100 pounds represents your 10 Repetition Maximum (10RM) for the bench press. Since most athletes training for outdoor sports have no need to test their 1RM, you will be referring to your RM number for a given weight in an exercise instead. For the training programs laid out in this book and for general outdoor sports training purposes, we see no need to train heavier than your 5RM. That does not mean, however, that you should not do sets of repetitions less than 5. It simply means that the weights you use probably should not be heavier than what you can lift when you are freshly warmed up and ready to try for a 5RM.

Training at high intensities requires more recovery time for the body's central nervous system (CNS). To avoid overtaxing your CNS, you should limit training intensities of 5RM or heavier for any particular muscle group to no more frequently than every 5 to 7 days. A 5RM means that you are lifting loads heavy enough to result in training to failure in 5 repetitions with a given weight. (Note that while some of the programs included later in this chapter include sets of 3 repetitions, the load is 6RM repeated multiple times.) While bodybuilders often train to failure, we recommend keeping a reserve of 1 to 3 repetitions (see definition on page 53) on any given exercise to permit higher frequency and greater training volume, both of which are conditions specific to the endurance needs for outdoor sports.

Time (Duration) of Training

The time, or duration, of your training is the length of each training session. It may or may not be proportional to the volume or workload per workout. Volume for this book is the total number of repetitions you perform during all sets for each exercise or muscle group multiplied by the weight lifted. For example, 3 sets of 10 repetitions completed with 100 pounds (45 kg) equals 3,000 pounds (1,360 kg) of volume, whereas 5 sets of 4 repetitions performed with 125 pounds (57 kg) equals 2,500 pounds (1,130 kg) of volume. The first example involves higher volume but has a shorter duration due to the lower number of sets. The second involves higher intensity and thus most likely requires more recovery time between sets.

The more sets you complete with heavier weights and lower repetitions, the stronger you can become. The more sets and more repetitions you complete with lighter weights, the more strength endurance you can build. Once you have completed a few warm-up sets, your strength workouts should not take longer than an hour. Stretching should not count toward your total strength time but should be included after every workout for at least 10 minutes. You may perform shorter, 15- to 30-minute workouts up to six times a week.

Type of Exercise

Generally, the exercises selected for a sport-specific program will include body resistance exercises (i.e., pull-up, push-up, or unweighted versions of the barbell back squat and dumbbell lunge), band exercises, or free-weight exercises using dumbbells, cables, barbells, loaded backpacks, rocks, or filled gallon jugs. Your exercise selection will vary widely according to your phase of training (preseason, in-season, postseason, off-season), sport-specific needs, training history, and assessment results from chapter 2.

Strength Guidelines

The guidelines in this section will help you select exercises (type), loads (intensity), repetitions, and sets that are specific to your goals, training age, and test results. By following these guidelines you will reach your strength goals more quickly and more safely than if you had not.

Exercise Selection

Incorporate the following recommendations when selecting exercises for your strength training program.

- Select free weights and cables over machines so that you can develop functional, three-dimensional strength and balance specific to your sport.
- Choose unilateral movements such as the one-leg deadlift or step-up for about half of your lower-body exercises and select a combination of unilateral and bilateral dumbbell exercises such as the one-arm dumbbell row and dumbbell overhead press for the upper body.
- Pick exercises that require you to stand or engage more of your body whenever possible. For example, you could do dumbbell overhead presses in a standing or seated position. In general, choose the standing version with the seated version for occasional variety. Prioritize the pull-up over the lat pull-down. Do the push-up instead of the bench press (you can vary the push-up intensity by using your feet instead of your knees, changing your hand spacing, or adding a weighted vest).
- Train the muscles you cannot see. People tend to emphasize the muscles they see in the mirror, such as the abdominals, chest, and biceps. For outdoor endurance sports, it is more important to strengthen the triceps, gluteals, hamstrings, and back.

Strength Terms

In order to build your strength program, you need to understand the terminology related to strength training. Following are basic definitions of terms that will appear throughout this chapter and throughout part II.

repetition—A single movement of an exercise through the whole range of motion and back again. For example, a pull-up performed from the straight-arm hang to the chin above the bar and back to the straight-arm hang is a single repetition.

set—A collection of repeated repetitions of one exercise.

straight sets—Completing multiple sets of an exercise (with resting between sets) before moving on to a different exercise. For example, in a workout calling for 3 sets of push-ups, 3 sets of pull-ups, and 2-minute rest intervals, the athlete does a set of push-ups, rests 2 minutes, repeats twice, and then moves on to 3 sets of pull-ups separated by 2 minutes of rest.

compound sets—Alternating sets of different exercises (with resting between sets). Typically, the two exercises work different parts of the body so that recovery from one exercise is affected minimally by the second exercise. For example, in a workout calling for 3 sets of push-ups, 3 sets of pull-ups, and 1-minute rest intervals, the athlete does a set of push-ups, rests 1 minute, does a set of pull-ups, rests 1 minute, and then repeats until the desired number of sets is completed.

body weight exercise—A strength movement that uses body weight as resistance; these include the push-up, pull-up, parallel bar dip, reverse torso curl, step-up, or reverse step-up, performed without external resistance.

free-weight exercise—A strength movement that uses dumbbells, barbells, cables, pulleys, backpacks, gallon jugs, or other forms of constant resistance that require balance and function in three-dimensional space. Such training loads the body similarly to the way it is loaded on a bike, in a boat, on a trail, on a ski slope, or on a rock ledge rather than requires the body to sit, lean, or lie down while moving an attached object.

machine exercise—A strength movement using exercise equipment that is limited to one- or two-dimensional movement patterns. For example, the leg press moves in a straight line (one dimension) and allows no deviation from that line. Athletes who are new to resistance exercise may find that machine exercises are easier to learn how to do. However, machines that do not fit the body properly can do more harm than good.

variable resistance—Bands, tubes, or elastics that offer great resistance at the end of the range of motion but very little resistance at the beginning.

training age—The number of years an athlete has been strength training consistently for two or more times per week.

unilateral exercise—A movement emphasizing a single limb in which one arm or one leg does most or all of the work. Examples include the one-arm dumbbell row (page 246) and one-leg deadlift (page 263). Such exercises engage the core and challenge stability in the supporting muscles much in the same way wilderness travel does.

bilateral exercise—A double-limb movement that involves both arms or both legs simultaneously, such as the barbell deadlift (page 261) or pull-up (page 242).

repetition maximum (RM)—The maximum weight load you can lift on a given exercise for a desired number of repetitions; attempting even 1 more repetition results in muscle failure. For example, if you can move 40 pounds (18 kg) on a dumbbell overhead press (page 251) for 5 repetitions but fail on the sixth repetition, 40 pounds (18 kg) is your 5RM.

repetition reserve (reserve)—The number of additional repetitions you could have performed in a set had you continued until you could no longer complete a lift in good form. For example, if you did 5 repetitions in a set and then felt that you could have completed the sixth but certainly not the seventh repetition, you have a repetition reserve of 1.

- When doing a full-body workout, select at least one exercise for upper-body pushing, one for upper-body pulling, and at least one lower-body movement, such as one of the exercises based around the squat, deadlift, lunge, or step-up. A categorized list of all the exercises discussed in part III is included in the exercise finder on pages 206 to 211.

Weight Selection

The amount of weight you can lift will vary greatly for each exercise. When working smaller muscle groups such as the rotator cuff and forearms, you will probably use just a small fraction of the weight you might use for a barbell leg exercise. Other exercises such as push-ups or pull-ups may primarily use your body weight for resistance. The larger the muscle groups you work and the longer you have been training, the more weight you will be able to lift.

Whenever you try a new exercise, select a weight you are certain you can lift and try a few repetitions to gauge how it feels. Err on the side of caution so that you do not overdo it in the first few workouts. If your goal for the one-arm dumbbell row is to complete 2 sets of 10 to 12 repetitions, try a few short, light sets of 4 to 6 repetitions as warm-ups to determine the approximate weight for each increment. Gyms vary widely in their equipment and machine lubrication. Inherent machine resistances and weight plate materials also differ, so resistance can vary among gyms; one weight stack labeled *50 pounds (22.7 kg)* may feel quite different from another stack labeled *50 pounds (22.7 kg)*. Note such differences so you can be consistent with your load selection at a given facility.

Taking a little extra time during your first few workouts will allow you to approach a suitable weight for each set more quickly in subsequent workouts. Once you can complete the highest number of repetitions within your specified range (e.g., 12 repetitions if your range is 10-12), see if you can go up to the next weight increment and still complete at least 10 repetitions with good form. In this way you can progress steadily, properly loading the muscles gradually and getting them to adapt more readily to the training. Whatever weight you use, make sure you perform each repetition with good form. If your form starts to degrade, terminate the set immediately.

Sets and Repetitions

All outdoor sports discussed in this book involve submaximal exertion over long durations ranging from an hour (biking or trail running) to several days or even weeks (backpacking or mountaineering) against various forms of resistance. Once you have determined your goals, training frequency, exercises, and length of training sessions, you can develop the appropriate amount of strength by adjusting the sets, repetitions, rest intervals, and number of exercises per workout. The sample strength programs at the end of this chapter provide real-life examples of how you can adjust all of these variables to fit your goal.

In general, the more repetitions you complete, the more localized muscular endurance you will build. On the other hand, the fewer repetitions you perform, the more strength you will develop, as long as you use a weight heavy enough to fatigue the targeted muscle fibers. As your training age increases, your neuromuscular system becomes more efficient and requires fewer repetitions at higher intensities to make continual strength gains. Table 4.1 shows how the number of repetitions affects training outcome. This table is not a prescription for all but merely an illustration of the relationship among repetition, training age, and training effect. You may find that you vary your repetitions depending on which muscle groups you are training, what stage of training you are in, and whether you are aiming for rehabilitation, endurance, stability, or pure strength development of the targeted muscle.

The repetitions in table 4.1 correspond to sets for which a reserve of 1 to 2 is maintained and an appropriate warm-up is followed. Repetition reserve is another

Table 4.1 Repetitions Based on Training Age and Desired Training Effect

	TRAINING AGE		
Desired outcome	<1 Yr.	1-3 Yr.	>3 Yr.
Maximum strength (not necessary for outdoor endurance athletes)	1-4	1-3	1-2
Strength	5-10	4-9	3-8
Mixed strength and endurance	8-12	7-11	6-10
Endurance	10-25	9-20	8-16

key factor to keep in mind when planning your sets. For warm-up sets you will want to keep many repetitions in reserve. The purpose of the warm-up sets is to prepare the mind and body for the proper form of an exercise. During the first few workouts when you are learning an unfamiliar exercise, keep several repetitions in reserve before you push yourself close to muscular failure so you learn how to perform the exercise correctly. During your regular training sets, the fewer repetitions you perform, the lower the reserve you need to keep. For example, in sets of 15 to 20, you might keep a reserve of 2 to 3, while for sets of 5 to 10, you might keep a reserve of 1 to 2. In addition, the more sets you do of a given exercise, the more cumulative the fatigue. Therefore, during the first set you will have more repetitions in reserve than you have during the last set, assuming you are using the same weight and the same number of repetitions each set. If you are doing 8 sets of 3 repetitions, you will want to start with a weight that you can lift 6 times (i.e., a 6RM weight), because by the time you get to the eighth set, you will probably be at a reserve of 1.

To control total workout volume, the more repetitions you do per set, the fewer sets you will complete, and vice versa. Table 4.2 suggests different combinations of sets and repetitions you can do per exercise.

Table 4.2 Total Repetitions per Exercise

Repetitions per set	Total sets	Repetitions per exercise
3-6	4-8	20-30
7-11	3-5	25-35
12-20	2-4	30-50

You may train your upper body and lower body differently. For example, you may want to increase upper-body strength while building lower-body endurance. It would be perfectly fine for you to complete sets of 6 to 8 repetitions for the upper body and 12 to 15 repetitions for the lower body if that scheme matches your goals. If you are moving your body or the weight explosively (as when doing plyometrics such as bounding, hopping, and jumping or performing dynos on campus boards), you should do more sets of fewer repetitions.

How quickly you complete a set of repetitions depends on your goals, but in general, lift the weight as fast as you can in order to recruit as much muscle as possible and then lower the weight for 1 to 3 seconds. Always remain in control; if your form starts to degrade, stop the set. Clearly, if you are working at your 15RM, you will be able to raise the weight quickly; a weight that is your 5RM will feel much heavier and will move much more slowly. Simply lift the weight with as much force as you can muster while remaining under control.

In general, the phase of your training program will help determine what outcome to target. For example, in the early preseason you might focus on mixed strength and endurance, in the middle of your preseason you might concentrate on strength, and toward the end of your preseason you might target endurance so that you can peak for specific goals. While in season you will probably be on a maintenance schedule in which you train moderate repetitions with a reserve of 2 to 3. Table 4.3 illustrates how your strength training might be periodized throughout the year.

Table 4.3 Sample Periodization

PRE-SEASON					
Early	**Middle**	**Late**	**In-season**	**Postseason**	**Off-season**
Lower volume with moderate repetitions	Moderate volume with lower repetitions focusing on strength	High volume with high repetitions focusing on strength endurance	Maintenance with moderate repetitions	Focus on imbalanced areas developed from sport-specific activities	Training of weak points

Rest Intervals

Rest intervals, or the amount of rest needed between sets, vary according to your goal. In general, training for strength involves heavier weights, fewer repetitions, and longer rests, while training for strength endurance involves lighter weights, more repetitions, and shorter rests. In addition, the rest required for recovery typically increases for exercises engaging larger muscles and with training age as a person grows in overall strength. Table 4.4 shows sample rest intervals for a person with a training age of 4 years who follows the repetitions in reserve guidelines for straight sets.

One way to optimize your training time is to alternate exercises in compound sets (see definition on page 52). Typically, compound sets allow you to cut your rest intervals in half since you will have two rest intervals between each set of the same exercise. Because of this time efficiency, all the sample programs at the end of this chapter use compound sets.

Table 4.4 Sample Rest Intervals

Repetitions in reserve	Squat and deadlift variations	Upper-body push and pull exercises	Core and limb isolation exercises
Strength: 1-2	3-5 min.	2-4 min.	1-3 min.
Mixed: 2-3	2-4 min.	2-3 min.	1-2 min.
Endurance: 3-4	1.5-2.5 min.	1-2 min.	1-1.5 min.

Gauging Intensity

A useful tool for gauging exertion in strength training is Perceived Exertion (PE). PE is a subjective rating of the feeling of exertion you experience during an exercise. It is based on your own perception of how hard you are working on the final repetition. On a 10-point PE scale, 10 is the highest PE. PE is assessed for each set, and the overall workout is assigned a score based on the average of the highest PE sets. Each repetition in a set should be executed with perfect form to minimize potential injury and undesired training effects. Following is a chart summarizing the 10-point PE scale for strength training. For strength endurance, keep the PE at 6 to 7; for strength, shoot for 8 and occasionally 9. For recovery or rehabilitation, aim for a PE of 4 or 5.

PE for Strength Training

Rating	Definition
10	Lifting to concentric failure under conditions of extreme physiological excitement (i.e., in competition). There is no reserve. The last repetition will probably take up to 5 seconds to complete.
9	Pushing to concentric failure. The last repetition lasts much longer than the other repetitions and the form may degrade slightly. Repetition reserve is 0 to 1.
8	Pushing to just short of concentric failure. The last repetition may slow but the form should remain the same through the entire set. Reserve is 1 to 2 repetitions.
7	Leaving 2 to 3 repetitions in reserve. The last repetition is easy and not very taxing.
6	Being able to do several more repetitions if desired. This is a recovery training level.
5-1	Leaving many repetitions in reserve. This is a warm-up level that serves to prepare the athlete for more intense exercise.

Training Equipment for Outdoor Sports

There are an infinite number of strength exercises you can do using just your body weight as resistance. However, for some individuals, an exercise such as a pull-up is too difficult to do, while an exercise like the squat requires far more resistance than body weight alone provides. Novice outdoor athletes can benefit from strength training without external weight, but intermediate and advanced athletes will receive greater gains, get more variety, and enjoy a lot more options if they have access to strength equipment. The guidelines on strength training mentioned previously in this chapter will help you determine what equipment will benefit your performance the most.

What you use for strength training will depend on your training age. If you are new to strength training, exercise bands, light dumbbells, and body weight exercises will challenge you sufficiently. As you gain more experience with strength training, your muscles will adapt to the stimulus. Every 3 to 6 weeks, you should change your program to keep making progress. You can lift heavier weights with lower repetitions, try variations of exercises you already know how to do, add repetitions or sets, rest less between sets, or learn more advanced training techniques and tips. The sample strength programs at the end of this chapter illustrate how you can change your program effectively as you increase your strength.

A gym membership may give you access to equipment; however, you certainly do not need one to gain the benefits of strength training. Variations on the push-up, pull-up, dip, lunge, squat, and handstand as well as yoga poses and abdominal exercises are all possible to do with body weight. Once working with your body weight feels easy, add a loaded backpack, a weight vest, gallon jugs filled with water, ankle or wrist weights, or adjustable dumbbells. This type of training can be accomplished on the most modest of budgets.

Developing Your Own Strength Program

You are now ready to put together a program tailored to your sport-specific goals. Compare your strength assessment results from chapter 2 with the sport-specific recommendations from table 1.1 on page 4 to determine whether you need to focus on upper-body, lower-body, or core training. You should combine this knowledge with the FITT parameters and the principles from chapter 1 in order to outline your program.

Following are additional concepts to consider when planning your personal strength training program. These include priority training, timing, combined training, and training progression.

Priority Training

In priority training, you emphasize what is most important to you at any phase of your program. When putting together a sport-specific strength workout, consider the following elements.

Importance Complete first the exercises that are the most important to your chosen sport. If you are a runner, cyclist, or backcountry skier, you should emphasize lower-body strength training. On the other hand, if you are a paddler or a technical climber, you should focus on developing upper-body strength, whether that means including additional sets of horizontal movements (paddlers) or vertical movements (climbers).

Balance Do any free-weight exercises requiring balance, such as the one-leg deadlift (page 263) or the one-leg version of the dumbbell lunge (page 273), before you do any exercises that put you in a seated or supported position, such as the leg press (page 278). As you progress through your workout, your body will fatigue, and therefore balance exercises will suffer more toward the end of a session than supported exercises would.

Weakness Complete the exercises that work weak areas of the body early or in separate workouts so that you recruit the most muscle fibers possible for them. This will help the weaker muscles catch up to the stronger muscles. To maintain strength in the strong muscle groups, include a set for them toward the end of the workout. Do this until you have reached better muscle balance. If one leg is weaker than the other, perform 2 sets of a single-leg exercise for the weak leg and 1 set for the strong leg until the legs are more even. Work the weaker limb first, and then finish by doing as many repetitions with the stronger limb as you could complete with the weaker limb. Stay even with your sets and repetitions whenever possible so that you do not perpetuate the problem.

Muscles Used Perform exercises that engage larger muscle groups before doing exercises that work smaller muscle groups. A smaller group, such as the biceps, assists larger groups when you perform a movement such as a pull-up. If you exhaust the muscle fibers in the biceps early in your workout so that they cannot assist in the pull-up, the larger, stronger latissimus dorsi will not perform optimally, and you will experience greater fatigue, lift less weight, and develop less strength. In general, you should place exercises in the following order: (1) exercises engaging the thighs, latissimus dorsi, or pectorals; (2) exercises engaging the deltoids or gluteals; (3) exercises engaging the triceps, biceps, calves, abductors, or adductors; and (4) exercises working the abdominals, spinal erectors, or muscles of the ankle, rotator cuff, and grip.

Imbalances Focus on areas that require more development and do minimal work for areas that are overdeveloped. Skiers, cyclists, climbers, or anyone who has stronger quadriceps than hamstrings should include the Romanian deadlift (page 262), the one-leg version of the machine leg curl (page 266), the good morning (page 265), the barbell deadlift (page 261), or other hamstring-dominant exercises for the first two-thirds of the workout and then balance the program with a set or two of the barbell back squat (page 270), the dumbbell lunge (page 273), calf work, and lower-back work. Hamstring work in the 4- to 8-repetition range with suitably heavy weight recruits the largest number of fast-twitch (strength) muscle fibers possible.

Timing

The best time to strength train is when you have the time to do it consistently. You need to do at least 20 minutes twice a week to gain benefits. Some people prefer exercising first thing in the morning; others like to do their strength training later in the day. Consider your back health when training early in the morning. Spinal experts recommend not doing any spinal flexion (forward-bending) exercises until you have been up and about for 1 to 2 hours. This is because the intervertebral disks absorb fluid throughout the night and are subject to more stress in the first hour or two of waking.

Experiment with the hours of the day that are convenient for you and see what your body prefers. If you are a morning person, you may want to strength train early; if you are a night owl, you may prefer late workouts. If most of your adventures have early starts (i.e., alpine starts for climbs, early race times for trail runs), you may decide you need to get used to functioning in the morning without coffee. Keep in mind that if you strength train one weekend afternoon and feel particularly strong, it may be due to timing and neural alertness rather than to a sudden increase in base strength.

Combining Strength and Aerobic Training

Combining strength and cardiovascular training into a single workout is popular for people pressed for time or for people unable to do multiple workouts in a day. However, performance in the second activity may be compromised if recovery time is insufficient. If your priority is to increase strength, complete your strength training before doing cardiovascular exercise; if you need to increase cardiovascular endurance, complete your endurance training before strength training.

Progressing Your Training

Try to improve in every workout. In order to make continual progress, you will need to vary the ways you adjust FITT parameters. Progressing may mean lifting more weight, completing more repetitions at a given weight, adding more sets for a specific exercise, doing the same volume in less time, speeding up a movement to make the muscles work that much harder, or making your body adapt to a given workload so that it becomes more efficient when moving a specific weight.

When you are doing a repetition progression, you add 1 repetition to each set the next time you do the same workout. When you are doing a weight progression of 2 percent, you complete the same number of repetitions per set but add 2 percent more weight. During a set progression, you add one more set of the same weight and repetitions, and during a rest progression of 5 seconds, you reduce the rest between sets by 5 seconds each time you do the same workout.

Sample Strength Programs

The *A, B, C, D,* and *E* letter-group denotations in the following sample strength workouts are used to tie the sample workouts to the sample training programs outlined in part II. Each letter group has several workouts associated with it (i.e., A1 and A2). The listed workouts for a single letter group are designed to be done in order, one on each day of the week you plan to do strength training. Each sample program in the sport-specific chapters in part II refers to the sample strength workouts listed in the following pages. When you see "A2 Strength" on day four of the first sample program provided in chapter 7, you should do all of the components of the strength workout identified by Workout A2 in as close to the order presented as possible.

The sample strength programs in this section list the sets to be done following a thorough warm-up. A common protocol is to do 2 warm-up sets, the first one with 50 percent of the planned weight and the second one with 75 percent of the planned weight. Each warm-up set should include about half the repetitions of the planned sets. If your workout calls for 3 sets of 8 repetitions of the barbell front squat with a target training weight of 95 pounds (43 kg), squat the 45-pound (20.4 kg) bar 5 to 6 times, add 15 pounds (6.8 kg) to each side, resting as long as it takes to change the weight, and do 3 to 4 more repetitions. Set the weight to the target weight and wait 1 minute before doing your first working set. After you have done a few exercises, you will probably be warmed up enough for the exercises that follow.

In the following sample programs, we also recommend a repetition reserve for the first set; these recommendations are meant as general guidelines to help you choose the appropriate weight for the exercise. If you do not know what weight you should be targeting, simply extend your warm-up by adding more weight on each set until you attain the desired repetition reserve. After your first session, you will have figured out what weight to use for the repetitions and sets indicated by the workout plan.

All the exercises included in the following strength programs are paired as compound sets. The labels in front of each exercise indicate the pairs and the order. For example, when you are doing 3 sets of 8 repetitions with 1 minute of rest, you would do exercise 1a and rest 1 minute, do exercise 1b and rest 1 minute, and then repeat this pair two more times before going on to exercises 2a and 2b.

While the following sample programs address needs that are common among outdoor sports, they are still generalizations. If you want to use them so you do not have to create programs from scratch but still desire individual customization, you can personalize them by trading some of the exercises. For example, imagine you are training for cross-country skiing. You learn from chapter 13 that the dumbbell lunge and its variations are a top priority for you, but your chosen sample program does not include them. You look in the exercise finder (page 210) and discover that the dumbbell lunge is a lower-body quadriceps-dominant exercise. You can now look for an exercise already listed in your program that is a quadriceps-dominant exercise, such as the barbell back squat, and swap this exercise with the dumbbell lunge. As another example, if you know you need to work on rotator cuff and hip abductor endurance in the off-season, you might select programs A1 and A2 and add a few sets of such exercises in the same repetition scheme. By switching exercises or adding targeted body stabilization movements, you will make the program more specific to your needs; by maintaining the other parameters (sets, repetitions, rest intervals, progression, and total number of exercises) you will achieve similar strength training outcomes.

Goal

Return to weights after time off

Schedule

Two weekly full-body sessions; alternate between A1 and A2

Workout A1

Do 2 sets of 12 repetitions with a reserve of 3 repetitions for the first set.

Rest 60 seconds between sets.

Use a progression of adding 1 repetition each time you do a workout.

1a	Barbell back squat	**1b**	Dumbbell overhead press (standing)
2a	Dirt digger	**2b**	Push-up
3a	Dumbbell shrug	**3b**	One-arm dumbbell row
4a	Ball leg curl (one-leg)	**4b**	Lat pull-down

Workout A2

Do 3 sets of 8 repetitions with a reserve of 3 repetitions for the first set.

Rest 90 seconds between sets.

Use a progression of adding 2 to 3 percent more weight each time you do a workout.

1a	Lunge step-up	**1b**	Bench press (incline dumbbell)
2a	Seated row with parallel grip	**2b**	Machine leg curl
3a	Bent-arm pullover	**3b**	Chin-up
4a	Decline crunch	**4b**	Standing calf raise

Goal

Build both strength and endurance

Schedule

Three weekly full-body sessions; rotate through B1, B2, and B3

Workout B1

Do 6 sets of 4 repetitions with a reserve of 3 repetitions for the first set.

Rest 120 seconds between sets.

Use a progression of adding 2 to 3 percent more weight each time you do a workout.

1a	Barbell deadlift	**1b**	Pull-up
2a	Bench press (flat barbell)	**2b**	Step-up

Workout B2

Do 4 sets of 8 repetitions with a reserve of 2 repetitions for the first set.

Rest 90 seconds between sets.

Use a progression of adding 1 repetition each time you do a workout.

1a	Bench press (incline dumbbell)	**1b**	One-leg deadlift
2a	Barbell front squat	**2b**	One-arm dumbbell row
3a	Rope face pull	**3b**	Push-up ball roll-in

Workout B3

Do 3 sets of 12 repetitions with a reserve of 2 repetitions for the first set.

Rest 60 seconds between sets.

Use a progression of decreasing rest intervals by 5 seconds each time you do a workout.

1a	Leg press	**1b**	Barbell military press (standing)
2a	Good morning	**2b**	Shrug (barbell)
3a	Horizontal pull-up	**3b**	Triceps push-down
4a	Forward barbell roll-out	**4b**	Biceps curl (dumbbells)

Goal

Maximize strength

Schedule

Four weekly sessions, upper and lower split; rotate through C1, C2, C3, and C4

Workout C1 (Lower)

Do 8 sets of 3 repetitions with a reserve of 3 repetitions for the first set.

Rest 90 seconds between sets.

Use a progression of adding 1 set per exercise each time you do a workout.

1a	Barbell back squat	**1b**	Standing calf raise
2a	Romanian deadlift	**2b**	Lunge step-up

Workout C2 (Upper)

Do 8 sets of 3 repetitions with a reserve of 3 repetitions for the first set.

Rest 90 seconds between sets.

Use a progression of adding 1 set per exercise each time you do a workout.

1a	Bench press (barbell)	**1b**	Pull-up
2a	Dumbbell overhead press (standing)	**2b**	One-arm dumbbell row

Workout C3 (Lower)

Do 4 sets of 6 repetitions with a reserve of 2 repetitions for the first set.

Rest 90 seconds between sets.

Use a progression of adding 2 to 3 percent more weight each time you do a workout.

1a	One-leg Bulgarian squat	**1b**	One-leg deadlift
2a	Reverse step-up	**2b**	Good morning
3a	Seated calf raise	**3b**	Saxon dumbbell overhead side bend

Workout C4 (Upper)

Do 4 sets of 6 repetitions with a reserve of 2 repetitions for the first set.

Rest 90 seconds between sets.

Use a progression of adding 2 to 3 percent more weight each time you do a workout.

1a	Barbell military press	**1b**	Seated row
2a	Bench press (narrow-grip barbell)	**2b**	Straight-arm standing lat pull-down
3a	Lying dumbbell triceps extension	**3b**	Biceps curl (EZ bar)

Goal

Maximize strength

Schedule

Two or three weekly full-body sessions; alternate between workouts D1 and D2

Workout D1

Do 5 sets of 5 repetitions with a reserve of 3 repetitions for the first set.

Rest 90 seconds between sets.

Use a progression of adding 2 to 3 percent more weight each time you do a workout.

1a	Barbell deadlift	**1b**	Parallel bar dip
2a	Step-up	**2b**	Pull-up
3a	Dirt digger	**3b**	External rotation (rotator cuff)

Workout D2

Do 3 sets of 8 repetitions with a reserve of 2 repetitions for the first set.

Rest 60 seconds between sets.

Use a progression of adding 1 set per exercise each time you do a workout.

1a	One-leg Bulgarian squat	**1b**	One-arm dumbbell row
2a	Dumbbell overhead press	**2b**	One-leg deadlift
3a	Standing calf raise	**3b**	Triceps push-down
4a	Dumbbell shrug	**4b**	Reverse torso curl

Goal

Build strength endurance

Schedule

Three weekly full-body sessions; rotate through workouts E1, E2, and E3

Workout E1

Do 4 sets of 8 repetitions with a repetition reserve of 2 for the first set.

Rest 60 seconds between sets.

Use a progression of decreasing rest intervals by 5 seconds each time you do a workout.

1a	Backward lunge	1b	Chin-up
2a	Hamstring pull-through	2b	Parallel bar dip
3a	Straight-leg sit-up	3b	Dumbbell overhead press (standing alternating)

Workout E2

Do 3 sets of 12 repetitions with a reserve of 3 repetitions for the first set.

Rest 45 seconds between sets.

Use a progression of adding 2 to 3 percent more weight each time you do a workout.

1a	Leaning lunge	1b	Bench press (flat dumbbell)
2a	One-leg deadlift	2b	Horizontal pull-up
3a	Seated calf raise	3b	Bent-over dumbbell raise
4a	Wood chopper	4b	Lying dumbbell triceps extension

Workout E3

Do 2 sets of 16 repetitions with a reserve of 4 repetitions for the first set.

Rest 30 seconds between sets.

Use a progression of adding 1 repetition each time you do a workout.

1a	Dumbbell lunge (walking)	1b	Dumbbell fly (flat)
2a	Romanian deadlift (dumbbells)	2b	Seated row (rotation)
3a	Reverse step-up	3b	Back extension
4a	Lat pull-down	4b	Medicine ball twist (decline)

Fueling for Outdoor Pursuits

Nutrition (more specifically, sport nutrition) is a complex topic on which there are literally hundreds of books and approaches. In this chapter, we provide basic nutrition guidelines that work well for outdoor athletes, including recommendations for the frequency, size, and timing of food intake. We also discuss how to adapt these general guidelines to your nutrition goals, such as staying healthy so you can continue to train, maintaining daily energy, supplying sufficient energy to prevent fatigue during endurance events, supporting continued effort at high altitude, and identifying nutritious, portable snacks for long trips.

Individual Variances

Every outdoor athlete has unique dietary requirements as well as individual goals, and there are probably as many suggested eating plans as there are individuals. Evidence (Price 2008) suggests that eating the foods your ancestors ate may be more important than following the "healthy diet" defined by government agencies. If your ancestors lived in tropical regions, you may perform well on a high-carbohydrate, low-fat diet, whereas if your ancestors grew up in harsh northern climates, you may do better on a diet high in protein and fat. You may already have discovered that certain foods leave you energized and satisfied, while other foods make you sluggish or otherwise uncomfortable. Such postprandial reactions can indicate which foods are best—and which are worst—for you.

The explanation for the way the optimal diet differs among individuals is that bodies vary greatly in how quickly they break down and convert food into energy. Some people break down food very quickly, while others take much longer to convert their food. If you eat a meal of pasta and tomato sauce (a high-carbohydrate, low-fat, low-protein meal) and feel a sudden surge of energy less than an hour after eating followed by lethargy, or if you still feel hungry shortly after eating a big meal, you may convert food to energy very quickly and your body might do best when fed foods high in protein and fat that take longer to metabolize. Conversely, if you feel sluggish after eating steak and a salad (a low-carbohydrate, high-protein, high-fat dinner) it is possible that you convert food to energy slowly. In this case, you may do better eating meals higher in carbohydrate since carbohydrate is processed more quickly than protein and fat are processed.

Nutrition Guidelines

When reading these guidelines, remember to consider your personal differences as well as your personal preferences. If you modify your nutrition program, add 1 or 2 of the guidelines at a time rather than trying to introduce all of them simultaneously. When you add a guideline, follow it at least 6 days out of the week for an entire month to establish your new habit before adding another one. To identify your macronutrient profile (ratio of carbohydrate to protein to fat) and track your caloric intake, consider using online resources such as those available through Weight Watchers or FitDay; the latter offers a free online tracking program.

Eat Frequently Every day, try to eat 5 to 6 equally sized meals or snacks every 3 hours or so. By eating smaller meals more frequently, you avoid getting too hungry or too full and you teach your body that it will receive nutritious food on a regular basis. This keeps your metabolic furnace stoked so that it releases fat stores more readily and provides you with energy all day long. When you are in the midst of endurance training that lasts multiple hours or exercising at altitude, you may find that you snack as often as every 45 to 60 minutes, although your snack size may be relatively small.

Choose Foods in Their Natural State Try to eat the majority of your foods in their original form. In other words, try to eat foods that grow, such as carrots or beans, or foods that move, such as fish or chicken. When shopping for groceries, stay on the outside aisles of the store, where the fresh produce, dairy, seafood, grains, and meats are located; avoid the interior shelves, where high-fat, high-sodium, canned, boxed, frozen, and manufactured foods all reside. Highly processed and refined foods including candy, chips, prepackaged or frozen meals, and crackers should play only a very small role in the outdoor athlete's diet. If you cannot easily pronounce all of the ingredients, avoid eating it!

Eat Protein With Every Meal Complete protein contains the essential amino acids that are necessary to every cell in the body. Protein tends to feel more satisfying because it controls the appetite for a longer time. Complete protein comes from animals and their dairy by-products. Most nonanimal sources of protein are incomplete, and you must combine them with other protein sources to get all the essential amino acids. See the discussion on protein on page 71.

Eat Vegetables With Every Meal Vegetables are packed with vitamins, minerals, and fiber essential for good health. Vitamin supplements are man-made attempts to supply the known vitamins and minerals that are used in the largest quantities by the body, but they are a poor replacement for the nutrients found in fresh vegetables and fruits. Fresh produce can reduce the acidity of your blood and thus can help prevent the loss of bone and muscle mass that can occur in acidic conditions.

Watch the Glycemic Index Try to keep the glycemic index (GI) of your meals low so you can maintain consistent energy levels. During and right after exercise, however, consume foods with higher GI values to create an insulin spike so you can replace depleted glycogen more quickly and minimize muscle breakdown. See the discussion of GI on page 69.

Eat a Variety of Foods Try to eat as many different types of foods as possible, as doing so enhances your chance of consuming all the required nutrients. It is easy to fall into a habit of eating the same 7 or 8 foods day after day. Select fruits and vegetables that vary enough in color to make up the entire spectrum of the rainbow at least once a week. Try a new whole grain or experiment with new herbs or spices on a regular basis. Instead of ordering the same item at restaurants, choose something new or have the waitstaff suggest a favorite dish.

Drink Plenty of Water Drink enough daily fluids to keep your urine nearly colorless. On your days off, that probably means drinking 64 fluid ounces (8 full cups, or 1.9 L) or more of water. On your exercise days, you may need to drink twice that amount. Your body is 60 percent water and requires water for a variety of physiological functions. Not drinking enough water can damage your health, reduce your performance, and increase your body fat. See the discussion on fluids on page 71.

Balance Your Fat Intake Most people function well if their fat intake is between 20 and 40 percent of their total calories. Balance your fat intake among saturated, monounsaturated, and polyunsaturated fats so that you are consuming them in approximately equal amounts. By replacing saturated fat (from animal products) with extra-virgin olive oil, avocado, fish, fish oil, and flax seeds, you can change your fat profile significantly. See the discussion on fat on page 70.

Adjust Nutrition to Training Your body handles food differently during exercise and during the hour or so immediately following exercise. You can enhance your training efforts by adjusting your intake during this time. Consuming a drink combining high-GI carbohydrate with protein in a 2-to-1 ratio (two-thirds carbohydrate, one-third protein) both during and after training can replenish glycogen, decrease protein breakdown, and increase protein synthesis. See the discussion on workout nutrition on the following page.

Allow Yourself to Cheat 10 Percent of the Time By allowing yourself to cheat occasionally, you acknowledge that you do not have to eat perfectly in order to eat well. Most people who are strict 100 percent of the time end up rebelling against their nutrition plan, making matters worse. If you eat five times a day, 7 days a week, you may allow yourself 3 to 4 cheat meals each week. By following such a strategy, you can go to a holiday party or attend a business lunch and partake in foods not on your plan without feeling guilty. By sticking with a nutrition plan 90 percent of the time, you will reap many health benefits over the long term.

Workout Nutrition

During and after exercise, your blood flow increases greatly. Since nutrients are delivered to the cells via the blood, this increased blood flow can be used to enhance nutrient delivery in order to promote recovery, increase the body's ability to build muscles, improve immune function, reduce muscle soreness, and increase bone mass.

To get your consumed nutrients into the blood as quickly as possible, drink fluids rather than eat solid foods, as nutrients in liquid form are absorbed far more quickly than those trapped in solid foods. Carbohydrate promotes an insulin response, since insulin is needed to carry the carbohydrate molecules and amino acids (from protein) to the cells. Studies indicate that consuming carbohydrate during exercise—anywhere from .2 to 1.2 grams of carbohydrate per 2.2 pounds (1 kg) of body weight—enables the athlete to postpone fatigue and perform at a higher level (Colgan 1993). A good starting point is 30 grams of carbohydrate for women and 40 grams for men. To get a good amount of protein into the blood, you should consume half as much protein in grams as you are consuming carbohydrate. You can sip this drink during your workout, consume half of it during and half of it after exercising, or drink all of it within an hour of completing your workout. While there are a number of specialized supplement mixes designed to be consumed during exercise, a simple, inexpensive, and effective way to get your liquid nutrition is to mix whey protein with Gatorade.

Carbohydrate

The best foods to consume after a strenuous workout are those that have relatively high GI values (see the suggested readings for GI values of various foods). In simple terms, the GI value measures how quickly food triggers arise in circulating blood sugar. Foods with a high GI value release glucose very quickly, while foods with a low GI value provide more sustained energy. Foods that are higher in protein and fat tend to have lower GI values, as these foods require more time to digest and do not cause as rapid a blood sugar response. Most simple sugars and highly refined carbohydrate foods, on the other hand, have higher GI values. During the day, consume carbohydrate foods with lower GI values so you can maintain your energy levels without creating spikes in your blood sugar levels.

Eating foods with lower GI values can also help you keep calm when handling emergencies or making important decisions. By regularly adding protein or small amounts of healthy fat to carbohydrate-rich foods, you can buffer the effect of any food with a high GI value, reduce the total GI value of the meal, and thereby control your body's insulin response. Add cream cheese or peanut butter to a bagel. Sprinkle some nuts on your yogurt. Add a small pat of butter to the pumpernickel toast or turkey sandwich. Avoid foods that list glucose, sugar, brown sugar, high fructose corn syrup, molasses, honey, or dextrose as one of the first two ingredients, *except* when you are consuming them as part of your posttraining nutrition.

Use the following guidelines to select foods with lower GI values and to reduce the glycemic load (the amount of carbohydrate in a serving of a particular food) of your meals:

- *Eat foods with fiber:* Foods with more fiber take longer to digest and absorb and hence have a lower GI value. For example, whole-grain wild rice has a lower GI value than instant white rice.
- *Eat food that takes more work to digest:* Any food containing protein or fat will take more time to digest and therefore will lower the total GI value of what you are eating.
- *Watch the specific sugars in your food:* Fructose is converted slowly, while maltose is metabolized more quickly.
- *Choose the best form of food:* Cooking or precooking raises the GI value of your food. Quick-cooking oatmeal has a much higher GI value than steel-cut or slow-cooked oatmeal has. This is also due in part to preprocessing and fiber content.
- *Watch out for enrichment:* Any food labeled as *enriched* has probably had the best parts removed during processing and returned afterward. Select whole, natural foods.

Fat

Fat is essential for skin health and important metabolic processes within the body. It should contribute 20 to 40 percent of your total daily calories. There are four main types of fat:

1. *Saturated fat.* Most animal products, including eggs, dairy, cheese, and butter, and coconut oil and palm oil contain saturated fat.
2. *Monounsaturated fat.* Most nuts and nut butters, olive oil, and avocado contain monounsaturated fat.
3. *Polyunsaturated fat.* Most nuts and nut butters, flax seeds and oil, vegetable oil, and fish oils contain polyunsaturated fat.
4. *Trans-fat.* Most margarine, vegetable shortening, partially hydrogenated vegetable oil, deep-fried snacks, fast foods, and commercially baked goods contain trans-fat.

Probably more important than watching your total caloric intake from fat is achieving a good balance among the different types of fat. Try to eat one-third saturated fat, one-third monounsaturated fat, and one-third polyunsaturated fat. Avoid consuming man-made trans-fat, as science shows us daily how dangerous such fat can be.

Polyunsaturated fats are broken down into omega-3 and omega-6 essential fatty acids. You should shoot for an equal balance of the two. Most Westerners consume 10 times more omega-6 than omega-3 fatty acids due to all the vegetable oils we consume. Two simple guidelines to follow to improve this ratio are to eat more monounsaturated fat like avocado and extra-virgin olive oil and to supplement your diet with high omega-3 foods such as fish, fish oil, and flax seeds. Implementing these two changes will help you approach the proper distribution of the different types of fat in your diet.

Fluids

Your goal for liquid consumption should be anywhere from 68 to 135 fluid ounces (2-4 L) of water per day, although this number varies greatly from person to person. In very hot weather and at high altitude, you should drink more often than you feel is necessary in order to avoid excessive thirst (a sign that you are already dehydrated). Because liquids are assimilated rapidly into the bloodstream, sport nutritionists and dietitians recommend consuming a beverage containing carbohydrate and protein immediately after a hard workout. This beverage will also help with total fluid replenishment.

On hot long-distance days, drink electrolyte-containing fluids such as Gatorade, Gookinaid, or Powerade. Mix your electrolyte fluids in the ratio of 1 gram of carbohydrate per ounce (30 ml) of water. Bring plenty of salty snacks such as pretzels, nuts, or trail mix for your workout. The salty snacks will not only replenish your salts but also encourage you to drink more frequently. Fresh fruits that replenish potassium and fluids are also great snack choices. If during your workout you experience nausea, muscle cramping, slurred speech, confusion, disorientation, or inappropriate behavior and yet have clear urine from your hydration efforts, you may need sodium rather than water. Severe hyponatremia (lack of sodium) is a true medical emergency and can result in seizure, coma, or even death.

Protein

Because muscle tissue is catabolized during distance activities, consuming additional protein can help you maintain aerobic metabolism and repair tissue damage. The dietary reference intake (DRI) of protein for adults is roughly .36 grams per pound (.8 g/kg) of body weight per day. Many sport nutritionists suggest that endurance athletes should consume .5 to .6 grams per pound (1.2-1.4 g/kg) per day. Since outdoor athletes are involved in endurance and strength training, we suggest that they shoot for .8 grams per pound (1.8 g/kg) per day. For a 150-pound (68 kg) athlete, this equates to 82 to 136 grams of protein per day, or 25 percent of a 2,000-calorie diet. Complete protein sources, such as animal and dairy products, contain all the essential amino acids that are required by every cell in the body. Most nonanimal sources of protein are incomplete and require you to combine them with other protein sources to get all the essential amino acids. Beans combined with corn or rice is an example of a meal that provides complete protein without including meat.

Top sources of protein are poultry, wild fish, wild game, grass-fed beef, eggs, and milk. Corn-fed beef and farm-raised fish also contain high amounts of protein; however, their fat profiles are considerably less beneficial than the profiles of their grass-fed or wild variations. Other foods such as yogurt and cheese contain protein, but their protein content (as a percent of total calories) is rather low. There are also many protein powders that contain casein, whey, or a combination of the two. Usually, protein accounts for most of the calories in these powders, but be sure to examine all the ingredients and the caloric makeup of any you are considering purchasing, since some actually contain junk carbohydrate calories.

Goal-Specific Guidelines

This section discusses strategies for reaching the five common nutrition goals that outdoor athletes might be pursuing at any given time in their training. These goals are (1) staying healthy to continue training, (2) maintaining energy levels during the day and keeping blood sugar levels stable, (3) fueling during long workouts to prevent fatigue, (4) reducing body fat while maintaining lean muscle mass, and (5) supporting continued effort at high altitude. If you identify with any of these goals, incorporate the following strategies into your nutrition plan.

Maintaining Health

Maintain your essential nutrients (vitamins and minerals) by eating a wide variety of raw, organic, fresh foods. A multivitamin or meal-replacement powder or snack bar may help certain individuals overcome deficiencies, but it is always best to try to get what you need from food sources rather than pills. The nutrients that are particularly important for strong, fit, healthy outdoor athletes are the following: protein (to encourage muscle development and repair), calcium (to speed bone repair and delay the onset of osteoporosis), iron (to prevent extreme fatigue as well as iron-deficiency anemia), and antioxidant vitamins E and C (to protect muscle cells from oxidative damage during endurance activities). Endurance athletes also need to replenish electrolytes (potassium and sodium) lost in sweating.

Outdoor athletes should strive for an intake of 1,200 to 2,600 milligrams of calcium daily (Gastelu and Hatfield 1997). In his book *Optimum Sports Nutrition*, Michael Colgan (1993) states that the small amount of calcium outside your bones, in your blood (1 percent), remains constant. "If your calcium intake is inadequate even a day, then your body cannibalizes its own skeleton to make up the deficit" (p. 190). By consuming 300 daily calories of calcium-rich foods such as yogurt, powdered or skim milk, broccoli, tofu, cheese, or pudding, you can supply your bones with the calcium needed to prevent stress fractures today and osteoporosis in the future. Dairy products provide ample amounts of calcium, phosphorous, and vitamin D. However, if you are lactose intolerant or vegan, be sure to consume lactose-reduced dairy products; nondairy foods such as calcium-rich tofu, calcium-fortified orange juice, broccoli, and other leafy greens; or even a supplement containing calcium carbonate or calcium phosphate, both of which are forms of calcium easily used by the body.

The recommended iron intake for active adults is 25 to 60 milligrams a day (Gastelu and Hatfield 1997). Backcountry athletes who train aerobically for more

Women and Iron-Deficiency Anemia: How to Check

Female athletes: If you tire earlier than usual during exercise or are unable to improve performance despite getting adequate rest, exercise, and proper nutrition, you may want to get a complete blood count (CBC) or serum ferritin test to measure your iron reserves and check for iron-deficiency anemia. The normal hemoglobin range for females is 12 to 16 grams per deciliter; normal hematocrit range is 37 to 47 percent (Harris 1994). The average ferritin value for young women is 30 micrograms per liter of blood; a value of 12 micrograms or less indicates complete depletion of iron stores in the liver (Harris 1994). You may have anemia if your values fall outside the normal ranges for hemoglobin and hematocrit relative to your baseline. In other words, if normal ferritin for you is 14 micrograms per liter and a measurement comes back at 13.5 micrograms, you may have anemia; a recurring measurement of 11.5 micrograms, on the other hand, may be your personal norm and not indicative of anemia even though it is lower than the norm. Even a healthy body does not take in iron very easily. Because of that, if you experience anemia you may be advised to take iron supplements for several months to a year.

than 6 hours a week, however, are more susceptible to iron deficiency because they lose a great amount of iron through intense training. Good food sources of iron include dried fruits such as raisins, figs, and dates; lean red meats; spinach, asparagus, kale, broccoli, and green, leafy vegetables; dried beans and peas; and seafood, poultry, and organ meats, including liver. Whole-grain breads and cereals fortified with iron are also good choices. Consuming calcium-rich foods, tea, coffee, or eggs with your iron-rich foods can inhibit iron absorption, whereas taking vitamin C when ingesting iron can increase iron absorption. Cooking in iron skillets can also be useful.

You should consume 1 gram of vitamin C (the cold prevention vitamin) daily. Vitamin C helps heal wounds, fight infections, and promote iron absorption. Most importantly, it helps protect cells from free-radical damage. One of nature's most important antioxidants is vitamin E, which promotes healthy nervous, cardiovascular, and circulatory systems by ensuring that they obtain enough oxygen from the red blood cells. Extensive aerobic exercise places additional demands on the free-radical scavengers of the body. At higher altitudes, where oxidative stress increases, vitamin E supplementation is even more important. Athletes recovering from injury or performing at altitudes higher than 5,000 feet (1,500 m) should shoot for 600 to 1,200 IU of daily vitamin E (Gastelu and Hatfield 1997). Good food sources of vitamin E are extra-virgin olive oil (or vegetable oils that are as unprocessed as possible) and whole grains, especially wheat. White flour, however, is usually stripped of vitamin E. Finally, bromelain, commonly found in fresh or dried pineapple, may assist with injury recovery.

Maintaining Energy

There is simply no way around it: Carbohydrate fuels endurance activity. Due to its small storage capacity for glycogen, the body needs a constant supply of carbohydrate, which it converts into glycogen for ready use during the day (Gastelu and Hatfield 1997). Complex carbohydrates found in starchy or fiber-rich foods such as fruits and vegetables, whole-grain breads, wild rice, and bran cereals provide you with sustained energy. They require more digestion time (have a lower GI value) and leave you feeling satisfied longer than simple carbohydrates do. Simple carbohydrates include white and brown sugars, molasses, corn syrup, fructose, honey, and other substances found in foods such as candy, pastries, colas, ice cream, and cookies. Such foods provide short-term energy in the form of empty calories that lack useful nutrients. Stick to foods with natural sweeteners and avoid artificial ingredients.

The outdoor athlete wishing to maintain energy levels throughout the day should begin with a diet consisting of 50 to 60 percent carbohydrate (the bulk of which should come from fruits, vegetables, and fibrous, colorful whole grains), 15 to 25 percent protein, and 25 to 35 percent fat. Experiment with this macronutrient ratio to discover what best fuels your activities. To adjust the ratio, modify the amount of complex carbohydrate you consume by 5 percent every few weeks as needed, particularly if you feel you do not have sufficient energy to fuel your endurance training. Keep adjusting until you hit the right ratio. As mentioned earlier, you may need to experiment to see if your body functions better on meals rich in fat and protein or meals abundant in complex carbohydrate.

Fueling Up for Long Workouts

The easiest way to sustain your energy during endurance workouts is to mix carbohydrate powders such as Cytomax, Powerade, Gookinaid, or Gatorade with protein powder and add them to your water bottle. This simple mixture can fuel your body during your exercise session as well as enhance your recovery afterward. For workouts lasting longer than 90 minutes, keep a few snack foods within easy reach so that whenever you experience a dip in energy, you can grab a few bites (every 30 minutes or so) to keep going. If you plan to do any sort of adventure race that requires hard exertion for longer than 2 hours, test your snack foods while you are training so you know how your body will react to them. Good snack suggestions are bananas, carbohydrate gels that are easily swallowed, mixed carbohydrate and protein drinks, dried fruits, jerky, orange sections, or foods you can suck on such as hard candies or licorice. If you will be gone longer than 2.5 hours, include protein in your snacks. Try tuna or turkey sandwiches, bagels with cream cheese, string cheese, or trail mix with nuts. These snacks require more digestion as well as chewing time and are more appropriate for long, sustained outings.

Reducing Body Fat While Maintaining Lean Muscle Mass

In order to lose a pound (.5 kg) of body fat, you need to burn 3,500 calories. The challenge in burning this many calories is maintaining lean muscle mass. You can increase your activity levels to burn an additional 250 calories per day and decrease your caloric intake by 250 per day in order to achieve a 3,500 (7 × 500) calorie deficit over the week. If you lose any more than 2 pounds (1 kg) per week, you are probably losing water weight and destroying lean muscle mass. If you have tried to lose weight, you already know that you may lose stamina as well, particularly if you embark on a low-carbohydrate plan. Chronic dieting (or undereating) decreases the amount of leptin in your body. You need to have leptin, the starvation prevention hormone, in abundance in order to steadily lose body fat. According to Joel Marion (2007) in *The Cheat to Lose Diet*, you should periodically include cheat meals or a cheat day in order to elevate your leptin levels so that the body can continue to release body fat.

If you restrict your daily caloric intake to less than 9 or 10 times your body weight in pounds, you will wreak havoc on your metabolism, hamper your performance, and destroy your psychological attitude. It is hard to stay motivated and focused when you are deprived of fuel! Plan your training around the end results you want. Start with a fat-burning workout plan for several weeks during which you reduce your caloric intake and include short, high-intensity anaerobic workouts and strength training to maintain your muscle mass and boost your metabolic rate. Then shift to your regular caloric intake and consume carbohydrate foods with a low GI value so you can sustain your endurance training and longer strength workouts. A day or two before your distance workouts, increase your consumption appropriate to your body weight and metabolic requirements (and choose the right foods, of course). Return to your nutrition plan the weeks following your event—after you have fully replenished your muscle glycogen—so you can keep your performance levels high while still getting the nutrition results you desire.

Supporting Effort at High Altitude

The simplest answer to the question, "What should I eat at high altitude?" is to eat whatever you will *be able* to eat consistently and abundantly at high altitude. Whenever possible, test foods while training at 10,000 feet (3,048 m) or higher so you learn what works best for you. Once you are at altitude, you probably will not want the foods and beverages you enjoy at sea level. Bring flavored drink mixes like Tang or Gatorade to mask the taste of treated water and to get the necessary carbohydrate calories. If you enjoy hot beverages, bring along a thermos of soup, cocoa, or tea.

Most high-altitude athletes prefer a high-carbohydrate, low-fat diet, finding fatty foods unpleasant or distasteful. Complex carbohydrate provides the ongoing fuel needed to replenish glycogen stores, while protein prevents excess deterioration of lean muscle mass. According to Carolyn Gunn, the author of the *Expedition Cookbook*, it is best to pack *at least* 4,000 calories per person per day for a high-altitude climbing expedition such as Mount McKinley, Alaska (Hanson and Hanson 2002, 17). These calories should be 50 to 60 percent carbohydrate, 15 to 25 percent protein, and 15 to 25 percent fat. Daily expenditures on climbing expeditions can be as high as 8,000 calories, depending on highest altitude, starting body weight, extreme

Women at Altitude

At least one research study has shown that at elevations above 14,109 feet (4,300 m), men use more carbohydrate to fuel exercise than they use at sea level. Women, on the other hand, oxidize less carbohydrate and more fat when at high altitudes. At high altitudes, women may also have a slight physiological advantage over men. Paraphrased from Colonel Askew, advisor for high-altitude military operations, women tend to suffer less severe symptoms of acute mountain sickness (AMS; see chapter 6), while men experience greater depression in appetite and food intake at high altitude (Askew 1996). Women, with their higher percentage of body fat and thus a better tolerance to the cold, may naturally demonstrate slightly superior performance in high-altitude environments.

temperatures, and performance requirements (Askew 1996). Keep snacks handy and store them close to your skin to keep them from freezing. For any expedition lasting longer than 2 weeks, you can expect to lose body weight, as you simply cannot tote enough food (nor will you feel like eating enough food) to maintain your starting weight. Since that is the case, plan to have as much muscle mass as possible and a few extra pounds of body fat going into your high-altitude excursion so that you have lean muscle mass and fat to spare without compromising performance.

Above all else, when at altitude, hydrate frequently. Dehydration exacerbates altitude sickness and diminishes appetite further. If you experience the first signs of a headache, try warding it off with a dilute carbohydrate-containing beverage. Drink a minimum of 100 to 135 fluid ounces (3-4 L) of liquid a day—consume even more in blistering heat or high humidity—and be sure that your daily beverages include 100 to 250 grams of carbohydrate that you consume in addition to your food calories. While water is the beverage of choice, flavorful carbohydrate drinks provide energy with each swallow and help prevent hyponatremia. Cider, juice mixes, cocoa, tea, lemonade, Gatorade, Gookinaid, soups, and the like all involve plenty of water and carbohydrate. The more fluid you get per meal, the better.

Hanson and Hanson (2002), members of the Seattle Mountaineers who have been to Mount McKinley, Alaska, several times and offer seminars on expedition preparation, recommend the following quick, light, totable foods for sustained energy at altitude:

- *For breakfast:* granola or energy bars, oatmeal, bagels, hot sweet rice, couscous, grape nuts, hot cocoa, tea, and cider
- *For lunch:* cheese and crackers, cookies, bagels, rolls, jerky, sausages, cheese sticks, nuts, candy bars, dried fruits, flavored juice drink mixes, fruit leather, fig bars, hard candy, and trail mix
- *For snacks on the go:* dried fruit, power gel packets, carbohydrate drinks, and cookies, along with other items recommended for lunch

- *For dinner:* cocoa, cider, soup, hot flavored gelatin, and tea to begin with; freeze-dried meals with rice, noodles, vegetables; instant rice, stuffing, or mashed potatoes; pudding or mousse for dessert

Consider the weight of all your food, especially if you will be hauling all of it yourself. Dehydrated food that is light in weight but dense in calories is highly desirable. Potato buds mixed with dried turkey, tuna, or other meat and hot water seem to go down pretty easily for many people at altitude. If you merely tolerate the taste of a snack at sea level, leave it behind, as taste sensitivity increases with altitude. Although some people find that the heat generated from curries or peppers helps them keep warmer, you should avoid exotic or spicy foods if you are not accustomed to them.

While fresh vegetables and fruits are great foods for health and energy, carrying them on your back on an extended trip is not feasible. Fresh fruits and vegetables can be heavy and are not very calorie dense. When you are traveling long distances in the backcountry, you will burn more calories than you can carry, and trying to keep up with the amount of calories you expend is more important than the type of food you eat. At some point you have to sacrifice food quality for increased calorie density. Consider dehydrated foods; calculate the number of calories they have per ounce. Some foods have less than 50 calories per ounce (2 kcal/g); others contain almost 200 calories per ounce (7 kcal/g). For a 10-day trip, you probably will not carry more than 20 pounds (10 kg) of food. If your food choices average 100 calories per ounce (3.5 kcal/g), you will be carrying 3,200 calories per day. However, on that same day you might expend 5,000 to 6,000 calories. Foods such as peanut butter or nut butters on crackers, string cheeses, dried jerky sticks, and trail mix with dried fruits and nuts are quite valuable for the outdoor athlete on extended trips.

Overcoming Environmental Challenges

Sometimes you train under ideal conditions and then have to perform under environmental factors that are beyond your control. This chapter provides tips for dealing with challenges such as heat, humidity, cold, precipitation, and high altitude. We discuss how to prevent illness, choose the correct clothing for anticipated conditions, acclimatize, fuel and hydrate to combat environmental maladies, and handle ever-changing landscapes. For scientific details on meeting environmental challenges, see Lawrence Armstrong's book, *Performing in Extreme Environments* (2000). Once you are armed with survival tips for handling extreme heat, cold, and altitude, you can combine this knowledge with the nutrition, cardiovascular training, strength training, and assessment information already provided to design an appropriate training program for your sport.

Heat

Different athletes react differently to heat. Those who train in heat and humidity generally fare better under such conditions than athletes who do not. Pushing too hard in hot, humid conditions can result in reduced muscular endurance and excessive sweating and can put you at risk for dehydration and heat illness. Hyperthermia shifts the body from aerobic to anaerobic metabolism, depleting carbohydrate stores and thus reducing exercise efficiency even more. To combat the heat, especially if you train in a moderate climate but plan to travel to hot regions for your adventures, incorporate the suggestions discussed in the following sections.

Prevent Heat Illnesses Heat cramps can occur if you become dehydrated during sustained exertion. Resting, massaging, or stretching the cramping muscles and drinking fluids can help. Heat exhaustion is the inability to continue to exercise in heat due to dehydration or inadequate electrolyte replacement. Symptoms include profuse sweating, cool, pale, and clammy skin, faintness, weakness, nausea, and rapid pulse. Treatment includes getting into the shade and out of the heat, resting with your feet elevated above your heart, and drinking electrolyte-replenishing liquids. Heatstroke is a very serious, potentially life-threatening heat illness. During heatstroke, the skin may be flushed, hot, and dry, indicating a rise in core body temperature to 105 degrees Fahrenheit

(41 C) or more. Symptoms include rapid pulse, weakness, headache, and altered mental state. An athlete experiencing heatstroke must cool down immediately: Shade, cool water, a change of clothing, a moist bandanna, or fanning can all help the body temperature drop. Watch for symptoms of heat cramps, heat exhaustion, and heatstroke in yourself and in your training partners or trip members. Dehydration can contribute to each of the three types of heat illness.

Fuel and Hydrate to Combat Heat A major challenge that outdoor athletes must avoid in all hot environments is dehydration. Signs of dehydration include very yellow or strong-smelling urine, extreme thirst that can lead to not wanting to drink, confusion and lack of coordination, and sluggishness. To combat the heat, drink more fluids more often, especially if you sweat profusely. If you do not plan to carry much water for your trip, research your route in advance. Bring a filter or iodine tablets to treat water that you get from streams, lakes, and glacial runoff to replenish your water supply. Extreme heat can mean high evaporation rates and little to no available running water in areas where you typically find snow pockets or flowing streams most of the year. Consider toting moisture-laden foods as a special but necessary treat; grapes, berries, and melon balls on a scorching day are far more satisfying than fruit leather or tough strips of dried jerky!

Hyponatremia is a low concentration of sodium in the blood. It occurs when athletes drink copious amounts of pure water without adequately replacing their electrolytes. It can also occur when athletes simply drink more often than necessary. It is more common during endurance events that last longer than 5 hours or are held in hot and humid weather, during which athletes attempting to rehydrate over several hours of exertion may end up compounding the problem of low electrolyte levels without realizing it. A study of 36 athletes competing in a triathlon lasting 3 to 4 hours compared with 64 athletes competing in an Ironman race lasting 9 to 15 hours found that while no athletes were hyponatremic following the shorter race, 27 percent were hyponatremic and dehydrated following the Ironman. To prevent hyponatremia, carry salty snacks to replenish the sodium lost in sweat, or add 25 grams of powdered carbohydrate sports-drink mix to every 32 fluid ounces (roughly 1 L) of water.

Being prepared for any environmental challenges you may face, such as extreme heat, is crucial for your comfort and safety.

Wear Appropriate Clothing Proper clothing is one of your first lines of defense against extreme elements. When choosing your clothing, always think in threes: (1) skin or base layer, (2) insulating layer, and (3) outer layer to protect against the elements. While insulation may be less crucial in extreme heat, the other two layers can make an enormous difference in how well you tolerate summer or desert conditions. Wear light-colored (beige, gray, or white) clothing to repel sunlight. Wear lightweight, loose-fitting, and breathable clothing, such as mesh or very thin layers of sunblock clothing, to prevent sunburn and stay as cool as possible. Include a wide-brimmed hat or visor to keep the sun off your face. Some hikers on the Pacific Crest Trail even carry a light umbrella to ward off the Southern California desert heat. Wear a bandanna around your neck that you can dip in cool streams and use to swab your neck and face. By always having appropriate base, insulating, and outer layers of clothing readily available, you will be better prepared for varying conditions. If you plan to be active for most of the day in a region where temperatures can change drastically, take a complete change of clothing so that you can remove sweat-drenched base layers and avoid being chilled by dropping temperatures.

Prepare for the Landscape If you must travel to a hot region for your adventure, arrive early so you have time to get used to the heat. You may need up to 2 weeks for full acclimatization (Armstrong 2000), much as you would need to adjust to high altitude. Some researchers suggest training in heated rooms, sweat suits, or dry heat saunas to get used to sweating and staying properly hydrated in higher temperatures, but this type of training can be dangerous unless you properly replenish your fluids. Weigh yourself before you begin exercising and drink at least 16 fluid ounces (2 cups, or 470 ml) of fluid for every pound (.5 kg) of weight lost during your workout. You may experience an initial decline in performance when you move from temperate to hot or humid conditions, but as your body adapts, your performance should return to its previous levels. An obvious way to avoid heat issues altogether is to participate in events located in hot regions of the country at times of the year that are cooler or less humid. If you do go in the hot season, train at dawn or dusk or during nonpeak sun hours. Perform any hard, high-intensity anaerobic workouts during cooler times early in the morning or late in the evening.

The worst heat of the day is typically between 12 and 4 p.m. The valley floor of the Grand Canyon, Arizona (United States), in July and August is a prime example of a place to avoid during the midday heat. In the middle of the summer, stick to shaded trails or north sides of mountains where the heat is less severe. Also keep in mind that a blistering day down in the valley may turn quite cool as you ascend a shady rock wall that is exposed to wind. In deserts, on glaciers, or in sun-drenched valleys where temperatures plummet as soon as the sun drops below the horizon, you can encounter changes of more than 40 degrees Fahrenheit (22 C). Be sure to dress appropriately for these climates.

Cold

Opposite of extreme heat conditions are extreme cold conditions. The human body strives to maintain a core temperature of 98.6 degrees Fahrenheit (37 C). During the winter, it has to battle wind, air temperature, and precipitation to stay warm. Cold affects physical coordination, mental facility, and performance. An obvious strategy for dealing with low temperatures is to wear lots of layers; however, multiple layers can hamper movement and increase sweating, which then puts a damp layer against your skin. Practicing your sport in cold weather and finding the right layering strategy for you are the first defenses against extreme cold. The strategies discussed in the following sections can also help you handle cold conditions.

Prevent Cold Illness Hypothermia develops whenever the body's core temperature drops below 95 degrees Fahrenheit (35 C). Wet clothing and wind exposure on even moderately cool days can cause your body to lose more heat than it can restore. Symptoms of hypothermia include shivering, awkward movements, chattering teeth, and diminished mental capacity. A person experiencing hypothermia should be warmed immediately. The person should get out of the wet and windy conditions to protective shelter, change out of wet clothes, drink fluids (warm fluids, although not necessary, may feel better in the mouth and on the hands), and if necessary move into direct contact with a warm body. Frostnip is localized freezing of the outer layer of skin, primarily at the extremities (fingers, toes, nose, and cheeks), whereas frostbite is far more serious and involves deep freezing of the blood vessels and skin tissues. Symptoms of frostbite include cold, hard, pale, or deeply discolored skin and loss of sensation. *Do not* rub or massage any area that you fear may be frostbitten, as doing so can cause greater damage. Only warm a frostbitten area if you know it will not freeze again; otherwise, the tissue may die.

Fuel and Hydrate to Combat Environmental Illness Eating regularly and staying hydrated are two strategies that stoke the metabolic furnace and keep you moving. Consume hot liquids (soup, tea, hot cocoa, cider) to supply carbohydrate, to restore fluids lost through increased exhalations in cold air, and to provide an external source of heat that can warm the fingers, face, and soul. Store snack foods close to your skin to keep them readily accessible and to prevent them from freezing. Since the brain utilizes glucose directly, make sure to ingest a steady stream of carbohydrate when you are in extreme cold. Without readily accessible fuel for the brain, coordination falters and the decision-making process becomes severely impaired.

Wear Appropriate Clothing Protect against cold illnesses by making educated, well-researched equipment choices. You want your clothing layers to provide you with adequate warmth without hampering your movements, preventing you from completing necessary tasks, or causing you to overheat.

Include base, insulating, and outer layers so you can discard or add clothing to stay comfortable as you move. Remove your outer layer before you start moving so you can minimize or delay the onset of sweating. If your base layer gets damp from sweat, change as soon as you stop moving. Merino wool, silk, and synthetic fabrics make good base layers. Avoid cotton shirts and pants, as they take a long time to dry and do not retain your body heat when damp.

Goose-down, synthetically insulated, and soft-shell coats of all weights are available to be used as an insulating middle layer, and the technology for wind and ultralight rain protection for the outer layer continues to advance every year even beyond Gore-Tex. While darker colors (blue and black) absorb sunlight and blend in with the environment more readily, a bright splash of color (orange, pink, or red) can make you more visible against snow and brush and may increase team visibility.

When embarking on multiday trips in cold environments, make sure each member in your party has at least one lightweight base layer, one dry, midweight change of clothing, one warm insulating layer, and one wind- and waterproof outer layer. Store your replacement dry clothing and sleeping bags in a water-resistant protective layer such as a trash compactor bag. Such bags can even double as temporary rain gear if needed.

As much as 80 percent of the heat lost from the body is due to wind (Armstrong 2000). Guard against the effects of wind by wearing breathable windproof layers, a protective hat, goggles or glasses with side shields (especially if ice pellets, debris, or rain are whipping around you), and mittens or gloves. Loose-fitting or comfortable knee or elbow athletic wraps can provide added warmth to joints during rest stops. As soon as you stop moving, add an insulating layer to fend off chill. Layered clothing will trap heat all around the body. Build extra strength and endurance so that you have added balance and stamina to combat wind. Whenever possible, start your trip by heading into the wind so that you do not have to face it at the end when you are fatigued.

Since a good portion of your body heat is lost through your head, always wear some sort of hat and ear protection. A balaclava is a wonderfully versatile and lightweight piece of clothing that all athletes can wear as a hat, neck warmer, and face protector in extreme wind. When pulled up to cover the mouth and nose, it can also help protect against frostnip in very cold temperatures. The hands and feet are just as crucial as the head. Mittens are far more effective at trapping warm air around each finger than gloves are, although gloves may allow greater dexterity. A good compromise is a five-fingered glove cut off at the fingertips with a mitten flap that covers the entire hand. This arrangement allows both for warmth and for dexterity in extreme cases when you need bare fingers, such as when tying or undoing knots, repairing equipment, or opening packages of food. If you have had issues in the past with frostnip, frostbite, or poor circulation such as Raynaud's disease, you should be especially conscientious about protecting yourself against cold exposure.

Avoid running or walking through the snow in low-cut shoes. Midlength and full-length gaiters keep snow out of your boots and add a layer of warmth to the lower legs. When worn over appropriate footwear (i.e., treated leathers, composite boots, or plastics) they can make the difference between soaking wet, freezing feet and comfortably dry feet. If your boots get wet, dry your feet thoroughly, put

Shivering and Age

Being fit, having a lot of muscle mass, and possessing a little extra insulating fat can help you stay warmer longer. Being fit means you can sustain activity for longer durations, which may give you the edge you need to return safely without freezing, while increased muscle mass provides greater metabolic heat production. Shivering is a protective mechanism we all have that generates heat and helps us warm up. However, shivering also burns valuable carbohydrate, precious fuel you need for your activity rather than for shivering (Armstrong 2000). Since aging can cause a decline in thermoregulation, people who are 55 years and older who experience any problems with cooler weather should take additional care to avoid excessive exposure to extreme cold.

on clean, dry socks, and put a small plastic bag around each foot before putting your boots back on. That thin layer of plastic is often enough to keep your feet dry when you start moving again so that you do not have to travel with cold, wet toes. Technology has advanced to such a degree that heat-fit bootliners come standard in most AT ski boots and are available for plastic mountaineering boots. Such liners are made from patented thermoplastic foam developed to be moldable, flexible, and durable for users at all skill levels. Athletes who spend days on end in such boots and who need comfortable bootliners that last longer than the standard will be delighted with such liners.

Prepare for the Landscape When exercising in cold weather, you may prefer to avoid activity in the early morning or late evening, when temperatures are at their lowest. Since there are fewer hours of daylight in the winter, you may have an abbreviated time span each day for your winter outing. Conversely, on a frigid, windy adventure like a mid-May climb of Mount McKinley in Alaska (United States), you may have nearly constant daylight but decide to wait to climb until midday to take advantage of slightly warmer temperatures. To avoid avalanches, rock falls, and ice falls that occur on steep routes as temperatures increase, many alpine travelers choose to get an early start, called an *alpine start,* in order to be back down the slope or into camp before snow bridges weaken or soft snow makes travel more difficult. Snowy slopes exposed to direct sunlight soon become slushy and slippery and make for surprisingly deep postholing. Finally, stream flow is at its lowest in the early morning after temperatures have dropped and melting has diminished. If you have to cross streams, do so early in the day or you may lose a day waiting for high runoff to subside.

Avoid Water Immersion Of particular importance to mountaineers crossing streams or traversing melting glaciers, trail runners embarking on early-season runs on high trails, thru-hikers, and paddlers are the effects of water immersion. Cooling by water is 20 to 25 times greater than cooling by air (Armstrong 2000). If you find that you will be anywhere near water that you might accidentally fall into, check water temperatures ahead of time. While wet suits may help cut down on heat loss somewhat, extra body fat can be even more beneficial as an insulating layer for the off-season or cold-water kayaker. If you find yourself immersed in water, maximize your leg movements to generate heat and get out of the water as quickly as possible. Puddle jumping and muddy trail riding may be exhilarating at first; however, cold air combined with high speed, moisture, and wind may make conditions ideal for hypothermia.

Altitude

At moderate altitudes of 7,000 to 14,000 feet (2,134-4,267 m), you face not only extreme temperature changes but also breathlessness and diminished coordination from the reduced atmospheric pressure. Arm yourself with the following tips and tricks so you can prevent mountain sickness and travel more effectively. At high altitudes above 14,000 feet (4,267 m), the altitude effects intensify and can vary greatly from person to person. Consult with your medical provider before leaving for any high-altitude trip.

Prevent Altitude Illnesses Acute mountain sickness (AMS) occurs when low-altitude residents ascend too quickly to moderate altitudes. Symptoms of AMS include headache, nausea, insomnia, coughing, loss of coordination, shortness of breath, and loss of appetite. Descent is the best treatment, although resting, drinking, eating, breathing deeply, and allowing a day of acclimatization usually helps. High-altitude pulmonary edema (HAPE) is a condition in which body fluids leak into the lungs, causing breathing difficulty, hacking, and racing pulse. The lips and nail beds may turn blue, indicating insufficient oxygen delivery to the rest of the body. High-altitude cerebral edema (HACE) results in brain swelling and manifests itself by lack of coordination and mental facility, headache, and loss of energy. Immediate descent is the best treatment for HAPE and HACE. In beginning stages of altitude illness, if any symptoms beyond a headache are experienced, monitor yourself and your partners carefully. If symptoms worsen, descend at least 2,000 feet (610 m) (Cox and Fulsaas 2003). If you have experienced altitude sickness on previous trips, headache medicine or physician-prescribed high-altitude medications such as acetazolamide may help with future altitude sickness. Gingko biloba may also be effective. A past bout of altitude sickness does not necessarily mean you will experience it again; conversely, previous success at altitude does not make you immune to altitude sickness on subsequent trips.

Fuel and Hydrate to Combat Environmental Illness In order to reduce chances of altitude-related maladies, stay thoroughly hydrated. To ward off a headache, make short, frequent drinking stops (every 30-45 minutes), especially on cold, overcast days when your tendency is to forget to drink or to wait until you reach your destination to have something warm. Drink 8 fluid ounces (240 ml) at each stop, and drink before you get thirsty, as thirst signals that you are already dehydrated. Bladder-and-tube hydration systems such as those by Camelbak and Platypus can keep a water source nearby, but you can also clip water bottles to a shoulder strap, fanny pack, or bike so you can grab a drink without having to stop. When you are above 10,000 feet (3,048 m), be sure to keep your water from freezing: Tuck a water bottle inside clothing, put an insulating sleeve on a drinking tube, or carry a spare collapsible water bottle so you have backup access to fluid. Avoid hydration systems that you have not tested in extreme weather and altitude conditions, as they may burst, leak, or freeze.

Whether you feel like it or not, keep eating. Your body works hard to go uphill, especially when carrying extra weight, and if you are traveling at altitude, the stresses on your body are even greater and you will feel less interested in food. Carry readily accessible snacks in inside pockets so they will not freeze and take bites every 20 to 30 minutes. Energy gel packets are great for high altitude, as they seldom freeze, do not require chewing, slide down the throat easily, and provide a good dose of simple carbohydrate for a boost of energy when you need it the most and feel like eating the least. Unless your group plans to take established eating breaks, be prepared to go most of your trip without a long break, nibbling along the way. Test your foods ahead of time and bring only what is palatable and satisfying at sea level, minus spicy or hard-to-chew foods. Include carbohydrate powders to add to your beverages. For long expeditions, make sure to bring a variety of foods and drinks.

Wear Appropriate Clothing Clothing recommendations for dealing with altitude are similar to those for dealing with cold: Wear proper base, insulating, and outer layers. To face the extremes of moderate and high altitudes, you may actually use several pieces of clothing to fulfill the insulation and outerwear requirements. Watch your body's core temperature, as extreme perspiration can sap your energy faster than you realize. When training in midday heat in areas where snow is readily available, try wrapping some in a bandanna and applying the compress to your forehead to cool down; if you carry extra water, a dash on your forehead can be refreshing.

Acclimate Learn how to use both pressure breathing and the rest step so you can benefit from them any time you start to feel nauseous or tired when above 7,000 feet (2,134 m). Since atmospheric pressure decreases the higher you go, the greater your altitude, the more difficult it is to get the oxygen you need into your lungs. By pursing your lips and exhaling forcefully and fully, you force out the carbon dioxide in your lungs, allowing for a more ready exchange with oxygen in the thinner air. To integrate this technique, called *pressure breathing*, into your pace, experiment with a pattern of stepping and breathing. Up to 10,000 feet (3,048 m), you may find yourself taking two steady steps for every breath, but extreme elevations may require 3 to 4 or even more breaths for every step.

The *rest step* is a method of hiking up a steep slope that allows the skeleton, rather than the muscles, to take the brunt of your weight. Lock out the bottom leg as you shift the other leg uphill and then pause in a full rest position. Then transfer your weight to the other leg, lock out the new bottom leg, and pause. Your torso should be upright and balanced over the downhill leg, and about 90 percent of your weight should be on the back leg. You can practice the rest step on stairs or any steep terrain at lower altitudes in order to help yourself develop a slower, smoother, and steadier rhythm. In this way, you avoid the exhausting hurry-and-wait gait of inexperienced climbers and find a comfortable pace that you can sustain for a very long time.

In order to make steady progress during your trip, listen carefully to your body, and start at a slower pace until you warm up. Both the rest step and pressure breathing will necessitate a slow pace. If you try to keep up with the fastest member of your party, you may never reach your goal. Use a heart rate monitor to gauge your relative intensity and try to stay within 65 to 75 percent of your MHR so that you can sustain effort for long durations. Include anaerobic workouts, pack carrying, and strength training in your conditioning program. While being in great shape does not guarantee success at altitude, it does increase your ability to endure sustained activity under challenging conditions.

Spend an extra day or night above 5,000 feet (1,524 m) if possible. For example, on the 14,411-foot (4,392 m) climb of Mount Rainier in Washington (United States), an overnight stay at the Paradise Inn on the way to Camp Muir or Glacier Basin Campground on the way to Camp Schurman can help with acclimatization. Allowing for additional time on a high-altitude trip can make it more comfortable and enjoyable. For proper acclimatization, you should gain no more than 2,000 feet (610 m) in any single day once you are above 10,000 feet (3,048 m). This climbing rate may not be an option for short trips where you quickly ascend and then descend as soon as you reach the summit. Climbers trying an ascent of Mount Rainier typically camp a night at 10,000 feet (3,048 m), attain the summit (4,400 foot gain) and return to base camp the next day, and then head for their cars later that afternoon or the next morning. Assuming you have adequate time and can carry the appropriate food to spend multiple nights above 10,000 feet (3,048 m), a general guideline is to climb high and sleep low, limiting increases in sleeping elevation to about 1,000 feet (305 m) per day (Cox and Fulsaas 2003). If you are cycling or trekking, you will likely go over high passes but return to lower elevations to sleep.

PART II

Conditioning for Specific Activities

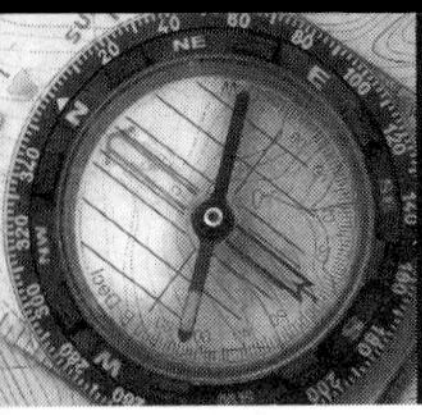

CHAPTER 7

Hiking, Trekking, and Backpacking

Hikers, trekkers, and backpackers all must cover great distances of nontechnical terrain while carrying a pack. For the purposes of this discussion, we define a hike as a 1-day outing that lasts at least an hour and potentially involves elevation gain on uneven terrain. A beginner hike might be 3 to 8 miles (5-13 km) on a sand or dirt trail that gains less than 1,500 feet (457 m) of elevation. An intermediate hike might be 8 to 14 miles (13-22.5 km) round-trip with 1,500 to 3,500 feet (457-1,067 m) of elevation gain. An advanced hike might have an elevation gain greater than 3,500 feet (1,067 m) and be 14 to 30 miles (22.5-48 km) round-trip. Carried gear for day hikes ranges from water and a snack (less than 10 pounds, or 4.5 kg) for easy hikes to a map, a compass, a change of clothes, a headlamp, additional water and snacks, and other essentials (15-20 pounds, or 6.8-9 kg) for intermediate to advanced hikes.

In this chapter, we define a trek as a series of day hikes linked together with overnight stays in huts, inns, or local bed and breakfasts. Treks range from beginning multiday desert tours or daily hikes en route to Machu Picchu in Peru to advanced multiweek high-altitude treks near Annapurna in Nepal, Gasherbrum in Kashmir, or even Mount Everest base camp in Nepal. The gear carried on such treks generally is limited to lunch, snacks, a camera, water, and clothing for the day's weather, while bedding, shelter, extra clothing, and fuel are carried by porters, Sherpas, or pack animals or are provided at each stop. Trekking is generally more taxing than hiking, requiring repeat endurance efforts with minimal recovery.

Backpacking, as defined in this chapter, also involves overnight stays, but when you are backpacking you must carry everything you need for the length of your trip. Backpacking can range from an overnight trip close to civilization to several weeks in remote backcountry. Extreme cases such as backpacking the Pacific Crest Trail, Continental Divide Trail, or Appalachian Trail in the United States involve months of continuous hiking, sometimes 20 to 30 miles (32-48 km) per day, with frequent breaks along the way to change gear and restock food.

Following are the fitness components required for hiking, trekking, and backpacking. A rating of 3 indicates that the component deserves the highest emphasis in your training program, while a rating of 1 indicates that the component is the lowest priority in your program.

Aerobic conditioning: 3

Anaerobic conditioning: 1 (2 if you plan to hike at high altitudes)

Upper-body strength: 1

Lower-body strength: 3

Flexibility: 2

Activity skill: 1

Cross-training: 2

Important areas of the body: quadriceps, gluteals, hamstrings, hips, core, calves, Achilles tendons, feet

Cardiovascular Needs

Hiking is one of the easiest ways to enjoy the great outdoors. Anyone who can walk, age 3 and up, is perfectly capable of hiking several miles. The most important component to include in a hiking, trekking, or backpacking program is cardiovascular endurance (which has a rating of 3). While day hikes can be enjoyed in and of themselves, they also form an important base for multiday high-altitude trekking, scrambling, climbing, and overnight backpacking trips. Walking while carrying a pack is an efficient and effective way to train for such adventures. If you do not have access to rolling hills or mountains, incorporate whatever varied terrain is available to you, such as stairwells, short hills, stadium steps, deserted parking ramps, and sandy dunes. If outdoor locations featuring elevation gain and loss are difficult to find, or if the weather precludes frequent outdoor training, use cardiovascular machines. Stair-climbers, elliptical machines, and incline treadmills develop endurance in the uphill propulsion muscles (gluteals, hips, calves, and hamstrings) while training the descending quadriceps muscles.

Once you have spent a month doing 3 to 5 weekly endurance workouts, try a hike within your capabilities and see how you feel during and after the trip. If your goal is to build hiking stamina in order to start trekking, backpacking, mountaineering, or climbing, add elevation gain on each hike until you can comfortably gain 1,000 to 1,500 feet (305-457 m) an hour or hike 2.5 miles per hour (4 kph) or faster for several hours. When you get comfortable with your beginning outings, try some intermediate trips with more gain, heavier loads, or greater distances. Study the hike ahead of time so you know what to expect and can select a trip that matches your current fitness level.

If you are ready to transition from hiking to overnight backpacking, start easy. Backpacking requires more gear and hence involves carrying more weight. The more equipment you carry, the greater the amount of strength endurance and training you need before your trip. While you can be ready for an easy 5-mile (8 km) hike in a few weeks, preparing for an enjoyable 15-mile (24 km) hike that requires you to gain 3,500 feet (1,067 m) and carry a pack of 30 pounds (13.6 kg) may take 3 months. Rather than making your first backpacking trip a rim-to-rim hike of the Grand Canyon in Arizona (United States), try an easier overnight trip to test your cooking gear, tent, footwear, conditioning, and mental preparation for the trip. All the extra gear will make your pack significantly heavier than it was during your

Include test hikes with gradually increasing pack weight so your muscles, tendons, and ligaments have adequate time to adapt.

beginning day hikes, so choose a shorter distance to see how your body handles the added weight. To prepare for successive days of hiking without recovery, add back-to-back training (repeat hikes on consecutive days) on your weekends as you near the start of your backpacking trip.

Once you have built up your aerobic stamina and speed, add 3 to 5 pounds (1.4-2.3 kg) to your pack each outing until you can carry your targeted trekking, backpacking, or mountaineering weight. The challenge is to maintain your base speed as your pack weight increases. The following sections discuss ways to build energy reserves, increase leg turnover rate, and maintain speed as you add weight to your conditioning outings.

Build Reserves If your goal trip requires you to maintain a steady pace for a set distance or elevation gain, include weekly distance training on comparable terrain. Distance training will help you develop reserves in your muscular and cardiovascular systems so that you can handle any additional distance, weight, or elevation gain encountered during your outing without jeopardizing your safety. Strive to be able to do 10 percent more than what your target pack weight, elevation gain, or mileage requires you to do. If your goal is to carry a 20-pound (9 kg) pack on a 10-mile (16 km) hike that gains 3,000 feet (914 m) of elevation and you can do one of the following, your body should be sufficiently prepared for your outing.

- 10 miles (16 km), 2,000 feet (610 m), and 25 pounds (11 kg), which is more weight but less gain;

- 12 miles (19 km), 3,000 feet (914 m), and 15 pounds (7 kg), which is more distance but less gain and less weight; or
- 8 miles (13 km), 3,400 feet (1,036 m), and 15 pounds (7 kg), which is more gain but less distance and less weight.

If you will have to carry a heavy pack on your goal trip but your training consists of hiking a few hours at a time with half the target weight and little to no elevation gain, expect soreness, aches, and discomfort during your backpacking adventure.

Increase Leg Turnover Rate Fartlek intervals can be applied to hiking training to increase leg turnover rate. During your training hikes, attack steeper portions of the trail with long, powerful strides. If you know the uphill stretch is short, push to the top as hard as you can and then relax to catch your breath as the terrain levels out. On pacing hikes, you can try this drill: Choose a short segment (no more than a few hundred yards or meters) midway through the outing and push yourself to 85 to 95 percent of your maximal effort. The remainder of the hike at base pace will feel easier in comparison, and you will have decreased your total hike time. The more you can include random bursts of speed among your bouts of steady hiking, the more fit you will become. As the weight of your pack increases, the natural tendency is to slow down. By establishing a benchmark in early season and comparing successive hikes with your initial outing, you will find that as your pack weight increases, your speed should match previous efforts or even increase as your fitness level improves.

Maintain Speed To increase your speed, use tempo training or pacing hikes to establish a pace similar to the one you will have on your goal trip. To gauge your speed improvement, pick a hike you can do every other week and compare your successive efforts. In early season, begin with a 10- to 15-pound (4.5-6.8 kg) day pack and then each time you repeat the hike, decrease your time or maintain your previous time with an additional 3 to 5 pounds (1.4-2.3 kg). If you choose, you can repeat a shorter elevation loop or route several times, striving to make the same time each lap. A long hill or set of stairs can provide a good challenge; try increasing your speed during each trip up and down, or try to complete more trips in a given period of time. As you increase your aerobic capacity and strength endurance, your speed and comfort level should increase while your hiking time decreases.

If you will be hiking above 8,500 feet (2,591 m), add weekly interval training at sea level as you approach your goal. Anaerobic training builds tolerance for work in thinner air and simultaneously increases your speed. Choose a hill or a set of stairs that will take 2 or 3 minutes to climb. Speed walk up it while using a heart rate monitor to gauge your effort. Walk back down at a comfortable pace and then repeat the climb. Try to equal or beat your first work interval with each successive interval in the workout. While these intervals can be done without weight, for hiking, trekking, and backpacking benefits, you should use pack weight, gradually increasing the amount until you can do a midweek pack workout with a weight that is 10 percent heavier than what you will carry on your trip. As you get more comfortable pushing yourself up steep inclines, decrease the amount of recovery time between work intervals. Once you are in the mountains, your anaerobic training will allow you to link together and complete harder trail segments with shorter recovery time, resulting in continuous movement with less effort.

If you live in a relatively flat area or in an area with uncooperative weather, you can do portions of your hiking-specific endurance training on cardiovascular machines such as the incline treadmill, elliptical trainer, VersaClimber, stair-climber, and StepMill. To gain 783 feet (239 m) of elevation per mile of walking, you need access to a treadmill that goes up to a 15 percent incline (an 8.5 degree slope). Most commercial treadmills only approach a 12 percent incline (a 6.8 degree slope), which is an elevation gain of 629 feet (192 m) per mile. If your goal is to hike a 3,400-foot (1,036 m) gain using a treadmill with a 12 percent incline, you need to cover 5.4 miles (8.7 km); at a pace of 2.7 miles an hour (4.3 kph), your hike would take you about 2 hours. When working on an elliptical machine, use the highest ramp setting and enough resistance to maintain a comfortable walking pace of 80 to 110 strides (40-55 complete leg turnover cycles) per minute. If you can, include segments of backward striding to work the quadriceps and mimic downhill walking. Flatland workout suggestions such as these can all be done using a loaded pack. To compensate for lack of high altitude or continuous elevation gain, plan to work up to slightly more weight (10 percent above recommendations) to add even more strength endurance than the athlete who has ready access to mountains for training. This will help prepare your body for the additional challenges you will face on continuous uphill terrain.

Strength Needs

The other major area of focus for hikers, trekkers, and backpackers is strength training. They need to train the quadriceps for descents; the hips for supporting pack weight over variable terrain; the shoulders, upper back, and trapezius for pack carrying, gear hoisting, and using trekking poles; and the lower back, obliques, and abdominals for transferring power from the legs into forward propulsion. While hikers, trekkers, and backpackers encounter less extreme terrain than scramblers or climbers do, they still need to be able to navigate short stretches across boulder, talus, or scree fields, cross streams, traverse heather slopes, or negotiate around tree roots, all of which challenge footing and balance and may require awkward or high steps.

Your preseason strength exercises should include single-limb movements that detect and correct weaknesses or imbalances in your legs and hips. The one-leg deadlift (page 263), the step-up (page 275), the reverse step-up (page 277), and the dumbbell lunge and its variations (page 273) will pinpoint whether both legs and hips are doing comparable work. During in-season training, you should focus on increasing your strength via exercises that work multiple muscle groups, such as the barbell front squat (page 271) and barbell deadlift (page 261). You should supplement these movements with 1 to 2 unilateral leg exercises to keep your legs balanced. As you increase your pack weight, you may feel fatigue in the sides of your hips; add body stabilization exercises such as the hip abductor band sidestep (page 235) or straight-leg raise abduction (page 236).

Use your weekly endurance and midweek pack hikes to refine your training program. If your shoulders fatigue when carrying a pack, add targeted upper-back or trapezius strengthening exercises such as the one-arm dumbbell row (page 246) or the dumbbell shrug (page 244). The solution to your tired shoulders could also be as simple as redistributing your pack weight to your hips with a hip belt, reducing your pack weight, or packing the heavier items at the bottom of your pack, closer to your core. You should evaluate other nonconditioning elements of your hike. For example, if you spent a lot of time looking at your feet on a rocky hike, you may have tensed up to keep yourself from losing your footing and caused yourself neck discomfort *not* because of the pack weight per se but because of factors related more to skill than to conditioning or equipment. By keeping a training journal in which you record your feelings, elevation gained, weight carried, distance traveled, times to mile markers, and performance of your fuel and hydration system for a particular hike, you can track what works for you and make appropriate adjustments.

Perhaps the most common complaint from hikers is of sore quadriceps the next few days after a hike. Both increasing mileage or weight too quickly can cause soreness. However, careful evaluation of training variables may point to other culprits. Steeper terrain or greater elevation change can also lead to leg soreness. If you included downhill trail running on the descent, the soreness may have been caused by the added eccentric loading. If you completed a tough strength workout for your legs the day before the hike, you may be experiencing DOMS from that strength session rather than from the hike. To load the quadriceps, perform exercises such as the reverse step-up (page 277), the one-leg Bulgarian squat (page 272), and the backward lunge (page 272). On steeper-than-average hikes, add water for weight (2 L bottles work well) and dump some at the top for the trip down. As you approach your goal outing, however, be sure that you can carry down whatever weight you carry up.

Flexibility Needs

Hikers, trekkers, and backpackers should stretch the calves, hips, trapezius, quadriceps, and lower back after each training session and outing. The calves tighten during long uphill climbs. The hips and trapezius will feel tired and sore if your backpack is loaded unevenly or if you add weight before they have adapted to previous loads. Descents overload the quadriceps. The following stretches can help your muscles: the trapezius stretch (page 219), the triangle pose (page 216), the bench hamstring stretch (page 218), the standing dowel torso rotation (page 214), the frog stretch (page 217), and the stair calf stretch (page 217). As you change out of your hiking boots, add the seated gluteal stretch (page 218) for a refreshing hip stretch.

Additional Considerations

Hiking, trekking, and backpacking can be enjoyed year round in all sorts of weather. Due to the increased amount of time that hikers and backpackers spend outside, they need to be familiar with how to handle the heat, cold, and other adverse weather conditions for their season. For high-altitude treks or advanced backpack trips such as the Continental Divide Trail or Pacific Crest Trail in the United States, you should consider carefully snow pack and pass closures in order to assess whether your route is even open to foot traffic. In areas where your goal trip involves low-lying valleys, you should consider hazards such as flooding, mudslides, stream crossings, or landslides that can make the trail dangerous or impassable at certain times of the year.

Take special care of your body by wearing appropriate footwear and a comfortable, well-fitting pack. Be aware of the ground cover you will be hiking on and choose your paths wisely if you are prone to foot ailments such as plantar fasciitis. Heavily visited hiking trails with well-compacted soil may be as hard on the feet as concrete is. Once you add the gear for a 4-day backpack trip, such terrain may become an invitation for extreme discomfort. Carry an adequate nutritional supply of 2 pounds (1 kg) of food per day (per person) to provide you with the 3,000 to 5,000 daily calories you will need for repeated effort on long backpacking trips. If you know that water resupply points are few and far between, carry a minimum of 100 fluid ounces (3 L) per person and at least one filter to take advantage of any running water.

Assessing Fitness and Gauging Improvement

Before you get started with a hiking program, do a ramp test on an elliptical trainer, a stair-climber, or an incline treadmill. Retest in a month to be sure that your heart rate numbers are dropping for identical test settings, and then shift to a field test on the same equipment so you can assess your pacing. On the four lower-body strength tests, note any weaknesses and include the appropriate exercises in your strength program. Once you have built your cardiovascular endurance to an hour or more, add monthly best-fit tests.

After at least a month of training, do a best-fit hiking test on a nearby trail with a pack weight that is at least 5 pounds (2.3 kg) heavier than what you have used so far. Within a month of your goal outing, use a weight similar to what you will need for your end objective. Hike for 2 hours to assess your average pace, elevation gain, and distance traveled. Each time you do the same route or distance, decrease your total travel time, including your breaks. A heart rate monitor can help you track uphill effort, and an altimeter can be useful to gauge your rate of ascent and descent.

As your comfort levels increase and your soreness diminishes, expand your effort 5 to 15 percent per week until you are able to do trips with more gains, heavier loads, or greater distances. As mentioned in chapter 2, if you perform loaded uphill best-fit testing, it may be tricky to determine what areas need the greatest focus. In most cases, assuming that you have adequate hydration and fueling, if you hike uphill

Advanced Considerations

A training book for outdoor sports would not be complete without mentioning the ultimate backpacking challenge: a transcontinental thru-hike such as the 2,665-mile (4,289 km) Pacific Crest Trail, the 2,168-mile (3,489 km) Appalachian Trail, or the 2,558-mile (4,117 km) Continental Divide Trail in the United States. People have even gone so far as to do yo-yos (Mexico to Canada and back again in 1 year) or the Triple Crown (all three trails in a single calendar year, as Brian Robinson did in 300 days in 2001). While the training principles remain the same for such a challenge, there are additional concerns to keep in mind.

Thru-hikers average 15 to 25 miles (24-40 km) per day for months on end. The Pacific Crest Trail requires that you be ready on day one for a 20-mile (32 km) stretch of desert in Southern California carrying 35 pounds (16 kg) and gaining 3,000 feet (914 m) to reach the first water resupply point. So unlike the Appalachian Trail, where you can train as you go, adding distance as your body adapts to hiking, for the Pacific Crest Trail, you need to be in peak physical condition from day one. The same holds true for the Continental Divide Trail. Allow at least 6 months to mentally plan and physically prepare for such a challenge. While the advanced high-altitude trek sample program included at the end of this chapter is a good training template, you should modify it by adding training pack weights of 35 to 40 pounds (16-18 kg). Doing so will ensure that you have the reserves needed for those stretches where you must carry additional food and water between resupply stations.

When doing your distance training, build to being able to complete a 1-day hike that is at least 10 percent longer than your longest day in the first week of hiking. Also, add at least a few 2- or 3-day overnight trips or back-to-back training days, preferably with your estimated starting pack weight, gaining 3,000 feet (914 m) and covering 15 to 20 miles (24-32 km) a day. Such trips will help you do a gear shakedown and make sure you are fully prepared for the first few weeks of your thru-hike.

with a light pack weight as specified in your program and quickly run out of breath, you need to increase your endurance; if you do well until you start adding weight and then you feel your legs have no pop, you need more strength. If both elements feel challenging, you need to build both strength and cardiovascular endurance.

Creating a Long-Term Program

To develop an appropriate training program, always start with your end goal. Then consider the distance you need to travel, the total elevation gain and loss, the highest elevation the hike will reach, the season of your goal event (winter and off-season trips will take more planning, gear, and weight), the terrain variability (goat trails are steeper, less traveled, and provide more challenging footing than well-used hiking trails), and your pack weight.

The FITT parameters, your personalized test results, the cardiovascular guidelines, and the strength guidelines are puzzle pieces that all fit together into a final picture that matches your body, lifestyle, goals, and needs. Once you have a well-defined goal, determine the amount of time you have available to train. The easier or shorter your goal, the less time you need to prepare, especially if you already have a good training baseline. Early in the season, focus on building the cardiovascular and strength endurance required for distance travel. Prioritize your training to address any weaknesses first. Include exercises that will help with muscle balance, joint integrity, overall stability, and appropriate range of motion.

If you add significant mileage or elevation change, altitude above 8,500 feet (2,591 m), multiple days of repeat effort, or pack weight beyond 35 pounds (16 kg), extend your timeline so that you will be able to prepare adequately. If you anticipate vacations or stressful workweeks that will interrupt your training, start earlier. After your adventure, allow for sufficient recovery and then shift into a routine that involves shorter, less-frequent workouts that maintain the training level you attained so that you can start at a higher baseline the next time you begin training to meet a specific goal. Your program should be fluid, always focusing on whatever needs improvement.

The following chart summarizes the training time you will need beyond your baseline training in order to prepare for a goal of a given difficulty, distance or duration, elevation change, and pack weight. Note that if your goal shares at least one variable with goals at the intermediate or advanced levels, include the training time suggested for the higher level indicated in the chart. In other words, if you will

Difficulty	Distance traveled; trip duration	Elevation change or top altitude	Pack weight	Training time above baseline
HIKES: SINGLE-DAY TRIPS WITH <20 LB. (9 KG) PACK				
Beginner	<8 mi. (13 km)	<1,500 ft. (457 m)	<10 lb. (4.5 kg)	4 weeks
Intermediate	<14 mi. (22.5 km)	<3,500 ft. (1,067 m)	<15 lb. (6.8 kg)	8 weeks
Advanced	<30 mi. (48 km)	>3,500 ft. (1,067 m)	>15 lb. (6.8 kg)	14 weeks
TREKS: MULTIDAY TRIPS OF SINGLE-DAY HIKES WITH <20 LB. 91 KG) PACK				
Beginner	<5 days	To 5,000 ft. (1,524 m)	<10 lb. (4.5 kg)	10 weeks
Intermediate	<14 days	To 10,000 ft. (3,048 m)	<15 lb. (6.8 kg)	14 weeks
Advanced	<21 days	To 19,000 ft. (5,791 m)	>15 lb. (6.8 kg)	16 weeks
BACKPACKS: MULTIDAY TRIPS WITH OVERNIGHT PACK AND SIGNIFICANT DISTANCE OVER VARIED TERRAIN				
Beginner	<10 mi. (16 km); 1 night	<2,000 ft. (610 m)	<20 lb. (9 kg)	6 weeks
Intermediate	<24 mi. (39 km); 4 days	<5,000 ft. (1,524 m)	<30 lb. (14 kg)	10 weeks
Advanced	>100 mi. (161 km); 2 weeks	>5,000 ft. (1,524 m); thru-hikes	>30 lb. (14 kg)	16 weeks

be doing a 14-mile (22.5 km) hike (intermediate level) with 1,500 feet (457 m) of elevation gain (beginner level) and a 15-pound (6.8 kg) pack (intermediate level), allow at least 8 weeks to train (the intermediate-level recommendation). While it may be possible to train in fewer weeks than suggested, in order to avoid strain and to properly prepare your muscles, tendons, ligaments, and cardiovascular system, you should allow for the suggested training time. Also, if you start training below the suggested baseline, you need to add more training time.

Add a week of training time for each 5 pounds (2.3 kg) of weight you are adding to the pack weight specified in the chart. The general conditioning recommendations for hiking, trekking, and backpacking are to build to the following weekly workloads (given your desired outcome) 2 weeks from goal. You should also include stretching with every workout.

Type	Number of weekly workouts 2 weeks from goal	Number of strength workouts	Number of cardiovascular workouts	Number of sport-specific weekly workouts	Weekly exercise time
Beginner hike	4	2 30 min. full body	2	1 hilly walk (>1 hr.), 12 lb. (5.4 kg), 2.5-3 mph (4-5 kph)	3-4 hr.
Intermediate hike	5	2 45 min. full body	3	1 beginner hike, 17 lb. (7.7 kg), 2-2.5 mph (3-4 kph) or 750 ft. (229 m) gain each hour	5-7 hr.
Advanced hike	6	2 1 hr. full body	4 (1 anaerobic)	1 intermediate hike, 22 lb. (10 kg), 1,000 ft. (305 m) gain each hour	8-12 hr.
Beginner trek	5	2 45 min. full body	3 (1 anaerobic)	1 beginner hike, 12 lb. (5.4 kg)	5-6 hr.
Intermediate trek	5	2 1 hr. full body	3-4 (1 anaerobic)	1 intermediate hike, 17 lb. (7.7 kg)	8-10 hr.
Advanced trek	6	2 1 hr. full body	4-5 (2 anaerobic)	1-2 intermediate hikes, 22 lb. (10 kg)	10+ hr.
Beginner backpack	4	2 45 min. full body	3	>1 beginner hike, 22 lb. (10 kg)	4-6 hr.
Intermediate backpack	5	2 45 min. full body	3-4	>1 intermediate hike, 27 lb. (12 kg); 1 B2B before goal	8-10 hr.
Advanced backpack	6	2 1 hr. full body	5 (1 anaerobic)	1-2 intermediate hikes, 37 lb. (16.8 kg); 1-2 B2B before goal	10+ hr.

B2B=back-to-back

Sample Goals and Associated Programs

The following sample programs introduce you to hiking, trekking, and backpacking programs that are designed to match specific goals. They include preparing for an intermediate hike (Mount Si in Washington), an intermediate backpack trip (Grand Canyon in Arizona), and an advanced high-altitude trek (Kilimanjaro in Tanzania). Training sessions at all levels should include 5 to 10 minutes of targeted stretching. Use the sample programs for insights into how you can manipulate training variables to fit your own goal. All three sample programs begin with the following baseline training: 2 to 4 weeks of at least four weekly workouts, including two 30-minute strength workouts (A1 and A2 on page 61), two cardiovascular workouts (one 45-minute distance at 65-75 percent MHR and one 30-minute tempo at 75-85 percent MHR), and one sport-specific hike of at least 4 miles (6.4 km) that involves an elevation gain of at least 700 feet (213 m) and a pack weight up to 10 pounds (4.5 kg). Suitable aerobic training options include walking stairs or hills; exercising on the incline treadmill, elliptical trainer, stair-climber, or StepMill; or hiking.

■ INTERMEDIATE HIKE

This program is suitable for a goal such as an 8-mile (12.9 km) hiking trip with a 17-pound (7.7 kg) pack on a well-established dirt trail that gains 3,400 feet (1,036 m), such as Mount Si. Choose cardiovascular modes specific to hiking and choose strength exercises that will prepare the calves, upper back, shoulders, and quadriceps for the elevation gain. This 8-week training program adds 7 pounds (3.2 kg) of pack weight to baseline 10 pounds (<4.5 kg) and increases elevation gain by 500 feet (152 m) each hike. While it may be challenging to find trails of comparable length and elevation gain, you can use the sample program as an illustration of how to manipulate the training variables according to what part of the training cycle you are in. The following numbers may be more helpful if you occasionally use machines for your pack endurance workouts, as you can program the specific distance, pace, and ramp height that meet your training needs.

Intensity Guidelines

Recovery	<65 percent MHR
Distance	65 to 75 percent MHR
Tempo	75 to 85 percent MHR
Interval	85 to 95 percent MHR

Week	Day 1	Day 2	Day 3	Day 4	Day 5	Weekend
BUILD STRENGTH						
1	30 min. tempo; A1 strength	Off	45 min. distance	A2 strength	Off	distance walk, 45 min., 8 lb. (3.6 kg)
2	33 min tempo; A1 strength	Off	50 min. distance	A2 strength	Off	distance hike, 1,000 ft. (305 m) gain, 6 mi. (9.7 km), 8 lb. (3.6 kg)
3	36 min. tempo; A1 strength	Off	55 min. distance	A2 strength	Off	distance hike, 1,500 ft. (457 m) gain, 8 mi. (12.9 km), 10 lb. (4.5 kg)
4	39 min. tempo; A1 strength	Off	60 min. distance	A2 strength	Off	distance hike, 2,000 ft. (610 m) gain, 6 mi. (9.7 km), 12 lb. (5.4 kg)
BUILD STAMINA						
5	45 min. recovery	40 min. tempo; E1 strength	50 min. distance, 15 lb. (6.8 kg)	E2 strength	Off	distance hike, 2,500 ft. (762 m) gain, 8 mi. (12.9 km), 13 lb. (6 kg)
6	50 min. recovery	40 min. tempo; E3 strength	60 min. distance, 18 lb. (8 kg)	E1 strength	Off	distance hike, 3,000 ft. (914 m) gain, 8 mi. (12.9 km), 15 lb. (6.8 kg)
7	55 min. recovery	45 min. tempo; E2 strength	70 min. distance, 20 lb. (9.1 kg)	E3 strength	Off	distance hike, 2,000 ft. (610 m) gain, 10 mi. (16.1 km), 19 lb. (8.6 kg)
8	45 min. distance	20 min. tempo; E1 strength	Off	45 min. recovery	Off	Goal: 8 mi. (12.9 km), 17 lb. (7.7 kg), 3,400 ft. (1,036 m) hike

■ INTERMEDIATE BACKPACK

This program is suitable for a person embarking on a goal such as a 3-night backpacking trip in the Grand Canyon that involves a rim-to-rim hike with a 35-pound (15.9 kg) pack over varied terrain and a 5,000-foot (1,524 m) elevation gain. Such a person would need to already have a suitable training foundation comparable to that established in the 8-week training program (pages 98-99) to embark on this 10-week program. In other words, the athlete who can comfortably hike 8 miles (12.9 km) carrying a 20-pound (9 kg) pack on a hike with 3,000 feet (914 m) of elevation gain can expect to start at week 1 of this program without too much difficulty or discomfort. While combining strength and anaerobic training into a single workout is good for building physical and mental stamina in latter months, such high-intensity workouts are physically and mentally demanding. If you prefer, add a sixth workout day and split the combination workout so that your performance will be higher during each session. Preferred aerobic modes include working on a high-ramp (>8 percent incline) treadmill, a StepMill, or an elliptical trainer; climbing stairs or hills; pack walking; and trail running.

Intensity Guidelines

Recovery	<65 percent MHR
Distance	65 to 75 percent MHR
Tempo	75 to 85 percent MHR
Interval	85 to 95 percent MHR

Week	Day 1	Day 2	Day 3	Day 4	Day 5	Weekend
			BUILD ENDURANCE			
1	45 min. distance	30 min. tempo; A1 strength	Off	20 min. uphill, 15 lb. (6.8 kg)	45 min. distance; A2 strength	6-8 mi. (9.7-12.9 km) round-trip, 3,000 ft. (914 m), 20 lb. (9 kg)
2	50 min. distance	30 min. tempo; A1 strength	Off	25 min. uphill, 18 lb. (8 kg)	50 min. distance; A2 strength	6-8 mi. (9.7-12.9 km) round-trip, 3,300 ft. (1,006 m), 22 lb. (10 kg)
3	55 min. recovery	30 min. tempo; A1 strength	Off	30 min. uphill, 20 lb. (9.1 kg)	55 min. distance; A2 strength	6-8 mi. (9.7-12.9 km) round-trip, 3,300 ft. (1,006 m), 25 lb. (11.3 kg)

Week	Day 1	Day 2	Day 3	Day 4	Day 5	Weekend
BUILD STRENGTH						
4	60 min. distance	30 min. tempo; D1 strength	35 min. repeat, 23 lb. (10.4 kg)	60 min. distance; D2 strength	Off	8-10 mi. (12.9-16.1 km) round-trip, 3,500 ft. (1,067 m), 28 lb. (12.7 kg)
5	30 min. recovery; D1 strength	60 min. distance	35 min. uphill, 27 lb. (12.2 kg); D2 strength	Off	30 min. tempo; D1 strength	8-10 mi. (12.9-16.1 km) round-trip, 3,500 ft. (1,067 m), 30 lb. (13.6 kg)
6	30 min. recovery; D2 strength	60 min. distance	35 min. repeat, 30 lb. (13.6 kg); D1 strength	Off	35 min. tempo; D2 strength	8-10 mi. (12.9-16.1 km) round-trip, 4,000 ft. (1,219 m), 30 lb. (13.6 kg)
BUILD STAMINA						
7	30 min. recovery; E1 strength	60 min. distance	30 min. uphill, 35 lb. (16 kg); E2 strength	Off	E3 strength	10-12 mi. (16.1-19.3 km) round-trip, 3.000-4,000 ft. (914-1,219 m), 35 lb. (15.9 kg)
8	30 min. recovery; E1 strength	60 min. distance	30 min. repeat, 38 lb. (17 kg); E2 strength	Off	E3 strength	B2B: day 1: 6 mi. (9.7 km), 3,000 ft. (914 m), 40 lb. (18 kg); day 2: 6 mi. (9.7 km), 2,000 ft. (605 m), 35 lb. (15.9 kg)
9	30 min. recovery	45 min. distance; E1 strength	30 min. uphill, 40 lb. (18 kg)	E2 strength	Off	10-12 mi. (16.1-19.3 km) round-trip, 3,500 ft. (1,067 m), 40 lb. (18 kg)
PEAK AND TAPER						
10	45 min. distance; E3 strength	Off	45 min. distance	30 min. recovery	Off	Goal: 3-day backpack trip to Grand Canyon

B2B=back-to-back

■ ADVANCED HIGH-ALTITUDE TREK

This program is suitable for a person with a goal such as a 6-day backpacking trip to the top of Kilimanjaro (19,340 feet, or 5,895 m) with a pack weight of 20 pounds (9.1 kg). What is unique about an African expedition is that porter assistance is mandated; hikers carry a day pack only. A training program to meet this backpacking goal needs to consider the following: (1) the goal is a repeated effort that includes 2,000 to 4,000 feet (610-1,219 m) of elevation gain on consecutive days and ends with more than 15 miles (24 km) of descent on days 5 and 6, (2) high-altitude exertion demands a greater level of fitness and will require anaerobic training starting in training week 9, and (3) additional acclimatization time (such as travel, extra day hikes, or even a safari) ahead of the trip is needed. The sample program illustrated here adds 8 weeks of strength, stamina, and taper blocks to the baseline and endurance training of weeks 1 through 8 of the program for the intermediate hike (the first sample program). Thus, this program requires 4 training months in all. Suitable cardiovascular training options include working on a high-ramp incline treadmill (with a 6-15 percent grade), an elliptical machine, a StepMill, or a stair-climber; trail running; or climbing stairs or hills.

Intensity Guidelines

Recovery	<65 percent MHR
Distance	65 to 75 percent MHR
Tempo	75 to 85 percent MHR
Interval	85 to 95 percent MHR

Week	Day 1	Day 2	Day 3	Day 4	Day 5	Weekend
1-8	Follow program for the intermediate hike (page 99)					
			BUILD STRENGTH			
9	30 min. uphill, 20 lb. (9.1 kg); C3 strength	C4 strength	75 min. distance, 15 lb. (6.8 kg)	45 min. tempo; C3 strength	Off	3,000 ft. (914 m) gain, 8 mi. (12.9 km) round-trip, 20 lb. (9.1 kg)
10	35 min. uphill, 20 lb. (9.1 kg); C4 strength	C3 strength	75 min. distance, 15 lb. (6.8 kg)	50 min. tempo; C4 strength	Off	3,000 ft. (914 m) gain, 8 mi. (12.9 km) round-trip, 23 lb. (10.4 kg)
11	40 min. uphill, 25 lb. (11 kg); C3 strength	C4 strength	75 min. distance, 20 lb. (9.1 kg)	55 min. tempo; C3 strength	Off	3,200 ft. (975 m) gain, 8-10 mi. (12.9-16.1 km) round-trip, 23 lb. (10.4 kg)

Week	Day 1	Day 2	Day 3	Day 4	Day 5	Weekend
			BUILD STAMINA			
12	45 min. uphill, 25 lb. (11 kg); E1 strength	30 min. recovery	75 min. distance, 20 lb. (9 kg)	60 min. tempo; E2 strength	Off	B2B: day 1: 6 mi. (9.7 km), 2,500 ft. (762 m), 25 lb. (11.3); day 2: 4 mi. (6.2 km), 1,500 ft. (457 m), 20 lb. (9.1 kg)
13	30 min. recovery	45 min. uphill, 30 lb. (13.6 kg); E3 strength	75 min. distance, 25 lb. (11.3 kg)	60 min. tempo; E1 strength	Off	3,400 ft. (1,036 m) gain, 8-10 mi. (12.9-16.1 km), 25 lb. (11.3 kg)
14	45 min. uphill, 30 lb. (13.6 kg); E2 strength	40 min. recovery	75 min. distance, 25 lb. (11.3 kg)	60 min. tempo; E3 strength	Off	B2B: day 1: 8 mi. (12.9 km), 3,000 ft. (914 m), 25 lb. (11.3 kg); day 2: 6 mi. (9.7 km), 2,500 ft. (762 m), 20 lb. (9.1 kg)
15	40 min. recovery	50 min. uphill, 20 lb. (9.1 kg); E1 strength	60 min. distance, 20 lb. (9.1 kg)	40 min. tempo; E2 strength	Off	2,000 ft. (610 m) gain, 5-6 mi. (8-9.7 km), 20 lb. (9.1 kg)
			PEAK AND TAPER			
16	45 min. distance; E3 strength, upper only	45 min. recovery	45 min. distance	Off or optional 30 min recovery	Travel	6-day hike Kilimanjaro, 19,340 ft. (5,895 m), 20 lb. (9.1 kg)

B2B=back-to-back

Alpine Scrambling and Mountaineering

Scrambling and mountaineering both involve attaining the top of a peak through nontechnical and technical means. In this chapter we define scrambling as nontechnical off-trail travel, often on snow or rock, requiring the occasional use of hands. A nontechnical summit is one that can be reached without a harness, rope, or protection hardware and does not involve extremely steep slopes or glacier travel. This category of mountain travel fills the gap between hiking, trekking, and backpacking on established trails and technical vertical climbing. Thus, scrambling can mean negotiating lower-angle rock; covering second- or third-class terrain; traveling over talus, scree, or boulder fields; crossing streams; maneuvering through dense brush; and walking on snowy slopes. Scramblers need full-body strength to cover such diverse terrain while carrying a pack and ice axe.

Mountaineering involves ropes, protection, and a harness to reach a summit and requires skill beyond that of scrambling. Mountaineers may handle fifth-class rock, hard snow, and low-angle ice or glacial terrain. Like scramblers, mountaineers need to handle greater ranges of motion that include squatting under downed logs while wearing a pack, stepping high to clear branches and rocks, pulling over chockstones, balancing while placing protection, or stopping quickly with an ice axe on steep slopes. If you are climbing low fifth-class rock in mountaineering boots, you should follow the mountaineering training guidelines in this chapter; if the climbing is difficult enough to require rock shoes, then you should add components from chapter 9 specific to a technical climbing program. If you need only one ice axe to ascend icy slopes of less than 40 degrees, train for mountaineering; terrain requiring two ice axes places you in the realm of ice climbing, for which you should use training information in chapter 9. For more information on ratings, see Cox and Fulsaas, 2003.

Following are the fitness components common to scrambling and mountaineering. A rating of 5 indicates components deserving the highest emphasis in your training program, while a rating of 1 indicates components that are the lowest priority in your program.

Aerobic conditioning: 3

Anaerobic conditioning: 3 (4 if you plan to travel at high altitudes)

Upper-body strength: 3

Lower-body strength: 4

Flexibility: 4

Activity skill: 3

Cross-training: 1

Important areas of the body: feet, trapezius, lower back, core, shoulders, calves, upper back, legs, hips

Scramblers and mountaineers (which collectively are called *alpinists)* share one major similarity with hikers, trekkers, and backpackers: covering varied terrain for great distances while carrying pack weight. Alpinists gain more elevation per unit of distance of travel, requiring additional stamina from the gluteals, hamstrings, hips, and calves for upward propulsion and greater strength from the quadriceps for steeper descents with heavier loads. Alpinists also need additional ankle stability and healthy feet, as the terrain they traverse is more uneven than the dirt trails most hikers, trekkers, and backpackers typically encounter. Mountaineers considering high-altitude expeditions should also include anaerobic training.

Challenging terrain requires additional stability in ankles and hips compared to most hiking terrain.

Cardiovascular Needs

While hikers focus on increasing mileage over established trails, scramblers and mountaineers work to gain more elevation per mile. The result is greater emphasis on developing uphill stamina over ever-steeper terrain. To prepare for such activity, you should be able to complete a beginner hike of carrying a 20-pound (9.1 kg) pack, covering 5 miles (8.0 km) round-trip, and ascending and descending 2,000 feet (610 m) in less than 2.5 hours.

In addition to having a base hiking capability, you should build up to doing 4 to 6 cardiovascular workouts per week as you approach your goal. While some of these workouts should be in the mountains or at least have an uphill emphasis, most can be done locally. The majority of your sessions should also load your spine and work your muscles in the same ways scrambling and mountaineering work them. The FITT parameters of your cardiovascular workouts will vary according to your goals and test results. The sample programs at the end of this chapter illustrate how to combine training variables to address different levels and goals.

As you plan your cardiovascular sessions, determine your goal for each one. Of the 4 to 6 weekly workouts, at least one should be distance training. Increase your distance gradually, adding 5 to 15 percent per outing. A second workout should emphasize higher intensity over a shorter distance (i.e., tempo) to focus on heavier pack weight, faster leg turnover, or travel on steep terrain. If you plan to be at altitude, add anaerobic training during a third weekly workout. Additional weekly cardiovascular workouts can be moderate to easy in terms of time, distance, and intensity, and recovery workouts following pack training should be short.

Once you have a focus for each cardiovascular workout, select your training modes. Suitable options include off-trail training, in-town training, spinal-loading cardiovascular machine training, step aerobics classes, and trail running. Note that suggested town or gym workouts will always be shorter than suggested sessions in the mountains due to the risks of overuse injury, the potential psychological burnout from spending hours training with the same view, and the lack of comparable training stimulus to being outside. If you *must* train for endurance indoors and are working toward intermediate or advanced goals, include several cross-training modes within your endurance workouts so that you use muscle groups in different patterns, prevent burnout, and avoid getting stale.

Off-Trail or In-Town Sessions

Ideally, you should include a hike, scramble, or mountaineering outing several times a month. You may find yourself on a steep learning curve when shifting from hiking to anything new such as scrambling, backpacking, or climbing, and it takes not only physical endurance but also mental stamina to adjust to the unfamiliar, more challenging terrain. If you do not have access to mountains, look for varied terrain that includes short, steep rolling hills, sandy dunes, or sloping wooded or countryside pastures. By walking over such terrain, you also develop stability in your ankles, strength in your hip flexors for high stepping, and uphill stamina in your gluteals and hamstrings. You may also find that including short bushwhacking stints on your hikes is a good way to train for the more challenging terrain you may encounter on steeper, off-trail alpine outings.

If you live near an inland lake or river, you may find a steep path or multiple flights of steps leading down to the beach or riverbank that you can use for your training. If you live near a public or school stadium, there might be a set of bleachers open to use. In cities, you may be able to find a multistory public building with several flights of stairs. Beaches, gravel beds, and the like can be used to work on the transition from hiking to off-trail activity in terms of developing endurance as well as integrity and agility in your ankles and feet.

To intensify your in-town workouts, replace continuous walks with uphill intervals. Choose a hill or set of stairs that takes 2 to 3 minutes to climb, and racewalk up it. Try to get your heart rate to 85 to 95 percent of your MHR as you approach the top. Time how long the interval takes you. Set a comfortable pace as you walk back down. Your heart rate should drop significantly on the return, providing sufficient rest as you descend to your starting point. Once it has dropped to roughly 65 percent of your MHR, turn around and head back up again. Try to equal or beat your initial climbing time on the first work interval with each successive interval.

To specifically target this workout for alpine travel, carry a pack, increasing the weight by 3 to 5 pounds (1.4-2.3 kg) per workout until you can do a midweek pack workout with 10 percent more weight than your goal outing weight. The more comfortable you are when pushing yourself up steep hills or stairs, the easier continuous uphill travel will feel.

Include fartlek training to simulate short, random bursts of energy. As you tackle a steep off-trail section, make your way uphill as quickly as you can, and then relax on the other side as you catch your breath. You can also clamber over and under downed logs similar to a natural obstacle course. Doing bursts of speed on heather, loam, shale, talus, sand, or scree slopes can enhance your skill and increase your confidence in your footing while simultaneously boosting your anaerobic capacity.

Cardiovascular Machines

Good machines for alpine training are elliptical machines, incline treadmills (up to 15 percent grade), VersaClimbers, Jacob's Ladders, StepMills, and stair-climbers. If you do alpine-specific endurance training on an elliptical machine, use the highest ramp setting possible with moderate resistance so that you can maintain a comfortable walking pace of 80 to 110 strides (40-55 complete leg turnovers) per minute. If your elliptical machine allows it, add backward walking to work the quadriceps as you would work them on descents. Elliptical machines with handles allow for upper-body training that is similar to what you may encounter on alpine outings.

Newer incline treadmill models that go up to 15 percent grade can provide a steady uphill climb. They can be a suitable substitute for mountainous terrain if the weather is bad or you do not have access to mountains. Backward walking at reduced inclines and lower speeds (hold on to the handrails for balance) can develop endurance in the quadriceps. VersaClimbers work both the upper and lower body in a near-vertical position and provide an efficient workout in a short amount of time. Revolving stair machines allow for comfortable foot positioning and replicate steeper alpine terrain. Look for models that duplicate the climbing motion, are comfortable for your stride, and allow for adjustable leg length and resistance to maintain knee health.

Step Aerobics

Group exercise classes that involve a 6- to 10-inch (15-25 cm) step are a great option for building endurance in the calves, hip flexors, gluteals, and hamstrings. Most classes involve upper-body movements and include upright spinal loading, making them good cross-training sessions that work the entire hip and leg area and provide a lot of variety.

Running

Running is another form of training commonly chosen by alpinists, though it is *not* necessary for optimal conditioning. By wearing a substantial pack on walks instead, you can target the legs, calves, and back and improve your ability to carry heavy weight up, down, and across steep slopes. The result is physical conditioning highly specific to alpine travel, as opposed to logging 30 to 40 running miles (48.3-64.4 km) a week. If you decide to run, keep in mind that your flat mileage will differ greatly from that of your trail runs or off-trail bushwhacks. Keep any pack weight light on trail runs to reduce eccentric loading of the quadriceps on descents, especially in early season. Keep track of time and elevation change by using an altimeter. Trail running can enhance ankle stability, increase balance and core stamina, and train the body effectively for ascents and descents.

Strength Needs

Scramblers and mountaineers benefit from strong upper-back, core, and leg muscles (rated 4); solid balance and agility; and flexibility in the calves, knees, torso, and ankles. You should do full-body strength training year round so you can maintain a baseline and then increase strength as needed. During the preseason, use single-limb free-weight exercises to correct any weaknesses in your legs and hips, particularly in the full range of motion you might encounter on alpine outings. Exercises such as the one-leg deadlift (page 263), step-up (page 275), reverse step-up (page 277), dumbbell lunge (page 273), and backward lunge (page 272) ensure that your legs and hips are evenly balanced and doing equal work. During the middle months of training, after you have established good muscle balance and core integrity and stability, incorporate full-body, full range of motion exercises, including variations on the barbell back squat (page 270), barbell deadlift (page 261), dumbbell overhead press (page 251), pull-up (page 242), and push-up (page 255). Core exercises include the plank (page 225), medicine ball twist (page 224), and wood chopper (page 227). Since the calves will take the brunt of the load when you are on steep terrain, include the standing calf raise (page 268) and other straight-leg variations of calf exercises. A few sets of the step-up (page 275) or other unilateral leg exercises in your latter training blocks will increase your range of motion and strength over what you developed in your early months of training.

Because of the dynamic and unpredictable nature of performing self-arrests with an ice axe, be sure you have full range of motion in your shoulders as well as good strength and joint integrity throughout the chest, shoulders, and core. Pull-ups, push-ups, and core exercises will enable you to get into position rapidly and hold your ice axe in place on icy slopes while you fight to stop yourself from sliding.

Try to anticipate which muscles will be involved in any upcoming activities and try to match your training movements to the movements that will be required for those activities. For example, if you know that you will be snowshoeing or telemark skiing on approaches for winter scrambles or mountaineering outings, develop strength endurance in the hip flexors for repeated high steps and sliding. Add ankle weights or ski boots to short anaerobic uphill or strength workouts. Do not, however, add ankle weights to long endurance workouts, as they can alter your natural stride, not to mention cause overuse injury.

Use your weekly outings as a guideline for refining your program. If you notice that your ankles get really tired on your fourth scramble, add unilateral balance exercises, especially if you have not yet done so or have removed them from your program. Analyze the terrain you chose for the outing that caused you difficulty. Traveling over particularly rough, steep, or rocky terrain; wearing different footwear with less ankle support; forgetting your trekking poles; or increasing mileage or elevation too quickly might all be responsible for your ankle problems rather than pointing to a lack in your training program. By tracking such variations in a training journal and noting for each trip your comfort level, elevation gained, weight carried, distance traveled, time to mile markers, and effectiveness of your nutrition and hydration system, you can determine what works best for you.

Flexibility Needs

Try the arm circles (page 214), tree hug stretch (page 219), and standing dowel torso rotation (page 214) after upper-body workouts specifically designed to strengthen muscles for ice axe use. The triangle pose (page 216), frog stretch (page 217), and 90-90 quadriceps psoas stretch (page 219) are a great follow-up for lower-body strength sessions. Just as we recommend doing a recovery workout after a hike, we suggest you get moving the day following any alpine outing to help restore your flexibility.

Additional Considerations

An alpinist who weighs 150 pounds (68.0 kg) will typically have an easier time carrying a 30-pound (13.6 kg) pack (20 percent of body weight) than a 120-pound (54.4 kg) climber will have carrying the same pack (25 percent of body weight). If the 120-pound (54.4 kg) climber can considerably increase her functional strength and muscle mass, she may very well outperform her heavier colleague, as ultimately she has less body weight to carry up the mountain. High-altitude climbers, on the other hand, will almost certainly lose 5 to 10 percent of their body weight on expeditions of 3 weeks or longer. Their strategy may be to add as much functional muscle mass as possible. They may also add a little extra fat right before their trip, not only to provide insulation but also to protect lean, active muscle tissue from being catabolized while they are on the mountain.

Due to the increased strenuousness of alpine travel, an alpine outing has a greater caloric requirement than a hike of the same distance has, as during the alpine outing it will take more time and effort to cover the same mileage. The recommended macronutrient ratios for scramblers and mountaineers remain the same as those for hikers, but in general, caloric quantities will need to be 10 to 15 percent greater. Hydration is as important for alpinists as it is for hikers; however, water resupply options may be fewer in off-trail routes (requiring more toted water and thus more weight) until the alpinist reaches snow. For extended high-altitude travel, it becomes more important to carry easily swallowed high-carbohydrate packets for quick energy.

Since alpine travel can be done year round, the range of weather conditions alpinists encounter is far greater than what most hikers, trekkers, or backpackers experience. Knowing how to read changing weather and slope conditions is vital to avoiding avalanches, whiteouts, and storms. Winter alpinists in particular need additional layers of clothing, a stove, fuel, and a small pot for boiling water (all adding to pack weight); they also need to be more alert for signs of hypothermia and frostbite. Winter conditions can affect the duration of the outing and therefore can play a significant role in how long you may be exposed to the elements and how much food and clothing you must carry. Even in the summer, alpinists traveling to extremely high altitudes can experience temperature swings as dramatic

Advanced Considerations

If you are training for an 8,000-meter peak, a high-altitude winter ascent, the Seven Summits, or other extreme ambitions, you need a baseline that is at the advanced mountaineering level (i.e., 21 weeks of training) or higher. For success with high-altitude climbing, get as strong as you possibly can and build as much stamina as you can to allow for several weeks (or even months, in the case of 8,000-meter peaks) at altitude.

As you plan your distance workouts, build to being able to do 10 percent more distance than your longest day in the first week of such a trip. You will lose 5 to 15 percent of your body weight, so plan to put on at least 5 pounds (2.3 kg) of body weight that you can easily afford to lose. In extreme high-altitude environments, adaptation to altitude plays a huge role in success. Some people tolerate altitude well; others do not. Acclimatization can vary widely from trip to trip. Eating frequently (even when you do not feel like it), staying hydrated, and knowing when to turn around are just as important as physical conditioning. Extreme weather conditions, group dynamics, and logistics of coordinating such attempts also play large roles in your success.

as 40 degrees Fahrenheit (22 C) from sunup to sundown. Try to train in weather conditions that match what you will experience on your goal outing. If you will be doing early alpine starts to avoid postholing, rock fall, melting snow bridges, or higher stream runoff, you will want to include early-morning training to get your body ready to perform at odd hours of the day.

Finally, while mountaineering and scrambling require greater technical skill than hiking requires, such as being able to perform a crevasse rescue, to travel in crampons while roped, and to use an ice axe for self-arrest, the actual physical skill required is relatively low when compared to that involved in technical climbing or skiing. For more on acquiring technical skills for alpine outings, see *Mountaineering: Freedom of the Hills* (Cox and Fulsaas 2003).

Assessing Fitness and Gauging Improvement

For scrambling and mountaineering, complete the 13-minute ramp test on a high-ramp elliptical trainer, a StepMill, a stair-climber, a Jacob's Ladder, a VersaClimber, or an incline treadmill that can go beyond a 10 percent grade. After a month of training, add a monthly 30-minute field test on the same equipment to gauge your progress. For alpine travel you can also use suitable equipment to assess elevation gain per unit distance, or pace. A benchmark for beginning scrambles is to travel at a pace of 2 miles per hour (3.2 kph) while carrying 25 pounds (11.3 kg) and gaining 750 feet (229 m) per mile (1.6 km), shooting for a 2,250-foot (686 m) gain to simulate a 3-hour, 6-mile (9.7 km) round-trip. Use your results on the lower-body strength tests from chapter 2 to select exercises that pinpoint weaknesses, and be sure that on your flexibility assessment you demonstrate normal range of motion throughout all your joints.

Once you have spent a month building up to 4 to 6 weekly workouts, select a scramble within your capabilities and see how you feel during and after the outing. As you get comfortable with beginner outings, expand your efforts by trying intermediate trips with more gain, heavier loads, or greater distances. Increase your workload (time, distance, elevation gain, pack weight) by 5 to 15 percent a week.

The best-fit test for alpine travel involves hiking steadily or scrambling for 2 hours to assess your average miles per hour, elevation gain, and distance. A sample test might be a local 8-mile (12.9 km) hike involving 3,000 feet (914 m) of gain, an ideal workout for scrambling, hiking, backpacking, and mountaineering. If such terrain is not available, use stadium stairs or smaller hills repeated as laps or high-ramp cardiovascular machines for the 2 hours. If you struggle with breathlessness while carrying a light pack, focus on adding endurance; if your legs feel heavy as soon as you increase pack weight, work on building strength.

A heart rate monitor can help you gauge how hard you are working when going uphill so you can estimate what your ascending pace would be on more challenging terrain. Take an altimeter to assess your rate of ascent and descent. Each time you do the same route, try to decrease your total travel time including breaks. Keep your average working heart rate at less than 75 percent of your MHR for most of your outing. This pace is comfortable enough that you can continue indefinitely without getting so tired that you have to stop frequently to rest. It also allows you to maintain energy reserves in case of emergency.

While assessing your improvement on hikes is a matter of keeping track of time, distance, and elevation gain, when you are assessing off-trail alpine outings, the terrain, altitude, and technical difficulty all become more important in determining your cumulative effort. If you are on an outing in which you alternate between easy walking and more challenging scree, boulder fields, heather slopes, stream crossings, and the like, your average rate of ascent and descent will reflect those difficulties. The amount of snow on your route can also affect your rate of ascent and descent. For example, if you are skilled at glissading or the snow is perfect for plunge stepping, you may find that your descent takes less time in the early season than it takes later on when you have to step carefully across slopes previously blanketed by a smooth layer of snow. By noting route conditions and seasonal variations in your training journal, you can more readily compare efforts on similar outings.

Creating a Long-Term Program

To develop your alpine program, start with the end goal. Consider the distance to travel, total elevation gain and loss, highest overall elevation, seasonality (for gear weight and route conditions), terrain variability, pack weight, and total time anticipated for the outing as well as the skill level and training required. If you determine from your flexibility and strength assessments that you need to focus on certain areas of the body, prioritize your preseason training to take care of those areas first. Include exercises that will help with muscle balance, joint integrity, and stability, and once you have built a solid foundation, add sport-specific bilateral exercises and alpine conditioning outings.

The following chart summarizes the training time you will need beyond your baseline training in order to prepare for a goal of a given sport, difficulty, distance, elevation change, terrain, and pack weight. Note that if your goal shares at least one variable with goals at the intermediate or advanced levels, you should include the training time suggested for the higher level indicated in the chart. In other words, if you will be doing a 5-mile (8 km) scramble (beginner level) gaining 2,500 feet (762 m; beginner level) of elevation but you intend to carry 30 pounds (14 kg; intermediate level) including heavy photography equipment, you will want to train for an intermediate objective and include at least 8 weeks of training to prepare for the additional weight. If you are new to scrambling and mountaineering, keep in mind the amount of skill necessary to master them; the training time recommendations made here are for preparing yourself physically once you have the necessary skills.

Difficulty	Trip duration; distance traveled	Elevation	Terrain	Pack weight	Training time above baseline
ALPINE SCRAMBLES: VARIED NONTECHNICAL 2ND- AND 3RD-CLASS TERRAIN WITH <40 LB. (18.1 KG)					
Beginner	Single day; <6 mi. (9.7 km)	<2,500 ft. (762 m) gain	Class 2 and 3	<20 lb. (9.1 kg)	6 weeks
Intermediate	Day or overnight; <10 mi. (16.1 km)	<3,500 ft. (1,067 m) gain	Class 2 and 3	<30 lb. (13.6 kg)	8 weeks
Advanced	2+ nights; >15 mi. (24.1 km)	<6,000 ft. (1,829 m) gain	Class 2 and 3; some snow travel	>30 lb. (13.6 kg)	12 weeks
MOUNTAINEERING: TECHNICAL 4TH- AND 5TH-CLASS TERRAIN					
Beginner	Single day; <6 mi. (9.7 km)	<2,500 ft. (762 m) gain	Class 5-5.2	<25 lb. (11.3 kg)	8-10 weeks
Intermediate	2- to 4-day; <30 mi. (48.3 km)	<7,000 ft. (2,134 m) gain	Class 5-5.5	<40 lb. (18.1 kg)	15-16 weeks
Advanced	>1 week; >30 mi. (48.3 km); expeditions	>7,000 ft. (2,134 m) gain	>Class 5.5	>40 lb. (18.1 kg)	24-26 weeks

Once you know how much time you need to train, break the weeks or months between your end goal and your starting point into training blocks. In addition to following all the other guidelines for developing your own program, include at least 1 or 2 back-to-back workouts with a pack if you are considering a multiday trip. Complete your final back-to-back outing no closer than 2 weeks before your trip so you have adequate recovery time. Make the day before your back-to-back conditioner an off day or a low-intensity cross-training cardiovascular workout to help you prepare your mind for the trip and keep your muscles limber. Include a rest or recovery day following a back-to-back conditioning bout. If on your goal outing you will be carrying a heavy pack for 5 or more days, gradually work up to carrying 10 percent more weight for several hours on end at least 2 days in a row.

The general conditioning recommendations for scrambling and mountaineering are to build to the following weekly workloads 2 weeks from goal. Be sure to include stretching with every workout.

Type	Number of weekly workouts 2 weeks from goal	Number of strength workouts	Number of cardiovascular workouts	Number of sport-specific weekly workouts	Weekly exercise time
Beginner scramble	4-5	2 30 min. full body	4 (1 anaerobic)	1 beginner hike, 20 lb. (9.1 kg)	6-7 hr.
Intermediate scramble	5-6	2 45 min. full body	5 (1 anaerobic)	1 intermediate hike, 25 lb. (11.3 kg)	8-10 hr.
Advanced scramble	6	2 1 hr. full body	5-6 (1 anaerobic)	1 intermediate hike, 30 lb. (13.6 kg)	11+ hr.
Beginner mountaineering	4-5	2 45 min. full body	4-5 (1 anaerobic)	1 beginner scramble, 25 lb. (11.3 kg)	7-9 hr.
Intermediate mountaineering	6	3 45 min. alt. upper and lower	5-6 (1-2 anaerobic)	1 intermediate scramble, 30 lb. (13.6 kg)	11-15 hr.
Advanced mountaineering	6-8	2 1 hr. upper and 2 1 hr. lower	5-6 (1-2 anaerobic sled/pack)	1-2 intermediate outings, >40 lb. (18.1 kg)	13-16 hr.

Sample Goals and Associated Programs

The following sample programs are designed to meet particular goals an alpinist might have. They include a beginner 1-day scramble, an intermediate 3-day mountaineering trip, and an advanced 3- to 4-week high-altitude mountaineering trip. Training sessions at all levels should include 5 to 10 minutes of targeted stretching. Use the sample programs for insights into how you can manipulate the training variables to create programs for yourself. The sample programs begin with the following baseline training: two 30-minute strength workouts; two cardiovascular workouts, one of which is a 45-minute distance session (at 65-75 percent MHR) and one of which is a 30-minute tempo session (at 75-85 percent MHR); and one 5-mile (8.0 km) hike with a 2,000-foot (610 m) elevation gain and a 13-pound (5.9 kg) pack. Cardiovascular modes specific to traveling over steep, uneven terrain include walking hills and stairs; using a stair-climber, StepMill, high-ramp treadmill, VersaClimber, or high-ramp elliptical trainer; taking step aerobics classes; trail running; and hiking.

■ BEGINNER 1-DAY SCRAMBLE

This program is suitable for a goal such as a 7-mile (11.3 km) scramble with a 20-pound (9.1 kg) pack covering an elevation gain and loss of 3,200 feet (975 m). The program should include the step-up (page 275) and reverse step-up (page 277), unilateral balance exercises for the ankles, and walks on beach dunes, in woods, or over railroad gravel where boulders, logs, and stumps can offer variable terrain. The 6-week scrambling progression shows how to transition from hiking to traveling over steeper terrain by increasing elevation gain by 300 to 500 feet (91-152 m) per outing and gradually increasing pack weight to 20 pounds (9.1 kg).

Intensity Guidelines

Recovery	<65 percent MHR
Distance	65 to 75 percent MHR
Tempo	75 to 85 percent MHR
Interval	85 to 95 percent MHR

Week	Day 1	Day 2	Day 3	Day 4	Day 5	Weekend
			BUILD STRENGTH			
1	40 min. tempo; B2 strength	60 min. distance, 15 lb. (6.8 kg)	Off	60 min. distance	B3 strength	2,300 ft. (701 m) gain, 5-6 mi. (8.0-9.7 km) round-trip, 16 lb. (7.3 kg)
2	40 min. tempo; B1 strength	60 min. distance, 17 lb. (7.7 kg)	Off	65 min. distance	B2 strength	2,600 ft. (792 m) gain, 5-6 mi. (8.0-9.7 km) round-trip, 16 lb. (7.3 kg)
3	45 min. tempo; B3 strength	30 min. uphill, 20 lb. (9.1 kg)	Off	70 min. distance	B1 strength	2,600 ft. (792 m) gain, 5-6 mi. (8.0-9.7 km) round-trip, 19 lb. (8.6 kg)
			BUILD STAMINA			
4	45 min. tempo; B2 strength	35 min. uphill, 22 lb. (10.0 kg)	Off	60 min. distance	B3 strength	2,900 ft. (884 m) gain, 6-8 mi. (9.7-12.9 km) round-trip, 19 lb. (8.6 kg)
5	45 min. tempo; B1 strength	40 min. uphill, 25 lb. (11.3 kg)	Off	65 min. distance	B2 strength	2,900 ft. (884 m) gain, 6-8 mi. (9.7-12.9 km) round-trip, 23 lb. (10.4 kg)
6	60 min. recovery	30 min. tempo; B3 strength	Off	45 min. distance	Off	3,200 ft. (975 m) gain, 7 mi. (11.3 km) round-trip, 20 lb. (9.1 kg)

■ INTERMEDIATE 3-DAY HIGH-ALTITUDE MOUNTAINEERING TRIP

This 15-week program is suitable for a goal such as a 3-day mountaineering trip up 14,411-foot (4,392 m) Mount Rainier in Washington (United States) with a 40-pound (18.1 kg) pack. It assumes you have the baseline aerobic capacity necessary to travel 7 miles (11.3 km) and gain 3,200 feet (975 m) of elevation while carrying 35 pounds (15.9 kg). If your goal pack weight will be considerably heavier than 35 to 40 pounds (15.9-18.1 kg), add 1 to 2 more months for such baseline building. High-altitude glaciated mountains in the Pacific Northwest of the United States, such as Mounts Hood (Oregon), Baker (Washington), Rainier (Washington), and Shasta (California), all generate their own weather. You should use a guide for safe crevasse navigation unless you have the skill set, knowledge, and experience to travel safely on your own.

Novice mountaineers attempting such a trip as a once-in-a-lifetime experience may end up carrying packs as heavy as 50 to 55 pounds (22.7-25 kg); you should plan accordingly so that you are ready to handle a heavier pack than the one suggested here if you go with a guide service that requires more or heavier gear. Also consider what time of year you plan to leave. Late in the season, when you have to navigate around crevasses that have opened up, your trip may last longer and involve a significantly greater amount of elevation gain and loss en route to the summit. Dropping 300 feet (91 m) on a hike may not seem like much, but having to regain what you already climbed at 12,000 feet (3,658 m) can be significant. Suitable cardiovascular modes for this program include working on the incline treadmill, elliptical trainer, StepMill, or stair-climber; trail running; stair and hill climbing; and hiking.

Intensity Guidelines

Recovery	<65 percent MHR
Distance	65 to 75 percent MHR
Tempo	75 to 85 percent MHR
Interval	85 to 95 percent MHR

Week	Day 1	Day 2	Day 3	Day 4	Day 5	Weekend
1-6	Follow training for beginner scramble program, but add 5 lb. (2.3 kg) each hike so by week 7 you can gain 3,200 ft. (975 m) with 35 lb. (15.9 kg)					
			BUILD STRENGTH			
7	45 min. distance; C1 strength	Off	30 min. uphill, 35 lb. (15.9 kg); C2 strength	60 min. distance	40 min. tempo; C3 strength	6-8 mi. (9.7-12.9 km) round-trip, 3,200 ft. (975 m), 35 lb. (15.9 kg)
8	Off	50 min. distance; C4 strength	45 min. tempo; C1 strength	35 min. uphill, 38 lb. (17.2 kg)	65 min. distance; C2 strength	8-10 mi. (12.9-16.1 km) round-trip, 3,500 ft. (1,067 m), 35 lb. (15.9 kg)

(continued)

Intermediate 3-Day High-Altitude Mountaineering Trip *(continued)*

Week	Day 1	Day 2	Day 3	Day 4	Day 5	Weekend
			BUILD STRENGTH *(continued)*			
9	55 min. distance; C3 strength	Off	45 min. tempo; C4 strength	35 min. uphill, 40 lb. (18.1 kg)	70 min. distance; C1 strength	8-10 mi. (12.9-16.1 km) round-trip, 3,500 ft. (1,067 m), 40 lb. (18.1 kg)
10	Off	45 min. recovery; C2 strength	50 min. tempo; C3 strength	40 min. uphill, 40 lb. (18.1 kg)	75 min. distance; C4 strength	8-10 mi. (12.9-16.1 km) round-trip, 3,500 ft. (1,067 m), 45 lb. (20.4 kg)
			BUILD STAMINA			
11	45 min. recovery; E1 strength	40 min. uphill, 45 lb. (20.4 kg)	75 min. distance	30 min. tempo; E2 strength; Tabata	Off	B2B: day 1: 6-8 mi. (9.7-12.9 km) round-trip, 3,000 ft. (914 m), 40 lb. (18.1 kg); day 2: <6 mi. (9.7 km), <2,300 ft. (701 m), 30 lb. (13.6 kg)
12	30 min. recovery	45 min. uphill, 50 lb. (22.7 kg); E3 strength	75 min. distance	35 min. tempo; E1 strength; Tabata	Off	8-10 mi. (12.9-16.1 km) round-trip, 4,000 ft. (1,219 m), 40-45 lb. (18.1-20.4 kg)
13	30 min. recovery; E2 strength	45 min. uphill, 50 lb. (22.7 kg)	75 min. distance	40 min. tempo; E3 strength; Tabata	Off	B2B: day 1: 8 mi. (12.9 km) round-trip, 3,500 ft. (1,067 m), 45 lb. (20.4 kg); day 2: 2,900 ft. (884 m) gain, 6-8 mi. (9.7-12.9 km) 35 lb. (15.9 kg)
14	30 min. recovery	40 min. uphill, 40 lb. (18.1 kg); E1 strength	60 min. distance	45 min. recovery; E2 strength	Off	2,000 ft. (610 m) gain, 5-6 mi. (8.0-9.7 km), 20 lb. (9.1 kg)
			PEAK AND TAPER			
15	45 min. distance; E3 strength	30 min. uphill or tempo	Off	45 min. recovery	Off	Goal: 3-day Rainier climb, 40 lb. (18.1 kg)

B2B=back-to-back

■ ADVANCED 3-WEEK MOUNTAINEERING TRIP

This program is suitable for a goal such as a 3-week high-altitude expedition up Mount McKinley in Alaska (United States) with a 50- to 80-pound (22.7-36.3 kg) pack and a 40- to 60-pound (18.1-27.2 kg) sled. This advanced program differs from the previous programs in its heavy carries and sled dragging, extreme altitude, frigid temperatures, and unpredictable weather. Alaskan alpine expeditions do not include porters, pack animals, or Sherpas. A mountaineer will carry 3 weeks of food and cold-weather gear totaling *at least* 60 pounds (27.2 kg) in a pack and 50 pounds (22.7 kg) in a sled for the first 2 days. After that, the trip involves multiple heavy carries as you ascend the mountain. The program should include several overnight trips, at altitude and in snow if possible, to test the logistics of attaching and toting sleds and dealing with cold conditions. If you can, drag tires or sleds on dirt, sand, or grass for training; the additional friction of such surfaces will make dragging the same weight on snow feel that much easier. Do sled dragging as interval training (1-2 minutes of dragging followed by recovery time to get the heart rate back below 65 percent MHR) on flat or slightly elevated terrain; the sled dragging will be on level to slightly inclined terrain on the approach to camp 1 on Mount McKinley. As you near your climb, be sure to do 1 to 2 trips with a full pack and loaded sled.

Intensity Guidelines

Recovery	<65 percent MHR
Distance	65 to 75 percent MHR
Tempo	75 to 85 percent MHR
Interval	85 to 95 percent MHR

Week	Day 1	Day 2	Day 3	Day 4	Day 5	Weekend
1-8	Follow weeks 3-10 of the intermediate mountaineering program or be able to hike 8-10 mi. (12.9-16.1 km), gaining 3,500 ft. (1,067 m) with 40 lb. (18.1 kg) at the start of the program suggested below					
			BUILD ENDURANCE			
9	40 min. uphill, 40 lb. (18.1 kg); D1 strength	D2 strength; Tabata; (Optional: 45 min. climbing gym)	60 min. distance and fartlek, 45 lb. (20.4 kg)	Off	45 min. tempo; D1 strength	3,500 ft. (1,067 m) gain, 8 mi. (12.9 km) round-trip, 45 lb. (20.4 kg)
10	30 min. recovery; D2 strength	D1 strength; Tabata	65 min. distance, 48 lb. (21.8 kg)	Off	50 min. tempo; D2 strength	4,000 ft. (1,219 m) gain, 10 mi. (16.1 km) round-trip, 45 lb. (20.4 kg)

(continued)

Advanced 3-Week Mountaineering Trip *(continued)*

Week	Day 1	Day 2	Day 3	Day 4	Day 5	Weekend
			BUILD ENDURANCE *(continued)*			
11	45 min. uphill, 45 lb. (20.4 kg); D1 strength	D2 strength; Tabata; (optional: 50 min. climb-ing gym)	70 min. distance and fartlek, 52 lb. (23.6 kg)	Off	55 min. tempo; D1 strength	3,000 ft. (914 m) gain, 6-8 mi. (9.7-12.9 km) round-trip, 50 lb. (22.7 kg)
12	30 min. recovery; A1 strength	A2 strength; Tabata	75 min. distance, 55 lb. (24.9 kg)	Off	60 min. tempo; A1 strength	3,500 ft. (1,067 m) gain, 8-10 mi. (12.9-16.1 km) round-trip, 50 lb. (22.7 kg)
			REST			
13	45 min. recovery; (optional 1 hr. climb-ing gym)	A2 strength, 2 sets of 16 reps for each	60 min. distance	30 min. recovery; (optional 45 min. climb-ing gym	Off	6 mi. (9.7 km) round-trip, 25 lb. (11.3 kg), gain not important
			BUILD STRENGTH			
14	40 min. uphill, 50 lb. (22.7 kg); C1 strength	60 min. distance; C2 strength OR 1 hr. climb-ing gym	90 min. distance, 45 lb. (20.4 kg)	45 min. fartlek; C3 strength; 20 min. 30 lb. (13.6 kg) sled drag	Off	B2B: day 1: 8 mi. (12.9 km), 3,000 ft. (914 m), 55 lb. (24.9 kg); day 2: 2,000 ft. (610 m) gain, 5-6 mi. (8.0-9.7 km), 35 lb. (15.9 kg)
15	30 min. recovery; (optional 1 hr. climbing gym)	40 min. uphill, 55 lb. (24.9 kg); C4 strength	90 min. distance, 45 lb. (20.4 kg)	50 min. pyramid; C1 strength	Off	4,000 ft. (1,219 m) gain, 8-10 mi. (12.9-16.1 km), 55 lb. (24.9 kg)
16	45 min. uphill, 55 lb. (24.9 kg); C2 strength	60 min. distance; C3 strength OR 75 min. climb-ing gym	90 min. distance, 50 lb. (22.7 kg)	55 min. fartlek; C4 strength; 20 min. 35 lb. (15.9 kg) sled drag	Off	B2B: overnight, >3,000 ft. (914 m) gain, >55 lb. (24.9 kg)
17	30 min. recovery; (optional 1 hr. climb-ing gym)	45 min. uphill, 55 lb. (24.9 kg); C1 strength	2 hr. distance, 30 lb. (13.6 kg)	40 min. tempo; C2 strength	Off	4,000 ft. (1,219 m) gain, 8-10 mi. (12.9-16.1 km), 60 lb. (27.2 kg)

Week	Day 1	Day 2	Day 3	Day 4	Day 5	Weekend
			BUILD STAMINA AND MENTAL TOUGHNESS			
18	E1 strength; (optional 1 hr. climbing gym)	75 min. distance, 55 lb. (24.9 kg)	45 min. uphill, 30 lb. (13.6 kg), focus on speed	45 min. tempo; E2 strength	Off	4,000 ft. (1,219 m) gain, 8-10 mi. (12.9-16.1 km), 55 lb. (24.9 kg)
19	E3 strength; (optional 1 hr. climbing gym)	90 min. distance	45 min. uphill, 55 lb. (24.9 kg)	30 min. sled drag, 40 lb. (18.1 kg); E1 strength	Off	B2B: sled shakedown, 50 lb. (22.7 kg) pack; 30 lb. (13.6 kg) sled
20	45 min. recovery; (optional 1 hr. climbing gym)	60 min. distance, 60 lb. (27.2 kg); E2 strength	60 min. uphill, 35 lb. (15.9 kg), focus on speed	50 min. tempo; E3 strength	Off	Rest: 6 mi. (9.7 km), 25 lb. (11.3 kg), gain not important
21	E1 strength; (optional 1 hr. climbing gym)	75 min. distance	45 min. uphill, 60 lb. (27.2 kg)	30 min. sled drag, 45 lb. (20.4 kg); E2 strength	Off	B2B: gear shakedown, >10,000 ft. (3,048 m), if possible
			PEAK AND TAPER			
22	30 min. recovery; E3 strength	45 min. tempo; (optional 45 min. climbing gym)	60 min. distance	E1 strength	Off	6 mi. (9.7 km) round-trip, 45 lb. (20.4 kg), gain not important
23	60 min. distance; E2 strength	40 min. sled drag, 40 lb. (22.7 kg)	45 min. recovery	Travel	Off	Travel to start climb of Mount McKinley

B2B=back-to-back

Rock and Ice Climbing

Technical rock and ice climbers have roughly the same aerobic conditioning needs as hikers and scramblers. They also require increased flexibility in the hips, shoulders, and core muscles in order to negotiate wide stems, twisting overhangs, and high mantels. Technique and skill play a far more important role for technical climbers than they play for hikers and scramblers, as does the strength needed for vertical travel with and without a pack. Anaerobic conditioning also is a much bigger component in the technical climber's program, becoming more important as the climber develops more advanced skills.

Rock climbing is technical fifth-class climbing that is steep enough to require sticky-soled, snug-fitting rock climbing shoes as well as helmets, protection, and ropes for the safety of the climbing party. Crag climbing (also referred to as *sport climbing)* is doing a technical climb of a group of numerous local climbing routes. On such routes, lead climbers clip into preset bolts for protection. Squamish in British Columbia and Red Rocks in Nevada, the Gunks in New York, and Smith Rocks in Oregon are such areas that afford good vertical climbs within minutes of walking distance of each other. Crag training is mentioned in this paragraph as a strength cross-training option for technical mountaineering; for more detail and for rating systems mentioned in this chapter, please see the list of suggested readings. Aid climbing, also known as *big wall climbing,* is seen at Squamish in British Columbia or at Yosemite National Park in California. While it may involve short approaches and gear lugging, its focus is purely vertical. It is gear intensive and requires specialized training with equipment and techniques.

Gym climbing is the scaling of man-made rocks at a climbing gym or an in-town outdoor venue. Often it comes with standard belay devices for climbing partners to use on fixed ropes or with padded floors that cushion falls. Many gym climbers do not wear helmets, though we advise that any time you use technical gear, especially outside on rock, you wear one. A fall is a fall, whether it occurs on fixed ropes, indoors, or outside. Bouldering is ropeless climbing focused on a small number of powerful moves. The climbing is limited to 5 to 10 feet (1.5-3 m) above the ground and may involve more lateral than vertical travel. Both gym climbing and bouldering can provide supplemental skills and strength workouts for technical alpine climbing.

Ice climbing is climbing on routes that require crampons and two ice axes or ice tools. It may be done on frozen waterfalls (water ice) or solid glacier ice that is steeper than 40 degrees. Dry tooling is a non-ice-conditioning exercise involving climbing on rock with two ice tools. Some indoor climbing gyms have dry tooling areas. Mixed climbing is a mixture of rock and ice climbing. Due to the varied climbing media, for which climbers need ice screws, ice and rock protection, and diverse anchor material, mixed climbing requires the most skill of all the technical climbing sports and can involve the most gear.

Following are the fitness components common to technical climbing. A rating of 5 indicates that the component requires the highest emphasis in your training program, while a rating of 1 marks the component as a low priority in your program.

Vertical water ice climbing requires a high level of conditioning in all the major components.

Aerobic conditioning: 3
Anaerobic conditioning: 5
Upper-body strength: 5
Lower-body strength: 3
Flexibility: 5
Activity skill: 5
Cross-training: 4

Important areas of the body: forearms, fingers, core, shoulders, triceps, calves, back, hip flexors

Cardiovascular Needs

Cardiovascular endurance is crucial for all technical alpine climbing with long and arduous approaches. The emphasis for this fitness component is to build uphill stamina over steep terrain such as goat and climbing trails. Such trails might involve grades of 1,500 feet (457 m) of elevation gain per mile (1.6 km). For this type of fitness training, you should be able to complete at least a beginner-level scramble of 6 miles (9.7 km), 2,500 feet (762 m) elevation gain, and 25 pounds (11.3 kg) of pack weight in less than 2.5 hours. If you do not have this baseline, see chapter 7 to build your hiking endurance and chapter 8 for tips on building tolerance for steeper terrain. If you are considering high-altitude technical expeditions, include weekly anaerobic conditioning.

In addition to achieving baseline mountaineering endurance, technical climbers need to work up to 3 or 4 aerobic-focused workouts per week as they approach their goal. The aerobic conditioning ranking of 3 for technical climbing reflects its *relative* importance compared with all the other variables. Anaerobic training (5), skill development (5), and flexibility (5) all become increasingly important as your routes grow more advanced. While some of your cardiovascular workouts will be uphill sessions in the mountains, most will be spinal-loading workouts in town. As you plan your cardiovascular workouts, determine what your goal is for each. At least one session should be a distance workout for developing climbing-specific endurance. Carry a pack (baseline requirements mentioned in the previous paragraph suggest at least 25 pounds, or 11.3 kg) and add 3 to 5 pounds (1.7-2.3 kg) per outing (an increase of 10 percent) until you reach your goal pack weight at least 2 weeks away from your goal. Another session should be an anaerobic workout focused on increased pack weight, faster leg turnover, or steep terrain. A third should be short, steady, high-intensity (tempo) training. Other workouts can be moderate to easy in terms of time, distance, and intensity, and recovery workouts following training with a pack should be short, low-intensity cross-training.

Once you have determined the focus of your cardiovascular workouts, choose your exercise modes. Suitable options for technical climbers include wilderness training, in-town training, spinal-loading cardiovascular machine training, trail running, and gym climbing.

Wilderness Training

Try to include a hike, scramble, or climb outside several times a month. Depending on where you live, this may or may not be possible. You can follow the recommendations provided in chapters 7 and 8; in addition, you should travel over short, steep rolling hills, sand dunes, or sloping wooded areas to build stability in the ankles, strength in the hip flexors for high stepping, strength in the gluteals and hamstrings for uphill propulsion, and strength in the quadriceps for descents. You can also use these outdoor workouts to develop climbing-specific endurance. Incorporate vertical crag climbing or bouldering into a circuit where you race-walk, trail run, or hike between boulder problems, and then drop your pack and spend a few minutes climbing. You can repeat such circuit activity for a desired amount of time. Because bouldering and circuit training can be done solo, you run an increased risk of overworking the tendons by not giving them enough rest. By building in a rest interval that is equivalent to belaying a climbing partner (or adding cardiovascular training as your rest interval between strength bouts), you decrease the chance of flash pumps and allow sufficient time for elbow and finger tendons to recover. Appropriate wilderness outings include trail running, hiking, snowshoeing, and cross-country skiing. During these workouts, you should build toward your target climbing pack weight by 5 to 15 percent per outing.

In-Town Outdoor Training

Appropriate in-town cardiovascular choices that take you outside include pack walking, stair-climbing, walking hills, jogging, trail running, biking, and in-line skating. If you live near an ocean, a lake, or a river, look for steep flights of stairs or paths that lead down to the water and might be suitable for local hiking. Tall public buildings with well-lit stairways or school bleachers can be good stair training. Beaches and local dirt or wood-chip paths with natural variation are great for developing strength in the feet, calves, and ankles while increasing the cardiovascular effectiveness of your running and walking with a pack. Even walking on the grass that lines urban paths provides a subtly varied terrain and a different training stimulus than walking on pavement provides.

Jogging, biking, and in-line skating all provide cross-training benefits that supplement the spinal-loading, climbing-specific cardiovascular workouts just mentioned. Look for outside climbing areas at local playgrounds or parks and combine climbing, hanging, and pull-up time with walking or jogging to create your own circuit. Such training develops climbing-specific stamina for approaches that mix scrambling and hiking. To intensify your wilderness or in-town workouts, replace walks with uphill intervals.

Cardiovascular Machines

The cardiovascular machines appropriate for technical climbers are similar to those used by scramblers and mountaineers: high-ramp treadmills, StepMills, and stair-climbers. VersaClimbers, elliptical trainers with moving arms, rowing machines, and cross-country ski machines all include upper-body movement and can be included for variety. Wear a weight belt, vest, or climbing pack on vertical climbers so that you get full-body anaerobic training specific to technical climbing. Use elliptical machines at the highest ramp setting to train for steep terrain. Use enough resistance to allow a sustainable pace of 80 to 110 strides (40-55 leg turnover cycles) per minute.

Rowing machines target the legs, lower back, and horizontal pulling muscles of the midback. A weekly rowing workout recruits the rhomboids, latissimus dorsi, core, and biceps in a pattern that complements the climbing muscles worked in the vertical plane. Cross-country ski machines build endurance in the torso, arms, and legs and are specific to preparing for winter approaches on snowshoes and skis. The more muscle mass the exercise involves, the higher your heart rate can get, especially if the exercise is new to you. During cross-training, keep track of your body's response to different modes of exercise so you can compare workouts and understand how they all work together to provide an adequate training stimulus.

Gym Climbing

If you have access to a commercial or private climbing gym, or if you are lucky enough to have one at home that you can adjust to your body's needs, there are low-intensity workouts you can do to enhance your anaerobic capacity while simultaneously building your climbing strength and endurance. Tie together several of the following drills into a workout focused on balance and footwork as opposed to trying the hardest route you can do. Keep your weight over your feet and find rest positions that allow you to stay in three-point balance while you look for another hold. Do not do dynamic moves or high-speed lunges; aim for constant movement and gradually build to 20 minutes at a time.

One-Hand Climbing Find an easy, nonvertical slab route and climb using both hands. Then climb the route a second time, keeping your nondominant hand behind your back or by your side. Place all your weight on your feet and use the hand merely for balance. Try the route a third time and use only your nondominant hand. The route will feel completely different each time.

Limited Features for Hands Use any holds or textured wall features for your feet, but use *only* the smaller features for your hands. This is a good drill for any climber who tends to rely on upper-body strength to power up a route. It also requires careful and deliberate foot placement.

Hands at Chest or Lower This drill works on stemming, manteling, underclinging, and pressing rather than hanging and pulling. Instead of looking for the highest holds you can reach, focus on finding lots of good footholds. Many times, the best way to move upward is to find a new foothold several inches higher than your current one that will allow you to inch higher just enough to access a hold previously out of reach.

If you are fairly new to technical climbing, you may find that your feet slip off holds or that you make a lot of noise when you drop a foot onto a hold. Highly experienced climbers look like they dance effortlessly on the wall. Add the following drills to improve your footwork.

Smooth, Quiet Climbing Pretend that the holds are made of delicate pumice and tread very softly as you climb. Look at the hold and choose one precise place to put your foot. Do not slide the foot onto the edge; place it and then do not let it move. This drill teaches you to be very exact with your footwork and will pay off handsomely when you get to harder routes.

Limited Features for Feet Use any feature for handholds, but use only the textured wall for your feet. This drill helps with friction or climbing slab faces and gets you used to using small holds that are similar to what you will have on harder, technique-focused routes.

Finding Rest Points The goal of this drill is to find a rest point every 5 or 6 moves. Shake out your arms between climbing series to prevent getting pumped. This is also a good technique to use when you are doing harder bouldering or traversing sequences.

Scramblers and mountaineers who want to incorporate some or all of the drills described above can try them on easier routes with their mountaineering boots. These drills will definitely feel more challenging in stiff-soled boots! The key to linking drills into a continuous workout is to climb down routes that are fairly easy to climb up, those that let you avoid getting a flash pump in your fingers and forearms. If you are at a rock gym, let your belay partner know that you want a little slack. Practicing these drills is helpful for when you lead an alpine route that is too difficult and you need to retrace your route to get back on track. By staying on the wall and moving continuously, both your respiration rate and heart rate may increase. Thus, this type of drill workout may provide low-intensity aerobic benefits as well.

Strength Needs

Climbers need stamina in their gluteal, hamstring, and gastrocnemius muscles for upward propulsion as well as in their quadriceps for steep descents with heavy loads. A climber's elevation gain per mile may match that of the mountaineer or scrambler; however, gain on the technical portion is primarily vertical. Because they must carry a lot of specialized gear and face a greater vertical component, technical alpine climbers need more strength in the entire body, particularly in the upper body (rating of 5), when compared with scramblers and mountaineers. The calves, forearms, fingers, shoulders, hips, and core are more heavily involved in technical climbing.

In the early weeks of your training, include unilateral free-weight strength exercises to correct weaknesses in your legs, hips, and upper body, particularly in the full range of motion you will need on technical climbs. Doing exercises such as the step-up (page 275), reverse step-up (page 277), dumbbell lunge (page 273), and one-leg Bulgarian squat (page 272) will ensure that both legs and hips are evenly balanced and doing equal work. Use body weight resistance and dumbbells for upper-body strength exercises such as variations on the dumbbell bench press (page 253), push-up (page 255), one-arm dumbbell row (page 246), horizontal pull-up (page 245), and pull-up (page 242).

After you have established good muscle balance and core integrity and stability, incorporate full-body, full range of motion exercises such as variations on the pull-up (page 242), seated row (page 247), triceps push-down (page 259), and barbell military press (page 252) to balance out the climbing muscles of the torso. For the lower body, include higher repetitions of the wide barbell back squat (page 270) to open up the hips, the barbell deadlift (page 261) to develop core strength and grip, and the one-leg deadlift (page 263) to enhance balance. Add a combination of challenging core exercises drawing from the dirt digger (page 222), forward barbell roll-out (page 230), reverse torso curl (page 228), back extension (page 233), and Saxon dumbbell overhead side bend (page 221). This is also a good time to add specialized strength exercises for forearms, fingers, rhomboids, and grip strength. These exercises include the Thor pronation (page 238), wrist extension (page 237), and rope face pull (page 240). Use your progress in the climbing gym as a guide for program refinement.

Once you have built a solid foundation of strength, add power moves and dynos in the bouldering caves or on tough climbing problems to advance to more difficult routes. Climbing with a weighted belt, vest, or secured pack is resistance training that can be used to build climbing-specific strength endurance at a rock gym. Bouldering is another excellent way to increase strength and power. Advanced climbers may add plyometric drills, campus board training, and fingerboard training.

As a general guideline, include at least 1 set of horizontal rowing and overhead pushing exercises for every 2 vertical pulling exercises you do. In other words, your strength work should include overhead pressing (for shoulders and triceps), horizontal pulling (for rhomboids and latissimus dorsi), forearm exercises, and targeted triceps work (for pain-free elbows). The tendons and ligaments require more time than the muscles require for strength development, and they also take an infuriatingly long time to heal due to limited blood supply. Be sure to give your support system enough time to adapt, because without proper time for adaptation to load and frequency, ligaments and tendons can be injured by climbing or vigorous strength training. Proper training of the tendons and ligaments increases their diameter and therefore their ability to withstand tension and tearing (Bompa and Cornacchia 1998; Lawrenson 2008).

Strength training should be a year-round endeavor for all technical climbers who want to make steady improvement. Many new climbers make the mistake of preparing well for their first season, making it through the season successfully but without doing regulated training, taking a break for several months, and then starting to climb exactly where they began a year ago. If instead of taking a long break you maintain your previous conditioning levels with a midweek strength workout throughout the season, take 2 weeks for active recovery in the late season, and launch into an off-season build, by the time the next season starts your initial conditioning will be so much higher than it was the previous year that you will see considerable improvement in your endurance, strength, and climbing ability come summer, even though you spend the same amount of time climbing.

As you gain new skills and try more difficult routes, the ability to sustain high-intensity muscular effort increases in importance. The strength needed for a single top-roped pitch is minimal compared with what you need to lead multipitch vertical rock or ice routes. If you are planning a climb that requires sustained effort in the fingers, calves, core, latissimus dorsi, biceps, or legs, use your off-season and preseason training to focus on building the necessary strength. Once you have a solid strength base, increase endurance by occasionally training in the 15- to 30-repetition range.

Your training should evolve seasonally. Once you are climbing every weekend, you probably will be getting all the leg and upper-body strength you need on the routes themselves. However, a maintenance strength routine can prevent injury. Alternate exercises for the lower and upper body so that one muscle group rests while the other works. Change your program every 4 to 6 weeks or whenever you feel you have reached a plateau. Repeating the same set of exercises or repetition scheme year round will not help you advance very far. A postseason program that strengthens the neglected areas of the body, such as the hamstrings, rhomboids, and pectorals, can be completed using body weight exercises, resistance bands, dumbbells and a weighted pack, or cables and free weights.

The endurance requirements for the fingers, forearms, and hands for technical climbing are the most specialized of any of the requirements for the outdoor sports in this book. Following are the unique grip and finger exercises that pertain to technical climbing. Climbers need phenomenal supporting grip strength for hanging on to hold after hold, especially while placing protection, as well as specific grip strength to enable holds on slopers and nubbins (Brookfield 1995). Add a few of these exercises to the end of your upper-body strength workouts or climbing gym sessions. This way you can complete your climbing and other pulling and grip exercises without being limited by a fatigued grip. Do your selected exercises for a few weeks, and then replace them with others. Keep rotating through the exercises as long as you continue to make progress. Certain exercises may help you more than others do; if you know your open-palm grip needs help, train it for 3 weeks, cycle off it for 2 weeks, and then return to it with a heavier weight.

Supporting Grip Strength

To develop supporting grip strength, use a thick grip of 2 to 2.5 inches (5-6.5 cm) when doing your pulling exercises. Use such a handle on cable weight stacks for the one-arm seated row (page 247) or lat pull-down (page 243). When at a home gym, you can attach a weight to a 2.5-inch (6.5 cm) diameter pipe that is roughly 10 inches (25.5 cm) long or wrap a cable handle with a washcloth to significantly increase its diameter. Another exercise that develops supporting grip strength is the farmer's walk (see figure 9.1). This exercise is so named because of its resemblance to farmers hauling heavy buckets over great distances. Simply hold heavy dumbbells in each hand and walk for a specified distance. Set the weights down during your rest interval, and then pick them up and repeat.

Figure 9.1 To do the farmer's walk, hold a significant dumbbell in each hand and walk for a specified time or distance.

Specific Grip Strength

To work on pinch grips, you can use homemade training devices made from 4- × 4-inch (10 × 10 cm) or 2- × 4-inch (5 × 10 cm) wood blocks or store-bought climbing grip attachments. Attach a large eye screw to each block so you can hook your blocks onto a cable pulley or attach a thin sturdy chain that you can loop around light weight plates. Load your blocks with a weight that you can hold for 15 to 60 seconds and then hold your blocks statically, do shrugs with them, carry them on the farmer's walk, or perform the one-arm seated row or lat pull-down with them. Also try pinching heavy books or dictionaries or partially inflated medicine balls. To make your own medicine ball, buy a playground rubber ball. Use a pair of needle-nose pliers to remove the plug and fill the ball with sand or tap water. The more fully you inflate the ball, the wider and stronger the pinch grip you will need to hold on to it. Use the pliers to reinsert the plug.

To develop hang grip strength, you can use a pull-up attachment to do pull-ups, or you can simply hang, trying to increase the amount of time you can hold on. Commercially available fingerboards can be hung in a squat rack, slung over a high pull-up bar, or crafted over garage rafters for home training. The narrow, bottom-most slots are very challenging, so build up your tendon endurance in the three- and four-finger deep pockets before doing single-digit crimpers.

To build grip strength for working with ice tools, drill a hole about 1 inch (2.5 cm) from the end of wooden dowels that are 1 foot (30.5 cm) long and the same diameter as your ice axe or tools. Wrap athletic tape around the dowels so your hands do not slip when you hold them. Thread cordelette or webbing through the holes and attach the dowels to a squat rack or pull-up bar. You can then hang from the wrapped dowels or do pull-ups from them. An exercise specific to ice climbing is the climber's ice flick (see figure 9.2). Grab light dumbbells (pick a weight slightly heavier than your ice tools; 2-5 lb., or 1-2.3 kg, should suffice) and stand with your arms stretched overhead as though you were facing a vertical wall of ice. Hold the dumbbells with your palms facing each other and lightly snap or flick the weight forward, keeping your upper arms still, to match the quick snap you would make into a wall of ice. Do 2 to 3 sets of 1 to 2 minutes of flicking to build shoulder, forearm, and wrist endurance.

Figure 9.2 Climber's ice flick, demonstrated with light hand weights held overhead with straight arms.

Flexibility Needs

To be fluid and catlike on the wall, you need dynamic flexibility (ranked 5) in the hips, shoulders, ankles, torso, and core. While daily yoga or stretching can help with all aspects of climbing, you can supplement climbing workouts with a good active warm-up that includes the movement patterns seen in wall climbing: stemming, manteling, drop knees, figure fours, high stepping, dynamic moves, climbing in balance, and shifting weight from side to side. Due to the intense repetitive focus on smaller upper-body muscles that is typical of vertical climbing, restorative flexibility is a high priority for climbers. Restorative flexibility is needed not only for the hips and thighs, but also for the back, biceps, triceps, forearms, ankles, and fingers.

To prepare for gym climbing, do the following dynamic stretches to increase blood flow to the targeted muscles and enhance range of motion specific to bouldering and top-rope or lead climbing: leg swings (page 213), arm circles (page 214), and unweighted lunge (page 273). Follow these stretches with several minutes of traversing and a few easy climbs before you start on your target problem. Include a few gym climbing drills (pages 123 to 125) in your workout to increase your mental focus.

At the end of every workout, do 1 to 2 easy routes during which you focus on footwork and form while removing the pumped feeling in your arms. The following static stretches can restore length to taxed muscles and release tension throughout the body: a one-arm version of the tree hug stretch (page 219), the straddle hamstring stretch (page 217), the frog stretch (page 217), the piriformis stretch (page 216), and the downward dog (page 215). These stretches target your forearms, hamstrings, calves, shoulders, and lower back. The trapezius stretch (page 219) is especially helpful following long stretches of belaying. The stretch protocol outlined above is also appropriate before and following strength training sessions.

Additional Considerations

Technical climbers want to maximize strength while minimizing muscle mass so that they have less weight to transport vertically. The finger and elbow tendons are particularly sensitive to additional weight; extra body mass can mean the difference between continuing to climb and being sidelined with overuse tendon injuries. On the other hand, high-altitude climbers need to prepare for the inevitable loss of body mass (5-15 percent on expeditions of 3 weeks or longer) and gain as much solid muscle mass as possible before their goal climb. They should also put on several extra pounds of fat to provide the body with extra subcutaneous fuel that can be burned instead of lean, active muscle.

Since the strength component of technical climbing is a high priority, consuming adequate protein for muscle growth and tissue repair is vital during training. Climbers should carry additional food supplies in case they are forced to bivouac due to long routes, poor weather, or tricky route finding. They should also plan to carry additional water during hot summer months when runoff is low and snow disappears.

The weather conditions that technical climbers encounter differ greatly between rock and ice climbing. Knowing how to read changing weather when climbing tall spires or peaks that generate their own weather systems, such as Wyoming's Grand Teton or California's Mount Whitney, is vital to avoiding exposure during electrical storms. Seasonal variation may mean postponing a climb until the late fall, when days are shorter but temperatures high up on southern exposures are more tolerable. Conversely, conditions may be such that a shaded route or climb with northern exposure requires additional clothing. If you will be climbing in the dark, include early-morning sessions at the climbing gym so you have a better understanding of how your body performs at odd hours of the day. Try a few alpine starts in the mountains to see how it feels to climb via headlamp.

Ice and mixed climbers can snowshoe or ski to travel to distant routes in winter conditions, making such climbing activities accessible and attractive in the off-season. Weather conditions can be trickier for ice climbing, as chilly and dry temperatures with stable weather conditions are needed to maintain ice routes. The weather conditions can also mean that the climber requires more clothing to be comfortable. When you go ice climbing, take additional clothing, a stove, fuel, and a small pot for boiling water and be alert for signs of hypothermia, frostnip, and frostbite. Winter conditions can change the duration of the outing and therefore play a role in how much food and gear you have to carry (additional weight) and how long you are exposed to the elements.

Assessing Fitness and Gauging Improvement

When possible, you should perform the ramp and field tests discussed in chapter 8 on machines with uphill and full-body components such as elliptical trainers with arms, VersaClimbers, Jacob's Ladders, StepMills, or stair-climbers. Both the ramp test and field test assess cardiovascular fitness; more important for climbers are the anaerobic, strength, and flexibility tests. While you should retest all eight strength movements every 4 to 6 weeks, the ones of particular relevance are the pull-up (page 242), step-up (page 275), medicine ball twist (page 224), and back extension (page 233). Focus on improving the frog stretch (page 217) and lying trunk rotation (page 215) if you struggled to perform suitably on these assessment tests.

Once you have spent a month building a foundation of 4 to 6 workouts a week, two of which are strength or gym climbing workouts, do a best-fit test such as a scramble, steep hike, or short climb to assess your progress. Look for a good bushwhacking route that requires the use of your hands and demands a lot from your calves, as technical rock and ice climbing involves the shoulders, core, ankles, and calves more than hikes and scrambles can assess. For hikes and scrambles, note your travel time from the trailhead. Then, each time you do the same distance, decrease your total time including breaks. An altimeter can be useful for measuring your rate of ascent and descent, particularly as the vertical technical difficulty increases. Maintain an average working heart rate of less than 75 percent of your MHR so you can keep energy in reserve in case of emergency. This heart rate suggestion no longer applies as soon as you start your vertical ascent, as factors such as adrenaline, exposure, belaying, and power moves will take you out of a steady state and may cause you to periodically tap into the anaerobic system.

While assessing improvement when hiking or scrambling is relatively straightforward, comparing technical outings involves the consideration of outside factors such as terrain, altitude, route finding, and weather. Note trail and route conditions, seasonal variations, and tricky navigational hints in your training journal so that you will be better able to compare previous efforts with future outings in the same spot. It may be easier to gauge improvement in your uphill and descending stamina on outdoor hiking and evaluate improvement in climbing stamina at the climbing gym.

If you find that you get winded going uphill without a pack, add cardiovascular training; if you struggle under the weight of a pack, add lower-body strength training. If you find it taxing or difficult to stay on rock without getting pumped, add upper-body strength training. If routes are changed frequently at your climbing gym, your bouldering, traversing, and endurance training may be affected. To gauge improvement at the climbing gym, keep track of route levels you can climb easily and assess how long you can stay on the wall without getting pumped forearms.

Creating a Long-Term Program

To develop a technical alpine climbing program, start with your end goal. The chart on page 132 suggests how long you should train to prepare for a rock or ice climb of a given difficulty, trip distance, elevation change, terrain, and pack weight. Note that if your goal shares at least one variable with goals at the intermediate or advanced levels, include the training time suggested for the higher level indicated in the chart. For example, if you will be doing a 12-mile (19.3 km; intermediate) technical climb that involves carrying an overnight pack weighing 30 pounds (13.6 kg; intermediate) but with a net gain of 1,500 feet (457 m; beginner), allow 12 weeks to prepare for the weight and length requirements. Climbers need years of experience to achieve the technical skill level required for advanced goals. Assuming you have the necessary skills and baseline fitness, the timelines suggested on the following page will suffice for physical conditioning.

In addition to using the guidelines from the previous sections on creating long-term programs found in chapters 7 and 8, consider the following for your climbing program: route finding, if your target route is relatively unknown; additional skills and training needed to complete your adventure; and preparing for the unknown, such as unplanned bivouacs or alternative objectives with higher technical difficulties. If you will be doing multiday trips with additional weight, a month from goal you should simulate repeat endurance by carrying 10 percent more weight for several hours at least 2 days in a row.

While you can include gym climbing from the start of your program, you should build a solid base of dynamic flexibility and full-body strength, particularly in the arms and fingers, before trying harder routes. Once you have spent at least a month working on your foundation, add sport-specific training exercises. To keep your muscles and joints in balance and avoid overuse injuries, include at least 10 minutes of pushing exercises for every 20 minutes you spend on vertical and horizontal pulling exercises.

Difficulty	Trip duration; distance traveled	Elevation	Terrain	Pack weight	Training time above baseline
	ALPINE ROCK CLIMBING: TECHNICAL 5TH-CLASS TERRAIN REQUIRING STICKY-SOLED SHOES				
Beginner	Single day; <6 mi. (9.7 km)	<2,000 ft. (610 m) gain	<6 pitches mixed with class 4 or scrambling	<25 lb. (11.3 kg)	8 weeks
Intermediate	Overnight; 6-15 mi. (12.9-24.1 km)	<3,000 ft. (914 m) gain	Multipitch 5.6-5.9	<35 lb. (15.9 kg)	12-16 weeks
Advanced	Multiday; emphasis on vertical, not horizontal	>3,000 ft. (914 m) gain or high altitude	Strenuous approach, >5.9	>35 lb. (15.9 kg)	18-26 weeks
	ALPINE ICE CLIMBING: TECHNICAL WATER OR GLACIER ICE REQUIRING CRAMPONS, TWO ICE TOOLS				
Beginner	Single day; <6 mi. (9.7 km)	<1,500 ft. (457 m) gain	<WI2 or 40-65 degree glacier ice	<25 lb. (11.3 kg)	8 weeks
Intermediate	Single day; 8-12 mi. (12.9-19.3 km)	< 2,500 ft. (762 m) gain	<WI3 or 65-80 degree glacier ice	<35 lb. (15.9 kg)	12 weeks
Advanced	Multiday; >12mi.(19.3km), emphasis on vertical gain	Above 10,000 ft. (3,048 m) altitude or >2,500 ft. (762 m) gain	Alpine mixed climbing >80 degree hard snow/glacier ice; WI4 or 5	>35 lb. (15.9 kg)	16-20 weeks

When you have built enough endurance to climb continuously for 10 to 12 minutes without getting pumped, you can increase the grade difficulty one notch to familiarize yourself with routes that have smaller or fewer holds. Since rating systems vary from one climbing locale to another and from gym to gym, you should be able to climb comfortably in the gym at 2 to 3 grades higher than what you intend to climb outdoors (i.e., be able to lead 5.10s at the gym before leading 5.7 outside). You can visit the climbing gym as frequently as every other day in the later phases of your training. Treat vertical climbing like any other training component and follow the 5 to 15 percent rule. Coaches in highly skilled sports such as gymnastics and figure skating suggest that the body first needs several years to adapt to increased training volume, with roughly twice as much time to attain full potential (Goddard and Neumann 1993). Advanced climbing is another sport that involves a high degree of skill and years of specific training; for the recreational climber, these numbers can easily double.

If you have had a break from vertical climbing or are just starting out with gym climbing, remember that it is very common for novice climbers to get excited about their new passion, progress to harder routes too quickly, and realize too late that rushing to greater and greater challenges may not be the best way to go about climbing. Just as you would not jump up a level in the weight stack between your very first and second session of strength training, you need to ease systematically into climbing, not only so that your muscles develop properly, but also so that your tendons and ligaments can adapt to the new stresses. While it is tempting to spend several hours at the climbing gym the first few times you go, discomfort and even strain may hit you the following days if you do so. Master a few basic techniques and build your hand, forearm, and finger tolerance gradually or run the risk of strain and injury.

The general conditioning recommendations for rock, ice, and mixed climbing are to build to the following weekly workloads 2 weeks from goal. Be sure to include stretching with every workout.

Type	Number of weekly workouts 2 weeks from goal	Number of strength workouts	Number of cardiovascular workouts	Number of sport-specific weekly workouts	Weekly exercise time
Beginner climb	4-5	2 30 min. full body	3	1 1 hr. climbing gym session; 1 2-3 hr. hike, 20 lb. (9.1 kg)	5-6 hr.
Intermediate climb	5-6	2 45 min. full body	4	2 1 hr. climbing gym sessions; 1 3-5 hr. hike, 30 lb. (13.6 kg)	10-12 hr.
Advanced climb	6-8	2 45 min. full body	4+ (1 anaerobic training)	Several 60-90 min. climbing gym sessions; 1 technical climb with a 2+ hr. approach, 40 lb. (18.1 kg)	14+ hr.

Sample Goals and Associated Programs

The following sample programs introduce you to technical climbing programs that are designed to match specific goals. Use them for insights into how you can manipulate training variables to design programs for yourself. The sample programs include a beginner 1-day rock climb, an intermediate 2-day rock climb, an intermediate high-altitude technical glacier climb, and an advanced mixed high-altitude climb. Each program assumes that you have established a baseline of at least 2 to 4 weekly workouts: two 30-minute strength sessions (such as A1 and A2 on page 61) and three cardiovascular sessions, including one 45-minute distance (65-75 percent MHR), one 30-minute tempo (75-85 percent MHR), and one 30- to 45-minute recovery (<65 percent MHR). Suitable aerobic training options include trail running; climbing stairs and hills; working on the elliptical trainer, stair-climber, StepMill, VersaClimber, or Jacob's Ladder; and hiking.

■ BEGINNER 1-DAY ROCK CLIMB

This program is suitable for a goal of a 5.4 three-pitch beginning rock climb with a 20-pound (9.1 kg) pack and a gain of 2,200 feet (671 m) of elevation in 5.5 miles (8.9 km). The training focus is to prepare the body to carry a pack for the alpine approach and the vertical gain. Add visits to the climbing gym if available (noted as optional in the following table); otherwise, focus on building lower-body endurance and upper-body strength. In your strength training, include the pull-up (page 242), one-arm dumbbell row (page 246), one-arm version of the lat pull-down (page 243), step-up (page 275), reverse step-up (page 277), and farmer's walk (page 127). Use weekly hikes to improve leg and core strength endurance. This 8-week program builds on the baseline suggested in the previous section.

Intensity Guidelines

Recovery	<65 percent MHR
Distance	65 to 75 percent MHR
Tempo	75 to 85 percent MHR
Interval	85 to 95 percent MHR

Week	Day 1	Day 2	Day 3	Day 4	Day 5	Weekend
			BUILD STRENGTH			
1	30 min. pyramid, 10 lb. (4.5 kg); D1 strength	45 min. distance	45 min. climbing gym (optional)	Off	30 min. tempo; D2 strength	Hike or hilly walk, 500 ft. (152 m) gain, 12 lb. (5.4 kg)
2	33 min. pyramid, 12 lb. (5.4 kg); D1 strength	50 min. distance	45 min. climbing gym (optional)	Off	33 min. tempo; D2 strength	Hike or hilly walk, 750 ft. (229 m) gain, 15 lb. (6.8 kg)
3	36 min. pyramid, 12 lb. (5.4 kg); D1 strength	55 min. distance	45 min. climbing gym (optional)	Off	37 min. tempo; D2 strength	Hike 4 mi. (6.4 km), 1,000 ft. (305 m) gain, 15 lb. (6.8 kg)
4	39 min. pyramid, 15 lb. (6.8 kg); D1 strength	60 min. distance	60 min. climbing gym (optional)	Off	40 min. tempo; D2 strength	Hike 4 mi. (6.4 km), 1,250 ft. (381 m) gain; 15 lb. (6.8 kg)
			BUILD STAMINA			
5	42 min. uphill, 15 lb. (6.8 kg); E1 strength	60 min. distance	60 min. climbing gym (optional)	Off	40 min. tempo; E2 strength	Hike 5 mi. (8.0 km), 1,500 ft. (457 m) gain, 15 lb. (6.8 kg)
6	45 min. uphill, 18 lb. (8.2 kg); E3 strength	70 min. distance	75 min. climbing gym (optional)	Off	43 min. tempo; E1 strength	Hike 6 mi. (9.7 km), 1,750 ft. (533 m) gain, 18 lb. (8.2 kg)
7	45 min. uphill, 20 lb. (9.1 kg); E2 strength	75 min. distance	60 min. climbing gym (optional)	Off	45 min. tempo; E3 strength	Hike 4-5 mi. (6.4-8.0 km), 2,000 ft. (610 m) gain, 18 lb. (8.2 kg)
8	30 min. recovery; E1 strength	45 min. distance	45 min. climbing gym (optional)	Off	Off	Goal: 3-pitch rock climbing 5.4, 20 lb. (9.1 kg), 2,200 ft. (671 m) gain, 5.5 mi. (8.9 km)

■ INTERMEDIATE 2-DAY ROCK CLIMB

This program is suitable for a goal such as a 20-pitch intermediate rock climb, perhaps the north ridge of the 9,415-foot (2,870 m) Mount Stuart in Washington. The 12-week training program follows the first 4 weeks of the sample program for the beginner rock climb and diverges from there to focus on getting the forearms, core, and calves ready for multipitch gain on rock. Since the goal climb is at a fairly significant elevation, anaerobic training serves a dual purpose: preparing the body both for altitude and for sustained climbing with individual moves up to 5.9.

If you are not certain you can do the whole route and descent of a climb like this in a day, you will need to carry bivouac gear and extra food, which may add 10 to 20 pounds (4.5-9.1 kg). Practice gym climbing and shorter technical alpine climbing with your goal climbing partners as often as feasible so you can increase your speed at details requiring skill such as placing protection, racking, and using rope. Focus on building lower-body endurance and upper-body strength. Your strength training should include varied exercises such as the standing calf raise (page 268), good morning (page 265), and farmer's walk (page 127). Use weekly hikes to develop leg and core endurance.

Intensity Guidelines

Recovery	<65 percent MHR
Distance	65 to 75 percent MHR
Tempo	75 to 85 percent MHR
Interval	85 to 95 percent MHR

Week	Day 1	Day 2	Day 3	Day 4	Day 5	Weekend
			BUILD ENDURANCE			
1-4	Follow first 4 weeks of beginner rock climb training program					
			BUILD STRENGTH			
5	35 min. pyramid, 20 lb. (9.1 kg); B1 strength	65 min. distance	75 min. climbing gym; B2 strength	Off	45 min. tempo; B3 strength	Day 1: hike 4-5 mi. (6.4-8.0 km), 1,600 ft. gain (488 m), 20 lb. (9.1 kg); day 2: 75 min. climbing gym
6	45 min. recovery	35 min. pyramid, 25 lb. (11.3 kg); B1 strength	60 min. climbing gym; B2 strength	Off	45 min. tempo; B3 strength	Day 1: hike 5-6 mi. (8.0-9.7 km), 2,000 ft. (610 m) gain, 24 lb. (10.9 kg); day 2: 90 min. climbing gym
7	60 min. recovery	40 min. pyramid, 30 lb. (13.6 kg); B1 strength	75 min. climbing gym; B2 strength	Off	40 min. tempo; B3 strength	Day 1: hike 6-8 mi. (9.7-12.9 km), 2,500 ft. (762 m) gain, 28 lb. (12.7 kg); day 2: 75 min. climbing gym

Week	Day 1	Day 2	Day 3	Day 4	Day 5	Weekend
			BUILD STAMINA			
8	45 min. recovery	45 min. pyramid, 35 lb. (15.9 kg); E1 strength	20 min. recovery; 90 min. climbing gym	Off	40 min. tempo; E2 strength	Day 1: 2 90 min. climbing gym; day 2: technical climbing 5 mi. (8.0 km), 25 lb. (11.3 kg)
9	45 min. recovery	45 min. uphill, 40 lb. (18.1 kg); E3 strength	25 min. recovery; 90 min. climbing gym	Off	45 min. tempo; E1 strength	Day 1: 6-8 mi. (9.7-12.9 km) hike, 3,000 ft. (914 m) gain, 33 lb. (15.0 kg); day 2: 90 min. climbing gym
10	45 min. recovery	45 min. uphill, 40 lb. (18.1 kg); E2 strength	30 min. recovery; 90 min. climbing gym	Off	40 min. tempo; E3 strength	Day 1: technical climbing 6 mi. (9.7 km), 30 lb. (13.6 kg); day 2: 8 mi. (12.9 km) hike, 3,000 ft. (914 m) gain
			PEAK AND TAPER			
11	40 min. recovery	40 min. uphill, 30 lb. (13.6 kg); E1 strength	60 min. climbing gym	Off	30 min. tempo; E2 strength	Hike 5 mi. (8.0 km), 2,000 ft. (610 m) gain, 20 lb. (9.1 kg)
12	30 min. tempo	45 min. distance	45 min. climbing gym (optional)	30min. recovery	Off	Goal: 2-day 20-pitch rock climbing 5.9

■ INTERMEDIATE 2-DAY ICE CLIMB

This program is suitable for a person embarking on a 2-day high-altitude ice climb (<70 degree snow and ice), such as the north ridge of Mount Baker in Washington, while carrying a 35-pound (15.9 kg) pack. This program could be considered to be on the cusp between intermediate and advanced due to the 10,781-foot (3,286 m) altitude of Mount Baker and the fact that most people climb it in 2 days due to the approach. Technical difficulty merits an intermediate rating. The recommended baseline is the end fitness level achieved in the beginner climb sample program: a weekly workload of at least one 60-minute distance session, one 45-minute uphill session, two 45-minute full-body strength training sessions (such as A1 and A2 on page 61 or D1 and D2 on page 64), one workout in the climbing gym, and one 6-mile (9.7 km) hike involving 2,000 feet (610 m) of elevation gain and a pack weight of 22 to 25 pounds (10.0-11.3 kg). If you are not at this level, add 6 to 8 weeks of training, using the beginner climb sample program as your guide. The program focus thereafter will be on getting the forearms, calves, core, and lungs used to additional work and high altitude. Appropriate cardiovascular modes include training on a stair-climber, a StepMill, a VersaClimber, a Jacob's Ladder, a high-ramp treadmill, or an elliptical trainer; hiking; trail running; or climbing stairs and hills.

Intensity Guidelines

Recovery	<65 percent MHR
Distance	65 to 75 percent MHR
Tempo	75 to 85 percent MHR
Interval	85 to 95 percent MHR

Week	Day 1	Day 2	Day 3	Day 4	Day 5	Weekend
			BUILD ENDURANCE			
1	30 min. tempo; B1 strength	60 min. climbing gym	60 min. distance, 20 lb. (9.1 kg)	Off	B2 strength	Hike 5-7 mi. (8.0-11.3 km), 2,300 ft. (701 m) gain, 15 lb. (6.8 kg)
2	35 min. tempo; B3 strength	70 min. climbing gym	70 min. distance, 20 lb. (9.1 kg)	Off	B1 strength	Hike 5-7 mi. (8.0-11.3 km), 2,600 ft. (792 m) gain, 20 lb. (9.1 kg)
3	40 min. tempo; B2 strength	75 min. climbing gym	60 min. distance, 25 lb. (11.3 kg)	Off	B3 strength	Hike 6-8 mi. (9.7-12.9 km), 2,900 ft. (884 m) gain, 25 lb. (11.3 kg)

Week	Day 1	Day 2	Day 3	Day 4	Day 5	Weekend
			BUILD ENDURANCE *(continued)*			
4	45 min. tempo; B1 strength	30 min. recovery; 60 min. climbing gym	70 min. distance, 25 lb. (11.3 kg)	Off	60 min. climbing gym; B2 strength	Hike 6-8 mi. (9.7-12.9 km), 3,200 ft. (975 m) gain, 30 lb. (13.6 kg)
			INCREASE STRENGTH			
5	30 min. uphill, 25 lb. (11.3 kg); C1 strength	30 min. recovery; 60 min. climbing gym	45 min. distance, 28 lb. (12.7 kg); C2 strength	Off	45 min. tempo; C3 strength	B2B: day 1: hike 6-8 mi. (9.7-12.9 km), 2,500 ft. (762 m) gain, 35 lb. (15.9 kg); day 2: 90 min. climbing gym
6	40 min. recovery; C4 strength	30 min. pyramid; 60 min. climbing gym; Tabata	50 min. distance, 30 lb. (13.6 kg); C1 strength	Off	45 min. tempo; C2 strength	Hike 8-10 mi. (12.9-16.1 km), 3,000 ft. (914 m) gain, 25 lb. (11.3 kg), focus on speed
7	35 min. uphill, 30 lb. (13.6 kg); C3 strength; 1 Tabata	45 min. recovery	60 min. climbing gym; C4 strength	60 min. distance, 35 lb. (15.9 kg)	45 min. tempo; C1 strength	Hike 6-8 mi. (9.7-12.9 km), 3,500 ft. (1,067 m) gain, 35 lb. (15.9 kg)
8	35 min. pyramid; C2 strength; Tabata	45 min. recovery; 60 min. climbing gym	45 min. uphill, 35 lb. (15.9 kg); C3 strength	45 min. tempo; C4 strength	Off	B2B: day 1: hike 6-8 mi. (9.7-12.9 km), 4,000 ft. (1,219 m) gain, 30 lb. (13.6 kg); day 2: hike 5 mi. (8.0 km), 3,000 ft. (914 m) gain, 25 lb. (11.3 kg)

(continued)

Intermediate 2-Day Ice Climb *(continued)*

Week	Day 1	Day 2	Day 3	Day 4	Day 5	Weekend
			BUILD STAMINA			
9	30 min. recovery	60 min. distance; E1 strength	40 min. pyramid, 40 lb (18.1 kg); 60 min. climbing gym	Off	45 min. tempo; E2 strength	Hike 6-8 mi. (9.7-12.9 km), 3,500 ft. (1,067 m) gain, 35 lb. (15.9 kg)
10	45 min. pyramid; E3 strength	65 min. distance	45 min. uphill, 40 lb. (18.1 kg); 60 min. climbing gym	45 min. tempo; E1 strength	Off	B2B: day 1, hike 6-8 mi. (9.7-12.9 km), 4,000 ft. (1,219 m) gain, 35 lb. (15.9 kg); day 2: hike 5 mi. (8.0 km), 3,000 ft. (914 m) gain, 30 lb. (13.6 kg), technical if possible
11	30 min. recovery; 60 min. climbing gym (optional)	60 min. distance; E2 strength	40 min. pyramid, 30 lb. (13.6 kg)	60 min. climbing gym	45 min. tempo; E3 strength	Hike 5 mi. (8.0 km), 2,000 ft. (610 m) gain, 25 lb. (11.3 kg), dry tool
			PEAK AND TAPER			
12	45 min. distance; 60 min. climbing gym	30 min. tempo; E1 strength	45 min. distance	30 min. recovery	Off	Goal: 2-day ice climb of Mount Baker north ridge, 10,781 ft. (3,286 m), 35 lb. (15.9 kg)

B2B=back-to-back.

■ ADVANCED MULTIDAY HIGH-ALTITUDE MIXED CLIMB

The following program is suitable for a challenging goal such as a mixed carryover climb of the North Mowich Headwall of 14,411-foot (4,392 m) Mount Rainier in Washington. This climb includes fifth-class (or A1) rock and hard snow or ice to 60 degrees and requires a pack of at least 40 pounds (18.1 kg). This climb differs from those in the previous sample programs in its high altitude, cold temperatures, committing route that is tough to back away from, unpredictable weather on a harsh mountain, steepness, and 2- to 4-day carryover requiring that all gear makes it up and over the mountain. A climber attempting the route needs ice screws, pickets, food for multiple days, bivouac gear, and clothing for any conditions, not to mention solid technical skills and a good head for making tough decisions. The program includes 4 months of training beyond baseline and a high-volume weekly workout regimen of three 45-minute cardiovascular sessions, two 45-minute full-body strength sessions, 1 to 2 sessions in a climbing gym, and a weekly hike, climb, or scramble at the intermediate level with 25 pounds (11.3 kg) of pack weight.

Intensity Guidelines

Recovery	<65 percent MHR
Distance	65 to 75 percent MHR
Tempo	75 to 85 percent MHR
Interval	85 to 95 percent MHR

Week	Day 1	Day 2	Day 3	Day 4	Day 5	Weekend
			BUILD FOUNDATION			
1	45 min. distance; A1 strength	60 min. distance	60 min. climbing gym	45 min. distance; A2 strength	Off	Hike 5-6 mi. (8.0-9.7 km), 2,500 ft. (762 m) gain, 25 lb. (11.3 kg)
2	45 min. distance; A1 strength	60 min. distance	60 min. climbing gym	30 min. tempo; A2 strength	Off	Hike 5-6 mi. (8.0-9.7 km), 2,500 ft. (762 m) gain, 28 lb. (12.7 kg)
3	45 min. distance; A1 strength	60 min. distance	60 min. climbing gym	45 min. distance; A2 strength	Off	Hike 5-6 mi. (8.0-9.7 km), 2,700 ft. (823 m) gain, 28 lb. (12.7 kg)
4	45 min. distance; A1 strength	60 min. distance	60 min. climbing gym	30 min. tempo; A2 strength	Off	Hike 6-8 mi. (9.7-12.9 km), 3,000 ft. (914 m) gain, 28 lb. (12.7 kg)

(continued)

Advanced Multiday High-Altitude Mixed Climb *(continued)*

Week	Day 1	Day 2	Day 3	Day 4	Day 5	Weekend
			BUILD STRENGTH			
5	45 min. distance; C1 strength	70 min. distance	30 min. uphill, 30 lb. (13.6 kg); C2 strength	90 min. climbing gym	40 min. tempo; C3 strength	Hike 6-8 mi. (9.7-12.9 km), 3,000 ft. (914 m) gain, 30 lb. (13.6 kg)
6	45 min. distance; C4 strength	60 min. distance	35 min. uphill, 30 lb. (13.6 kg); C1 strength	90 min. climbing gym	45 min. tempo; C2 strength	Hike 8-10 mi. (12.9-16.1 km), 3,000 ft. (914 m) gain, 30 lb. (13.6 kg)
7	45 min. distance; C3 strength	75 min. distance	40 min. uphill, 35 lb. (15.9 kg); C4 strength	90 min. climbing gym	50 min. tempo; C1 strength	Hike 6-8 mi. (9.7-12.9 km), 3,000 ft. (914 m) gain, 30 lb. (13.6 kg)
8	45 min. distance; C4 strength	60 min. distance	45 min. uphill, 40 lb. (18.1 kg); C3 strength	90 min. climbing gym	55 min. tempo; C4 strength	Hike 8-10 mi. (12.9-16.1 km), 3,000 ft. (914 m) gain, 30 lb. (13.6 kg)
9	45 min. distance; C1 strength	75 min. distance	45 min. uphill, 40 lb. (18.1 kg); C2 strength	90 min. climbing gym	60 min. tempo; C3 strength	Hike 6-8 mi. (9.7-12.9 km), 3,000 ft. (914 m) gain, 30 lb. (13.6 kg)
			RECOVERY WEEK			
10	45 min. recovery; A1 strength	30 min. recovery	45 min. distance	60 min. climbing gym, easy technique	Off	Hike 1,000 ft. (305 m) gain, 20 lb. (9.1 kg), 10-12 mi. (16.1-19.3 km)
			BUILD ENDURANCE			
11	60 min. distance; B1 strength	45 min. pyramid, 30 lb. (13.6 kg)	90 min. climbing gym	60 min. tempo	75 min. distance; B2 strength	B2B: day 1: hike 6-8 mi. (9.7-12.9 km), 3,000 ft. (914 m) gain, 35 lb. (15.9 kg); day 2: technical climb
12	30 min. recovery or off	45 min. uphill, 45 lb. (20.4 kg); B3 strength	90 min. climbing gym	60 min. tempo	75 min. distance; B1 strength	Technical climb (single day)

Week	Day 1	Day 2	Day 3	Day 4	Day 5	Weekend
			BUILD ENDURANCE *(continued)*			
13	30 min. recovery or off	45 min. pyramid, 35 lb. (15.9 kg); B2 strength	120 min. climbing gym	65 min. tempo	80 min. distance; B3 strength	B2B: day 1: hike 6-8 mi. (9.7-12.9 km), 3,000 ft. (914 m) gain, 40 lb. (18.1 kg); day 2: climbing gym
			BUILD STAMINA			
14	30 min. recovery or off	45 min. repeat, 35 lb. (15.9 kg); E1 strength	120 min. climbing gym	90 min. distance, 25 lb. (11.3 kg); E2 strength	75 min. tempo	B2B: day 1: hike 6-8 mi. (9.7-12.9 km), 3,500 ft. (1,067 m) gain, 40 lb. (18.1 kg); day 2: technical or climb gym
15	30 min. recovery or off	45 min. uphill, 45 lb. (20.4 kg); E3 strength	120 min. climbing gym	90 min. distance, 30 lb. (13.6 kg); E1 strength	75 min. tempo	Technical climb (single day)
16	30 min. recovery or off	45 min. repeat, 40 lb. (18.1 kg); E2 strength	120 min. climbing gym	90 min. distance, 35 lb. (5.9 kg); E3 strength	75 min. tempo	Overnight with partners 4,000-6,000 ft. (1,219-1,829 m) gain, 40-50 lb. (18.1-22.7 kg)
17	30 min. recovery or off	45 min. uphill, 50 lb. (22.7 kg); E1 strength	120 min. climbing gym	90 min. distance, 40 lb. (18.1 kg); E2 strength	45 min. distance	B2B: day 1: hike 6-8 mi. (9.7-12.9 km), 3,000 ft. (914 m) gain, 40 lb. (18.1 kg); day 2: technical climb
			PEAK AND TAPER			
18	30 min. recovery or off	45 min. uphill, 30 lb. (13.6 kg); E3 strength	75 min. climbing gym	45 min. distance, 30 lb. (13.6 kg); E1 strength	Off	Hike 5-6 mi. (8.0-9.7 km), 2,000 ft. (610 m) gain, 30 lb. (13.6 kg)
19	45 min. distance	30 min. pyramid; E2 strength	60 min. climbing gym	30 min. recovery	Off	Mount Rainier mixed climb

B2B=back-to-back

Trail Running

Trail running allows the outdoor athlete to explore remote terrain while unencumbered by a heavy pack. It includes running on varied surfaces such as dirt, sand, water, grass, and gravel; obstacles such as rocks, tree roots, and potholes; and irregular slopes. It is solitary running that is not done on roads, pavement, tracks, or treadmills and can be mountain running at high altitude, snowshoe racing, orienteering, adventure racing, and ultradistance racing. It often combines fast walking on steep uphill segments with springy downhill running and allows for great freedom of movement unhindered by weight.

Following are the fitness components common to trail running. A rating of 5 indicates a component deserving the highest emphasis in your training program, and a rating of 1 assigns a component to the lowest priority in your program.

Aerobic conditioning: 5

Anaerobic conditioning: 2 (3 if you plan to run at high altitudes)

Upper-body strength: 1

Lower-body strength: 2

Flexibility: 1

Activity skill: 2

Cross-training: 4

Important areas of the body: quadriceps, gluteals, hamstrings, hips, core, calves, Achilles tendons, feet

Trail runners can cover a decent amount of ground in a relatively short time when compared with laden hikers who may take hours to cover similar distances. Conditioning needs for this group revolve around cardiovascular training: Trail running has a rating of 5 for aerobic conditioning and 2 to 3 for anaerobic conditioning, especially for athletes planning to include high-altitude runs. Because of the high-impact nature of the sport, the need for cross-training for muscle balance and prevention of injury is also quite high (rating of 4). Due to the uneven terrain, trail running requires moderate leg strength (rating of 2) as well as balance, coordination, mental focus, and moderate skill (rating of 2) to master travel without falls. Compared with the other sports featured in this book, trail running places a low emphasis on upper-body strength (rating of 1) and flexibility (rating of 1).

Cardiovascular Needs

You can train for trail running in one of several ways. If you are already fairly comfortable running 10 to 15 miles (16.1-24.1 km) a week on flat local terrain, you can try some easy trail runs of 3 to 5 miles (4.8-8.0 km) with mild hills. When you are preparing to embark on trail runs of similar lengths to your flat runs (i.e., 3 m or 4.8 km), at least one of your in-town training runs should be longer distance, ranging from 4 to 6 miles (6.4-9.7 km).

Another way to start training is to walk briskly on a trail and jog gently for 1 or 2 minutes at a time, walk to catch your breath, and then repeat until you have accumulated 20 to 30 minutes on your first outing. On each subsequent workout, you jog a little longer until you can jog 5 minutes at a stretch. Then you begin reducing your walking intervals until you are comfortable jogging 5 minutes and walking 1 minute. Until you can jog for 30 minutes on varied terrain, consider walking up hills and jogging flats and gentle downhill segments. Avoid carrying too much weight on downhill sections at first. The biggest mistake you can make on a trail running program is to turn a loaded hike into a downhill dash to the car, unless you want to feel your quadriceps for the next 3 days. Trail running puts high stress on the quadriceps even before the added pack weight.

When you add trail runs to an existing program, you are in essence starting a new sport. Throw out any preconceived ideas you have about mileage and speed based on your experience on flat terrain so you can establish new backcountry goals. Since many trails do not have mile markers, carry a pedometer or wear a watch and run for time. Head out about half the time you plan to be gone and allow the other half to return. If you start by running steadily uphill, you may be able to go out for two-thirds of the time and leave the last one-third for coming back down. While faster, more experienced runners may be able to cover a wilderness mile in 8 minutes, it is perfectly normal to see trail miles take 15 minutes or longer depending on the terrain. If you are gaining 1,000 feet (305 m) per running mile, you may find that the time it takes you to a run a mile doubles or even triples. On flat terrain you may be able to cover 6 miles (9.7 km) or more an hour, whereas on steep grades you may cover only 2 to 3 miles (3.2-4.8 km) in the same time.

Trail running requires greater anaerobic training (a rating of 2-3) compared with track or road running, as trails in some areas can involve significant uphill travel. Athletes planning on running above 7,000 feet (2,137 m) should include anaerobic training to increase their tolerance for the thinner air. While such training can be done on the trail, it is okay and at times even preferable to do speed work on a track or road in order to avoid falling or rolling an ankle from trying to move too quickly over challenging turf.

When building your program, keep in mind that in addition to having a base running capability, you want to build up to doing 4 to 6 weekly aerobic workouts as you approach your target outing. While some of these workouts should be on trails, they all do not need to be running and they all do not need an uphill component. Your workouts will vary in FITT principles according to your current fitness level and unique goals. A city runner might start with a weekly regimen of two aerobic workouts of 30 to 45 minutes, one endurance workout of an hour, and one short, high-intensity anaerobic workout that includes hills, sprints, stairs, or intervals on a stair-climber or an elliptical trainer. The endurance distance workout will vary according to the end goal. The sample programs at the end of this chapter illustrate how you can combine various aerobic sessions with anaerobic workouts and strength training to address different levels and goals for trail running.

After you have determined the duration, intensity, and goal of your cardiovascular workouts, you can select training modes that support those parameters. Suitable options vary according to what phase of training you are in (in-season, preseason, or postseason). In-season choices include spinal-loading options that can be done in the mountains, outside in town, or at the gym. Low-impact cross-training options for the off-season can aid recovery, increase muscle balance, and maintain flexibility.

In-Season Training

Many trail runners venture to the backcountry for the solitude and beauty of the outdoors. While your ability to train in the wilderness depends somewhat on your location and seasonality, when you get out there you can include a variety of training options that load the spine and legs the same way that trail running does. Include several of these options on a regular basis for a healthy, well-rounded program.

Challenging mountain conditions require additional training beyond in-city preparation.

Flat Running Clearly the best training for trail running is trail running. But if you are unable to get to your favorite trail, running on grass, sandy beaches, railroad ties, gravel paths, or cinder tracks challenges the ankles, hips, and feet while also being more forgiving than paved roads. If most of your training is done indoors on treadmills with rubberized, forgiving surfaces, start with a lower total mileage on paved surfaces until your body adapts to the pavement in order to avoid shin splints, plantar fasciitis, stress fractures, or other lower-extremity ailments. Flat runs in town recruit muscles differently than trail runs do, and both tap into your aerobic and anaerobic energy systems differently.

Uphill Running An alternative to flat running that helps with both the ascending and the descending portions of trail running is running repeats on hills or stairs. Keep your torso upright and relaxed, and take smaller steps as needed to maintain your pace. When running downhill, let gravity be your friend rather than your enemy. Avoid braking with each step, as constant braking is what leads to sore quadriceps. Uphill terrain will challenge the gluteals and hamstrings, while flat and downhill running will develop the quadriceps. When doing uphill intervals, use mileage in town and time in the mountains. Keep in mind that terrain difficulties such as grades, elevation changes, and obstacles will affect your time from trail to trail.

Incline Treadmill This forgiving indoor option allows you to train the uphill component without getting out to the trails. It also gives you the option of working tempo and uphill intervals into training, although if you frequently do your workouts on a treadmill, allow yourself plenty of time in your program to adapt to added mileage on the trail. When used for cross-training that is combined with road and trail running, the treadmill works well. Add backward walking or jogging (see page 107) for quadriceps-dominant training.

High-Ramp Elliptical Trainer Elliptical trainers set on higher ramp settings are great nonimpact alternatives that help develop the uphill propulsion muscles in the gluteals and hamstrings. Machines with handles also develop upper-body stamina. Stride on a resistance that is lower than what you might use for hiking training so you can maintain a comfortable jogging cadence of 150 to 180 steps per minute.

In-Line Skating Skating is an excellent in-town, low-impact option that allows you to cover a significant amount of ground while using many of the same muscles used for running. It also allows you to work the abductors and gluteals in a movement similar to skate skiing. These are the muscles that can help with sidestepping to avoid obstacles on the trail and can power you up hills. Training in a forward leaning position (as in speed skating) also builds endurance in the core musculature crucial for maintaining upright posture and good balance in running.

Hiking Walking on varied terrain while wearing a pack is an excellent low-impact way to see some of the same scenery you may access when running, and is a suitable cross-training mode for building quadriceps, core, and ankle strength on descents and gluteal strength on ascents. Using trekking poles can build upper-body endurance that will give you additional strength when running uphill.

Stations One way to add mild upper-body strength training is to intersperse jogging with strength training stations. For the stations you can use natural obstacles that you encounter on the trail or on town routes: ducking under or climbing over downed logs, jumping across stream beds, dropping down to do push-ups, pulling yourself onto a low tree branch, doing calf raises on the curb while waiting for the light to change, and so forth. Get creative by including strength stops and you will enjoy nature's playground even more.

Off-Season Training

One goal of pre- and postseason training is to keep your muscles in balance while you maintain your aerobic stamina for your sport. Another is to recover fully before you ramp up the training volume and intensity for the next season. Suitable modes for the off-season include Pilates, low-impact aerobic exercise classes, step classes, yoga, swimming, and aqua jogging. Cross-country skiing and snowshoeing provide great winter training for the trail runner. Cross-country skiing is excellent for increasing stride length and core strength. Snowshoeing is a wonderful way to build hip flexor strength for high uphill steps. Both also incorporate upper-body movements that transfer into added uphill propulsion come springtime.

Adding biking or its many variations during the off-season enables you to include nonimpact distance training to maintain your cardiovascular stamina. Biking at 100 revolutions per minute or more on an easy gear is a great way to include higher volume without putting added strain on the knees, feet, or ankles. Mountain biking requires balance and core stability similar to that needed for trail running and is a low-impact, quadriceps-dominant sport performed on terrain similar to that of trail running. Spinning classes, with their races and chases, provide excellent anaerobic training. Training videos and DVDs are available for home cycle training. Finally, indoor biking on a wind trainer is a good option on days when it is too icy, cold, or treacherous to run. You may find that any of these modes also benefit in-season recovery as an occasional cross-training day.

Strength Needs

In trail running, lower-body strength (a rating of 2) is important in the ankles and calves (for preventing rolls and sprains and absorbing high-impact steps), core and lower back (for promoting upright posture and balance), gluteals and hamstrings (for providing uphill propulsion), and quadriceps (for managing descents). Moderate strength in the abductors and adductors helps maintain muscle balance and facilitates lateral movements around obstacles such as rocks and roots. While the dirt surfaces of most trails are relatively forgiving to your body and therefore can be considered more healthful than pavement, the fact remains that with every step, the feet, legs, and spine absorb impact 2 to 4 times your body weight.

Upper-body strength increases uphill power. Trail runners may encounter widely varied terrain that ranges from relatively well-maintained, even, and obstacle-free trails to steeper goat or climbing trails overgrown by brambles. Some trails even require you to use your hands on roots or brush to avoid stumbling. The more challenging the terrain, the more helpful it can be to have a strong upper body. However, in general, leg and core strength and stability should receive higher priority than upper-body strength.

While weekly hill training and sprinting intervals can build strength for hill climbs, two well-designed full-body strength workouts per week will drop your run time, increase your power on uphill segments, put spring in your step, and give you more confidence—not to mention faster reaction times—on rugged terrain. Sport-specific strength training keeps your body in balance and enhances your performance.

Include strength training to balance out any disparities in the lower limbs, particularly any strength difference between the quadriceps and the hamstrings. You should spend equal time training the front and back of the thighs. An imbalance can shorten your stride and set you up for additional tightness that ultimately leads to injury. Since trail running is a high-impact sport, the gastrocnemius muscles in the calves carry the brunt of the force. Adding a few exercises to strengthen the anterior tibialis (front of the shin) can prevent shin splints and keep the lower extremities balanced and pain free.

The unilateral exercises that are especially valuable for developing both strength and balance are the step-up (page 275), reverse step-up (page 277), dumbbell lunge and its variations (page 273), one-leg Bulgarian squat (page 272), standing calf raise (balancing on one leg; page 268), one-leg deadlift (page 263), and dorsiflexion (page 239). The band clam abduction (page 235) and ball adduction (page 232) are good for targeting the muscles in the hips. A great exercise to strengthen the hamstrings while simultaneously stretching and elongating the entire back of the body is the Romanian deadlift (page 262). Early-season lower-body strength training programs should include *at least* two quadriceps-dominant unilateral exercises as well as two hamstring-dominant movements (train them evenly to prevent imbalances). They should then be rounded out with one calf, core, lower-back, and gluteal exercise. The upper-body strength program should include multiple-muscle movements, including at least one horizontal pushing exercise such as the push-up (page 255) or the dumbbell bench press (page 253), one vertical pressing movement such as the dumbbell overhead press (page 251), one horizontal pulling exercise such as the horizontal pull-up (page 245) or one-arm dumbbell row (page 246), and other movements that work the core, shoulders, and arms.

Flexibility Needs

Trail runners need to maintain normal flexibility in the calves, Achilles tendons, hamstrings, groin, quadriceps, gluteals, hip flexors, and ankle muscles. Stretching these muscles aids in recovery, prevents injury, and restores flexibility to areas that are heavily stressed during running. The muscles in the upper and lower back, not to mention the smaller muscles in the feet, also take a beating from running.

A properly designed flexibility program can increase stride length. Greater stride length translates into greater speed with reduced risk of strain, particularly in the hamstrings.

Dynamic stretches suitable for warming up for trail running include leg swings (page 213), the unweighted walking lunge (page 273), and standing dowel torso rotation (page 214). Good active stretches include the downward dog (page 215), straddle hamstring stretch (page 217), and stair calf stretch (page 217). Suitable static stretches vary from person to person, but doing the listed dynamic and active stretches along with the 90-90 quadriceps psoas stretch (page 219), seated gluteal stretch (page 218), and bench hamstring stretch (page 218) at the end of a session will sufficiently target the lower body.

If you are susceptible to foot ailments caused by overuse, such as plantar fasciitis, add gentle foot stretches first thing in the morning and consider using a tennis ball to massage the soles of your feet before taking a step. If stretching and rest do not help your recovery, you may need to cross-train in a nonimpact sport such as cycling as your feet recover.

Additional Considerations

While the best training for trail running is trail running, there are numerous benefits to cross-training (rated as 4). Many trail runners enjoy participating in at least one other sport to help keep their muscles strong and bodies balanced and agile. The trail runner typically gets out in the backcountry once or twice a week and supplements longer trail runs with flat running, uphill intervals, treadmill or elliptical workouts, and strength training—all examples of workouts designed to complement training for outdoor sports. A runner who can comfortably run 10 to 15 miles (16.1-24.1 km) per week in town is ready to embark on some basic trail runs, although it is not essential to be at such weekly mileage to begin gradual training on trails.

Due to the increased strenuousness of wilderness travel, you will burn more calories on a trail run than you will use on a flat road run of the same distance. Experiment with bringing different foods on longer runs, keeping them as light and portable as possible. For ultradistance runs, take light snacks that will not freeze on colder outings, and at altitude, bring foods that will not require nimble fingers to eat, since swelling from reduced atmospheric pressure can make you feel clumsy or awkward.

A snugly fitting lumbar pack or fanny pack with tight loops for water bottles is a worthwhile investment to hold snacks and liquids close to the body. You might prefer having a hydration pack with a bite valve in order to keep your hands free and be able to sip on the go. If you like flavored electrolyte solutions, consider a multibottle carrier, as Camelbak or Platypus hydration tubes can be challenging to clean. Drink at least 5 to 10 fluid ounces (148-296 ml) of water for each 15 minutes you run.

Trail runners, perhaps more so than other outdoor athletes, need to be prepared for environmental changes, as they tend to carry less emergency supplies than hikers, skiers, or mountaineers carry. Take at least one windproof outer layer for the torso in case you need to stop and walk part of the way. Always leave your planned route and end destination with someone back home, and whenever possible, run with a partner in case of emergency. If you participate in snowshoe running, take a lumbar pack large enough to carry the layers you will strip off as you warm up. Also be aware that snow can add significant weight to snowshoes, requiring more strength endurance from the hip flexors. If you train in extreme weather conditions, know the signs of heat and cold injury. Always plan for more water than you think you will need, especially when in the desert, even if that means carrying a water filter. Have a complete change of clothes, extra water, and snacks waiting in the car, along with a pair of dry shoes and a first aid kit.

Assessing Fitness and Gauging Improvement

Once you are familiar with all the conditioning and concerns specific to your sport, it is time to start training. Since trail running requires repeat uphill and downhill performance, a good machine to use for your 13-minute ramp test is the incline treadmill. Start at a 6 to 8 percent incline to simulate steeper terrain. Maintain your initial speed as you increase the ramp height 1 to 2 percent every 3 minutes. After a month or more of training, you can begin periodic 30-minute field tests. Find a portion of a challenging trail that you would like to repeat every 3 to 4 weeks and run at the fastest pace you can sustain for the entire test. The initial lower-body strength assessment can point you to areas that you can improve dramatically with strength work. If you identify that you are weak in the upper-body strength tests, you can focus on the weak areas during the pre- and off-season to help increase your speed and balance.

The best-fit test for trail running is a monthly assessment that involves running for at least an hour on a hilly course with an elevation gain or terrain similar to that of your goal. Choose a readily accessible trail that you know well and can use to improve your weaknesses. If your weakness is ascending hills, choose a well-maintained trail with challenging uphill sections unencumbered by dangerous roots or rocks. If you need to add endurance, increase your volume each week by 5 to 15 percent, or 1 to 2 miles (1.6-3.2 km), on long runs. To improve downhill technique, find an in-town hill and do repeats, keeping your body upright and your footfalls light while avoiding braking with each step. On longer runs, practice fartlek running, gradually linking longer sprints with shorter recovery times until you achieve a new steady pace.

Use a heart rate monitor and pedometer to assess your average pace, elevation gain, and distance traveled. Note any outings that go slower than usual and try to determine whether poor fueling, weather conditions, or navigation errors lengthened your time. Ultimately, you should gauge your improvement needs by what you find most challenging, whether it is speed, endurance, performance on tricky terrain, pacing, heart rate, or muscle soreness the next day. Improvement may include running a given length faster than before, running it in same time but with a lower average heart rate, or experiencing less discomfort afterward.

Creating a Long-Term Program

Begin planning by starting with your end goal. Also consider the time your have available to train, the total time anticipated for your goal run or race, the elevation gain and loss as well as the highest elevation you will reach, and the terrain variability. Also take into account the season of the planned run, as you will want to have enough time to practice in any extreme cold, snow, or heat before your event. As you develop your program, backtrack from the event and count the weeks available for training so that each of your training segments has a distinct goal.

The following chart takes into account your past running experience as well as the difficulty, anticipated distance, and elevation change of your chosen goal to summarize how much time you will need for training. These suggestions can be especially helpful if you are new to trail running. If you are already running flat marathons, you may be able to spend less than the suggested time when preparing for an advanced trail run of a shorter distance, although to avoid overdoing it and to properly prepare the muscles, you should try to train for the recommended time. Note that if your goal shares at least one variable with goals at the intermediate or advanced levels, include the training time suggested for the higher level indicated in the chart. For example, if you are a beginner trail runner who will be doing a 6-mile trail run (intermediate level) with 750 feet of elevation gain (beginner level), allow 12 weeks (intermediate time) to train for the distance.

Difficulty	Years of experience	Single-run distance traveled	Elevation	Training time above baseline
Beginner	<1	<4.5 mi. (7.2 km)	<800 ft. (244 m) gain	8 weeks
Intermediate	1-3	4.5-13 mi. (7.2-20.9 km)	<3,000 ft. (914 m) gain	12 weeks
Advanced	>3	>13 mi. (20.9 km), including ultras	>3,000 ft. (914 m) gain	16-20 weeks

Early in the season, prioritize your training so that you minimize imbalances or weaknesses first. Include exercises that will help with joint integrity and stability, particularly if your off-season program or cross-training sport does not work the same muscle groups mentioned in the section on strength training. After you can run on a trail for at least 45 minutes, perform your first 30-minute field test.

A well-rounded training program will help you prevent strain and injury and avoid plateaus and psychological burnout. To progress your workouts, determine how your body reacts to the FITT parameters from chapter 1. Learn how to pace yourself and train smarter, not harder. As we age, we need longer recovery times following distance training. You may find that as you age, the mileage you ran when you were younger is no longer appropriate. You may also find that you can do one decent anaerobic workout per week but that coupling two or more high-intensity workouts with your weekly long trail runs compromises your immune system and leaves you more susceptible to illness.

Your pace on any longer runs should be a few minutes per mile slower than your current short (i.e., 5K) race pace, and the steeper the terrain, the slower your pace will be until your body gets accustomed to the additional strain and load. When increasing your distance, add 1 to 2 miles (1.6-3.2 km) to your long runs at no greater than 5 to 15 percent per week. Finally, if you always repeat the same route, distance, and time, vary your program for optimal progress as well as for more challenge and enjoyment.

Planning a program for ultradistance running takes special considerations. To complete a 50K, 50-mile (80.5 km), 100K, or 100-mile (161 km) event or longer, focus on completing the distance comfortably before you start adding time goals. Trail running is different from road running. If you are able to complete a road marathon nonstop, then adding several miles to your long run on trail terrain and a midweek hilly workout may give you enough training to complete a 50K with some walking on uphill portions. While people normally train up to 23 miles (37 km) for a marathon, you should build only to 26 miles (41.8 km) on trails if you are training for a 50K trail run. The principle of specificity holds for ultradistance training: There is nothing like running on trails to train for a trail race. Your pace may be closer to 15 minutes per mile (1.6 km) on ultradistance trail runs, and you may end up snacking on those portions of the trail that you walk. You may also find yourself running at night, so plan accordingly and test different lighting options to see what provides the most illumination for the least weight.

The general conditioning recommendations for trail running are to build to the following weekly workloads by the time you are 2 weeks from goal. Be sure to include stretching with every workout.

Type	Number of weekly workouts 2 weeks from goal	Number of strength workouts	Number of cardiovascular workouts	Number of sport-specific weekly workouts	Weekly exercise time
Beginner trail run	4	2 30 min. full body	3	1 flat distance run; 1 60 min. trail run	4-6 hr.
Intermediate trail run	5-6	2 30 min. full body	3-5 (1 anaerobic)	1 distance run; 1 cross-train	6-10 hr.
Advanced trail run	6	2 45 min. full body	5 (1 anaerobic)	2 distance runs; 1 cross-train	10+ hr.

Sample Goals and Associated Programs

The following sample programs introduce you to trail running programs designed for specific goals. They include preparing for a beginner trail race and for an intermediate backcountry trail run with significant elevation gain. Use these programs for insights into how you can manipulate the training variables to create your own program. Suitable baseline training for trail running is at least four weekly workouts that comprise two 30-minute full-body strength sessions (such as A1 and A2 on page 61), two 45-minute distance sessions, and one 30-minute recovery workout.

■ BEGINNER TRAIL RUN

This program is suitable for a runner embarking on a goal such as the 6K Canmore Challenge trail run in Alberta, Canada. It prepares the novice trail runner who has a suitable baseline of 10 miles (16.1 km) a week on flat terrain for an off-road race along the Bow River in Banff, Alberta, against top runners and local ski racers. Cardiovascular training options for this program include trail running, training on an incline treadmill or elliptical trainer, and walking hills or stairs. Anaerobic workouts added in the second month should focus on building speed and preparing for the varied and unstructured nature of wilderness terrain.

Intensity Guidelines

Recovery	<65 percent MHR
Distance	65 to 75 percent MHR
Tempo	75 to 85 percent MHR
Interval	85 to 95 percent MHR

Week	Day 1	Day 2	Day 3	Day 4	Day 5	Weekend
			BUILD ENDURANCE			
1	30 min. tempo	A1 strength	Off	45 min. distance	30 min. tempo; A2 strength	Off
2	35 min. tempo	A1 strength	Off	50 min. distance	35 min. tempo; A2 strength	Off
3	40 min. tempo	A1 strength	Off	40 min. tempo; A2 strength	Off	55 min. distance
4	40 min. tempo	A1 strength	Off	45 min. tempo; A2 strength	Off	60 min. distance
			BUILD STRENGTH AND SPEED			
5	40 min. tempo; D1 strength	45 min. recovery	Off	30 min. uphill	D2 strength	60 min. distance
6	45 min. tempo; D1 strength	45 min. recovery	Off	35 min. uphill	D2 strength	65 min. distance
7	45 min. tempo; D1 strength	50 min. recovery	Off	40 min. uphill	D2 strength	45 min. distance
8	30 min. tempo; D1 strength	30 min. fartlek	30 min. recovery	Off	Off	6K trail run race

■ INTERMEDIATE TRAIL RUN

This program is suitable for a goal such as an intermediate 6-mile (9.7 km) trail run with a 4,000-foot (1,219 m) elevation gain such as Mailbox Peak in Washington. The 12-week training program is designed to prepare the intermediate runner for challenging terrain on a steep goat or climbing trail that may require walking up the steep portions and selecting slow and careful footing on the way down. Preferred aerobic training options for this program are trail running; hiking; training on an incline treadmill, StepMill, stair-climber, or high-ramp elliptical trainer; and walking hills or stairs. The anaerobic workouts added in week 6 should include a midweek light pack component on very steep terrain in order to build appropriate strength endurance in the legs.

Intensity Guidelines

Recovery	<65 percent MHR
Distance	65 to 75 percent MHR
Tempo	75 to 85 percent MHR
Interval	85 to 95 percent MHR

Week	Day 1	Day 2	Day 3	Day 4	Day 5	Weekend
			BUILD ENDURANCE			
1	45 min. recovery	B1 strength	60 min. distance	30 min. tempo; B2 strength	Off	1 60 min. distance
2	45 min. recovery	B3 strength	65 min. distance	30 min. tempo; B1 strength	Off	1 trail run, 1,000 ft. (305 m) gain
3	50 min. recovery	B2 strength	70 min. distance	35 min. tempo; B3 strength	Off	1 trail run, 1,250 ft. (381 m) gain
4	55 min. recovery	B1 strength	75 min. distance	35 min. tempo; B2 strength	Off	1 trail run, 1,500 ft. (457 m) gain

Week	Day 1	Day 2	Day 3	Day 4	Day 5	Weekend
			BUILD STRENGTH			
5	60 min. recovery	30 min. uphill; D1 strength	60 min. distance	Off	40 min. tempo; D2 strength	1 trail run/hike, 2,000 ft. (610 m) gain
6	60 min. recovery	35 min. fartlek, 8 lb. (3.6 kg); D1 strength	75 min. distance	Off	45 min. tempo; D2 strength	1 trail run/hike, 5-6 mi. (8.0-9.7 km), 2,500 ft. (762 m) gain
7	60 min. recovery	40 min. uphill, 10 lb. (4.5 kg); D1 strength	80 min. distance	Off	45 min. tempo; D2 strength	1 trail run/hike, 6-8 mi. (9.7-12.9 km), 2,750 ft. (838 m) gain
			BUILD STAMINA			
8	60 min. recovery	40 min. fartlek, 10 lb. (4.5 kg); E1 strength	90 min. distance	45 min. tempo; E2 strength	Off	1 trail run/hike, 5-7 mi. (8.0-11.3 km), 3,000 ft. (914 m) gain
9	60 min. recovery	40 min. uphill, 12 lb. (5.4 kg); E3 strength	100 min. distance	50 min. tempo; E1 strength	Off	1 trail run/hike, 6-8 mi. (9.7-12.9 km), 3,250 ft. (991 m) gain
10	50 min. recovery	45 min. pyramid, 12 lb. (5.4 kg); E2 strength	75 min. distance	50 min. tempo; E3 strength	Off	1 trail run/hike, 7-9 mi. (11.3-14.5 km), 3,500 ft. (1067 m) gain
			PEAK AND TAPER			
11	45 min. recovery	45 min. uphill, 14 lb. (6.4 kg); E1 strength	60 min. distance	45 min. tempo; E2 strength	Off	1 trail run/hike, 8 mi. (12.9 km), 3,750 ft. (1,143 m) gain
12	30 min. tempo	30 min. uphill, 10 lb. (4.5 kg); E3 strength	Off	30 min. recovery	Off	Goal: trail run, 6 mi. (9.7 km), 4,000 ft. (1,219 m) gain

Off-Road Biking

Off-road biking offers outdoors enthusiasts a way to cover a large amount of territory in a short time. It also offers a huge variety of terrain challenges, including climbing steep trails, crossing streams, traveling over boulders and logs, descending hair-raising chutes, soaring off drop-offs, and even carrying your bike over sections you simply cannot ride. However, there are also touring trails allowing leisurely rides through beautiful scenery that are only marginally more difficult than a ride on flat, paved roads. The varied forms of off-road biking can be broken down into four types, which are described in the following paragraphs.

Cross country is the most popular form of off-road biking. It generally refers to riding from one point to another over unpaved, varied terrain, requiring many gear combinations and wide, knobby tires. The frame of the mountain bike is shorter than that of a road bicycle to allow for extra clearance between the legs during travel over rough terrain. The bikes are shorter so the rider can lift the front wheel off the ground more easily. The bottom bracket is elevated for additional clearance over obstacles. A typical cross-country bike may weigh 18 to 25 pounds (8.2-11.3 kg).

Marathon, or 24-hour (enduro), and epic biking require extreme endurance. Cross-country marathon riding involves point-to-point biking over 37 to 62 miles (60-100 km) of mountainous terrain. Usually, 24-hour races are held overnight with 4-person teams. Epic riding includes all-day or multiday adventures in remote wilderness areas.

Downhill biking is akin to resort skiing. Riders drive or take a lift to the top of a hill or mountain and ride downhill at high speed through rough terrain. To negotiate obstacles at race speed, riders must possess a unique combination of total-body strength, aerobic and anaerobic fitness, and mental control. The rider usually wears shin guards and a full face helmet with goggles; he might wear even more, depending on the terrain. The bikes are typically heavier to provide the rider with more control during high-speed downhill rides. They are stiff so a rider gets a faster response when steering. Shock absorbers can be added to both the front and back wheels to provide the rider with more control when navigating bumpy terrain.

Dirt jumping and trials riding are akin to trick riding and obstacle course riding. Dirt jumping involves riding over groomed dirt mounds and going airborne. Trials is hopping onto any and all suitable obstacles while riding a very small, low-framed bike and requires excellent balance. Freeriding (what many downhill riders do for fun) can include downhill riding, crossing elevated bridge and log rails, and performing stunts considered more aggressive than those performed in typical cross-country biking. This chapter focuses on cross-country off-road biking and defines the advanced rider as being one who can handle more obstacles and varied terrain than the beginner can take on.

Because of the extremely varied terrain involved in off-road biking, your training should be tailored to your goals. Since many people enjoy off-road biking as a cross-training option for the other sports discussed in this book, we focus on both the seasoned off-road biker and the novice rider with high levels of conditioning in another backcountry sport.

Following are the fitness components common to off-road biking. A rating of 5 indicates a component that requires the highest emphasis in your program and a rating of 1 identifies a component that needs the lowest priority in your program.

Aerobic conditioning: 4

Anaerobic conditioning: 4 (varied terrain) or 2 (touring)

Upper-body strength: 3

Lower-body strength: 5 (varied terrain) or 3 (touring)

Flexibility: 2

Activity skill: 4 (varied terrain) or 2 (touring)

Cross-training: 1

Important areas of the body: core, upper and lower back, quadriceps, calves

Cardiovascular Needs

Aerobic conditioning ranks high (rating of 4) for all types of off-road biking, as the rider needs to be able to sustain continuous travel over long durations, switching among different terrain types. The requirements for anaerobic conditioning differ significantly among the various types of off-road biking; riders gravitating toward highly varied, steep, or technical terrain will rank anaerobic conditioning a 4, while those preferring less varied, wider, compact but unpaved trails will rank it a 2. On a relatively flat touring outing, a biker may encounter long stretches of sustained travel that demand strong aerobic endurance and occasional steep terrain that taxes the anaerobic system. Other routes may require the opposite: rolling hills that feel like sprints to go uphill and occasional flat areas that allow the rider to relax and recover somewhat before the next hill.

A solid aerobic baseline provides a training foundation for strength and anaerobic components that follow later in the program. Trips in flat, remote areas with compact trails require primarily aerobic conditioning, which can be developed through endurance rides in town or on comparable trails. If you already enjoy road biking, the transition to touring will be easy: Just allow for more varied surfaces requiring greater vigilance, slower speed, and somewhat lesser mileage until your body adapts to the terrain. If you are new to biking, begin training on flat to moderate terrain and build to being able to sustain 30 to 45 minutes of continuous riding before choosing routes that add elevation or obstacles. Rides involving steep grades, mud, sand, or lots of obstacles require greater anaerobic conditioning than touring requires. Once you can navigate moderately challenging terrain for longer than an hour, increase the elevation gain and add uphill training to enhance your anaerobic capacity.

After you have determined the duration, intensity, and goal for each cardiovascular workout, you can choose training modes that will support those parameters. Suitable in-season options for bikers include wilderness training, in-town outdoor training, Spinning classes, cross-training, and training on indoor cardiovascular machines.

Wilderness and In-Town Training Many off-road bikers venture outdoors to enjoy the beauty of nature and experience the thrill of steep descents. Instead of biking on flat ground or gentle hills in town, you can do much of your training on dirt, gravel, or sand if available. You can also train in the wilderness if you have ready access. While your choice of terrain depends on your location and seasonality, there are other exercise modes you can add to your training that involve wilderness elements. These include road biking, skateboarding, trail running, and snow travel.

Road Biking If you cannot get to the mountains, you can still train appropriately, particularly for touring, by distance road cycling. Add hilly terrain or local races to incorporate anaerobic or sprint training. Do uphill repeats to simulate mountainous terrain.

Skateboarding Modes of training that incorporate balance and develop lower-back, hip, and leg endurance include skateboarding and in-line skating. Whenever possible, include gently rolling slopes to simulate the varied terrain you will encounter on your bike; when you are on wheels, such terrain will really challenge your legs during anaerobic training sessions.

Trail Running Trail running develops balance and core stability that is similar to that needed for off-road biking. Including running in your

©Whit Richardson/Aurora Photos

The best way to train for off-road biking is to get used to varied terrain similar to what you will encounter on your goal trip.

training will help you when you have to hop off your bike and push or carry it over obstacles. Since trail running and off-road biking are performed on similar terrain, athletes generally choose one over the other, while riders who love the thrill of descents may include snowboarding, randonee, downhill, or telemark skiing during the snow season.

Snow Travel Snowshoeing, cross-country skiing, snowboarding, and backcountry skiing all provide full-body cross-training for the off-road biker. They develop upper-body endurance for pulling up on the handles when going uphill and for supporting the bike when crossing obstacles. They also enhance core strength for better balance and stability when cruising down a mountain. Finally, they build lower-body strength in the gluteals and hamstrings that comes in handy for uphill propulsion.

Spinning Classes A Spinning class is a good training option that can be done in town and is good for when the weather is bad, you are pressed for time, or you want to add anaerobic training to your workout. If you have a home Spinning bike or wind trainer, you may find that training with Spinning exercise tapes is a great way to combat boredom in a routine and include lots of variety in a cardiovascular session. Some videos offer motivating, upbeat music and attractive background scenery. Riding at home using a bike trainer eliminates any coasting you might experience on an outdoor ride and provides a great sport-specific workout.

Cardiovascular Machines and Cross-Training Suitable cardiovascular machines for the off-road biker include upright, Spinning, and recumbent bikes, though the latter should be used less frequently given postural considerations and muscle recruitment patterns. To enhance three-dimensional balance and increase core stability in patterns similar to off-road biking, jog or racewalk on incline treadmills, particularly if you can incorporate backward walking into your program to develop the quadriceps. Cross-country skiing machines, VersaClimbers, Jacob's Ladders, elliptical trainers with handles, and other multiple-muscle group cardiovascular machines are all suitable cross-training options for the biker.

Strength Needs

When going up steep hills, the rider must propel both body and bike upward at a certain minimum speed in order to keep going. While doing so, you load the muscles of the upper legs as well as the upper body and core. The higher your strength-to-weight ratio, the less frequently you will shift into your anaerobic zone when going uphill. Therefore, leg strength is given highest priority (rating of 5) for riders attacking varied terrain. Unilateral compound movements can be used to correct any strength imbalances during the preseason, and bilateral compound movements can be added as the biking season approaches. Exercises such as the barbell back squat (page 270), barbell deadlift (page 261), backward lunge (page 272), and one-leg Bulgarian squat (page 272) will be key to leg strength development. Leg and core strength remain important for touring and distance bikers, but since their highest emphasis is on developing endurance, leg strength ranks a 3 for them.

Incorporate single-leg cycling drills to smooth out your stroke and work on both the downward drive and upward lift. Performing these drills at a low gear is also useful in cross-training for any other sport if you are recovering from a leg injury. Use a wind trainer or Spinning cycle with pedal clips, and have a stool nearby and out of the way to support the nonworking leg. Once you have warmed up both legs, complete 6 to 8 series of 30 to 45 seconds of work for each leg with 1 to 2 minutes of bilateral recovery. In other words, work the right leg, then the left, and then spin easily with both legs to recover before repeating. Of the single-leg drills, 3 to 4 should begin with the left leg and the other 3 to 4 with the right so you train the legs under similar aerobic and anaerobic conditions. Focus on making each leg stroke as deliberate and smooth as possible. This technique allows you to develop the hamstrings and quadriceps simultaneously and get a sense of how the leg pulls the crankshaft *upward* as well as pushes it down.

While upper-body strength does not directly contribute to bike propulsion, it is important for stabilization, so it ranks a 3 for cross-country and distance bikers. The upper body absorbs a lot of jarring forces as the biker travels over rough terrain; it also controls the position of the bike frame. The heavier the bike, the more impact it has on the upper body. Since beginner riders tend to overgrip the handlebars, resulting in pain or, in extreme cases, numbness in the wrists, it is important to develop suitable upper-body strength and find rest or relief positions when riding to occasionally stretch out the forearms and wrists. Women may find that they have stellar balance but insufficient upper-body strength; including exercises for the deltoids, pectorals, wrists, and triceps in preseason will help you feel more comfortable completing early season rides.

As in lower-body strength training, in upper-body training the off-road biker will benefit from using compound exercises, both bilateral and unilateral, for the chest, back, shoulders, arms, and core. Basic exercises such as the dumbbell bench press (page 253), the pull-up (page 242), the one-arm dumbbell row (page 246), the standing dumbbell overhead press (page 251), the plank and its variations (page 225), the decline crunch (page 223), and the dirt digger (page 222) provide a good foundation.

Another type of supplemental training that is excellent for lower-body strength is tire or sled dragging, either on flat dirt or slight hills. Load weight onto a sturdy child's sled or use an oversized tire. Attach a 1-inch (2.5 cm) thick rope and either grab the free end with your hand or attach it to a weight belt or harness around your waist. Find an area that allows you to walk forward or backward while dragging the sled or tire for 30 to 50 feet (9.1-15.2 m). Forward dragging challenges the hamstrings and gluteals; backward dragging loads the quadriceps. This sort of training develops the core and leg strength necessary for pushing, carrying, or maneuvering your bike over and around obstacles in challenging terrain.

Flexibility Needs

While flexibility is important for all sports because it helps maintain muscle balance and normal range of motion, it ranks fairly low (a rating of 2) for all types of off-road biking. After a long day of riding on varied terrain, you may find that stretching provides restorative effects, particularly for the lower back, middle back, calves, and quadriceps and also, perhaps surprisingly, for the forearms, which act as shock absorbers through the handlebars. In your program, include the downward dog (page 215), 90-90 quadriceps psoas stretch (page 219), lying trunk rotation (page 215), tree hug stretch (page 219), and stair calf stretch (page 217).

Additional Considerations

There are three ways to increase your ability to climb while on the bike: improve your climbing technique, decrease the weight of your bike and body, and increase your power output via appropriate strength training. It makes sense that the athlete who maintains strength while dropping excess body fat will see dramatic effects due to increased relative strength (strength divided by body weight). Studies have shown that an increase in leg strength can also affect power output dramatically. Dr. Burke (2008) of the University of Illinois conducted a study in which, during 10 weeks of training, eight individuals increased their average 1RM leg strength in the squat by 43 percent, going from 220 pounds (9.8 kg) to 318 pounds (144.2 kg). This strength gain resulted in a 47 percent increase in time to exhaustion (which went from 4:18 to 6:17) while riding at 100 percent peak oxygen consumption with no increase in $\dot{V}O_2max$. What makes this finding more impressive is that each of these subjects had already been training in cycling for several years.

Riding over terrain with greater variability requires a higher level of skill (a rating of 4) for successful downhill and obstacle navigation when compared with the skill required for touring (a rating of 2). According to *Trail Solutions: IMBA's Guide to Building Sweet Singletrack* (2004), beginner cross-country off-road bike trails may be compact gravel paths that are 6 to 10 feet (1.8-3.0 m) wide, have a 5 to 10 percent grade, and are free of obstacles. A short and narrow, well-defined flat path with no obstacles may still be classified as a beginner trail. Intermediate trails are considerably more challenging: 2 to 6 feet (.6-1.8 m) wide, up to 10 percent grade, with obstacles to navigate. Advanced bike trails may be less than 2 feet (.6 m) wide and steep (up to a 20 percent grade) and may feature numerous obstacles. Confronting such environmental hazards takes skill and practice and is one of the draws of this sport.

Natural obstacles include tree roots, gravel, downed logs, sand, water, rocks, and ruts in water run-off areas. To handle wet tree roots, try to get your bike to cross the root at a right angle, as any other angle may cause the front wheel to turn to one side and toss you off your bike. Steer straight across the root, as turning can cause a skid. Cross as quickly as possible so that you can get back onto dirt surfaces that provide greater traction. Practice shifting your body weight back to unload the front tire as it goes over tree roots and then shifting your weight forward to unload the back tire.

Brace yourself mentally and physically for a change in speed whenever you change surfaces. For example, if you ride into a sandy stretch too quickly, you may be catapulted off your bike. Get ready to add power as soon as both tires hit the sand, or you may end up grinding to a halt. Gear down and pedal as fast as you can to propel yourself forward. If the sand stops you, simply pick up your bike, find a shallower or more compact area of sand that you can ride through, or walk (or run) through the sand while pushing your bike. If you have to cross water, pick a path with the least amount of rocks and brake lightly before entering to lessen the impact of the water. As soon as both tires are in the water, apply smooth strokes to power across. If you enter a rocky area, your challenge will be crossing the rocks without getting jostled about. Hovering just over the saddle will allow you to shift your body backward, forward, or sideways to navigate the terrain.

Proper clothing can be critical in off-road biking. While some sections of the trail may require extreme exertion and cause profuse sweating, others may be gradual descents demanding minimal effort. Moving between these two extremes can lead to great changes in body temperature and may even cause hypothermia. Wear a base layer of clothing that maintains your body heat even when you are sweating. Materials that work well are Merino wool, silk, and synthetic fibers. Avoid wearing cotton next to the skin. Another critical layer to have readily available is a water- and windproof outer layer that can be worn on long high-speed descents, at rest stops, or when the weather turns cooler or wetter. A third insulating layer of down or a synthetic can be useful for rest stops or unforeseen events such as bike problems that necessitate an unplanned night in the wilderness.

Assessing Fitness and Gauging Improvement

The assessments that are most important for all off-road bikers are the lower-body strength and field tests. Repeat these tests every 4 to 6 weeks. If you score below target in any area, prioritize your training to address these weaknesses first. While the upper-body, ramp, and flexibility tests help establish a baseline for strength and cardiovascular fitness, you may retest them every 6 to 8 weeks rather than monthly.

After a month of baseline training, try a best-fit test, which for off-road bikers is the 30-minute field test using a known trail on a relatively dry day. Record how far you go in 30 minutes using a bike computer or GPS and keep track of the elevation gained in the 30 minutes. Note the conditions of the trail, as the previous day's weather can change the difficulty of the terrain. Also note how you felt during and following the test so you can adjust your training program accordingly. If your legs failed to power you uphill, focus on lower-body strength training; if your lungs gave out before your legs, build aerobic and anaerobic endurance.

To assess your aerobic capacity and improvements therein, select an exercise mode that you can improve in some way each week. This may mean completing a favorite off-road route faster than before, completing the route in the same time but with less effort, or moving at the same speed but maintaining a lower working heart rate, all of which indicate improved cycling fitness. Once you have a fitness baseline, add a monthly field test that consists of a 15-mile (24.1 km) road ride or a 60-minute indoor cycle. Warm up for at least 5 to 10 minutes so that you feel limber in all your targeted muscle groups before you do your test. On an indoor cycle, try to cover more distance with each retest. For an outdoor test, try to reach the same end point in less time. To gauge the effectiveness of your anaerobic training such as Tabata intervals, chart the distance you cover in a 4-minute indoor cycle ride set to a specific resistance level. In subsequent workouts, try to increase the distance traveled as an indicator of your adaptation to your anaerobic training modes.

For each week's distance ride, add 10 to 15 minutes over the last week until previous distances become easier and more comfortable. While it may be more gratifying to exercise on cardiovascular machines that provide immediate feedback on mileage, caloric use, or vertical feet traveled, the miles you put in on your bike will benefit your sport directly. With a bike computer or a GPS, you can chart your distance, though keep in mind that GPS numbers will not reflect your battle with the changing terrain and conditions. It may be easier to gauge yourself on a measurable piece of stable trail and leave harder trails with more varied terrain for high-intensity fartlek intervals.

Another gauge of your improvement is how easy it becomes to climb specific hills. You may find that certain hills are so difficult in the beginning that you have to get off and push your bike up them. As you train, note how difficult certain hills feel and observe how your ability changes. Improved hill climbing leads to improved overall performance.

A final way to gauge your improvement is to assess your energy level, soreness, and stiffness following outings. If you feel stiff, sore, lethargic, or worn-out for several days after your ride, you may have worked too hard, or you may have neglected your warm-up or stretching. If you feel great, have energy to do more, and experience no aches or pains following a ride that previously caused a lot of discomfort, then you are adapting beautifully to the workload and increasing your overall biking fitness.

Creating a Long-Term Program

The first chart on page 166 summarizes the amount of training time you will need to prepare for a goal of a given difficulty, distance, elevation change, and terrain. Note that if your goal shares at least one variable with goals at the intermediate or advanced levels, include the training time suggested for the higher level indicated in the chart. For example, if you will be doing a 2-hour trip (intermediate level) with few obstacles and a wide path (beginner level) gaining 800 feet of elevation (just beyond beginner level), allow at least 10 weeks to train for the trip duration. Though not specified in the chart, if you will be doing overnights that involve carrying additional weight, add training time to handle the increase in the weight of the bike and panniers. For baseline training, off-road bikers should do 2 to 4 weeks of three or more weekly workouts, including two 30-minute full-body strength sessions (A1 and A2 on page 61) and at least two 30-minute cardiovascular workouts, to build biking endurance. Suitable cardiovascular options for all levels of off-road biking include variations on biking as well as uphill training (biking or running), sled dragging, hiking with a pack, or Spinning classes.

Difficulty	Duration	Terrain	Steepness; elevation gain	Training time above baseline
Beginner	<1 hr.	No obstacles, 6+ ft. (1.8 m) wide	<10% grade; <600 ft. (183 m) gain	6-8 weeks
Intermediate	1-3 hr.	Moderate obstacles, 2 ft. (.6 m) wide in parts	10%-15% grade; <2,500 ft. (762 m) gain	10-12 weeks
Advanced	>3 hr.	Unavoidable obstacles, 6-12 in. (15-30 cm) wide in parts	>15% grade; >2,500 ft. (762 m) gain	16 weeks

The general conditioning recommendations for off-road biking are to build to the following weekly workloads by the time you are 2 weeks from goal. Be sure to stretch with every workout.

Type	Number of weekly workouts 2 weeks from goal	Number of strength workouts	Number of cardiovascular workouts	Number of sport-specific weekly workouts	Weekly exercise time
Beginner mountain bike	4	2 45-min. full body	3 (1 anaerobic)	1 distance bike; 1 flat bike	4-6 hr.
Intermediate mountain bike	5	2 1 hr. full body	3-4 (1-2 anaerobic or sled drag sessions)	1 beginner mountain bike ride; 1 distance road bike ride	6-8 hr.
Advanced mountain bike	6	2 1 hr. full body	4-5 (2 anaerobic or sled drag sessions)	1 intermediate mountain bike ride; 1-2 distance rides	8-12 hr.

Sample Goals and Associated Programs

The following sample programs are designed to meet particular goals an off-road biker might have. They include a beginner 7-mile bike ride and an intermediate 14-mile bike trip. Training sessions at all levels should include 5 to 10 minutes of targeted stretching. Use the sample programs for insights to how you can manipulate the training variables to create programs for yourself. The sample programs begin with the following baseline training: two 30-minute strength workouts and three cardiovascular workouts, two of which are 30- to 40-minute distance sessions (at 65-75 percent MHR) and one of which is a 30-minute tempo session (at 75-85 percent MHR).

■ BEGINNER OFF-ROAD BIKE

This program is suitable for a person with a goal such as a 7-mile (11.3 km) ride with a 250-foot (76 m) elevation gain along Laurel Gap Trail near Mount Mitchell, North Carolina. The objectives for these 6 weeks of training beyond baseline are to test various dirt and rooted terrains that are similar to what is expected on the ride as well as to build endurance suitable for at least an hour of riding with mild elevation gain.

Intensity Guidelines

Recovery	<65 percent MHR
Distance	65 to 75 percent MHR
Tempo	75 to 85 percent MHR
Interval	85 to 95 percent MHR

Week	Day 1	Day 2	Day 3	Day 4	Day 5	Weekend
			BUILD ENDURANCE			
1	30 min. distance; A1 strength	Off	30 min. tempo	A2 strength	Off	40 min. distance
2	35 min. distance; A1 strength	Off	33 min. tempo	A2 strength	Off	45 min. distance
3	40 min. distance; A1 strength	Off	36 min. tempo	A2 strength	Off	50 min. distance, 100 ft. (30 m) gain
			BUILD STRENGTH			
4	30 min. uphill; D1 strength	Off	40 min. tempo	D2 strength	Off	4 mi. (6.4 km) ride, 150 ft. (48 m) gain
5	35 min. uphill; D1 strength	Off	45 min. tempo	D2 strength	Off	5.5 mi. (8.9 km) ride, 200 ft. (62 m) gain
6	40 min. uphill; D1 strength	Off	30 min. recovery	D2 strength	Off	Goal: 7 mi. (11.3 km) ride, 250 ft. (76 m) gain

■ INTERMEDIATE OFF-ROAD BIKE

This program is suitable for a person who wishes to ride the 14-mile (22.5 km) Buffalo Creek mountain bike trail (Pine, Colorado) and cover a 2,400-foot (732 m) elevation gain in less than 3 hours. During these 10 weeks, you will familiarize yourself with the different types of terrain expected on the ride, including slickrock, loose crushed rock, and sand, and otherwise practice descending and fast riding. As an alternative to the sled dragging suggested in week 4 (drag 1-2 minutes, recover to below 65 percent MHR, repeat for the duration), pack-loaded uphill walking (or even biking repeats with panniers or backpack weight) is a suitable anaerobic training mode that can build strength for the uphill portions of the ride.

Intensity Guidelines

Recovery	<65 percent MHR
Distance	65 to 75 percent MHR
Tempo	75 to 85 percent MHR
Interval	85 to 95 percent MHR

Week	Day 1	Day 2	Day 3	Day 4	Day 5	Weekend
			BUILD ENDURANCE			
1	45 min. recovery; B1 strength	Off	60 min. distance	B2 strength	Off	60 min. bike, 500 ft. (152 m) gain
2	50 min. recovery; B3 strength	Off	65 min. distance	B1 strength	Off	75 min. bike, 750 ft. (229 m) gain
3	55 min. recovery; B2 strength	Off	70 min. distance	B3 strength	Off	90 min. bike, 1,000 ft. (305 m) gain
			BUILD STRENGTH			
4	60 min. recovery	30 min. uphill; D1 strength	75 min. distance	Off	20 min. sled drag, 15 lb.; D2 strength	90 min. bike, 1,250 ft. (381 m) gain
5	60 min. recovery	35 min. uphill; D1 strength	80 min. distance	Off	30 min. tempo; D2 strength	2 hr. bike, 1,500 ft. (457 m) gain

Week	Day 1	Day 2	Day 3	Day 4	Day 5	Weekend
			BUILD STRENGTH *(continued)*			
6	60 min. recovery	40 min. uphill; D1 strength	90 min. distance	Off	20 min. sled drag, 17 lb.; D2 strength	2.5 hr. bike, 1,750 ft. (533 m) gain
			BUILD STAMINA			
7	45 min. recovery	45 min. uphill; E1 strength	90 min. distance	Off	35 min. tempo; E2 strength	3 hr. bike, 2,000 ft. (610 m) gain
8	60 min. recovery	30 min. uphill; 20 min. sled drag, 20 lb.; E3 strength	75 min. distance	Off	40 min. tempo; E1 strength	10 mi. (16.1 km) bike, 2,000 ft. (610 m) gain
9	45 min. recovery	50 min. uphill; E2 strength	60 min. distance	Off	45 min. tempo; E3 strength	12 mi. (19.3 km) bike, 2,200 ft. (671 m) gain
			PEAK AND TAPER			
10	40 min. tempo; E1 strength	45 min. distance	Off	30 min. distance	Off	Goal: 14 mi. (22.5 km) bike, 2,400 ft. (732 m) gain

Canoeing, Kayaking, and Rafting

Paddling sports allow athletes to explore areas of the world unreachable on foot, such as islands, bays, glacier terminuses, high-walled valleys, and beaches exposed only at low tides. Canoeists, kayakers, and rafters have unique conditioning needs in that they require great core strength and upper-body endurance and less cardiovascular conditioning or leg strength. Flexibility also plays a more vital role for paddling than for other sports in this book.

A canoe is an open-hulled boat with bow and stern seats and can be paddled in tandem by two or solo by one. Each canoeist paddles primarily on one side of the boat, although on agreement paddlers can switch sides every 25 to 30 strokes or switch places so the stern paddler remains in command of the boat. The J, sweep, and draw strokes are down and backward pull power strokes that the bottom hand performs while the top hand affords paddle control and stability with a slight forward push.

Kayaking involves tandem or solo travel in either an enclosed-hull touring sea kayak (ideal for lakes and ocean travel) or a nimble white-water kayak designed for high maneuverability on swift rivers. The paddle has two blades that can be positioned ranging from parallel to a 90-degree angle for easier feathering and paddling. The kayak stroke combines pulling with one hand with stabilizing and pushing somewhat with the other. The core musculature as well as the shoulders and back engage heavily to propel the craft forward. The quadriceps and hips are involved in stabilizing the craft and performing Eskimo rolls.

River rafting requires good swimming endurance as well as core and upper-body strength for paddling. Commonly, rafting involves 4 to 8 people propelling a rubberized craft. Its conditioning needs and stroke requirements overlap strongly with those of canoeing and less so with those of kayaking.

The term *portage* applies to all three sports and refers to carrying gear or craft between bodies of water or around obstacles. A portage can range in length from 50 yards (46 m) to several miles (or km). You must have the core strength as well as the leg strength and endurance to pull or carry your craft or gear on whatever length of portage you encounter. In this chapter we discuss canoeing, lake, sea, and white-water kayaking, and rafting in conditions up to class IV (difficult) river rapids.

The following is a summary of the fitness components that are common to paddling. A rating of 1 indicates a fitness component that has a low priority in a conditioning program and a rating of 5 is given to those components receiving the highest emphasis.

Aerobic endurance: 3

Anaerobic endurance: 3

Upper-body strength: 4

Lower-body strength: 1

Flexibility: 3

Activity skill: 3

Cross-training: 5

Important areas of the body: obliques, lower back, upper back, chest, shoulders, arms, forearms, and wrists and the quadriceps and hips for stabilization

Canoe outings may be leisurely several-mile afternoon paddles or they may be marathon-like ventures, lasting many days and involving massive several-mile portages, such as in the case of a 3-week Canadian boundary waters trip. Kayak trips can range from explorations on calm lakes to adventures on class IV (or higher) rapids. River rafting can take you through some of the most stunning terrain in the world. Paddlers who like to explore remote destinations on foot benefit from spinal-loading cardiovascular training, while all paddlers require core and upper-body strength conditioning (rated 4) specific to paddling.

©Bridget Besaw/Aurora Photos

Unlike most other outdoor sports, paddling requires significant upper-body propulsion to reach your destination.

Cardiovascular Needs

The desired baseline cardiovascular conditioning needs clearly increase as the length of your target trip and portages increases. Also, the longer your trip, the greater is your need for stamina in the arms, shoulders, chest, back, and torso. Jan Nesset, editor of *Canoe & Kayak Magazine,* refers to sea kayaking as "hiking with your arms." Canoeists, kayakers, and rafters all benefit from aerobic training as a foundation for the high-intensity anaerobic and strength components required in a well-rounded paddling program. While spinal loading helps with general fitness preparation, it is critical for comfortably handling portages. If you have difficulty accessing bodies of water for regular training, suitable cross-training increases in importance.

A solid aerobic baseline (rating of 3) establishes the foundation on which subsequent training is built. If you enjoy lake canoeing, sea kayaking, or river paddling in conjunction with exploring remote areas on foot, include spinal-loading cardiovascular cross-training (rating of 5) at the appropriate level for a secondary activity such as hiking, scrambling, or trail running. If your focus is paddling itself, emphasize anaerobic training (3) in cardiovascular sessions, especially if you travel on waters of class II or higher. Because the working musculature of the upper body is smaller than that of the lower body, the maximum heart rates you experience in your sport may be lower than those you see while doing cross-training that engages the larger leg muscles.

During the first month of training, your baseline cardiovascular conditioning should include 20- to 30-minute aerobic sessions at least 2 or 3 times a week at 65 to 75 percent of your MHR. These workouts need not all be in a canoe, kayak, or raft, although the more time you spend in your craft, the more sport-specific your training will be. At least one aerobic session should include lower-body spinal loading to assist with portages outside your boat and stabilization and balance within your boat.

After a month of training, add 1 to 2 anaerobic sessions per week, preferably selecting a mode involving the upper body, and extend one aerobic session to 45 to 90 minutes depending on your end goal. For your anaerobic training, you can perform repeat efforts of paddling, swimming, or rowing on an ergometer, working hard for a set duration and recovering for a set duration. Fartlek training is a good mode for paddling, as its random nature mimics the random distances found between eddies, swells, wind gusts, and rocks. While in a canoe or kayak, pick a spot to race toward and put forth your greatest effort to get there; recover before repeating. When swimming, you can do more traditional tempo or speed training, going hard for a certain number of laps or amount of time, recovering, and trying to repeat your effort on previous intervals. Finally, on a full-body cardiovascular machine such as the rowing or kayak ergometer, include Tabata sprints, particularly if you race or guide. These anaerobic training sessions will help you prepare for rough water, fast and challenging river conditions, and emergencies. The sample training programs at the end of this chapter illustrate how you can combine various aerobic and anaerobic sessions with strength training to address different levels and goals for paddling.

Once you have determined the focus for each cardiovascular workout (aerobic or anaerobic), select your training modes. If possible, select exercises that incorporate trunk and arm movements to help develop stamina and strength specific to paddling. Suitable options include boat, water, wilderness, and indoor full-body training.

Boat Training For boat training, you should spend time in your canoe, kayak, or raft. But even spending time in a rowboat or dragon boat and sculling or rowing can provide excellent paddling training with direct carryover to your sport. If boat training classes in an indoor pool are available, you can practice wet exits and entries, Eskimo rolls, high and low braces, and emergency rescues. If you have access to a nearby body of water such as a bay or small lake, you may be able to paddle as often as 4 days a week. Vary your training so you are not always covering the same distance or time in each workout. Consider combining shorter, high-intensity boating workouts with a low-intensity land-based aerobic workout such as jogging or in-line skating. Combination training can also help as a warm-up or cool-down for accessing boat-launch areas.

Water Training Paddling is the one outdoor sport for which we endorse swimming as a necessary cross-training activity. It can save you during the times you find yourself in the water, whether by choice or accident. While swimming may be an off-season or recovery option for all other sports, for paddling it can be an in-season component, since it is a nonimpact training option that requires the upper-body and trunk stamina demanded by paddling. Be certain you can swim at least 170 feet (50 m) in full paddling garb. Developing such skills and endurance can be attained by swimming as little as once every 1 to 2 weeks in order to maintain swimming stamina. If you do not know how to swim when you start paddling, take lessons and *always* wear a life jacket in the craft. Water polo, synchronized swimming, or water aerobics are training options that allow you to work the upper body while developing stabilization ability in the hips and trunk.

Wilderness Training Each sport discussed in this book has suitable cross-training benefits for paddling. People often paddle when they have access to water and choose another outdoor sport when they do not. Mountain biking, hiking, and backpacking can be combined naturally with paddling without either sport detracting from the other. Trail running is a good option for increasing agility and balance. Since trail running requires high steps over limbs, roots, and rocks, it provides excellent conditioning for the hip flexors and quadriceps, muscles strongly recruited for stability when kayaking and rafting. On shorter boating trips, you may even find yourself docking your craft and jogging or biking back to the put-in location to retrieve your car—if you anticipate such travel, include trail running or mountain biking regularly in your training. Scrambling, cross-country skiing, and climbing complement paddling, as all four sports recruit the upper body in different patterns, and this maintains muscle balance. If you plan to explore the backcountry while on paddling trips, add a weekly distance spinal-loading cardiovascular workout to train for hiking or scrambling.

Indoor Full-Body Training Rowing or kayak ergometers (such as those by Vasa) are the cardiovascular machines with the greatest similarity to paddling. Also suitable are other machines that train the upper body, including VersaClimbers, cross-country ski simulators, Jacob's Ladders, elliptical trainers with moving handles, and upper-body cycles that allow you to train the push and pull component simultaneously. If you anticipate having long portages where you will have to carry your canoe, kayak, or gear, include several elliptical or moderately inclined treadmill workouts with a pack to prepare the lower back, shoulders, and legs for such portages.

Strength Needs

While paddlers have a unique conditioning need for great core strength and upper-body endurance, their need for lower-body strength is less critical. While other sports in this book involve direct propulsion from the legs, paddling requires propulsion from the torso and upper body, so lower-body strength, while mildly important for stability and balance, is de-emphasized (given a rating of 1).

Kayaking, rafting, and canoeing rely heavily on the strength endurance and integrity of the muscles around the shoulder joint, including the pulling muscles of the latissimus dorsi, rhomboids, rear deltoids, and biceps as well as the core muscles (abdominals, lower back, and obliques) and forearms (for gripping). Arm movements provide fine motor control in the boat, while the larger muscles in the torso and trunk provide stability. Avoid focusing solely on the biceps, triceps, and forearm muscles; include them in a well-rounded program that incorporates the chest, shoulders, back, obliques, and abdominals.

The lower body provides a balanced and stable base from which to paddle. It is also needed during significant portages to, from, and between waterways. If your trip includes any long portages, develop a plan for transporting your gear. Strap systems can hook your craft onto your frame pack for easier carrying and stability. Portage-specific wheels can be strapped to your canoe or kayak for easier transport, although when you will be traversing unknown or uneven terrain, carrying remains a valid lighter-weight option. The more weight you have in your craft, the more drag you will experience and the harder you will have to work, so choose wisely. Whether you carry or pull your craft and gear, you need at least mild backpacking conditioning in order to handle the additional weight. If you intend to do vehicle-supported trips or to launch near your home so you can forego portages, your emphasis should remain core and upper-body endurance.

The muscles that are often neglected in strength training for paddling are the pectorals and triceps (pushing muscles), the lower-back muscles, and the forearm extensors. Since paddling is repetitive and has distinct ranges of movement, balanced training for unused areas of the body is important, especially as you increase the time spent paddling. Train pulling *and* pushing muscles in order to maintain integrity of the shoulders, rotator cuff, and postural muscles. Strength of the opposing muscle groups is crucial for injury prevention; you run a higher likelihood of injury if you neglect your nonpaddling muscles.

Sport-specific exercises to include in a canoeing or rafting program are the one-arm dumbbell row (page 246), the one-arm seated row rotation (page 247), the straight-arm standing lat pull-down (page 249) for both paddle drive and front crawl in swimming, the paddling oblique twist (a variant of the medicine ball twist; page 224) for developing strength in the obliques and hip flexors, the push-up (page 255) and dumbbell bench press (page 253) for simultaneous development of pushing and core strength, and the plank and its variations (page 225). Early in the season, workouts should also include variations of the external rotation (page 234) to ensure that the smaller rotator cuff muscles will be able to handle increased load. The wrist extension (page 237) and Thor pronation (page 238) can help prevent forearm and elbow tendon strain from repetitive use.

Even without significant upper-body strength, a kayaker can expect to maintain a steady pace at 3 miles per hour (4.8 kph) in low wind and little current. In wind or swift-moving water, core strength and stability become more important for maneuvers such as the hip snap, low brace, and high brace (Krauzer 1995). Kayaking exercises that condition the core to work in conjunction with the upper body include the Saxon dumbbell overhead side bend (page 221), which is a good exercise for the high brace; the wood chopper (page 227), the medicine ball twist (page 224), and the paddling oblique twist (a variant of the medicine ball twist; page 224), which are good both for paddling endurance and for the low brace; the straight-arm standing lat pull-down (page 249); and the plank and its variations (page 225). About 90 percent of kayak strokes involve a power stroke, requiring work from the arms, shoulders, and core and control and stability from the hips. In fact, much of the torso rotation in a forward kayak stroke comes from the quadriceps (Mattos 2002). Train the hips and legs with the one-leg deadlift (page 263) and the barbell back squat (page 270) with a wide stance for lateral stability, the Romanian deadlift (page 262) for lower-back and hamstring strength, and the barbell front squat (page 271) for quadriceps and torso strength. For the hip abductors, include the band clam abduction (page 235) and hip abductor band sidestep (page 235).

An effective training method for building anaerobic and strength endurance is a total-body barbell strength circuit that includes six strength exercises, with 10 repetitions performed per exercise, done nonstop in succession for 20 minutes. The easiest way to gauge your strength improvement is to add a few pounds each time or to complete more sets, repetitions, or total circuits (with no breaks between exercises) in the allotted 20 minutes. For the barbell circuit, perform these six exercises in the following order: the bent row with a barbell (a variation of the one-arm dumbbell row on page 246), the barbell back squat (page 270), the barbell military press (page 252), the barbell deadlift (page 261), the barbell shrug (a variation of the dumbbell shrug on page 244), and the barbell front squat (page 271). Simply move from one exercise to the next without setting down the bar. The weight can range from a 9-pound (4.1 kg) Body Bar for the novice strength trainer to a barbell weighing 25 to 45 pounds (11.3-20.4 kg) for the seasoned paddler; in most cases, the military press and shrug will dictate what weight to use for the entire circuit.

This circuit will give you the extra mental toughness you will need for any competition and will also prepare the body for the barrage of strokes and movements you will need to perform in tough current or wind conditions.

Flexibility Needs

Flexibility training for the hamstrings, quadriceps, shoulders, core, hips, lower back, forearms, and wrists should receive moderate emphasis (a rating of 3), especially for anyone who discovers notably tight areas in any of the five flexibility assessments. Sitting with the legs outstretched for long durations can have serious repercussions. Kayakers who fail to maintain proper posture in the craft are prone to lower-back problems. A balanced program that includes flexibility training on land as well as active stretching and warm-up movements in the boat will help prevent strain and injury. Paddling requires greater areas of the body to move through larger ranges of motion than a sport such as trail running requires.

As an increasing number of athletes aged 45 and older gravitate toward paddling as a nonimpact way to enjoy the backcountry, stretching to prevent injury and preserve suppleness grows in importance. Your flexibility will decrease with age unless you have a specific program designed to maintain it. Paddlers of all ages will benefit from an active warm-up and cool-down, both in the gym and beside the water, including arm circles (page 214), leg swings (page 213), and standing dowel torso rotation (page 214). If you start to feel tight in the upper back and neck, do the trapezius stretch (page 219). Other stretches appropriate for gym training are the triangle pose (page 216), the one-arm version of the tree hug stretch (page 219), the 90-90 quadriceps psoas stretch (page 219), and the downward dog (page 215).

Additional Considerations

Skill level is rated a 3 for paddlers, as it takes time to master the various strokes, Eskimo rolls, wet exits and entries, rescue methods, and navigation skills and to become familiar with currents, high and low tides, eddies, water patterns, and paddling in high winds. While a beginner paddler can prepare for a successful half-day trip in about 10 weeks, becoming proficient requires several seasons of boating to attain the necessary skills to make water travel second nature.

When it comes to macronutrient intake, canoeists and kayakers require additional protein for tissue repair and slightly lower carbohydrate; the remainder of the diet is fat. Hydration provides a different challenge for paddlers: Unless you use a Camelbak hydration system, you will need to take frequent breaks from paddling to hydrate. Drink at least 20 fluid ounces (600 ml) every hour that you paddle. For refueling, take easily accessible snack foods in waterproof containers that can float if accidentally dropped. Keep snacks protected from waves and cold weather in baggies in oversized pockets or under your spray skirt.

The heavier the paddler and gear, the lower the craft sits in the water. Competitive racers want to be as light as healthily possible to improve maneuverability in rapids. However, one advantage of additional body fat is a greater likelihood of survival in the case of immersion in frigid waters. Hypothermia from exposure to wet, windy conditions is a leading cause of death among sea kayakers. Bring extra clothing in a waterproof bag, a thermos of soup or a hot beverage, a fire starter, and a sleeping bag if you will be adventuring in off-season or cooler climes. A neoprene wet or dry suit can keep you warm while paddling or in the event of immersion, and you may find that it is a requirement for participating on a guided trip. Water-resistant gloves or hand protectors such as pogies, which allow you to keep bare skin on the paddle, are crucial in colder weather in order to prevent stiff, cold, or frostbitten fingers. Thick-soled neoprene booties may help keep your feet warm. Avoid footwear that can get caught on foot pegs (such as sandals) or can fill up with water in the event of capsizing (such as rubber boots).

Advance knowledge of water conditions, navigational obstacles, tide charts, approaching storms, and pullout points can all be helpful in preventing spills or other trouble. Pay attention to wind speed and direction and currents so you can progress steadily toward your goal. Winds less than 10 knots (18.5 kph) will probably not affect your travel. However, if your top speed is 3 knots (5.6 kph) and you are paddling directly into a 20-knot (37.0 kph) headwind, you will quickly tire without ever reaching your destination. If you will be traveling in a canyon, knowing the regional weather patterns and escape routes is imperative so that you know what to do in case of flash flooding.

Your program would not be complete without planning for physical discomforts or difficulties you might experience on your trip. Research ahead of time what local wildlife you might encounter. If necessary, you can bring appropriate hanging bags or protective gear such as bear cannisters, which will add to your weight. If you will be paddling near popular salmon runs or on rivers where flooding has made certain sections impassable, you may need alternative plans for route closures, adding to portage or paddling distances. If you plan to use downed logs as fuel, include a heavy-duty adze or axe. Chopping wood adds both weight and additional physical exertion beyond paddling to your trip. In the continental United States, you need to know ahead of time where there are fire pits in designated camp spots; you can also bring a small stove and appropriate fuel.

If you do popular paddling trips that require permits months ahead of time, consider what options are available to you if your targeted campsites are already full. Practice using any wheeled portage devices ahead of time; use a terrain and grade that are similar to what you may encounter to determine whether you may need two people to maneuver over and around rocks, roots, and slopes. Finally, plan to deal with black flies, mosquitoes, or other biting bugs, especially in boggy, slow-moving water. By building more strength and stamina than you think you will need, you will be better prepared to survive whatever unusual circumstances you might face.

Assessing Fitness and Gauging Improvement

The upper-body strength and flexibility tests are the most important assessments for all three paddling sports, and they should be repeated every 4 to 6 weeks. After a month of baseline training, it is time for a best-fit test. For paddlers, this is the 30-minute field test performed on a known stretch of flat water on a calm day. Record how far you go in 30 minutes, whether you are doing laps around a small lake or distance along the shore of a larger lake. For river travel, select a favorite stretch that is accessible in both high and low water conditions. Note the time it took you to complete your test stretch of water as well as any obstacles or changes (i.e., wind speed, direction, or currents) that might have affected your results. Also note how you felt during and following the performance so you can adjust your training program accordingly.

If you score below target in upper-body strength or flexibility, prioritize your training to address these weaknesses first. The lower-body strength tests, ramp test, and field test can be completed every 6 to 8 weeks to establish a baseline for lower-body strength and cardiovascular fitness.

To assess aerobic capacity, select an exercise mode that you can improve in some way each week. This may mean completing a favorite paddling route faster than before, completing the route in the same time but with greater ease, or completing it at the same speed but lower working heart rate, all of which indicate improved paddling fitness. Once you have a fitness baseline, add a monthly field test of a 6,660-foot (2,000 m) rowing or kayak ergometer piece or a continuous half-mile (.8 km) swim. Warm up for at least 5 to 10 minutes so that you feel limber in all your targeted muscle groups before doing your test. On the ergometer, try to cover more distance with each retest. When rowing or swimming, try to reach the same initial end point more quickly each time. To gauge the effectiveness of your anaerobic training such as Tabata intervals, chart the meters you cover in a 4-minute workout on a rowing ergometer. In subsequent workouts, try to increase the distance traveled as an indicator of your adaptation to your training.

Add 10 to 15 minutes to each week's distance paddle until your previous distances become easier and more comfortable. While it may be more gratifying to exercise on cardiovascular machines that provide immediate feedback on distance traveled or caloric use, the nautical miles that you travel in your craft will provide the most direct benefit for your sport. With good navigation skills or a GPS unit, you can chart your paddled distance, though you should keep in mind that GPS numbers will not reflect your battle with the tide, current, or wind, any of which may add to your total time and distance if you undergo serious drift. It may be easier to use a measurable, reproducible route (such as an easy river or lake) under calm conditions for testing and to leave harder river excursions and windy sea travel for high-intensity fartlek intervals.

A final way to gauge your improvement is to assess your energy levels following an outing. If you feel great, have energy to do more, and have no residual aches or pains following a workout that may have previously caused extreme soreness or stiffness, then you are making significant progress in adapting to the workload and increasing your paddling fitness.

Creating a Long-Term Program

When creating a long-term paddling program, consider your destination, the required mileage or duration, the required days of travel, the type of paddling (solo, tandem, sea, lake, or river), the class of water (A or I-IV; for more on classes, see the suggested readings for paddling resources) and inherent skill level required, the weather and water conditions, and the cross-training to include with paddling.

The recommended baseline conditioning for paddlers includes three elements: being able to paddle at low intensity for at least 3 to 4 hours in a canoe, raft, or kayak; being comfortable paddling hard in windy conditions for at least 30 minutes at a time; and having the skills to handle capsizes should they occur. The following chart summarizes the training time you will need beyond your baseline training in order to prepare for a paddling trip given its difficulty, distance, and speed; water conditions and class; and nonpaddling elements such as portages, trail running, or hiking. If you plan to pursue other outdoor sports in addition to paddling, see the appropriate chapters for suitable training programs. Note that if your goal shares at least one variable with goals at the intermediate or advanced levels, include the training time suggested for the higher level indicated in the chart. For example, if you will be doing a leisurely 3-night (intermediate) flat water (beginner) canoe trip with short days (<6 miles / 10K per day; beginner) and two portages linking three lakes together (intermediate), you will want to allow at least 10 weeks of training to prepare for successive days of exertion and moderate weight portages.

Difficulty	Trip duration; distance traveled; speed	Water conditions	Nonpaddling considerations: hikes, portages	Training time above baseline
Beginner	Single day (5 hr.); <12 mi. (19.3 km); <2.25 mph (3.62 kph)	Flat water, little current, no wind, (class A-II)	None	6-8 weeks
Intermediate	Short overnight trip; <20 mi. (32.2 km); 2.25-3 mph (3.62-4.83 kph)	Moderate river, sea, or lake (class II-III)	Several, <1.5 mi. (2.4 km) hikes, <400 ft. (122 m) gain	10-12 weeks
Advanced	Multiple days; >15 mi. (24.1 km) each; >3 mph	Obstacles, swiftly flowing currents, extreme weather (<class IV)	May include long distances on foot	16 weeks

Early in the season, include unilateral full-body strength training and short aerobic sessions in your program. During the midseason, incorporate sport-specific upper-body and core strength training sessions or circuits as well as anaerobic training. The further into the season you get, the longer your paddling workouts should be, with recovery days following multiday trips or high-intensity sessions that tax the whole body. Off-season training might include an entirely separate sport or indoor cross-training with maintenance strength training so that you can begin paddling at a higher starting point the next season. The off-season is also a great time to include yoga if your flexibility needs improvement.

If your goal involves a multiple-day outing, gradually add 5 to 15 percent distance or time per week as you approach your goal trip. Include enough training time so that 6 weeks from your goal you can try a few back-to-back outings, either overnight trips or successive day trips, to get accustomed to less recovery time between paddling workouts. This may mean that you spend the early season building to long day trips, add a few overnight or weekend trips in the midseason, and then during the late season embark on a several-day or weeklong goal that you have built up to over several months. A training program for a weeklong trip clearly requires more training, advanced elements, and more time (4 months) than a program for a 5-hour day trip requires (6 weeks). When not working toward a goal, all paddlers should do a baseline training regime of three weekly workouts that include at least one 45-minute full-body strength session, one 30-minute spinal-loading tempo session (on a strength day), one 45-minute paddling-specific cardiovascular distance session, and one 2-hour paddle.

Type	Number of weekly workouts 2 weeks from goal	Number of strength workouts	Number of cardiovascular workouts	Number of sport-specific weekly workouts	Weekly exercise time
Beginner paddles	4	2 30 min. full body	3	1 45 min. paddling-specific workout; 1 2-3 hr. paddle	5-7 hr.
Intermediate paddles	5	2 45 min. full body	3-4 (1 anaerobic)	1-2 paddling-specific workouts; 1 3-5 hr. paddle	6-10 hr.
Advanced paddles	6	2 1 hr. full body	4-5 (1 anaerobic)	2 1 hr. paddling-specific workouts; 5-7 hr. paddle with at least 2 back-to-back outings	10-12 hr.

The general conditioning recommendations for paddling at different levels are to build to the following weekly workloads by the time you are 2 weeks from goal. Be sure to include stretching with every workout.

Sample Goals and Associated Programs

The following sample programs introduce you to paddling programs that are designed to match specific goals. Use them for insights into how you can manipulate training variables yourself to create your own training program. They include programs for a beginner sea kayaking trip, an intermediate overnight kayaking or canoeing trip, and an advanced rafting trip.

■ BEGINNER KAYAKING TRIP

This program is suitable for a person embarking on a goal such as a 1-day 10-mile (16.1 km) sea kayaking trip. This basic program adds 6 weeks beyond baseline to prepare you for a beginner trip with minimal wind or current. Include core exercises specific to paddling in each strength workout and perform hamstring and lower-back stretches with every workout.

Intensity Guidelines

Recovery	<65 percent MHR
Distance	65 to 75 percent MHR
Tempo	75 to 85 percent MHR
Interval	85 to 95 percent MHR

Week	Day 1	Day 2	Day 3	Day 4	Day 5	Weekend
			BUILD STRENGTH			
1	45 min. recovery	30 min. tempo; D1 strength	Off	45 min. distance; D2 strength	Off	2 hr. paddle
2	45 min. recovery	33 min. tempo; D1 strength	Off	50 min. distance; D2 strength	Off	2.25 hr. paddle
3	50 min. recovery	36 min. tempo; D1 strength	Off	55 min. distance; D2 strength	Off	2.5 hr. paddle
			BUILD STAMINA			
4	30 min. fartlek; E1 strength	60 min. distance	Off	40 min. tempo	E2 strength	2.5 hr. paddle
5	35 min. fartlek; E3 strength	60 min. distance	Off	45 min. tempo	E1 strength	2.75 hr. paddle
6	40 min. fartlek; E2 strength	60 min. distance	Off	30 min. recovery	Off	Goal: 10 mi. (16.1 km) sea kayak

■ INTERMEDIATE OVERNIGHT CANOEING OR KAYAKING TRIP

This program is suitable for a person aiming for a 9-day paddle on the 73-mile (117.5 km) Bowron Lake canoe circuit in British Columbia, Canada. It incorporates 12 weeks of training beyond baseline. While the water conditions on this circuit in the Cariboo Mountains are not especially challenging, the circuit's length and duration qualify it as an intermediate trip. It has a number of portages, some as long as 1.5 miles (2.4 km), and if you use wheels, you are restricted to 65 pounds (29.5 kg) of gear in the craft to discourage deep rutting in portage tracks. If you bring weight beyond the set limit, you will have to make multiple trips or carry the extra weight on your back. If you opt to include as a side trip a scramble up the 6,745-foot (2,056 m) Wolverine Mountain, your training program should also include a hiking component. Suitable cardiovascular training options for this program are training on rowing ergometers, VersaClimbers, or elliptical trainers with arms; swimming; paddling; or hiking.

Intensity Guidelines

Recovery	<65 percent MHR
Distance	65 to 75 percent MHR
Tempo	75 to 85 percent MHR
Interval	85 to 95 percent MHR

Week	Day 1	Day 2	Day 3	Day 4	Day 5	Weekend
			BUILD ENDURANCE			
1	45 min. tempo; B1 strength	Off	60 min. distance	B2 strength	40 min. recovery	2.5 hr. paddle
2	50 min. tempo; B3 strength	Off	60 min. distance	B1 strength	45 min. recovery	2.75 hr. paddle
3	55 min. distance; B2 strength	Off	65 min. distance, 10 lb. (4.5 kg)	B3 strength	50 min. recovery	3 hr. paddle
4	60 min. distance; B1 strength	Off	70 min. distance, 12 lb. (5.4 kg)	B2 strength	55 min. recovery	2 hr. paddle, 4 mi. (6.4 km) hike, 15 lb. (6.8 kg)

Week	Day 1	Day 2	Day 3	Day 4	Day 5	Weekend
			BUILD STRENGTH			
5	30 min. pyramid; B3 strength	60 min. recovery	75 min. distance, 15 lb. (6.8 kg)	Off	45 min. tempo; D1 strength	3.5 hr. paddle
6	20 min. pyramid; D2 strength; Tabata	45 min. recovery	75 min. distance, 18 lb. (8.2 kg)	Off	45 min. tempo; D1 strength	3 hr. paddle, 5 mi. (8.0 km) hike, 15 lb. (6.8 kg)
7	30 min. pyramid; D2 strength	60 min. recovery	80 min. distance, 20 lb. (9.1 kg)	Off	45 min. tempo; D1 strength	4.5 hr. paddle
8	25 min. pyramid; D2 strength; Tabata	45 min. recovery	85 min. distance, 22 lb. (10.0 kg)	Off	45 min. tempo; D1 strength	4 hr. paddle, 5 mi. (8.0 km) hike, 20 lb. (9.1 kg)
			BUILD STAMINA			
9	45 min. recovery; E1 strength	90 min. distance	35 min. pyramid, 30 lb. (13.6 kg)	60 min. tempo; E2 strength	Off	B2B: day 1: 5 hr. paddle; day 2: 6 mi. (9.7 km) hike, 25 lb. (11.3 kg)
10	45 min. recovery	E3 strength	90 min. distance, 25 lb. (11.3 kg)	45 min. tempo; E1 strength	Off	B2B: 3 hr. paddle each day
11	45 min. recovery; E2 strength	75 min. distance	40 min. fartlek, 30 lb. (13.6 kg)	45 min. tempo; E3 strength	Off	B2B: day 1: 2 hr. paddle; day 2: 4 mi. (6.4 km) hike, 20 lb. (9.1 kg)
			PEAK AND TAPER			
12	Off	30 min. tempo; E1 strength	45 min. distance	30 min. recovery	Off	Goal: Bowron Lake trip

ADVANCED RAFTING OR KAYAKING TRIP

This program is suitable for a person who wishes to take a class IV, 277-mile (365.3 km) rafting trip down the Colorado River in the Grand Canyon (Arizona). A dream trip such as this requires permits months in advance and at least 10 days of travel time to go the entire distance from Lees Ferry to Lake Mead. You should add more days if you intend to enjoy some of the numerous side trips that lead you to sparkling streams, pristine pools, green fern glens, and ancient Anasazi ruins. This training program requires 16 weeks to prepare you sufficiently for the trip. If you will not be able to do any specific rafting training, include workouts on a rowing ergometer, VersaClimber, or elliptical trainer with arms; swimming; paddling; trail running; or hiking for general cardiovascular conditioning.

Intensity Guidelines

Recovery	<65 percent MHR
Distance	65 to 75 percent MHR
Tempo	75 to 85 percent MHR
Interval	85 to 95 percent MHR

Week	Day 1	Day 2	Day 3	Day 4	Day 5	Weekend
			BUILD ENDURANCE			
1	45 min. recovery	A1 strength	60 min. distance	Off	30 min. tempo; A2 strength	2 hr. paddle *or* 30 min. erg plus 30 min. walk, 15 lb. (6.8 kg)
2	45 min. recovery	A1 strength	60 min. distance	Off	33 min. tempo; A2 strength	2.5 hr. paddle *or* 35 min. erg plus 30 min. walk, 18 lb. (8.2 kg)
3	50 min. recovery	A1 strength	65 min. distance	Off	36 min. tempo; A2 strength	3 hr. paddle *or* 40 min. erg plus 35 min. walk, 20 lb. (9.1 kg)
4	55 min. recovery	A1 strength	70 min. distance	Off	40 min. tempo; A2 strength	3.5 hr. paddle *or* 45 min. erg plus 40 min. walk, 20 lb. (9.1 kg)
			BUILD STRENGTH			
5	45 min. recovery	C1 strength	30 min. uphill, 20 lb. (9.1 kg); C2 strength	75 min. distance	45 min. tempo; C3 strength	4 hr. paddle *or* 45 min. erg plus 45 min. walk, 20 lb. (9.1 kg)
6	30 min. recovery	C4 strength	35 min. pyramid, 20 lb. (9.1 kg); C1 strength	75 min. distance	45 min. tempo; C2 strength	3-5 hr. paddle

Week	Day 1	Day 2	Day 3	Day 4	Day 5	Weekend
BUILD STRENGTH *(continued)*						
7	45 min. recovery	C3 strength	35 min. uphill, 22 lb. (10.0 kg); C4 strength	75 min. distance	50 min. tempo; C1 strength	5 mi. (8.0 km) hike, 1,500 ft. (547 m) gain, 15 lb. (6.8 kg)
8	30 min. recovery	C2 strength	40 min. pyramid, 23 lb. (10.4 kg); C3 strength	80 min. distance	50 min. tempo; C4 strength	4 hr. paddle
9	45 min. recovery	C1 strength	40 min. uphill, 25 lb. (11.3 kg); C2 strength	85 min. distance	55 min. tempo; C3 strength	4-6 mi. (6.4-9.7 km) hike, 2,000 ft. (610 m) gain, 18 lb. (8.2 kg)
BUILD STAMINA						
10	35 min. recovery	45 min. pyramid, 25 lb. (11.3 kg); E1 strength	85 min. distance	55 min. tempo	E2 strength	B2B: day 1: 5 hr. paddle; day 2: 5 mi. (8.0 km) hike, 2,000 ft. (610 m) gain, 20 lb. (9.1 kg)
11	30 min. recovery or off	45 min. fartlek, 25 lb. (11.3 kg); E3 strength	90 min. distance	60 min. tempo	E1 strength	Hike 2,300 ft. (701 m) gain, 5 mi. (8.0 km) round-trip, 23 lb. (10.4 kg)
12	30 min. tempo; E2 strength	45 min. pyramid, 28 lb. (12.7 kg)	90 min. distance	60 min. tempo	E3 strength	B2B: day 1: 4 hr. paddle; day 2: 3 hr. paddle
13	30 min. recovery or off	45 min. fartlek, 30 lb. (13.6 kg); E1 strength	90 min. distance	60 min. tempo	E2 strength	Hike 2,500 ft. (762 m) gain, 6 mi. (9.7 km) round-trip, 25 lb. (11.3 kg)
14	30 min. tempo; E3 strength	50 min. pyramid, 25 lb. (11.3 kg)	75 min. distance	60 min. tempo	E1 strength	B2B: day 1: 5 hr. paddle; day 2: 3 hr. paddle
PEAK AND TAPER						
15	30 min. recovery or off	40 min. fartlek, 20 lb. (9.1 kg); E2 strength	65 min. distance	30 min. tempo; E3 strength	Off	Hike 1,500 ft. (547 m) gain, 4 mi. (6.4 km) round-trip, 15 lb. (6.8 kg) *or* 2 hr. paddle
16	E1 strength	30 min. tempo	45 min. distance	30 min. recovery	Off	Goal: Colorado River rafting trip

B2B=back-to-back
erg=rowing ergometer as dryland replacement for boat training

Snowshoeing, Cross-Country Skiing, and Backcountry Skiing

Conditioning programs for the snow sports overlap those of trekking and mountaineering in that all three categories require great cardiovascular endurance and moderate leg strength. However, each snow sport emphasizes different muscle groups and varies in the suggested priority for each fitness component. Proper conditioning will make your snow outings safer and more enjoyable.

Snowshoeing is a low-impact winter hiking activity that requires little more equipment than snowshoes strapped onto your feet. Snowshoes allow you to walk on deep snow without sinking as far as you would in boots alone. Adjustable trekking poles are optional but can be helpful in deep snow.

Classic cross-country skiing (Nordic skate skiing) involves free-heel skiing with short, soft boots on long, thin skis lacking metal edges. Cross-country skiers often use groomed trails at ski resorts. Free-heel gear, similar to but not as strong as telemark gear, is lighter and faster and requires less energy but does not accommodate aggressive downhill skiing. Bindings lock in the toe, but because there is no cable, they are less stable and lack good edge control. Often, these skis have fish scales for traction when pushing back. This low-impact sport requires good balance and high endurance throughout all the major muscle groups.

Backcountry telemark skiing (Nordic downhill skiing) involves free-heel skiing on metal-edged skis designed to accommodate steep, aggressive slopes. Telemark skiers add skins and use heel elevators to provide a comfortable resting position for backcountry climbing. Since the heels of the boots come off the skis, downhill turns require the inside knee to drop low and the inside ski to drop back, creating fore-aft stability. The cable on the back helps keep the heel in place, adding to the stability of the gear on slopes. Backcountry telemark skiers may travel significant distances, and they carry greater pack weight and encounter more varied terrain when compared with cross-country skiers. This type of skiing also includes high-altitude touring, requiring more anaerobic conditioning and lower-body strength than cross-country skiing requires.

Randonee (alpine touring, AT) gear is lighter than alpine downhill gear but heavier than telemark gear. Randonee skiers use their gear for the backcountry (versus resorts with lift serve) by using skins for ascending, much like telemark skiers do. The binding allows the heel to be free for climbing or for crossing flat land but locked in place for parallel turns. Such skis are suitable for rugged and steep backcountry terrain.

Following are the fitness components common to snow sports. A rating of 5 indicates a fitness component that requires the greatest emphasis in your conditioning program and a rating of 1 is assigned to fitness components requiring the lowest priority in your program.

Aerobic conditioning: 4

Anaerobic conditioning: 2 (3 if you plan to be at high altitudes)

Upper-body strength: 3

Lower-body strength: 4 (telemark or AT skiing), 3 (snowshoeing), 2 (cross-country skiing)

Flexibility: 3

Activity skill: 4 (skiing), 1 (snowshoeing)

Cross-training: 3

Important areas of the body: core, shoulders, upper back, legs, hips, calves, hip flexors

Snow sport athletes should focus on developing cardiovascular endurance (a rating of 4) as well as muscular endurance in the shoulders, upper back, core, and legs. Telemark and AT skiers especially need decent lower-body strength. Maintaining flexibility in the shoulders, core, and hips ranks medium priority (rating of 3) for all types of skiers. Snowshoeing usually requires less instruction and skill (rating of 1) than cross-country, telemark, and AT skiing (rating of 4), all of which take more time and effort to master. High-altitude backcountry skiers need more anaerobic training (3) than snowshoers and cross-country skiers require (2).

Conditioning programs for snowshoers are quite similar to those of hikers and trekkers, with additional focus in the following areas: (a) strength in the hips and hip flexors for kicking steps, stepping high in deep snow, and combating heavy snow sitting on top of snowshoes; (b) stamina in the hip abductors, hip adductors, hamstrings, and gluteals for upward propulsion, sidestepping up steep slopes, and maintaining the wider gait required for walking in snowshoes; (c) strength in the shoulders and upper back for poling up steep hills; and (d) strength in the core for handling heavier winter loads.

Programs for cross-country skiers resemble those of trail runners but have additional focus in the following areas: (a) poling strength and stamina in the upper back, shoulders, triceps, and core; (b) stamina in the hip abductors and hamstrings for herringbone and skate skiing; and (c) flexibility in the hip flexors, hamstrings, latissimus dorsi, core, and shoulders. Training for telemark skiers overlaps that of mountaineers but has additional focus in the following areas: (a) quadriceps strength for the unique free-heel downhill ski turn and (b) flexibility in the calves, hip flexors, hamstrings, and shoulders.

Finally, programs for randonee skiers share conditioning elements with mountaineering programs but also require high-impact exercises to help with rapid descents. Randonee skiers should include (a) plyometric exercises for any jumps or rough terrain they encounter, (b) high-altitude anaerobic training for ski touring at elevation, and (c) flexibility in the quadriceps, hamstrings, hips, calves, shoulders, and lower back.

Cardiovascular Needs

Deep snow and cold temperatures increase the cardiovascular requirements for snow sport athletes compared with summer athletes who travel similar distances. Thus, snow sport athletes must develop uphill stamina over steep terrain with heavier pack weight and footwear. To prepare for this type of training, these athletes benefit from starting with a good foundation of being able to complete a 5-mile (8.0 km) hike while carrying a 20-pound (9.1 kg) pack and gaining 2,000 feet (610 m) of elevation in less than 2.5 hours. If you lack this baseline of endurance conditioning, turn to chapter 7 to build it.

In addition to possessing baseline snow travel capability, you need to be performing 3 to 6 aerobic workouts per week as you approach your target outing. At least some of these workouts should be in the snow; ideally, they involve an uphill component. They should all be spinal-loading options that work your muscle groups the same ways that snowshoeing and skiing work them. These workouts will vary in FITT principles according to your current fitness level and personal goals. The sample programs at the end of this chapter illustrate how you can combine aerobic and strength sessions to address different levels and goals for snow sports.

Depending on your goal distance and round-trip elevation gain and loss, your cardiovascular targets may vary considerably. Since backcountry skiing is largely an aerobic activity with anaerobic bursts mixed in whenever hills need to be climbed, the more of an aerobic base you have, the better you will feel on your outings. Start with three weekly cardiovascular workouts lasting 45 minutes each and add one longer endurance workout of 1 to 2 hours after a month of training. The lengths of your distance workouts will vary according to your end goal and beginning fitness. If you will be doing trips lasting several hours, start with 45 minutes and add 5 to 15 minutes to each distance workout until you can go at least 90 minutes. If you plan on doing long cross-country or multiday backcountry ski tours, start with an hour of continuous movement in the range of 65 to 75 percent of your MHR and add 15 to 20 minutes to each outing until you can go several hours. Include spinal-loading training such as in-line skating, treadmill walking or jogging, hiking, and elliptical training. Hills and stair-climbing will help with hilly ascents. You can also incorporate time on an indoor cross-country ski machine.

As you plan your cardiovascular sessions, determine what your goal is for each. Include at least one distance elevation-gaining workout a week. Build to your target distance gradually, adding 5 to 15 percent per week. For a second weekly workout, emphasize higher intensity over a short distance to focus on pack weight, steeper terrain, or speed. A third weekly workout, particularly if you will be traveling at altitude, should be a high-intensity anaerobic session. One of your workouts should focus on the unique characteristics of your sport discussed earlier in this chapter. For snowshoeing, that may mean including sessions of sidestepping up steep slopes to increase stamina in hip adductors and abductors; for randonee skiing, add anaerobic training combined with plyometric exercises to prepare for the rough terrain. Additional cardiovascular sessions can be moderate to easy in terms of time, distance, and intensity. Include a low-intensity cross-training workout for recovery after distance training.

Include snow scrambling for those portions of your travel you may have to make on foot rather than skis or snowshoes. These approaches, which are often uphill, include crossing over bare faces, ridges, or shoulders; navigating terrain that is too steep for skins or that is more conducive to crampons; handling exposed patches in early winter or late spring; and confronting snow or ice that is too hard for ski edges to get decent purchase.

Once you have a focus for each cardiovascular workout, select your training modes. Suitable options include wilderness training, in-town outdoor training, and indoor spinal-loading cardiovascular machine training.

Wilderness Training The best training for backcountry snow travel is getting out to the snow. If you have to travel far to reach snow, or if the snow season is limited where you live, hiking and scrambling are great warm-weather activities that have excellent carryover to snowshoeing. The heavier your pack during your late-season hiking or scrambling, the easier the transition to your snow sport will be. Mountaineering, with its travel across variable terrain, is useful for telemark and AT conditioning.

Trail running is a conditioning option that will help you increase agility, balance, and stability. Since trail running requires high steps over limbs, roots, and rocks, it provides excellent preseason hip flexor conditioning for snowshoers. Using poles on trail runs helps with balance, increases cardiovascular effectiveness due to the additional muscle recruitment, and is excellent for cross-country skiers who need power for propulsion on flat terrain.

Mountain biking is a popular cross-training option that develops endurance in the lower back and quadriceps, which is valuable for the cross-country skier who uses the double-pole technique. It is also useful for anyone who wants to build cardiovascular endurance but has knee issues or wishes to avoid high-impact running.

In-Town Outdoor Training Telemark and randonee skiing both require hamstring-dominant endurance training for strong uphill propulsion. Bounding up hills, inline skating, and roller skiing with ski poles are all suitable outdoor training options, as are hill running, hill walking with trekking poles and a pack, and stair-climbing (walking with a pack or running without). You can walk on grass, hills, sand, or dirt and use poles to increase upper-body endurance. Unlike using trekking poles when hiking (striking the ground slightly ahead of you for balance), pole walking involves striking the ground with the tip angled behind you for forward propulsion so that you are using the poles much the same way you use them in skiing. To target the quadriceps, add backward walking or running uphill for short stints. If there are small snowy hills in your neighborhood, race up them (or partway up them) on your skis and practice downhill techniques on the way down.

Indoor Training To target the quadriceps, you can walk or run backward on a treadmill, but because you have to face forward to set your target pace, you may find it awkward to set the appropriate speed and then reverse your position. Elliptical trainers allow you to stride forward *or* backward, targeting the gluteals, hamstrings, and calves during forward motion (on high ramp) and emphasizing the quadriceps during backward motion. The stair-climber, StepMill, incline treadmill (that goes to 15 percent grade or greater), cross-country ski machine, VersaClimber, and Jacob's Ladder all train the uphill propulsion needed for backcountry snow travel. Slide boards and ski machines such as the Skier's Edge can also be incorporated into a suitable training program.

To intensify your indoor workouts, add weight. Weighted vests can weigh up to 80 pounds (36.3 kg) or more and place the weight around your entire torso instead of concentrating it on your back like a pack does. You can also use your backpack, filling it with water jugs, sandbags, clothing, books, and the like to increase your pack weight. Avoid using dumbbells, weight plates, and rocks, as they put too much pressure in one spot and can damage your pack, not to mention strain your neck and shoulders.

Strength Needs

In the early weeks of your strength training, include unilateral exercises to correct any imbalances in your hips and legs. Since snow travel requires the large core and leg muscles to work in coordination with the muscles of the shoulders, upper back, and arms for extended durations, do sets of higher repetitions during the midseason. Rotate through exercises that target the gluteals and hamstrings, such as the one-leg deadlift (page 263), machine leg curl (page 266), ball leg curl (page 267), hamstring pull-through (page 264), and bridge (page 231). Include upper-back strength exercises such as the floor-assisted pull-up (page 242) and bent-over dumbbell raise (page 250). The straight-arm standing lat pull-down (page 249) and bent-arm pullover (page 258) are particularly helpful for the double-pole technique, and the dumbbell shrug (page 244) and its variations will help strengthen the trapezius for carrying heavy packs.

After improving your muscle balance, core integrity, and stability, add full-body exercises that cover the full range of motion, such as the Romanian deadlift (page 262) for the hamstrings, the barbell front squat (page 271) for the quadriceps, and the dumbbell overhead press (page 251) for the shoulders. Also add sport-specific movements such as ski training and muscle conditioning on a roller board or Total Gym or the following targeted exercises suggested for each backcountry sport.

Snowshoeing

The wider the snowshoe and the deeper, wetter, or heavier the snow, the harder the psoas and abductor muscles of the hip have to work. To prepare the psoas for snow-laden snowshoe steps, do several sets of high marches for 1 to 2 minutes at a time while wearing heavy ski boots or 5- to 10-pound (2.3-4.5 kg) ankle weights or holding a dumbbell against each thigh near the knees. Adding ankle weights for distance cardiovascular exercise may alter your gait and is not advised. To target the outer hip, used for duckwalking and sidestepping, include the hip abductor band sidestep (page 235), band clam abduction (page 235), and straight-leg raise abduction (page 236). Look for steep grassy hills or several flights of stairs and practice doing the same wide steps and traverses you make with snowshoes. Steep ascents require you to travel on the balls of your feet (which can tire the calves) or drop the heels (which stretch the calves). In each strength workout, build endurance in the calves and ankles by including one-leg standing calf raises (page 268) or seated calf raises (page 269).

Cross-Country Skiing

Efficiency in cross-country skiing requires arm strength to help maintain glide. Skiers using the diagonal technique require core stability, complete range of motion in the shoulders and legs, and strength endurance in the gluteals, hamstrings, triceps, and deltoids. The triceps push-down (page 259), bent-arm pullover (page 258), and dumbbell overhead press (page 251) can increase upper-body strength; the dumbbell lunge (page 273), leaning lunge (page 274), and one-leg Bulgarian squat (page 272) are suitable lower-body exercises. To target the lower back, hamstrings, and core, try the good morning (page 265), Romanian deadlift (page 262), dirt digger (page 222), push-up ball roll-in (page 229), or wood chopper (page 227).

The skating technique requires abductor and gluteal endurance in conjunction with flexible adductors and hip flexors. This technique is more advanced than the diagonal technique and requires greater balance and lateral stability in the core. Suitable exercises include the one-leg deadlift (page 263), the hip abductor band sidestep (page 235), the one-arm lat pull-down (page 249), the straight-leg raise abduction (page 236), the dirt digger (page 222), and the barbell back squat (page 270) with a wide stance.

Randonee Skiing

To handle steep terrain and remote backcountry, AT skiers need additional endurance in the shoulders, core, and upper back. You should include exercises such as variations of the dumbbell bench press (page 253) or the push-up (page 255), the barbell military press (page 252), the seated row (page 247), the one-arm dumbbell row (page 246), the back extension (page 233), and the forward barbell roll-out (page 230). You can add lower-body plyometric exercises following a solid month of base training with traditional strength training. Plyometric exercises added to bilateral work develop explosive strength and prepare the legs for going airborne or tackling extreme downhill terrain. Add 1 or 2 of the following exercises into your program for several weeks and work up to doing all four (2 to 3 sets each) in a single workout. Perform for number of footfalls or for set time. You will feel these in your calves and quadriceps, not to mention your heart and lungs. In each workout, see if you can add 5 seconds of work or 4 to 5 jumps to each set. Start with 30 seconds of jumping for 2 sets per exercise and build to sets of 60 seconds as your fitness increases.

Lateral Hops Jump sideways over a line, back and forth, with your feet as close together as they would be on skis. Keep your torso upright and do not stay on the floor for too long—try to be up in the air as long as you can.

V Jumps Jump forward and left and then back to start, and then jump forward and right and back to start, as though you are drawing the letter *V* with your feet. Hold your arms as if you were holding ski poles.

Square Jumps Imagine you are standing in a square with all four corners fair game for jumping. Keep your feet close together and jump forward, left, backward, and right, or jump in other combinations to create Z or X patterns. If fancy footwork confuses you, simply jump rope to gain plyometric benefits for your calves and quadriceps.

Tuck Jumps As you jump, lift your feet as far off the ground as possible and try to tuck your knees into your chest. You may feel more comfortable jumping twice to each tuck (jump, jump, tuck, repeat). Reach your hands to your shins with each tuck jump as your knees come up to the chest in order to encourage high jumps.

Telemark Skiing

Telemark ski preparation parallels that of AT skiing, with two notable exceptions. To prepare the quadriceps for the free-heel downhill turn, shorten the stride of the dumbbell lunge (page 273) so that you touch the back knee to the forward heel when lunging. Doing the lunge with the back or front foot elevated requires more from the abductors and adductors and mimics the position you need when going downhill on free-heel skis. Plyometric training is not as important for telemark skiing, since such training is predominantly for fixed-heel AT or alpine downhill skiing.

Flexibility Needs

In skiing and snowshoeing, a full range of motion through the shoulders, hip flexors, and hamstrings enables high steps, awkward gait, double poling, skate skiing, ascents, and descents. Since some of these movements are not easily duplicated on dry land, a good stretching routine can help to prepare you for snow challenges as well as restore flexibility following a day of snow play. Stretches for the hamstrings, abdominals, and lower back are especially useful for the double-pole technique, which generates forward movement from the arms and torso.

The following stretches are particularly helpful for snowshoers and backcountry skiers: leg swings (page 213), arm circles (page 214), standing dowel (ski pole) torso rotation (page 214), stair calf stretch (page 217), bench hamstring stretch (page 218), and 90-90 quadriceps psoas stretch (page 219). As in all sports, get moving the day after any snow outing, as a low-intensity recovery workout can reduce muscle soreness and restore flexibility. This workout can take the form of a short walk followed by the recommended stretches, a yoga session, a swim, or a bike ride.

Additional Considerations

For any long-day or multiday tours, skiers and snowshoers may carry greater weight than their summer counterparts carry due to cold weather needs: more gear, food, clothing, and emergency supplies. Since snow travel has a limited window of opportunity in many parts of the world, snow sport enthusiasts may participate in complementary summer sports such as hiking or mountain biking. You should include strength training year round to maintain and increase your strength for your chosen sports at appropriate times.

Due to the increased strenuousness of the snow sports (additional weight, colder weather, wetter conditions) the caloric needs will be greater for winter alpine travel than for a warm-weather hike of the same distance. You should eat the same recommended macronutrient ratio during the summer and the winter except that your quantities should be 10 to 15 percent greater for your winter sport. A 170-pound (77.1 kg) male skier carrying a 40-pound (18.1 kg) pack may expend 3,500 calories in 6 hours. At altitude, where an appetite may drop to 50 percent of that at sea level, it becomes even more crucial to eat regularly and frequently. Hydration is very important for snow sports. In cold weather it can be less obvious when you need to stop to refuel. By drinking 20 fluid ounces (600 ml) of liquid per hour, you should consume 136 fluid ounces (4 L) per half day of skiing. The skier inhales cold, dry air that has to be heated within the body, which requires additional energy. At the same time, the skier releases moisture-laden air with every exhalation, adding to dehydration simply by being in colder

©Jimmy Chin/Aurora Photos

Winter ski mountaineering requires careful selection of appropriate gear and clothing to confront cold, wind, and moisture.

air. Factor in the extra work required by exercising and shivering to keep the body warm, and the energy and carbohydrate requirements of snow sport athletes increase even more.

Backcountry athletes need to know how to read changing weather, snow, and slope conditions in order to avoid avalanches, whiteouts, and storms. They also need additional layers of clothing, particularly since their sports involve high degrees of aerobic activity (and hence sweating); stove, fuel, and a small pot for boiling water; and a shovel and avalanche gear, all of which add to winter pack weight. Skiers need to select proper clothing to confront cold, wind, and moisture; they also need to be alert for signs of hypothermia and frostbite.

Assessing Fitness and Gauging Improvement

In many cases, snowshoers and skiers train and perform fitness evaluations on dry land before they ever see snow. The most applicable fitness tests for the different snow sports vary since the training components and needs vary widely, but all snow sport athletes should periodically assess their long-distance endurance. AT and telemark skiers can include the ramp test and should perform the lower-body strength tests more frequently than snowshoers and cross-country skiers perform them. The best-fit test for snowshoers, telemark skiers, and AT skiers is a 30-minute field test on a high-ramp elliptical trainer, a StepMill, a stair-climber, or an incline treadmill (that reaches a 10 percent grade or higher). Cross-country skiers can in-line skate or roller ski on a fixed-distance track or use the NordicTrack. Upper-body strength tests can pinpoint weaknesses in assistance muscles and should be done monthly, particularly for cross-country skiers.

After a month of training and every 4 weeks thereafter, do a best-fit test on a nearby hilly, snowy course with a pack weight aligned with your end objective. Be sure the area is a low avalanche risk so that you can repeat the test often. For the test, ski or snowshoe for 2 hours to assess your average pace, elevation gain, and distance traveled. Each time you do the same route, try to decrease your total travel time including breaks or maintain previous performance with increased pack weight. A heart rate monitor can help you track your uphill effort, and an altimeter can gauge your rate of ascent and descent. To determine your relative improvement in both strength and endurance, alternate between flatter outings that involve fast and light travel and steeper outings that involve a heavier pack. As your comfort level increases and soreness diminishes, expand your effort by 5 to 15 percent per week until you are able to do moderately difficult trips with more gain, heavier load, or greater distance.

Keep track of snow conditions as you train: Heavy wet snow can slow you down and cause significant soreness in the hip flexors and hips. Fresh powder may make travel easy. Icy conditions can result in nearly impossible ascents or super fast descents. Poor footing and backsliding are expected when snowshoeing on steep or icy slopes or for the beginner first learning proper snowshoe technique. The same terrain that is easy to cross in summer may take additional time and effort in winter. Breaking trail through deep, fresh powder can feel harder for snowshoers than kicking steps under icy conditions feels for mountaineers. Sometimes traveling a half mile (.8 km) an hour on rolling terrain can feel fast, while other times it may be possible to travel upwards of 3 miles per hour (4.8 kph). A slower-than-usual outing may result from improper fueling, from snow, or from poor weather; it may also indicate inadequate preparation or undertraining.

Creating a Long-Term Program

Always start your planning by focusing on the end goal. Consider the distance of your goal trip, the total elevation gain and loss, the highest elevation, the terrain variability, the pack weight, the total time anticipated for the outing, the skill level and training required, and, perhaps most importantly, the season of your trip, as you will want to time your training to match the season of abundant snowfall. If your assessment points to particular areas that need strengthening, prioritize your preseason training to address these weaknesses first. Include exercises that will help with muscle balance, joint integrity, and stability, particularly if your off-season training or cross-training sport does not require the same muscles or movements.

The following chart summarizes the amount of training time you will need in order to prepare for a goal given the sport, difficulty level, trip duration, elevation change, and pack weight. If you are new to a snow sport, keep in mind the amount of skill you will need to master it. The following training time recommendations are only for physical preparation once you have attained the necessary skill. The heavier your pack, the longer your trip, or the more elevation change you expect to encounter, the more time you will want to allow for preparation. Note that if your goal shares at least one variable with goals at the intermediate or advanced levels, include the training time suggested for the higher level indicated in the chart. For example, if you will be doing a 6-mile telemark ski trip (9.7 km; intermediate) carrying a 15-pound pack (6.8 kg; beginner) for just over 3,200 feet of elevation gain (975 m; advanced), you will want to allow 12 to 16 weeks to prepare for the distance and elevation gain.

Difficulty	Trip duration; distance traveled	Elevation	Pack weight	Training time above baseline
SNOWSHOEING: VARIED NONTECHNICAL ALPINE TERRAIN				
Beginner	Single day; <5 mi. (8.0 km)	<1,200 ft. (366 m) gain	<20 lb. (9.1 kg)	6 weeks
Intermediate	Single day; <12 mi. (19.3 km)	<3,000 ft. (914 m) gain	<30 lb. (13.6 kg)	10 weeks
Advanced	Overnight; >12 mi. (19.3 km)	>3,000 ft. (914 m) gain	>30 lb. (13.6 kg)	16 weeks

(continued)

(continued)

Difficulty	Trip duration; distance traveled	Elevation	Pack weight	Training time above baseline
CROSS-COUNTRY SKIING: LIGHT PACK, RELATIVELY LEVEL TERRAIN				
Beginner	Single-day; <6 mi. (9.7 km)	Negligible	<15 lb. (6.8 kg)	6 weeks
Intermediate	Single day; 6-12 mi. (9.7-19.3 km); 10K, 15K races	<600 ft. (183 m) gain	<20 lb. (9.1 kg)	12 weeks
Advanced	Multiple successive days; >12 mi. (19.3 km) each; 30K, 50K races	>600 ft. (183m) gain	>20 lb. (9.1 kg)	16 weeks
TELEMARK OR RANDONEE SKIING: STEEP, REMOTE BACKCOUNTRY TERRAIN				
Beginner	Single-day; <5 mi. (8.0 km)	<1,000 ft. (305 m) gain	<20 lb. (9.1 kg)	6 weeks
Intermediate	Single-day; 5-12 mi. (8.0-19.3 km)	<3,000 ft. (914 m) gain	<30 lb. (13.6 kg)	12 weeks
Advanced	Multiday tour; >12 mi. (19.3 km) each	>3,000 ft. (914 m) gain	>30 lb. (13.6 kg)	16 weeks

If you participate in multiple snow sports, design a well-rounded program that has training components for each sport. Include several combination outings before leaving for a multisport adventure. Such a combination outing might include a lift-serve, a strength-dominant day the first day, a distance day the second, and a recovery or off day the third.

Your in-season and off-season training routines will look considerably different, especially if you participate in multiple sports. Off-season skiers may choose to train for strength 3 days a week (i.e., Monday, Wednesday, and Friday) while training longer cardiovascular sessions twice weekly and taking backcountry trips or off days on weekends. In-season skiers may opt to switch to strength training twice a week, a long midweek cardiovascular session, a shorter high-intensity session, and skiing on the weekends, with a day off before or after the weekend ski or both, depending on how much recovery is needed. Include 5 to 10 minutes of stretching with any workout or outing. The general conditioning recommendations for snowshoeing, cross-country skiing, and backcountry skiing are to build to the following weekly workloads by the time you are 2 weeks from goal. Be sure to stretch with every workout.

Type	Number of weekly workouts 2 weeks from goal	Number of strength workouts	Number of cardio-vascular workouts	Number of sport-specific weekly workouts	Weekly exercise time
Beginner snowshoe	4	2 30 min. full body	3	2 hr. hilly walk, hike, or snowshoe	5-6 hr.
Intermediate snowshoe	5	2 45 min. full body	3-4	1 beginner snowshoe, 3-4 hr.	6-9 hr.
Advanced snowshoe	5-6	2-3 45 min. full body	3-4	1 intermediate snow-shoe, 4-6 hr., at least 1 B2B before overnight trip	8-15 hr.
Beginner cross-country ski	4	2 30 min. full body	3	2-hr. hike or short ski	5-6 hr.
Intermediate cross-country ski	5	2 45 min. full body	3-4	1 beginner 3-4 hr. cross-country ski, 15 lb. (6.8 kg) pack	8-10 hr.
Advanced cross-country ski	6	2 1 hr. full body	4-5 (1 anaerobic)	1 all-day intermediate cross-country ski tour, 20 lb. (9.1 kg) pack	12+ hr.
Beginner backcountry ski	4	2 30 min. full body	3	1 beginner 2-3 hr. hilly walk or snowshoe, 20 lb. (9.1 kg) pack	5-6 hr.
Intermediate backcountry ski	5	2 45 min. full body	4	1 beginner backcountry ski outing or snowshoe, 30 lb. (13.6 kg) pack	8-10 hr.
Advanced backcountry ski	6	2 1 hr. full body	5 (1 anaerobic)	1 midweek pack workout; 1 intermediate backcountry ski outing or snowshoe, 40 lb. (18.1 kg) pack	10-15 hr.

B2B=back-to-back

Sample Goals and Associated Programs

The following sample programs introduce you to snow sport programs designed to match specific goals. Use these for insights into how you can manipulate training variables to design your own program. The sample programs address a beginner cross-country ski outing, an intermediate one-day snowshoe adventure, and an advanced backcountry ski trip. Each program assumes that you have established a baseline of at least two weekly distance sessions of 45 minutes each, two 30-minute strength sessions, and a 1-hour hike or ski of 4 to 6 miles (6.4-9.7 km) with 15 pounds (6.8 kg).

■ BEGINNER CROSS-COUNTRY SKI

This program is suitable for a person embarking on a goal such as a 5.5-mile (8.9 km) flat tour around Keechelus Lake, Washington, that involves traveling along the railroad grade while carrying 15 pounds (6.8 kg). For a beginner cross-country ski trip with minimal gain, include a 3-week strength block and a 3-week stamina block to prepare the hips, lower back, and upper body for such full-body effort. Suitable cardiovascular training options for this program include working on a NordicTrack or an elliptical trainer with arms, in-line skating, roller skiing, trail or treadmill running, and walking with a pack.

Intensity Guidelines

Recovery	<65 percent MHR
Distance	65 to 75 percent MHR
Tempo	75 to 85 percent MHR
Interval	85 to 95 percent MHR

Week	Day 1	Day 2	Day 3	Day 4	Day 5	Weekend
			BUILD ENDURANCE			
1	45 min. recovery	30 min. tempo; A1 strength	45 min. distance	Off	A2 strength	1 ski 3 mi. (4.8 km) *or* walk 45 min., 10 lb. (4.6 kg)
2	50 min. recovery	33 min. tempo; A1 strength	50 min. distance	Off	A2 strength	1 ski 3.5 mi. (5.6 km) *or* walk 45 min., 12 lb. (5.7 kg)
3	55 min. recovery	36 min. tempo; A1 strength	55 min. distance	Off	A2 strength	1 ski 4 mi. (6.4 km) *or* walk 50 min., 15 lb. (6.8 kg)
			BUILD STRENGTH AND SPEED			
4	45 min. recovery	40 min. pyramid, 15 lb. (6.8 kg); B1 strength	60 min. distance	Off	B2 strength	1 ski 4.5 mi. (7.2 km) *or* walk 50 min., 18 lb. (8.2 kg)
5	45 min. recovery	45 min. pyramid, 18 lb. (8.2 kg); B3 strength	60 min. distance	Off	B1 strength	1 ski 5 mi. (8.0 km) *or* walk 1 hr., 20 lb. (9.1 kg)
6	Off	45 min. tempo; B2 strength	45 min. distance	30 min. recovery	Off	Goal: ski 5.5 mi. (8.9 km), 15 lb. (6.8 kg)

■ INTERMEDIATE SNOWSHOE

This program is suitable for a person attempting a 10-mile (16.1 km) winter snowshoe trip up Mount Pilchuck, Washington, that involves a 2,900-foot (884 m) gain and a 25-pound (11.3 kg) pack. When leaving for such a winter trip, be certain there are no avalanche hazards at the time you go or else choose your route wisely. After attaining the baseline suggested earlier, you can safely embark on this kind of intermediate program. Suitable cardiovascular training modes are similar to those for hiking and include training on a high-ramp treadmill (8-15 percent grade), an elliptical trainer, a stair-climber, or a StepMill; trail running; climbing stairs or hills; skiing; or snowshoeing.

Intensity Guidelines

Recovery	<65 percent MHR
Distance	65 to 75 percent MHR
Tempo	75 to 85 percent MHR
Interval	85 to 95 percent MHR

Week	Day 1	Day 2	Day 3	Day 4	Day 5	Weekend
			BUILD ENDURANCE			
1	60 min. distance	45 min. tempo, 15 lb. (6.8 kg); B1 strength	Off	60 min. distance	B2 strength	1 hike, ski, or snowshoe 4-6 mi. (6.4-9.7 km), 1,500 ft. (457 m) gain, 18 lb. (8.2 kg)
2	60 min. distance	45 min. tempo, 18 lb. (8.2 kg); B3 strength	Off	65 min. distance	B1 strength	1 hike, ski, or snowshoe 4-6 mi. (6.4-9.7 km), 1,750 ft. (533 m) gain, 21 lb. (9.5 kg)
3	60 min. distance	45 min. tempo, 21 lb. (9.5 kg); B2 strength	Off	70 min. distance	B3 strength	1 hike, ski, or snowshoe 4-6 mi. (6.4-9.7 km), 2,000 ft. (610 m) gain, 24 lb. (10.9 kg)
			BUILD STRENGTH			
4	45 min. recovery	30 min. uphill, 24 lb. (10.9 kg); D1 strength	75 min. distance	Off	45 min. tempo; D2 strength	1 hike, ski, or snowshoe 5-7 mi. (8.0-11.3 km), 2,000 ft. (610 m) gain, 24 lb. (10.9 kg)

Week	Day 1	Day 2	Day 3	Day 4	Day 5	Weekend
			BUILD STRENGTH *(continued)*			
5	45 min. recovery	30 min. uphill, 27 lb. (12.2 kg); D1 strength	80 min. distance	Off	45 min. tempo; D2 strength	1 hike, ski, or snowshoe 5-7 mi. (8.0-11.3 km), 2,250 ft. (686 m) gain, 26 lb. (11.8 kg)
6	50 min. recovery	35 min. uphill, 30 lb. (13.6 kg); D1 strength	85 min. distance	Off	50 min. tempo; D2 strength	1 hike, ski, or snowshoe 5-8 mi. (8.0-12.9 km), 2,500 ft. (762 m) gain, 28 lb. (12.7 kg)
			BUILD STAMINA			
7	55 min. recovery	40 min. repeat, 25 lb. (11.3 kg); E3 strength	90 min. distance, 20 lb. (9.1 kg)	Off	50 min. tempo; E1 strength	1 hike, ski, or snowshoe 6-8 mi. (9.7-12.9 km), 2,500 ft. (762 m) gain, 30 lb. (13.6 kg)
8	60 min. recovery	40 min. uphill, 28 lb. (12.7 kg); E2 strength	90 min. distance, 25 lb. (11.3 kg)	Off	55 min. tempo; E3 strength	1 hike, ski, or snowshoe 7-9 mi. (11.3-14.5 km), 2,600 ft. (792 m) gain, 32 lb. (14.5 kg)
9	45 min. recovery	45 min. fartlek; E1 strength	90 min. distance, 30 lb. (13.6 kg)	Off	60 min. tempo; E2 strength	1 hike, ski, or snowshoe 5 mi. (8.0 km), 1,500 ft. (457 m) gain, 15 lb. (6.8 kg)
			PEAK AND TAPER			
10	45 min. distance; E3 strength, upper only, 3 sets of 16 reps	30 min. tempo	45 min. distance	30 min. recovery	Off	Goal: 10 mi. (16.1 km) round-trip, 2,900 ft. (884 m) gain, 25 lb. (11.3 kg)

■ ADVANCED RANDONEE SKI

This program is suitable for a person preparing for a 1-day ski tour up the 8,365-foot (2,550 m) Mount Saint Helens (Washington) in April with a gain of 4,500 feet (1,372 m) in 10 miles (16.1 km) and a pack weight of 30 pounds (13.6 kg). Although the single-day status and rather moderate terrain for skiing (less than 30 degrees) may qualify this trip as an intermediate ski, the amount of elevation gain in a single day also qualifies it as an advanced ski, setting this objective right on the cusp between intermediate and advanced. Such a trip requires significant endurance and familiarity with snow travel but does not require a high degree of technical ski skills. The 16-week program builds from the baseline suggested earlier and includes cardiovascular training options that range from working on the NordicTrack, elliptical trainer, incline treadmill, stair-climber, StepMill, VersaClimber, or Jacob's Ladder to in-line skating or roller skiing to climbing stairs or hills. Plyometric exercises can be included in lower-body sessions during weeks 9 through 14.

Intensity Guidelines

Recovery	<65 percent MHR
Distance	65 to 75 percent MHR
Tempo	75 to 85 percent MHR
Interval	85 to 95 percent MHR

Week	Day 1	Day 2	Day 3	Day 4	Day 5	Weekend
			BUILD FOUNDATION			
1	45 min. distance	20 min. uphill, 12 lb. (5.4 kg); A1 strength	Off	30 min. tempo; A2 strength	Off	1 ski or hike 4 mi. (6.4 km), 1,000 ft. (305 m) gain, 15 lb. (6.8 kg)
2	50 min. distance	20 min. uphill, 12 lb. (5.4 kg); A1 strength	Off	35 min. tempo; A2 strength	Off	1 ski or hike 4 mi. (6.4 km), 1,250 ft. (381 m) gain, 15 lb. (6.8 kg)
3	50 min. distance	25 min. uphill, 15 lb. (6.8 kg); A1 strength	45 min. recovery	35 min. tempo; A2 strength	Off	1 ski or hike 4-5 mi. (6.4-8.0 km), 1,500 ft. (457 m) gain, 18 lb. (8.2 kg)
4	55 min. distance	25 min. uphill, 15 lb. (6.8 kg); A1 strength	50 min. recovery	40 min. tempo; A2 strength	Off	1 ski or hike 5 mi. (8.0 km), 1,750 ft. (533 m) gain, 18 lb. (8.2 kg)

Week	Day 1	Day 2	Day 3	Day 4	Day 5	Weekend
			BUILD ENDURANCE			
5	60 min. distance	30 min. uphill, 20 lb. (9.1 kg); B1 strength	Off	75 min. distance	45 min. tempo; B2 strength	1 ski or hike 6-7 mi. (9.7-11.3 km), 2,000 ft. (610 m) gain, 20 lb. (9.1 kg)
6	60 min. distance	33 min. uphill, 20 lb. (9.1 kg); B3 strength	Off	75 min. distance, 10 lb. (4.5 kg)	45 min. tempo; B1 strength	1 ski or hike 6-8 mi. (9.7-12.9 km), 2,300 ft. (701 m) gain, 20 lb. (9.1 kg)
7	65 min. distance	30 min. pyramid, 20 lb. (9.1 kg); B2 strength	Off	75 min. distance, 15 lb. (6.8 kg)	50 min. tempo; B3 strength	1 ski or hike 6-8 mi. (9.7-12.9 km), 2,600 ft. (792 m) gain, 20 lb. (9.1 kg)
8	70 min. distance	33 min. pyramid, 20 lb. (9.1 kg); B1 strength	Off	75 min. distance, 20 lb. (9.1 kg)	50 min. tempo; B2 strength	1 ski or hike 6-8 mi. (9.7-12.9 km), 3,000 ft. (914 m) gain, 23 lb. (10.4 kg)
			BUILD STRENGTH			
9	35 min. repeat; C1 strength	75 min. distance, 25 lb. (11.3 kg)	45 min. recovery; C2 strength	Off	45 min. tempo; C3 strength	1 ski or hike 10 mi. (16.1 km), 2,500 ft. (762 m) gain, 25 lb. (11.3 kg)
10	38 min. repeat; C4 strength	75 min. distance, 28 lb. (12.7 kg)	45 min. recovery; C1 strength	Off	45 min. tempo; C2 strength	1 ski or hike 6-8 mi. (9.7-12.9 km), 3,500 ft. (1,067 m) gain, 28 lb. (12.7 kg)
11	40 min. repeat; C3 strength	60 min. distance, 28 lb. (12.7 kg)	50 min. recovery; C4 strength	Off	45 min. tempo; C1 strength	1 ski or hike 10 mi. (16.1 km), 2,500 ft. (762 m) gain, 28 lb. (12.7 kg)
			BUILD STAMINA			
12	45 min. repeat; E1 strength	80 min. distance, 30 lb. (13.6 kg)	60 min. distance	Off	45 min. tempo; E2 strength	1 ski or hike 6-10 mi. (9.7-16.1 km), 4,000 ft. (1,219 m) gain, 30 lb. (13.6 kg)
13	35 min. recovery; E3 strength	90 min. distance	75 min. distance, 30 lb. (13.6 kg)	Off	45 min. tempo; E1 strength	1 ski or hike 10 mi. (16.1 km), 3,500 ft. (1,067 m) gain, 25 lb. (11.3 kg)

(continued)

Advanced Randonee Ski *(continued)*

Week	Day 1	Day 2	Day 3	Day 4	Day 5	Weekend
			BUILD STAMINA *(continued)*			
14	50 min. repeat; E2 strength	60 min. recovery	90 min. distance, 33 lb. (15.0 kg)	Off	45 min. tempo; E3 strength	1 ski or hike 6 mi. (9.7 km), 2,500 ft. (762 m) gain, 35 lb. (15.9 kg)
			PEAK AND TAPER			
15	45 min. recovery; E1 strength	30 min. fartlek	75 min. distance, 25 lb. (11.3 kg)	40 min. tempo; E2 strength	Off	1 ski or hike 6 mi. (9.7 km), 2,000 ft. (610 m) gain, 20 lb. (9.1 kg)
16	E3 strength	45 min. distance	35 min. tempo	30 min. recovery	Off	Goal: Mount Saint Helens skin ski, 10 mi. (16.1 km), 4,500 ft. (1,372 m) gain, 30 lb. (13.6 kg)

Exercises for Peak Performance

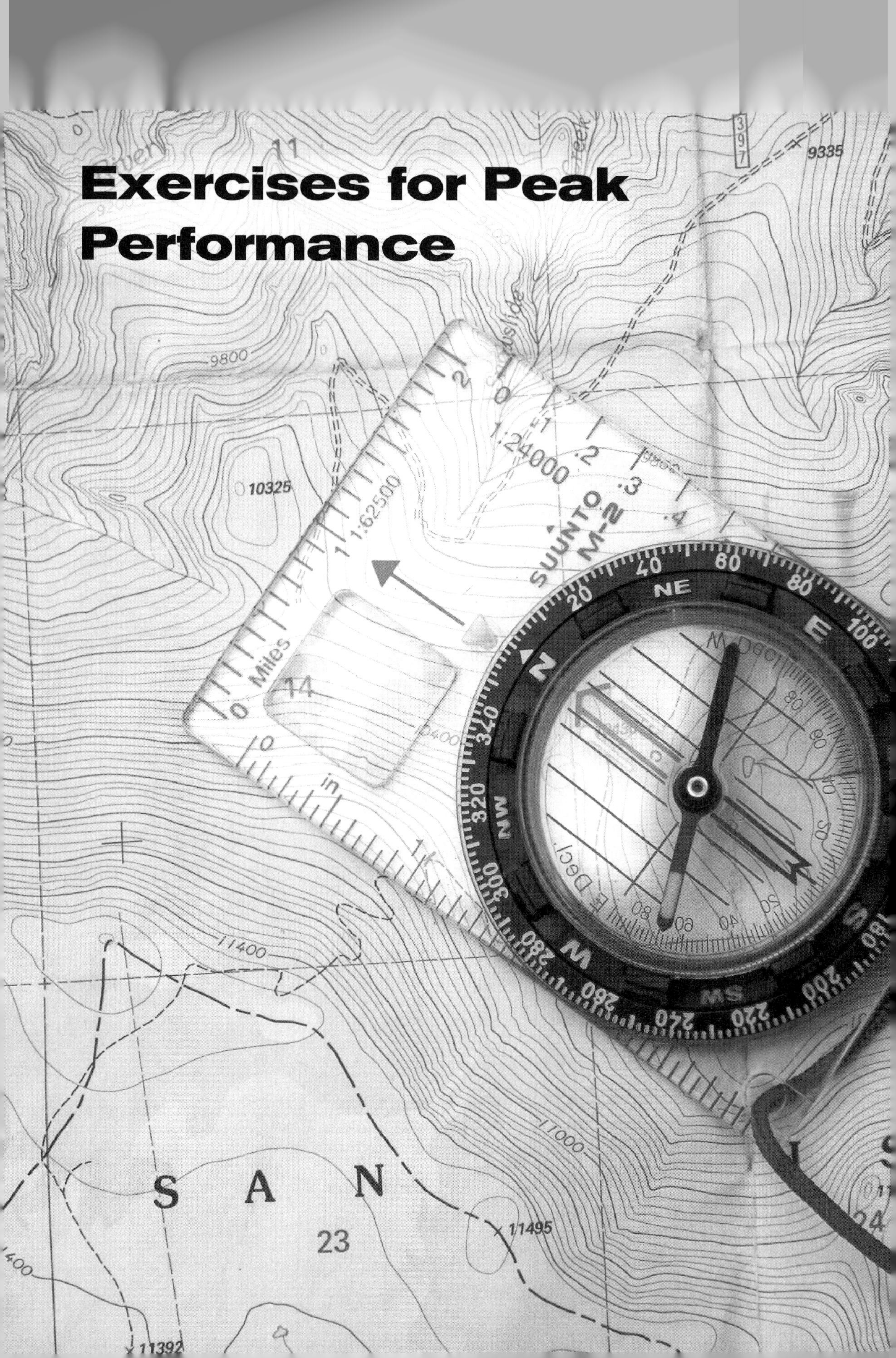

Exercise Finder

Category	Exercise name	Page number	TYPE OF EXERCISE: Primary (P) or secondary (S)	Unilateral (U) or bilateral (B)	Horizontal (H) or vertical (V) (for push/pull exercises)
CHAPTER 14: FLEXIBILITY AND MOBILITY					
Dynamic stretches	Leg swings	213	P	U or B	N/A
	Arm circles	214	P	U or B	N/A
	Standing dowel torso rotation	214	P	U or B	N/A
	Lying trunk rotation	215	S	U or B	N/A
Active stretches	Downward dog	215	P	U	N/A
	Triangle pose	216	P	U	N/A
	Piriformis stretch	216	S	U	N/A
	Straddle hamstring stretch	217	S	B	N/A
	Stair calf stretch	217	S	U or B	N/A
	Frog stretch	217	P	B	N/A
Static stretches	Seated gluteal stretch	218	P	U	N/A
	Bench hamstring stretch	218	P	U	N/A
	90-90 quadriceps psoas stretch	219	P	U	N/A
	Tree hug stretch	219	S	U or B	N/A
	Trapezius stretch	219	S	U	N/A
CHAPTER 15: BODY STABILIZATION AND SUPPORT					
Core stability exercises	Saxon dumbbell overhead side bend	221	S	U	N/A
	Dirt digger	222	P	U	N/A
	Decline crunch	223	S	B	N/A
	Medicine ball twist	224	P	U	N/A
	Plank	225	S	B	N/A
	Straight-leg sit-up	226	P	B	N/A
	Wood chopper	227	P	U	N/A
	Reverse torso curl	228	S	B	N/A
	Push-up ball roll-in	229	S	B	N/A
	Forward barbell roll-out	230	P	B	N/A
	Bridge	231	S	U or B	N/A
	Ball adduction	232	S	B	N/A
	Back extension	233	P	B	N/A

APPLICABLE OUTDOOR SPORTS						
Hiking	Mountain-eering	Climbing	Trail running	Off-road biking	Paddling	Snowshoeing and skiing
CHAPTER 14: FLEXIBILITY AND MOBILITY						
		X	X		X	X
	X	X			X	X
X	X		X		X	X
		X		X		
		X	X	X	X	
X	X				X	
		X				X
		X	X			
		X	X	X		X
X	X	X			X	
X			X			
X			X			X
	X		X	X	X	X
	X	X		X	X	
X	X	X			X	X
CHAPTER 15: BODY STABILIZATION AND SUPPORT						
		X			X	
		X		X		X
	X			X		
	X	X			X	
	X			X	X	
		X			X	
	X				X	X
		X				
		X				X
		X		X		X
X	X	X	X	X	X	X
			X			X
X	X	X	X	X	X	X

Category	Exercise name	Page number	TYPE OF EXERCISE: Primary (P) or secondary (S)	Unilateral (U) or bilateral (B)	Horizontal (H) or vertical (V) (for push/pull exercises)
CHAPTER 15: BODY STABILIZATION AND SUPPORT					
Body stabilization exercises	External rotation	234	S	U	N/A
	Hip abductor band sidestep	235	S	U or B	N/A
	Band clam abduction	235	S	U	N/A
	Straight-leg raise abduction	236	S	U	N/A
	Wrist extension	237	S	U or B	N/A
	Thor pronation	238	S	U	N/A
	Dorsiflexion	239	S	U or B	N/A
	Rope face pull	240	S	U or B	N/A
CHAPTER 16: STRENGTH					
Upper-body pull exercises	Pull-up, chin-up, floor-assisted pull-up	242	P	B	V
	Lat pull-down	243	P	U or B	V
	Shrug: dumbbell, barbell, pack	244	S	U or B	V
	Horizontal pull-up	245	P	B	H
	Row: one-arm dumbbell, bent, two-arm, rhomboid	246	P	U or B	H
	Seated row, rotation	247	P	U or B	H
	Biceps curl: EZ bar, hammer, traditional	248	S	U or B	N/A
	Straight-arm standing lat pull-down	249	S	U or B	N/A
	Bent-over dumbbell raise	250	S	B	N/A

APPLICABLE OUTDOOR SPORTS						
Hiking	Mountain-eering	Climbing	Trail running	Off-road biking	Paddling	Snowshoeing and skiing
CHAPTER 15: BODY STABILIZATION AND SUPPORT						
	X	X			X	X
X	X				X	X
			X		X	X
X						X
	X	X			X	
		X			X	
			X			X
		X				X
CHAPTER 16: STRENGTH						
	X	X			X	X
		X				X
X	X					X
	X	X	X		X	
X	X	X	X	X	X	X
		X			X	X
		X			X	
X					X	X
			X	X		X

Category	Exercise name	Page number	TYPE OF EXERCISE: Primary (P) or secondary (S)	TYPE OF EXERCISE: Unilateral (U) or bilateral (B)	TYPE OF EXERCISE: Horizontal (H) or vertical (V) (for push/pull exercises)
CHAPTER 16: STRENGTH					
Upper-body push exercises	Dumbbell overhead press: standing, sitting	251	P	U or B	V
	Barbell military press, standing push press	252	P	B	V
	Dumbbell bench press	253	P	U or B	H
	Narrow-grip barbell bench press	254	P	B	H
	Push-up	255	P	B	H
	Dumbbell fly	256	S	U or B	H
	Parallel bar dip	257	P	B	V
	Bent-arm pullover	258	S	B	H
	Triceps push-down	259	S	U or B	V
	Lying dumbbell triceps extension, standing (variation)	260	S	U or B	V
Hamstring-dominant lower-body exercises	Barbell deadlift	261	P	B	N/A
	Romanian deadlift	262	P	B	N/A
	One-leg deadlift	263	P	U	N/A
	Hamstring pull-through	264	P	B	N/A
	Good morning	265	P	B	N/A
	Machine leg curl	266	S	U or B	N/A
	Ball leg curl: two-leg, one-leg	267	S	U or B	N/A
	Standing calf raise	268	S	U or B	N/A
	Seated calf raise	269	S	B	N/A
Quadriceps-dominant lower-body exercises	Barbell back squat	270	P	B	N/A
	Barbell front squat	271	P	B	N/A
	One-leg Bulgarian squat	272	S	U	N/A
	Backward lunge	272	S	U	N/A
	Dumbbell lunge, walking lunge	273	P	U	N/A
	Leaning lunge	274	S	U	N/A
	Step-up	275	P	U	N/A
	Lunge step-up	276	P	U	N/A
	Reverse step-up	277	S	U	N/A
	Leg press	278	S	U or B	N/A

N/A=Not applicable

APPLICABLE OUTDOOR SPORTS						
Hiking	Mountaineering	Climbing	Trail running	Off-road biking	Paddling	Snowshoeing and skiing
CHAPTER 16: STRENGTH						
X	X	X	X	X	X	X
		X			X	
		X	X	X	X	X
		X			X	X
	X	X	X			X
		X	X	X		
		X				
					X	X
	X	X				X
X					X	
X	X	X		X		
			X		X	X
X	X	X	X		X	X
	X			X		X
		X				X
			X	X		X
		X				X
X	X	X	X			X
			X			X
	X	X		X	X	X
X					X	X
X		X	X	X		X
X	X			X		
X	X	X	X			
	X	X				X
X	X	X	X			
	X	X		X		X
X	X	X	X			
			X	X		

Flexibility and Mobility

The 15 exercises in this chapter are dynamic, active, and static stretches specific to the sports discussed in part II. Studies indicate that stretching done before a workout should incorporate dynamic stretches geared toward warming up the body and increasing range of motion. Since statically held stretches done *before* strength training can prevent maximal firing of the muscles, you should perform static and active stretches at the end of workouts or right *after* working a certain muscle group to help restore flexibility to the targeted muscles. Dynamic stretches start out with small movements and, as the muscles warm up and stretch, ever increasing range of motion through a joint. Active stretches engage muscles to hold a fixed position while static stretching involves passively lengthening a muscle in a held position; both are relatively ineffective for warm-ups but can be used to help the body cool down and the muscles elongate following exercise.

To save time, select strength exercises that will strengthen your body while simultaneously increasing your range of motion. Such exercises include the Romanian deadlift (page 262) for the lower back and hamstrings and the bent-arm pullover (page 258) and dumbbell fly (page 256) for the chest and shoulders. Stretches that include a mild strength component are the triangle pose (page 216) for the hamstrings, obliques, and chest; the downward dog (page 215) for the shoulders, hamstrings, and calves; and the frog stretch (page 217) for the hips, calves, and lower back. Remember these five stretching tips:

1. Learn when to strengthen rather than stretch. If you have excessively mobile joints (e.g., in the ankles, shoulders, or lower back); if you hyperextend your back, elbows, or knees; or if you know you are quite flexible, rather than stretching you may need strength training in order to tighten the muscles that protect the joints.
2. Keep stretches pain free. Avoid rapid movements unless you are performing dynamic stretches. Perform dynamic stretches for 30 to 60 seconds until your joints are warm.
3. Hold static and active stretches for at least 30 seconds. During the first 15 seconds of a stretch, your body tries to protect you from stretching too far by tensing the muscle (the opposite of what you want), but after the first 15 seconds your body will relax and allow you to deepen the stretch. Holding for too short a time does not allow you to enter the relaxation phase.

4. Coordinate breathing with stretching. Take advantage of your body's natural relaxation process. Inhale deeply to begin, and exhale fully as you deepen the stretch.
5. Stretch your tightest areas first. Tight areas may inhibit areas that are naturally looser. Within tight regions, begin by stretching the larger groups and then move to the smaller ones: hamstrings, gluteals, quads; lower back, abs; chest, latissimus dorsi; shoulders, arms; and forearms, calves.

Eccentric muscle contractions can cause inflammation, muscle spasms or cramps, fluid retention (swelling), or even tiny tears in muscle tissue. These tears cause damaged cells to release chemical substances that stimulate nerve endings and register pain. Thus, such pain is caused by tissue inflammation rather than lactic acid buildup. As soon as the tissues recover, the pain subsides. Stretching immediately after eccentric training sessions and as part of an active recovery following sessions of intense exercise may help reduce DOMS, as can performing several weeks of strength training before beginning any eccentric training such as downhill trail running, scrambling, hiking, or climbing. Establish a good daily stretching routine and maintain full range of motion for as long as possible.

Dynamic Stretches

LEG SWINGS

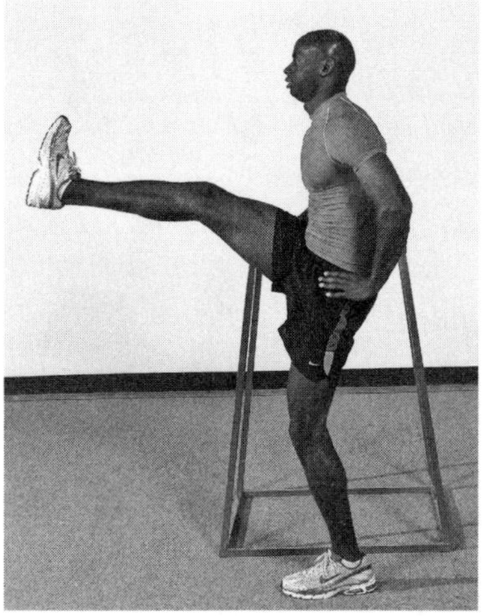

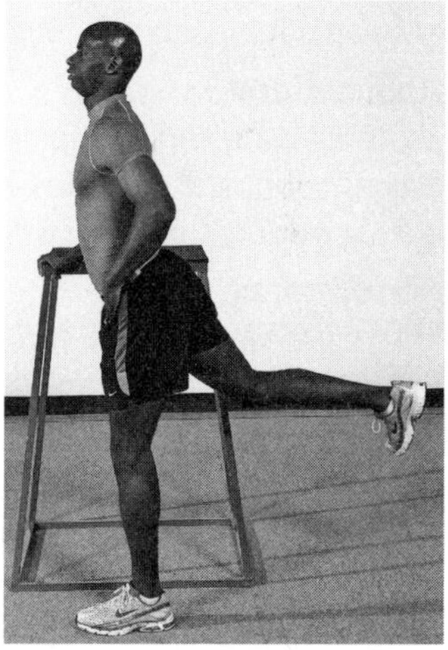

Muscle Groups Stretched

Hamstrings, hip flexors, abductors, adductors (to side)

Applications

Benefits biking, trail running, skiing, and climbing; helps with shortened hamstrings

Performance

Stand next to a wall or high support that allows you room to kick forward and backward. Hold the support and balance firmly on one leg. Gently swing your other leg forward and backward, letting it kick higher in both directions with each repetition. Keep your torso still and eyes focused on a point in front of you so you can gauge how high you kick with your first leg; duplicate that range of motion when working the other leg. For additional range of motion in the hip abductors and adductors (especially for technical climbers and skate skiers), face the wall or support and then swing the non-weight-bearing leg side to side. With practice you should be able to abduct (move the foot away from the body) up to hip level without leaning excessively sideways.

Dynamic Stretches

ARM CIRCLES

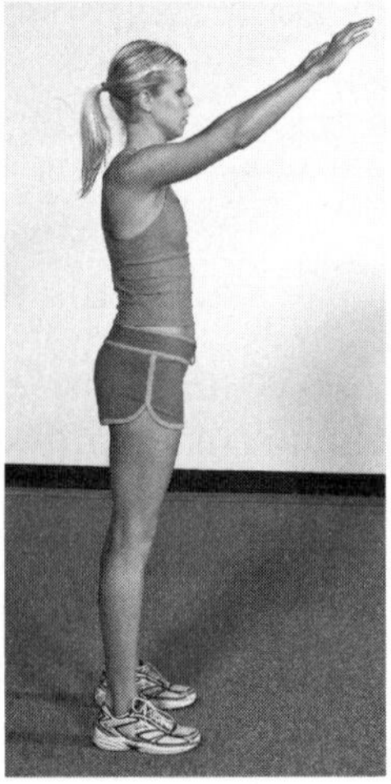

Muscle Groups Stretched
Pectorals, rhomboids, deltoids

Applications
Benefits paddling, climbing, cross-country skiing, and swimming; makes a good addition to upper-body strength sessions

Performance
Lift your arms straight out to your sides, holding them parallel to the ground. Make small backward circles, rotating through the shoulder joint, gradually increasing the circumference of the circle until your arms are rotating in giant circles that reach above the head and down to the thighs. Complete 30 seconds of easy backward circles and then repeat going forward.

STANDING DOWEL TORSO ROTATION

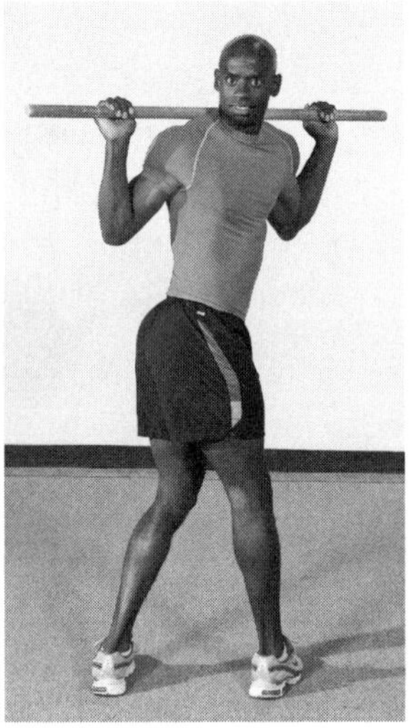

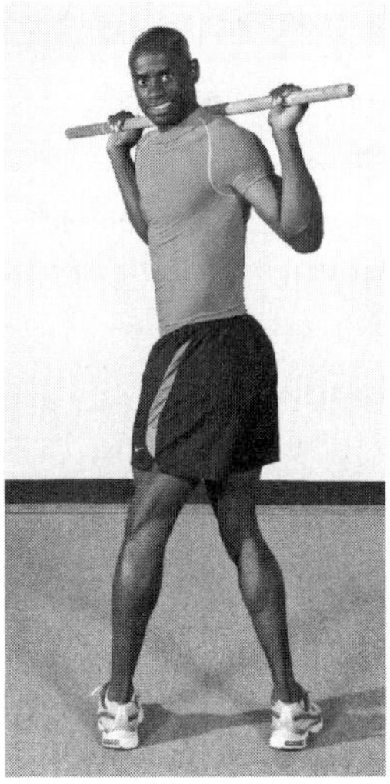

Muscle Groups Stretched
Obliques, latissimus dorsi, pectorals, lower-back muscles

Applications
Benefits paddling, climbing, skiing, trail running, and activities requiring excessive torso mobility

Performance
Place a dowel across the back of your shoulders and stand with your feet shoulder-width apart with arms outstretched and hands lightly clasping the dowel. Extend tall out of the spine and gently rotate your torso right and left. Allow the head to turn with the shoulders so that you activate all the trunk and hip muscles. Start with small movements and gradually increase the range of motion, keeping your shoulders level and eventually allowing your feet to pivot as you near the end of your warm-up.

LYING TRUNK ROTATION

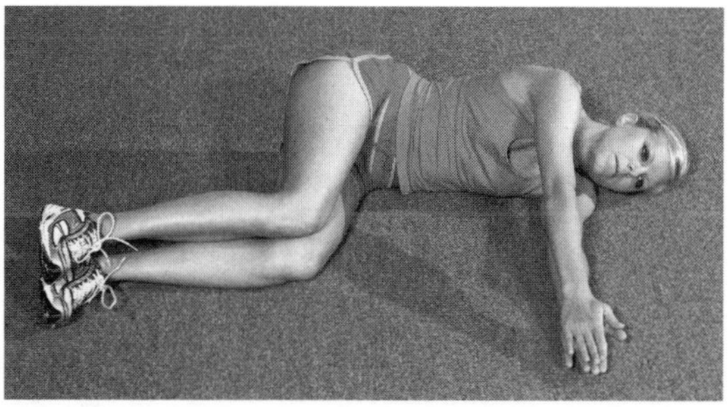

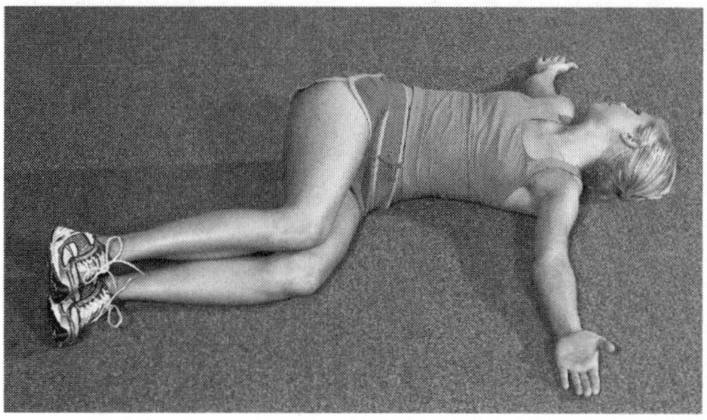

Muscle Groups Stretched
Obliques, lower back, pectorals, deltoids

Applications
Great for all sports; helps anyone feeling tight in the upper, mid-, or lower back (this stretch provides relief similar to that of chiropractic adjustments without adding strain to the hips or lower back)

Performance
Lie on your left side with your arms extended straight out in front of you and your legs drawn toward your chest so that they from a right angle to your torso; place a pillow between the stacked knees. Keep your legs relaxed and your left shoulder on the floor throughout the movement. Inhale. As you exhale, raise your right arm and rotate your upper torso until your right shoulder touches the floor; return to the starting position and repeat the desired number of times. Then turn onto your right side and repeat the entire stretch.

DOWNWARD DOG

Muscle Groups Stretched
Hamstrings, lower-back muscles, pectorals, deltoids, calves

Applications
Benefits running, paddling, and climbing

Performance
Get down onto your hands and knees on a mat. Curl your toes underneath you and gently lift your hips, pressing back onto both feet so that your heels press down to the floor. Straighten your arms and lower your head, pressing your chest toward the thighs so that you form an inverted V. Contract the quadriceps to increase the stretch through the hamstrings. To modify this stretch for tight hamstrings, place your hands on a low step or bend one leg and press only one heel to the floor at a time. If you feel any discomfort in the shoulders, lower back, or hamstrings, try the triangle pose instead.

Active Stretches

TRIANGLE POSE

Muscle Groups Stretched

Pectorals, deltoids, obliques, latissimus dorsi, hamstrings

Applications

Benefits climbing, paddling, and skiing

Performance

Stand with your legs several feet apart, with your right toes slightly turned in and left toes turned to the side so that your left heel lines up with your right arch. Keep both legs straight and open the arms wide apart, keeping your hands level with the shoulders. Shift your right hip to the right as you lean directly to the left and place your left hand on your knee, shin, or ankle or onto a yoga block. Extend your right arm toward the ceiling, palm facing forward, expanding across the front of the body. Repeat to the other side, turning your left toes slightly inward and your right toes to the side.

PIRIFORMIS STRETCH

Muscle Groups Stretched

Piriformis, gluteals, hip muscles

Applications

Benefits hiking, mountaineering, climbing, running, and skiing

Performance

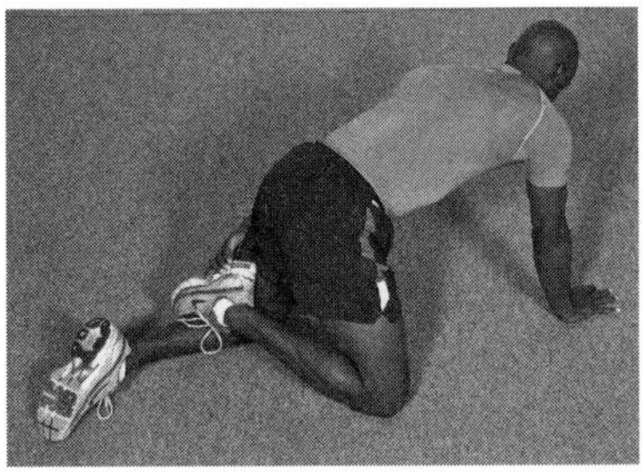

To stretch the right hip, start on your hands and knees with your right ankle resting directly behind your left knee and at a right angle to both knees. Move your right hand off to the right and simultaneously shift your hips and shoulders smoothly to the right until you feel a stretch in the right hip. Avoid lateral flexion or rotation of the pelvis or trunk. Reverse and repeat for the left hip. Move into this position rhythmically as a dynamic stretch in a warm-up or hold it for an active stretch as part of a cool-down.

STRADDLE HAMSTRING STRETCH

Muscle Groups Stretched
Hamstrings, lower-back muscles, adductors

Applications
Great for running, paddling, and climbing

Performance
Stand in a straddle position with your feet as wide apart as comfortable and your toes pointing forward. Bend forward at the hips, keeping your weight in your heels. Use a bench for torso support as needed. Work toward touching your hands, forearms, or elbows to the floor.

STAIR CALF STRETCH

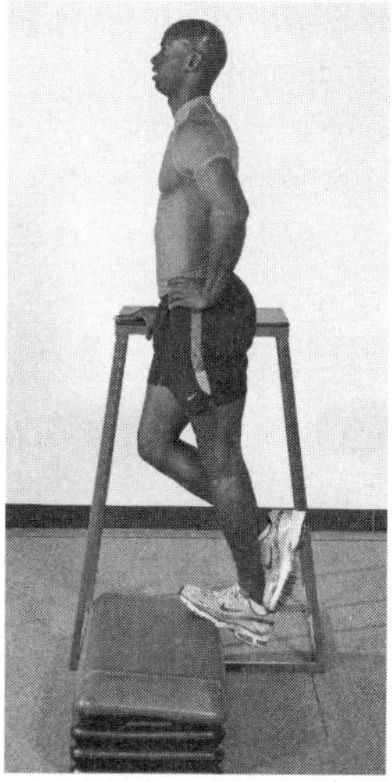

Muscle Groups Stretched
Gastrocnemius

Applications
Benefits running, climbing, hiking, and skiing; particularly useful following crampon work, friction slab climbing, or dynamic high-impact movements

Performance
Stand with the ball of one foot on the edge of a step or curb and hold onto a stable object for balance. Lower the heel while contracting the gluteals. Reposition your foot if it starts to slip. Start with the tighter calf first. To deepen the stretch, perform it (on one leg or two) with a pack or barbell across your shoulders.

FROG STRETCH

Muscle Groups Stretched
Hips, lower-back muscles, adductors, calves

Applications
Good for skiing, mountaineering, and technical climbing

Performance
Stand with your feet shoulder-width apart and sink into a full squat, keeping your heels flat on the floor and allowing your torso to lean forward slightly without collapsing over your knees. Press your elbows against your knees to increase the stretch in your hips and inner thighs. Extend the torso upward. As your flexibility increases, begin this stretch in a wider stance. If you cannot keep your heels down, start with the stair calf stretch to stretch tight calves or press your knees open while sitting on a bench. If you experience knee discomfort in a low squat position, try the straddle hamstring stretch instead.

SEATED GLUTEAL STRETCH

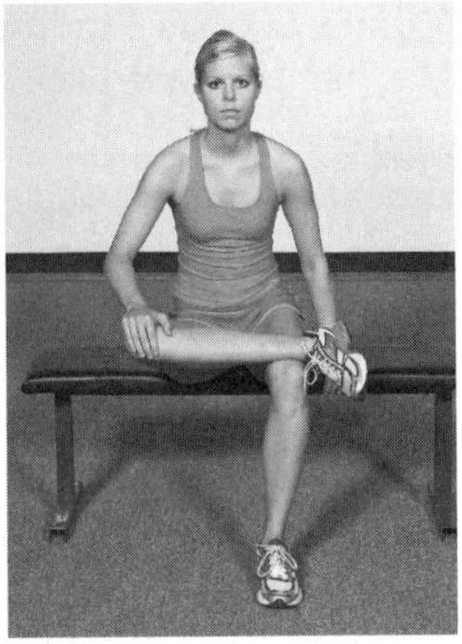

Muscle Groups Stretched
Gluteals, lower-back muscles

Applications
Benefits hiking, biking, trail running, snowshoeing, mountaineering, and skiing

Performance
Sit on a bench with your right ankle over your left knee. Press the chest forward, keeping your back flat, and press the right knee down gently to open up the hip. To vary the stretch, bring the knee up toward your chest. To do this stretch while lying on the floor, place the right ankle over the left knee and reach through the window of your leg; clasp your hands under the left thigh or on the left shin and draw the leg close to your chest. Repeat with the left side. If you have a history of hip dysfunction, this may not be the best stretch for you; seek professional guidance to get a suitable recommendation for your particular needs.

BENCH HAMSTRING STRETCH

Muscle Groups Stretched
Hamstrings, gluteals, lower-back muscles

Applications
Good for paddling, running, and skiing; particularly useful in cold weather when hamstrings start to tighten

Performance
Use a car bumper, log, or bench to elevate one leg and place your hands on your hips. With your chest lifted, back flat, and hips squared forward, bend forward at the waist so that you feel the pull in your hamstrings, not your back. The toes of the standing leg should point toward the bench rather than point to the side. Press the tailbone back and pull your toes up to increase the stretch through your hamstrings.

90-90 QUADRICEPS PSOAS STRETCH

Muscle Groups Stretched

Quadriceps, hip flexors, lower-back muscles

Applications

Benefits running, biking, skiing, snowshoeing, and climbing

Performance

While on a mat, sit on your left hip and bend your left leg 90 degrees in front of you. Ease your right leg behind you and gently pull your right foot toward your buttocks. Rotate your torso to the left until you can rest on your elbows. Press the right hip forward and feel a stretch through the quadriceps and hip flexors. Repeat to the other side.

TREE HUG STRETCH

Muscle Groups Stretched

Latissimus dorsi, deltoids, arm muscles, lower-back muscles, hamstrings

Applications

Good for climbing, paddling, and skiing; useful following upper-body strength workouts

Performance

While standing, face a small tree or a vertical pole. Wrap your hands around it a little below shoulder level. Bend forward and lean back with straight arms and legs until you feel a good pull along the back of your body. Position your hands at different levels to target various areas of your back. Perform with one arm at a time for a more intense stretch.

TRAPEZIUS STRETCH

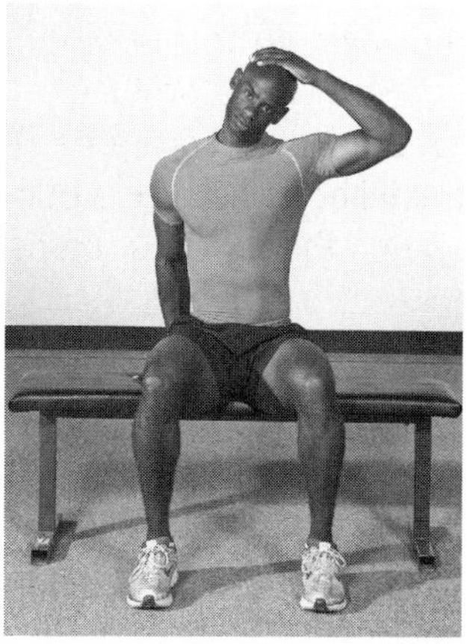

Muscle Groups Stretched

Trapezius

Applications

Benefits hiking, mountaineering, climbing, paddling, and skiing; good for anyone carrying excessive tension in the upper back and neck

Performance

Sit tall on a bench with knees at a right angle to your torso. Place your left hand on the side of the head near your right ear while your right hand rests on the bench just behind your back. Gently draw your left ear toward your left shoulder until you feel a good stretch along the right side of the neck. To increase the stretch, tilt your head to look down toward the fingers and lean your head slightly forward. Repeat to the other side.

Body Stabilization and Support

Outdoor sports are dynamic, three-dimensional activities for which core stability forms the foundation for developing strength throughout the entire body. Core stability exercises will help you develop sport-specific strength in the abdominals, obliques, and lower back. The body stabilization exercises included in this chapter will help you shore up inherently weaker areas that might limit your strength development from the exercises in chapter 16. The descriptions, performance cues, and pictures for the exercises in chapters 15 and 16 should be used as reminders for someone who is already familiar with these exercises. If a specific exercise is new to you, seek professional guidance on attaining the proper form. For future reference, a listing is provided in the exercise finder (page 206).

Always maintain good posture and a neutral spine when performing strength exercises. Complete each movement through its entire range of motion so your muscles gain full benefit. Control both the concentric (lifting) and eccentric (lowering) portions of every repetition. If you experience pain or discomfort when performing any exercise, reduce the weight, try a variation with a smaller range of motion and then work up to a full range of motion, or try another exercise for the same muscle group. Master form before adding weight, increasing range of motion, or attempting variations. Start with an assessment of your current strength levels and select exercises from these two chapters to address your weak areas before embarking on an overall sport-specific strength program. Always include an active warm-up before strength training and always stretch afterward.

SAXON DUMBBELL OVERHEAD SIDE BEND

Muscle Groups Involved

Obliques

Performance

Hold one dumbbell in both hands or a light dumbbell in each hand, with your arms straight up into the air and the weights directly over your shoulders. Stand with your feet shoulder-width apart, knees slightly bent, and abdominals tight. Inhale and stretch to one side as far as feels comfortable; exhale as you return to center. Repeat to the other side and alternate for the desired number of repetitions.

Precautions

- If you feel discomfort in your lower back, reduce or eliminate the weight.
- Avoid bending forward or backward on this exercise.
- Extend tall, out of the spine, from start to finish so you can fully engage the obliques.

Variations

- Use a weight plate, light barbell, or medicine ball in place of the dumbbells.
- To perform the one-arm side bend, hold one dumbbell or loaded EZ bar at your side. Stand with your feet shoulder-width apart and place your other hand behind the head. Inhale and lower straight to the side as far as you feel comfortable. Exhale and return to vertical.

DIRT DIGGER

Muscle Groups Involved

Quadriceps, gluteals, hamstrings, obliques, spinal erectors, deltoids, biceps, grip muscles

Performance

Stand with your feet shoulder-width apart. Cup a fairly substantial dumbbell in both hands and hold it in front of your body. Squat as though to touch the dumbbell to the floor just in front of you, keeping your chest up and forward, your eyes up, and your back flat (not vertical); your weight should be in your heels. Exhale and stand, gently rotating to one side, your eyes and torso following the weight as you raise the dumbbell to your shoulder. Alternate side to side.

Precautions

- Avoid hyperextending the back at the top of the movement; keep your torso long and extend out from the crown of the head. Be sure you have built core strength before performing this exercise, as it involves torso rotation and multiple muscle groups.
- Keep the dumbbell fairly close to your body to avoid shoulder strain.

Variation

To work the spinal erectors, legs, and entire abdominal wall, try vertical swings: Lift a dumbbell or medicine ball straight up overhead, as though you might throw it. Contract your abdominals intensely to prevent yourself from overextending.

DECLINE CRUNCH

Muscle Groups Involved

Rectus abdominis

Performance

Lie flat on your back on a slant board with your feet looped under the ankle support, your legs elevated higher than your head, your knees bent, and your hands across your chest or behind your head with your elbows out to the side. Exhale and peel your shoulders off the board while pressing the small of your back into the board. Keep your elbows back to prevent pulling on the neck. To protect the lower back, keep your trunk slightly flexed throughout and avoid resting completely at the bottom position. Inhale and return to the starting position, keeping your muscles contracted.

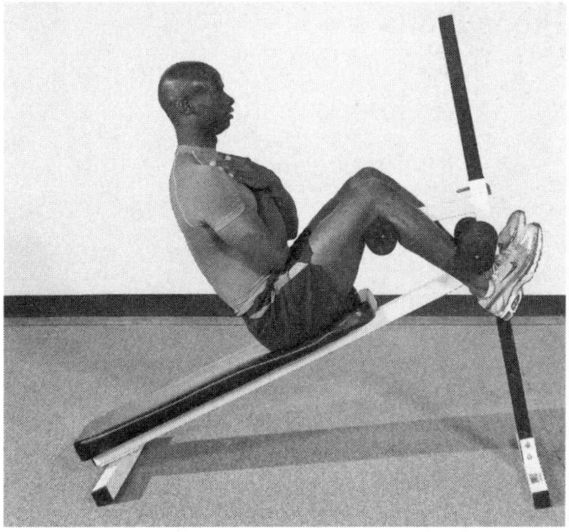

Precautions

- If exercises involving forward flexion are contraindicated for you, perform pelvic tilts (contract and relax with the abdominals) rather than peeling your shoulders off the board.
- Perform floor or ball crunches if you experience any discomfort in your lower back.

Variations

- For the floor crunch, lie on a mat on the floor with your knees bent 90 degrees, your feet resting on the floor or on a bench, and your hands across the chest or behind the head. Exhale as you lift your shoulder blades off the bench, pressing the ribs toward the hips and navel toward the floor. Inhale as you lower.
- To perform the ball crunch, choose a ball of appropriate size: If you are 60 to 66 inches (152-168 cm) tall, use a 22-inch (55 cm) ball, and if you are 67 inches (170 cm) or taller, use a 26-inch (65 cm) ball. Lie across it, adjusting until the ball is at the small of your lower back. With your hands behind your head, exhale and peel your shoulders off the ball, simultaneously pressing your navel down into the spine and curling your hips up. Inhale and relax down until your shoulder blades touch the ball. Stretch through the full range of motion with each repetition.

MEDICINE BALL TWIST

Muscle Groups Involved

Rectus abdominis, obliques

Performance

Sit on the floor and lean back 10 to 30 degrees with your knees bent and feet remaining flat on the floor. Hold a medicine ball, dumbbell, or weight plate in your hands. Keep your abdominals tight to protect the lower back as you lean back. Inhale as you twist gently to one side and exhale as you return to center. Rotate to the other side and repeat side to side for the desired number of repetitions.

Precautions

- Keep your feet solidly on the floor and avoid rotating too far.
- Hold a slightly curved spinal position to help protect the lower back from hyperextension.
- If twisting while flexing is contraindicated for you, choose other exercises.

Variations

- For the twisting dumbbell exchange, start with a dumbbell in your left hand and twist left to place it directly behind you on the mat. Without the weight, quickly rotate to the right and pick up the weight with your right hand; transfer the weight to your left and repeat. Be sure to reverse directions to do the same number of repetitions to the other side.
- For the decline Russian twist, do the same basic motion on a slant board. Your feet should be higher than your hips. Keep the weight closer to your body instead of making a rainbow arc over your torso.
- For the paddling oblique twist, place your palms facing down and 18 to 24 inches (46-61 cm; about the same width you would use with a kayak paddle) apart on a Body Bar, dowel, ski pole, paddle, or light EZ bar. Lean back 30 degrees to activate the abdominals. As you dip the left end of the bar toward the floor, pull down and back slightly with the left hand, push up and forward with the right, and twist your shoulders and torso left to follow the paddle movement, keeping your eyes forward. Repeat with the right end and right hand dipping to the right side.

PLANK

Muscle Groups Involved

Rectus abdominis, lower-back muscles, obliques; variations involve the deltoids, triceps, pectorals, gluteals, or hamstrings

Performance

Start by lying facedown on a mat. Lift onto (a) your elbows, forearms, and knees; (b) your elbows, forearms, and toes; (c) your hands and knees; or (d) your hands and toes. Distribute your weight evenly among the points touching the floor. Hold your abdominals tight to support the lower back, and keep your head aligned with neutral spine by looking down at the floor without dropping your head forward. Build to holding this position for 30 seconds before attempting more advanced versions.

Precautions

- Avoid letting the hips sag. Try the easiest version first and build to advanced versions once you master form.
- If you feel any shoulder discomfort on the elbow versions, try the hand versions instead. If you feel wrist discomfort on the hand versions, use hex dumbbells or push-up stands to allow a neutral position of the wrists.

Variations

Planks are some of the most versatile exercises in your repertoire. By placing your hands or legs on a step or ball, you can increase the intensity for both the core and the upper body; by adding a weight vest or ankle weights, you can increase the challenge for the core, gluteals, and hamstrings.

- Ball plank: Position your knees, shins, or toes on the ball and place your hands shoulder-width apart on the floor. The closer the ball is to your feet, the harder the exercise; start with the ball at your thighs or knees and work toward placing your toes on the ball.

- Elbow circles on ball: Kneel on the floor with your forearms on top of the ball. Inhale, contract the abdominals firmly, and rise onto your toes, holding your arms together tightly. Make 5 to 8 small, slow circles in each direction with your elbows.
- Side plank: Begin on your hands and toes, and then lift one hand off the floor and reach that arm toward the ceiling as you rotate your torso to that side. Stack one foot on top of the other while keeping the hips lifted. Hold that position for 1 to 2 seconds and then rotate back down to the starting plank and rotate to the opposite side.

(continued)

Plank ***(continued)***

- Reverse plank: For this variation, sit with your legs straight out in front of you. Place your palms on the floor behind and outside of your hips. Straighten your arms, exhale, and lift the hips until your body forms a straight line from heels to shoulders. Stop if you experience any shoulder discomfort.

STRAIGHT-LEG SIT-UP

Muscle Groups Involved

Rectus abdominis, psoas

Performance

Sit on a Roman chair or hyperextension rack with your ankles secured, a slight bend in your knees, and your hips supported by the bench but slightly suspended to allow full range of motion. Hold your hands across the chest (beginner) or behind the head (intermediate); you can also hold a weight (at chest for intermediate, behind head for advanced). Inhale as you lower your torso to just above parallel to the floor, keeping a slight curve in the trunk. Exhale as you lift to the starting position.

Precautions

- Keep your abdominals tight and trunk curled throughout this very advanced movement. Do not lower below parallel to the floor.
- If you have any history of lower-back pain, select other exercises.

Variation

If your apparatus allows your feet to rest below waist level, lower your torso backward only until the legs and trunk are aligned; if your feet are even with your waist, lower your torso until you are parallel to the floor.

WOOD CHOPPER

Muscle Groups Involved

Obliques, erector spinae, deltoids

Performance

For this exercise, use a top-attachment cable stack. With a slightly wider than shoulder-width stance, stand with the working side away from the high cable and place your far hand on the handle or rope first. Place your near hand on top of the far hand. Keeping your arms straight and your legs slightly bent, bring the band, weighted cable, or rope across the body on a descending diagonal and end the movement at or slightly below knee level. Allow the hips and trunk to swivel to duplicate a chopping movement.

Precautions

- Since the obliques can handle more weight than the deltoids can handle, if you feel any discomfort in the shoulders, hold the weight or handle close to the body like you do for the dirt digger.
- If you are using free weights (see the following variations), avoid hyperextending at the top position. Control the weight at all times.

Variations

- Perform a free-weight version using medicine balls, dumbbells, or a weight plate.
- Experiment with the reverse wood chopper, holding a low-cable attachment and moving upward diagonally across the body.

REVERSE TORSO CURL

Muscle Groups Involved

Lower abdominals, hip flexors

Performance

Lie on your back on a mat, floor, or slant board with your ankles crossed and your feet lifted above the knees. Your legs should be fairly straight. Exhale and lift your hips straight up toward the ceiling. Avoid using momentum; use muscle. Inhale as you lower your hips and repeat.

Precautions

- If you experience any discomfort in the lower back, bend the knees.
- Hold onto a heavy bench with your hands if you need assistance lifting the hips off the floor.

Variation

The dead bug is a rehabilitative exercise to help increase lower abdominal strength. Position a band or a shirtsleeve directly under the small of your back and pull on it laterally to be sure that your abdominals remain contracted and the band does not slip. Legs should be bent at the knees at a right angle to allow you to keep your feet close to the buttocks throughout. Contract the abdominals tightly to keep your knees close to your chest. Then, alternating legs, lower one foot to the floor, exhale and return it to the starting position, and lower the other foot to the floor. As your strength increases and you can maintain the pelvic tilt, gradually walk your feet farther away until this becomes a bicycle exercise. If you lose tension in the band under your back, you have moved the feet too far away from your body.

PUSH-UP BALL ROLL-IN

Muscle Groups Involved

Psoas, rectus abdominis; also triceps, deltoids, pectorals (as stabilizers)

Performance

Start in a push-up position with your palms on the floor and your thighs, shins, or toes on the ball. Keep abdominals tight and maintain a straight body line from shoulders to knees in starting position. The closer the ball is to your feet, the harder this exercise will be. Exhale and draw your knees in toward your chest, lifting your hips toward the ceiling. Inhale and return to the starting position.

Precautions

- Keep your hips raised in order to prevent hyperextending the back.
- Use hex dumbbells or push-up bars on the floor to keep the wrists in a neutral position.

FORWARD BARBELL ROLL-OUT

Muscle Groups Involved

Rectus abdominis, hip flexors, triceps, pectorals

Performance

Kneel and place your hands 1 to 2 feet (30-61 cm) apart on a lightly loaded barbell on the floor in front of you. Keeping your abdominals tight, inhale and roll the barbell forward as far as you can while maintaining control, and then exhale as you roll back to start position.

Precautions

- If forward flexion is contraindicated for you, *do not* do this exercise.
- Include this exercise in the late stages of core training once you have built a solid foundation of core strength.
- Avoid letting the back hyperextend at the start or end position.
- Keep your arms straight but not locked to prevent the upper body from fatiguing before the core muscles do.

Variation

To perform the forward ball roll-out, start on your knees facing a ball. Place your palms facedown on the ball, cup hands into fists with knuckles together and heels of hands on the ball, or clasp hands together with pinkies on the ball. Keep your abdominals tight and maintain a straight line from your shoulders to your hips to your knees as you roll the ball forward. As your strength increases, try doing this exercise on your toes.

BRIDGE

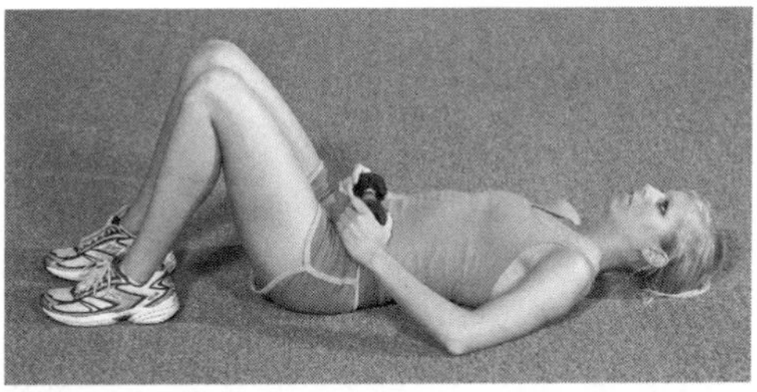

Muscle Groups Involved

Hamstrings, gluteals, erector spinae

Performance

Lie on your back on a mat with your feet shoulder-width apart and about 18 inches (45 cm) from your buttocks. Exhale and raise your hips off the mat by pressing your heels evenly into the floor. Inhale and lower your hips to the floor. To target the gluteals, keep your feet closer to the buttocks; to target the hamstrings, move your feet 24 inches (61 cm) away from the buttocks. Hold a dumbbell, medicine ball, ankle weight, or weight plate at the hips for increased resistance.

Precaution

If you experience neck pain, place a thin, rolled towel under your neck and perform this exercise on a mat.

Variations

- For the unilateral one-leg bridge, lie on your back with your right ankle resting on your left knee or straight up in the air, your left foot flat on the floor about 2 feet (61 cm) from your buttocks, and your arms on the outside of either hip for balance. Exhale and press down on the left foot to raise the hips off the floor. Keep your hips parallel to the floor.
- For the bench bridge, place a step, chair, or weight bench a few feet from your buttocks and rest both heels on the bench, and then lift using one or both legs.
- For the ball bridge, place both feet on a ball and allow the ball to move slightly as you bridge the hips upward until your body forms a straight line from shoulders to ankles.

BALL ADDUCTION

Muscle Groups Involved

Hip adductors, gluteals, hamstrings, erector spinae, anterior tibialis

Performance

Lie on your back on the floor or a mat. Place your feet on the ball and your hands at your sides. Position the feet on either side of the ball like salad tongs; your toes should point up and ankles should press into the ball. Squeeze inward as though to pop the ball. Exhale and raise your hips several inches off the floor until your body forms a straight line from shoulders to ankles, and then inhale and lower back to the floor without relaxing the muscles.

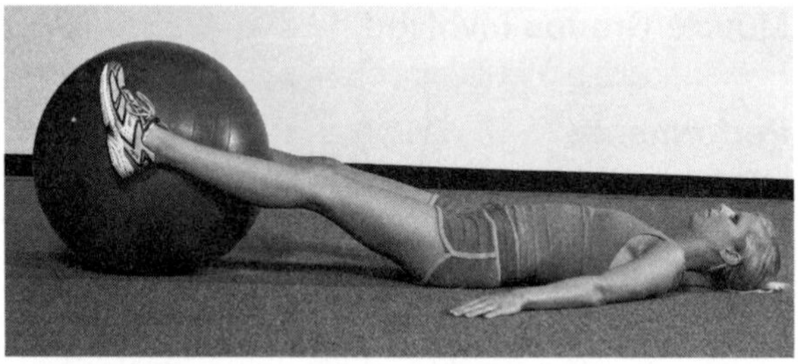

Precaution

If your feet start to slide off the ball, place them above the midline of the ball so that the largest part of the ball is just below your ankles.

Variation

For increased intensity, hold a dumbbell or weight plate against your hip bones with the hands.

BACK EXTENSION

Muscle Groups Involved

Spinal erectors, gluteals, hamstrings

Performance

Position yourself on a hyperextension bench to allow for as much range of motion through the lower back as possible. Secure your ankles under the pad or top roller so that your legs are almost straight. Hang down until your torso is nearly perpendicular to floor. Place your hands at the small of your back, across your chest, or behind your head. Exhale as you lift, inhale as you lower. Lift until torso is parallel to the floor.

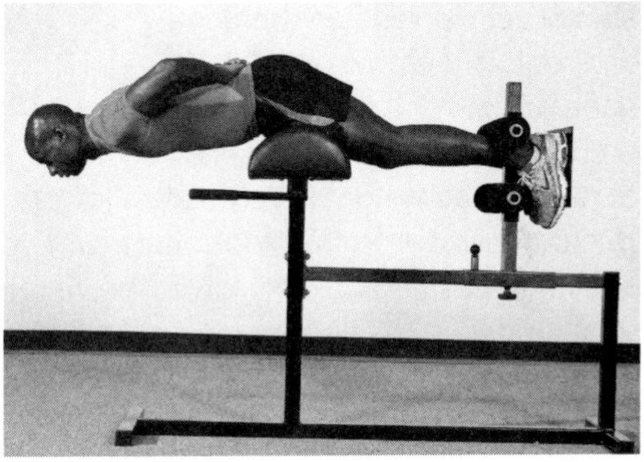

Precautions

- If back hyperextension is contraindicated for you, choose other exercises.
- If you use a bench that positions your hips higher than your feet, only lift until your torso and thighs are aligned; avoid hyperextending the back. Look at the floor to keep the head in neutral alignment.
- If you have low blood pressure, be slow and cautious getting off the bench.

Variations

- For the quadruped variation, kneel with your hands under the shoulders and your knees under the hips. Extend one arm and the opposite leg, keeping your hips and torso still and abdominals tight. Add light dumbbells to each hand or ankle weights to each leg to increase difficulty. Avoid excessive lateral movement of the hips as you raise the limbs. If this is a really weak area, beginners can also start with one leg or arm and go "around the world" one limb at a time.
- For the ball back extension, lie across a ball with your legs wide, feet braced against a wall, and ball at your abdomen. Place your hands at your lower back (beginner) or chest (intermediate) or behind the head (advanced). Exhale and raise your torso up to straighten your body, and inhale as you lower.

EXTERNAL ROTATION (ROTATOR CUFF)

Muscle Groups Involved

External rotators: supraspinatus, infraspinatus, teres minor, subscapularis

Performance

For all rotator cuff exercises, use very light weights and keep the repetitions slow and controlled. Sit on a bench with one knee bent and rest your elbow on your knee. Your foot should be propped in front of you so that when the weight is completely lowered at the end of the repetition, the upper arm remains parallel to the floor. Start with your forearm vertical and hand neutral (arm wrestling position). Slowly lower the weight in an arc toward the midline of your body (maintaining a 90 degree elbow throughout) until your forearm is just above parallel to the floor. Exhale and lift the hand to just shy of vertical and repeat. When finished, do the other side.

Precautions

- Start with your weaker or nondominant arm first and do the same number of repetitions on both sides.
- Keep your torso still; if your torso rocks, reduce the weight.
- If you feel discomfort with very little weight, try the exercise with no weight; if that still causes pain, try another variation or consult a physician.

Variation

For the side-lying rotator cuff rotation, lie on your side on the floor with a towel held snugly between your upper arm and side for support. Start with your elbow bent at 90 degrees and hand facing navel. The upper arm will remain glued to your side, and your elbow should remain at 90 degrees throughout the movement. Exhale and arc the weight upward, stopping just shy of vertical to keep constant tension on the rotator cuff muscles rather than deltoids. Slowly return to your navel and repeat.

HIP ABDUCTOR BAND SIDESTEP

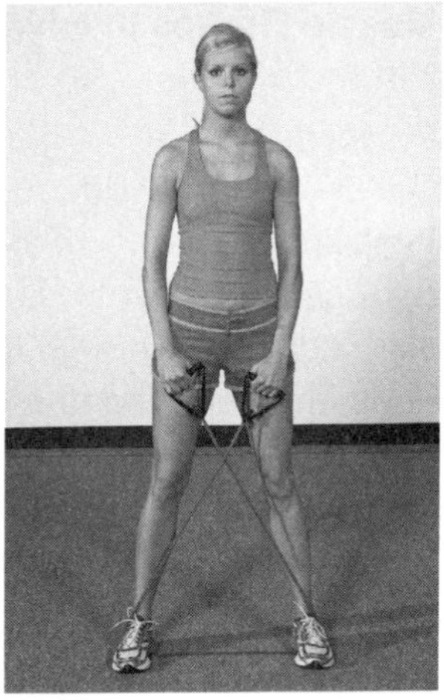

Muscle Groups Involved

Hip abductors

Performance

Stand with both feet on an exercise tube or looped band. Hold the ends in your hands and cross your arms so the band forms an X. Step to the side for 4 to 8 steps, keeping the toes straight forward and pausing with the leg abducted (lifted out to the side) for a second before returning it to the floor and taking your next step. Keep your torso vertical and still throughout the set to avoid lateral rocking.

Precaution

Keep hips squared forward and toes pointing straight ahead.

Variations

- Try sidestepping across a room and back for time.
- Balance on one leg and repeat the desired number of repetitions on one leg before shifting to the other.
- Lower your body into a semisquat and perform the sidestep as described above.

BAND CLAM ABDUCTION

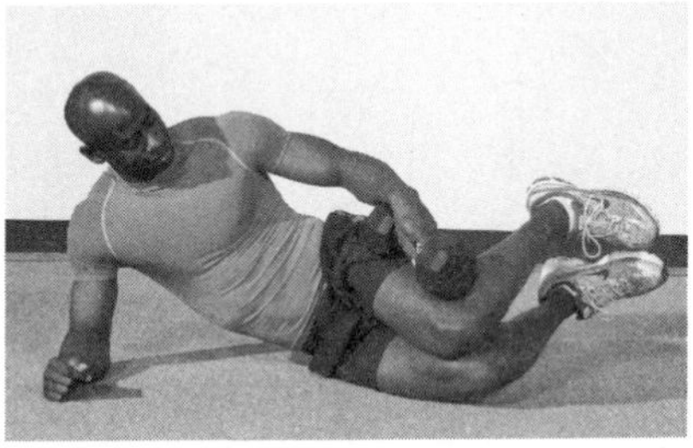

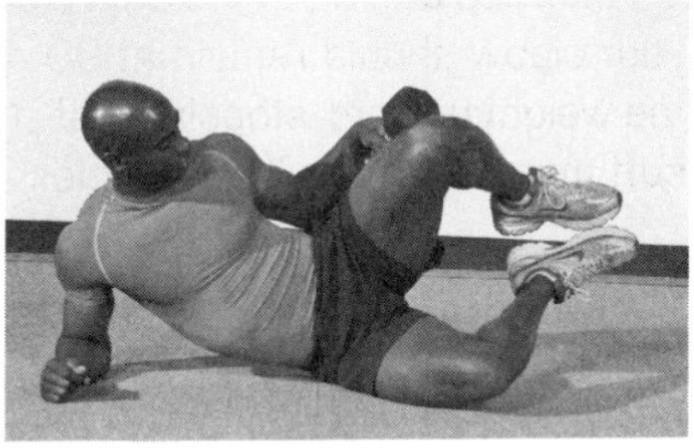

Muscle Groups Involved

Hip abductors, obliques

Performance

Lie on one side on your elbow as shown or with your head resting on your bottom hand, elbow propped on the floor. Your knees should be bent and at a 45-degree angle from your torso. The bottom knee remains on the floor and the ankles stay in the air throughout the exercise. Keeping the feet together, rotate the top knee as if it were opening like a clamshell, squeezing the buttocks to initiate the movement. When you can perform 15 repetitions on each leg, add a looped exercise band around both knees or hold a dumbbell as pictured against the outer thigh close to the knee for increased resistance.

Precaution

If you feel discomfort in your back or neck, lower onto the floor on your arm rather than elbow in order to keep your head and neck in line with the spine. Extend tall out of the shoulder joint and keep abdominals held tight throughout.

STRAIGHT-LEG RAISE ABDUCTION

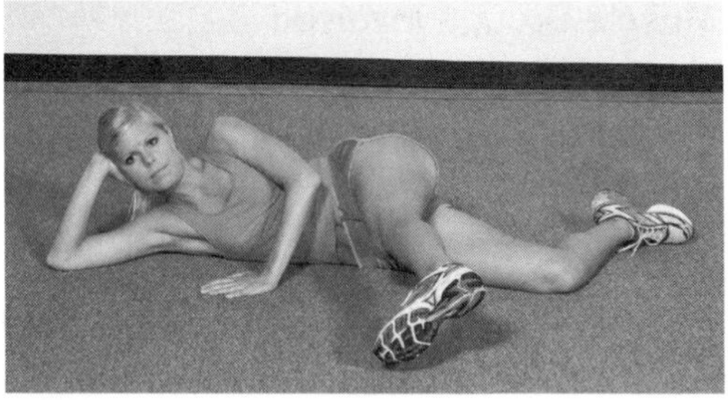

Muscle Groups Involved

Hip abductors

Performance

Lie on one side with your bottom knee bent and top leg extended straight at a right angle to your torso. Keep your hips stacked and your lifted heel above the toes. Avoid rocking the body backward as you raise the leg.

Precaution

If it is difficult to hold the leg at a right angle to the body, include hamstring stretches daily.

Variation

Wear a ski boot or ankle weight or hold a dumbbell at the outer thigh near the knee to add intensity when it becomes too easy to lift the leg without resistance.

WRIST EXTENSION

Muscle Groups Involved

Wrist extensors, biceps

Performance

Sit on a chair or bench and hold very light dumbbells in each hand. Your palms should be facing down. Rest your forearms on the knees and keep your forearms still throughout the movement. Hands hang over the kneecaps. Keep your thumbs alongside the fingers (i.e., all five digits on the same side of the dumbbell rather than overlapping) to allow maximum movement through the wrists. Exhale as you lift your knuckles above the horizontal plane; inhale as you lower.

Precaution

Keep the repetitions high to build endurance in the muscles as well as the tendons and ligaments. If you experience any discomfort, reduce the weight. Use 3 to 8 pounds (1.4-3.6 kg) less weight than what you can use for regular wrist curls (see below).

Variations

- For the regular wrist curl (wrist flexors), turn the palms face up, keep the thumbs alongside the fingers, and lift the weights through the same range of motion you used for the reverse wrist curl.
- For the wrist roll-up, use a dowel attached to a weight by a string at least 3 feet (1 m) long. Start with 3 to 5 pounds (1.4-2.3 kg) and increase by 1 to 2 pounds (.5-.9 kg). Hold the dowel in both hands, palms facing down, dowel parallel to the floor, and arms stretched out in front of the body with upper arms parallel to the floor. Use the forearms to twist the rope onto the dowel in all four directions, controlling weight on the way up and down; avoid letting gravity unravel the weighted cord.

THOR PRONATION

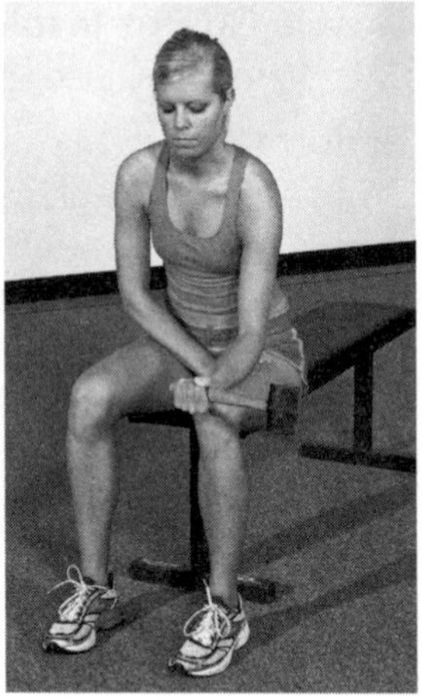

Muscle Groups Involved
Wrist pronators

Performance
Hold an uneven adjustable dumbbell or heavy hammer in one hand. Sit on a bench with your forearm resting on your thigh and the end of the hammer just in front of your kneecap. Hold the weight at one end and allow the rest of it to stick out between the thumb and forefinger. Start at neutral position (hammer pointing straight up) and rotate your hand in a gentle arc from one side to the other. Take care to avoid overextending beyond parallel to the floor in either direction.

Precautions

- For this rehabilitation exercise, keep the weight light and repetitions high.
- If you experience any pain in the elbow, reduce the weight.

Variation
Perform the exercise while kneeling on the floor so that the elbow and wrist are on the floor. This position naturally prevents you from overextending beyond parallel to the floor in either direction.

DORSIFLEXION

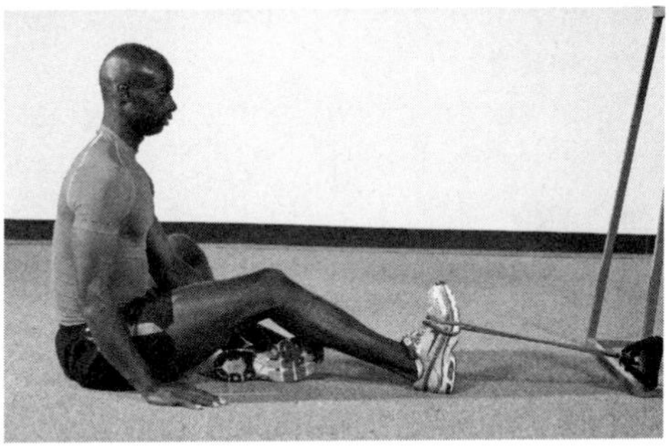

Muscle Groups Involved

Anterior tibialis

Performance

Sit on a bench or the floor with a looped band around your toes. Anchor or tie the other end of the band around a sturdy bench or weight stack. Pull your toes back against the band, moving through your full range of motion.

Precaution

Make certain the band is secure around your anchor and toes so it does not slip off.

Variations

- Turn the foot inward and outward against resistance to work ankle eversion and inversion. This variation is especially helpful in rehabilitating sprained ankles.
- Stand on your heels, hold the wall for support, and perform toe raises for very high repetitions (1-3 minutes) to increase endurance in the front of the shins for racewalking and running.
- For ball dorsiflexion, sit on the floor with legs extended. Cradle a stability ball above your ankles, between the shins and toes of both legs. Heels remain on the floor throughout. Sit with knees slightly bent and abdominals tight. Pull your toes into the ball while pressing against the ball with your hands (arms straight). Perform very high repetitions (20 or more) or add a pause in the fully contracted state.
- If using a weight plate instead of a band, place one end on the floor against a wall so the weight will not move off your foot. Sit on a bench or chair facing the wall with the other end of the plate against the toes. Always wear shoes for the weighted variation.

ROPE FACE PULL

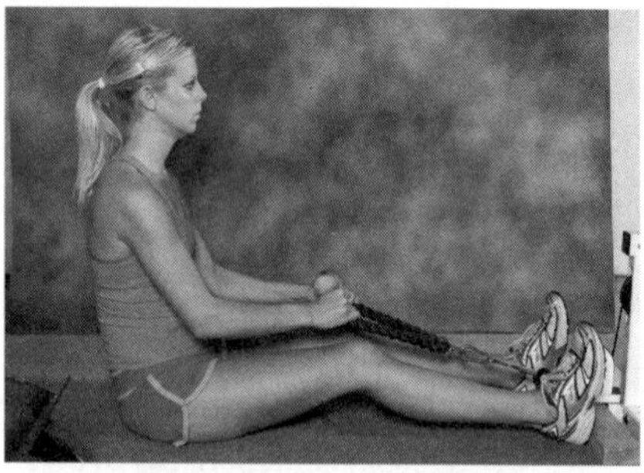

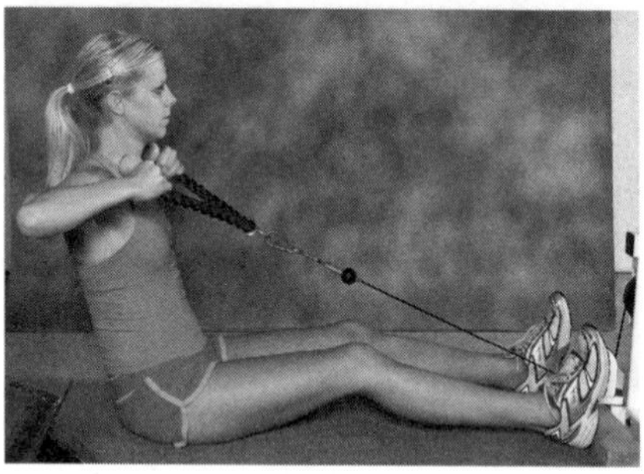

Muscle Groups Involved

Rhomboids, deltoids, biceps

Performance

Sit at a seated row or low pulley system with a rope attachment. Grasp the rope knot between the thumbs and the forefingers. Keep the wrists neutral, shoulders relaxed and away from the ears, and elbows above shoulder level as you pull the hands and rope toward your face. Squeeze the shoulder blades together.

Precaution

Use a weight much lighter than what you can use for seated rows.

Variation

Perform unilaterally with a single hand, your palm facing the floor and your torso still or rotating only slightly.

Strength

Your body can move in many ways, and trying to work all the major muscle groups during one strength workout may take more time than you have available for a single session. In this chapter we describe comprehensive free-weight exercises that provide the highest possible training stimulus by engaging multiple muscle groups simultaneously. These exercises are arranged into the following categories: upper-body pull and push exercises, which are subdivided further (when appropriate) into movements in the horizontal (H) or vertical (V) plane; lower-body hamstring-dominant exercises; and lower-body quadriceps-dominant exercises. The various exercises are either multi-joint (primary, P) or single-joint (secondary, S) movements and are unilateral (U, single limb) or bilateral (B, both limbs). The description for each exercise lists the targeted muscle groups, describes the proper performance, explains the possible variations, and suggests precautions you can take when you feel any discomfort during the exercise. For easy future reference, these exercises, as well as the stretches in chapter 14 and body stabilization and support exercises in chapter 15, are listed in the exercise finder (page 206).

In addition to adhering to the performance tips suggested in chapter 15, be sure to emphasize weak areas while including at least one primary exercise for the other three movement categories; work in both the horizontal and the vertical planes. By doing all types of movements and working in both planes, you will maintain strength and muscle balance. Master the form of each exercise before adding weight, increasing the range of motion, or attempting a more complex variation.

Upper-Body Pull Exercises

PULL-UP, CHIN-UP, FLOOR-ASSISTED PULL-UP

Muscle Groups Involved

Latissimus dorsi, biceps, abdominals

Performance

Stand in front of a pull-up bar and grip the bar with your palms facing forward and your hands shoulder-width apart. Exhale as you pull your body up until your chin clears the bar. Inhale as you smoothly lower yourself into a straight-arm hang. Do not allow the elbows to lock out at the bottom position or the shoulders to lift toward the ears.

Precautions

- To protect your shoulders, stop just shy of full extension in the elbows and shoulders to keep muscular tension at the bottom of the movement.
- If the palms-forward position is uncomfortable for your shoulders, try a reverse grip (with your palms facing your chest, known as chin-ups) or a neutral grip (with your palms parallel).
- To protect the lower back, avoid swinging the legs or whipping the body upward.

Variations

- To perform a floor-assisted pull-up, position an empty barbell in a squat rack at nose level and use your feet to provide assistance to help raise yourself up. At the start position, knees should be slightly forward of the barbell so you can avoid hyperextending the back at the top.

- Use grip devices, rock rings, or dowels (to mimic movements in ice climbing) to work on particular grips.
- To progress to the full pull-up, once a week do negatives, which focus on the eccentric (lowering) portion of the movement, until you can lower yourself slowly over 20 to 30 seconds.
- To increase resistance as needed, hold a dumbbell between your knees or ankles, add ankle weights, use a hip belt with attached plates, or use a weight vest.
- Perform a weight-assisted pull-up on a Nautilus or a Gravitron machine.

LAT PULL-DOWN

Muscle Groups Involved

Latissimus dorsi, biceps, deltoids

Performance

Sit facing a weight stack with your knees secured and your torso vertical or leaning back slightly. Grip the bar hanging overhead. A narrow grip recruits the biceps more directly and feels like a stronger position, while a wider grip targets the latissimus dorsi and feels more difficult at the same weight. Exhale as you pull the bar to an end point between your chin and sternum. Inhale and return the bar to the starting position.

Precautions

- Always pull the bar to the chest instead of behind the head to reduce the risk of shoulder injury. Keep your shoulders retracted at the top of the movement to prevent shoulder strain.
- Avoid pulling the bar any lower than the sternum, as this movement engages the wrists strongly in an awkward position. Keep the wrists neutral to prevent wrist strain.

Variations

- Use a handle attachment to work one arm at a time for unilateral balance and stability.
- Lean back to a 45-degree angle and pull the bar to midsternum to more effectively recruit the abdominals (this move is great for overhanging climbs).
- Use a palms-parallel or a reverse grip to emphasize the biceps.

DUMBBELL SHRUG

Muscle Groups Involved

Trapezius

Performance

Hold a fairly heavy dumbbell in each hand. Stand with your feet shoulder-width apart and your arms at your sides. Exhale and raise the shoulders straight up toward the ears as far as feels comfortable. Inhale as you lower. Press the weight down rather than letting gravity pull it down.

Precautions

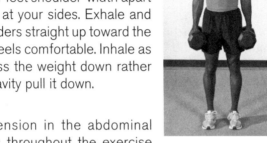

- Keep tension in the abdominal muscles throughout the exercise and relax the neck.
- Use lifting straps if your grip tires before your trapezius does.

Variations

- For barbell shrugs, hold a barbell in front of your thighs. Your palms should be facing down. Pull the shoulders up and slightly back to counter the forward position of the bar.
- Put a loaded backpack on the shoulders or hold the backpack in both hands by its straps. Complete the movement as with dumbbells.

HORIZONTAL PULL-UP

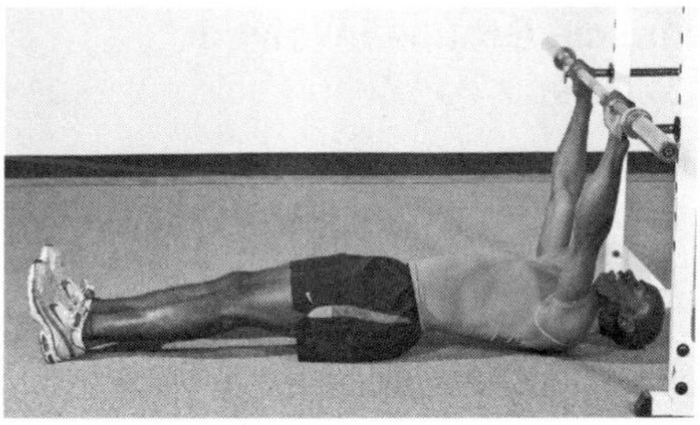

Muscle Groups Involved

Latissimus dorsi, rhomboids, biceps, abdominals

Performance

Position a pull-up bar in a doorway or a barbell on the safety pins or brackets of a squat rack. The bar should be 2 to 3 feet (.6-.9 m) above the floor. Lie down on your back on the floor and slide underneath the bar so that your shoulders can barely touch the floor when you grasp the bar with arms straight. Keep your knees slightly bent when you first begin this exercise and then straighten the legs as you progress. Pull your torso up as much as you are able or until your chest touches the bar.

Precaution

If you find it too difficult to do a few repetitions with straight legs, bend your knees and bring your feet toward your torso to provide assistance.

Variation

Perform this exercise with the feet slightly elevated (on a bench, step, or ball) to change the angle at which the latissimus dorsi and rhomboids are recruited as well as the difficulty for the abdominals and obliques.

ONE-ARM DUMBBELL ROW

Muscle Groups Involved

Latissimus dorsi, rhomboids, biceps

Performance

To work the left arm and left side of the back, stand on the left side of a bench. Place your right hand and knee on the bench for support and clasp a heavy dumbbell with your left hand. Use a neutral grip, with your palm facing the body. Keeping a neutral spine, exhale and pull the dumbbell up toward the left hip, and then inhale as you lower. When finished with the desired number of repetitions, repeat with the right arm.

Precautions

- Avoid rounding or rotating the spine during the movement.
- Keep the standing leg slightly bent and next to the supported knee to reduce strain on the back and knee joint.

Variations

- Perform this exercise with a dumbbell in each hand, maintaining a neutral spine and slightly bent knees, or use a barbell for bent rows.
- To more heavily target the rhomboids in a rhomboid row, turn the palm to face the feet and move your arm out at a right angle to the torso as though to make a half T. Complete as above with a lighter weight than you would use for the regular version.

SEATED ROW

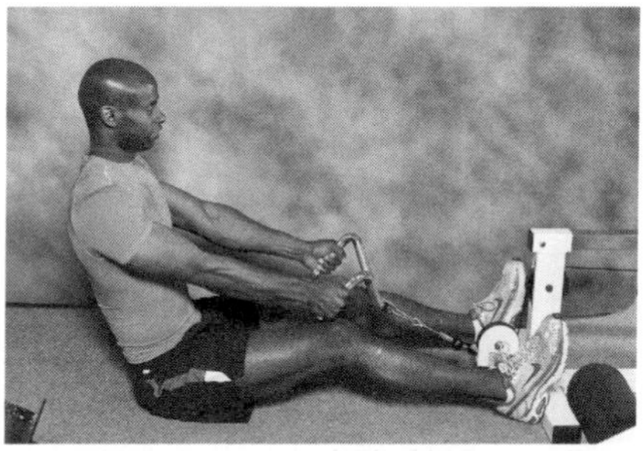

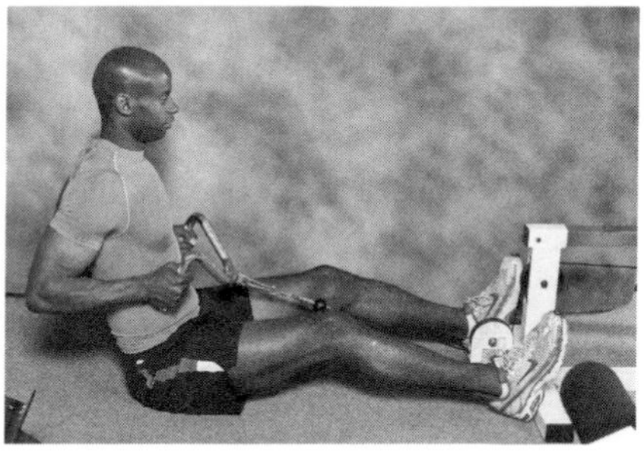

Muscle Groups Involved

Latissimus dorsi, rhomboids, biceps

Performance

Sit on a low bench or the floor in front of a row machine or cable machine. Keep a slight bend in the knees and the torso nearly vertical. Grasp a parallel grip attachment. Exhale and draw the attachment toward the rib cage, squeezing the shoulder blades together without allowing them to move up toward the ears. Inhale and release your hands slowly forward, allowing the back to stretch but keeping the torso steady.

Precautions

- Try another grip or a different attachment if you feel pain in the shoulders.
- Control the weight as you complete each repetition.
- Keep the shoulders down to recruit the muscles in the middle back rather than the trapezius.

Variations

- When you are at home or just beginning with this exercise, you can try the band row. Sit on a floor with a heavy resistance band (or several light bands) looped around your feet. Grasp the fee ends of the band with your hands and keep your knees slightly bent. With your palms parallel or facedown, relax the shoulders and pull your hands toward the ribs, keeping your torso still.
- For unilateral training, use a single handle and slightly rotate the torso to the side as you pull the handle toward your ribs.

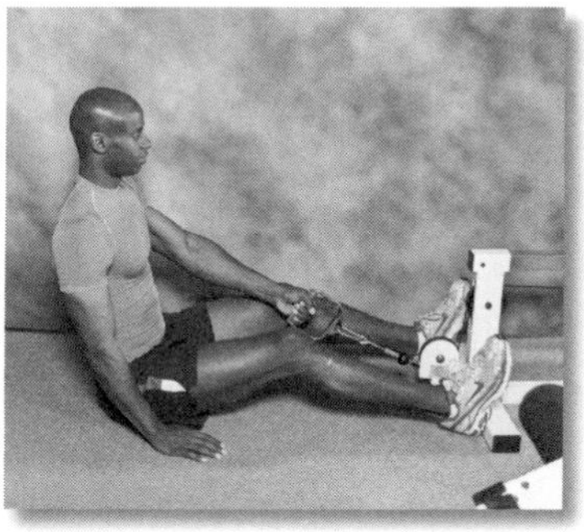

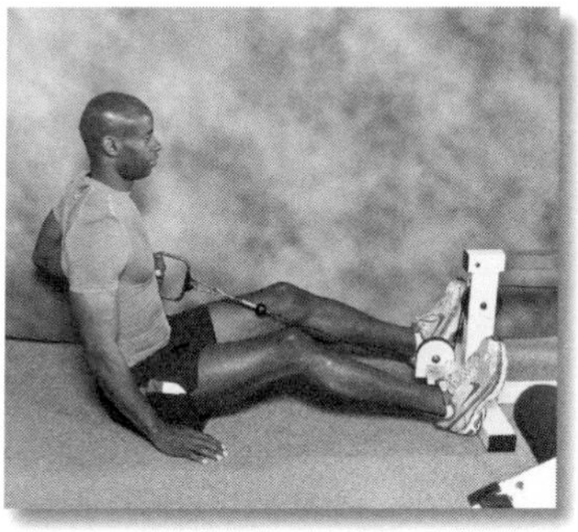

Upper-Body Pull Exercises

BICEPS CURL

Muscle Groups Involved

Biceps, forearms

Performance

Stand with your feet shoulder-width apart and hold a dumbbell in each hand. Your palms may face forward and away from the body (for traditional curls) or toward the thighs (for hammer curls). Keep your elbows close to your body; do not allow them to come forward of the shoulders or away from the sides. Exhale and lift the weights up toward the shoulders. Inhale and lower the weights to the thighs. Control the weight in both directions.

Precautions

- Avoid using too heavy a weight to prevent yourself from swinging the dumbbell.
- Reduce the weight if you feel discomfort.

Variation

- Use a barbell or an EZ bar, palms forward. Exhale to lift; inhale to lower.

STRAIGHT-ARM STANDING LAT PULL-DOWN

Muscle Groups Involved

Latissimus dorsi, chest, triceps, abdominals

Performance

Stand facing a lightly loaded top-attachment cable stack. Your feet should be hip-width apart, your abdominals tight, your arms nearly straight, and your body upright. Grasp the bar above your head and exhale as you arc it toward your thighs, stopping just in front of the legs without allowing it to touch. Inhale as you return the bar to the start position. Keep a light, open grip on the bar to prevent pulling.

Precautions

- Avoid leaning excessively forward to recruit the abdominals.
- Avoid bending the elbows, as this turns the exercise into a triceps exercise.
- Limit your top range of motion to the bar just below shoulder level if you have any shoulder issues.
- To prevent discomfort in the lower back, stagger your feet (one in front of the other) for a more stable platform.

Variations

- Use a lat bar or whatever attachment feels most comfortable to you.
- Use single-handle attachments for unilateral training for paddling, climbing, or skiing.

BENT-OVER DUMBBELL RAISE

Muscle Groups Involved

Rear deltoids, rhomboids

Performance

From a standing position, hinge forward at the hips until your torso is parallel to the floor. Hold light dumbbells with your palms facing each other and your elbows slightly bent. Initiate the lifting movement from your back and shoulders by squeezing the shoulder blades together and raising the arms out to the side (think of a big bird spreading its wings) to target rear deltoids and rhomboids. Exhale as you lift and inhale as you lower.

Precautions

- Avoid using excessive momentum or too much weight.
- Keep your legs soft, back flat, chest lifted, and head neutral to avoid straining your hamstrings or lower back.

Variations

- To perform the seated dumbbell raise, sit with your torso leaning over your thighs and your hands hanging down and facing your shins. Exhale and squeeze the shoulder blades together as you raise your arms to shoulder level. Inhale and lower.
- Perform the incline dumbbell raise by sitting facing into an incline bench (at an angle of 30-45 degrees). Keep your arms slightly curved and exhale to bring your elbows up toward the ceiling, squeezing your shoulder blades together. Inhale as you lower.

DUMBBELL OVERHEAD PRESS

Muscle Groups Involved

Deltoids, triceps, abdominals, spinal erectors

Performance

Stand with your feet shoulder-width apart, a dumbbell in each hand with your palms parallel or facing forward, and your knees slightly bent. Exhale as you press the dumbbells overhead and slightly forward, keeping your abdominals tight and your shoulders directly over your hips. Inhale as you lower the weight.

Precautions

- If you feel discomfort in the lower back, find a neutral spine by tightly contracting your abdominals and keeping your back relaxed.
- If you feel discomfort in the shoulders, change hand positions (from parallel to facing forward or vice versa) or use a lighter weight.

Variations

- Stagger your stance (one foot in front of the other) or perform this exercise against a wall with your gluteals and shoulders touching the wall.
- Complete the exercise while sitting on a bench with or without vertical back support.
- The Arnold dumbbell press targets both medial and anterior deltoids; start with reversed palms in front of your chest and rotate the palms forward at the top of the movement.

BARBELL MILITARY PRESS

Muscle Groups Involved

Deltoids, triceps; also abdominals, spinal erectors (as stabilizers)

Performance

Stand inside or in front of a squat rack with the barbell held in brackets or safety pins just below shoulder level. Keep your abdominals tight, spine neutral, and knees soft. Position your hands on the bar several inches wider than shoulder-width apart; allow them to face forward. Exhale as you press the barbell up overhead without locking out the elbows. Inhale as you lower the barbell to your sternum.

Precautions

- If you have any shoulder instability, try this exercise with dumbbells, palms parallel.
- Avoid using too heavy a weight to prevent overextending the back.

Variations

- Experiment with using an EZ bar or dumbbells for this exercise.
- For the standing push press, stagger your stance for increased stability and use a very small leg push to increase power through the core, shoulders, and legs.

DUMBBELL BENCH PRESS

Muscle Groups Involved

Pectorals, triceps, deltoids

Performance

Lie on a bench with your feet wide and flat on the floor and dumbbells in both hands. Start with the weights directly over your shoulders; your palms may be parallel or may face your feet. Inhale and lower the weight toward your shoulders by bending the elbows; exhale as you lift the weight back up with control. Trace the letter *A* with the dumbbells, bringing them together without clinking at the top.

Precautions

- If you have a tall bench or short legs and your back arches or your feet cannot stay flat on the floor during the exercise, raise your feet either on the bench, on a step, or on weight plates to keep your upper thighs parallel to the floor, your feet flat, and your spine neutral.
- If you experience any shoulder discomfort, reduce the load to enable full range of motion, try an incline or a decline bench, or try a different hand position.
- For low repetitions (less than 5) involving heavy weight, use a spotter to help you get into position.

Variations

- Like the plank, the bench press has numerous variations that depend on the angle of the bench (incline, flat, decline), the equipment used (dumbbells, barbells, bands), the width of the grip, and the thickness of the barbell or dumbbells.
- The wider your grip on the barbell, the lighter the weight you should use; a wider grip directly hits the outer pectorals, less so the triceps. Always use a spotter for safety when lifting a heavy barbell.
- Perform the bench press on an incline bench to target deltoids and upper pectorals.
- Perform the bench press on a decline bench to target the lower pectorals.

NARROW-GRIP BARBELL BENCH PRESS

Muscle Groups Involved

Triceps, deltoids, pectorals

Performance

Lie on a bench with your feet wide and flat on the floor. Position your hands just outside your rib cage in a narrow grip of 10 to 16 inches (25-41 cm) on a barbell. Inhale and lower the barbell, tucking your elbows in close to the rib cage. Exhale as you press up. The weight will be lower on your sternum than it is during a standard bench press.

Precautions

- Keep your wrists neutral and support the bar on the pads of your hands, not your palms or fingers.
- If you experience lower-back pain, place your feet on the bench, on a step, or on weight plates to maintain a neutral spine and keep the upper thighs parallel to the floor and feet flat.

Variation

To perform the same exercise with dumbbells, keep your palms parallel (in a neutral grip) and your elbows tucked in close to your ribs. Your forearms should remain perpendicular to the floor throughout the exercise.

PUSH-UP

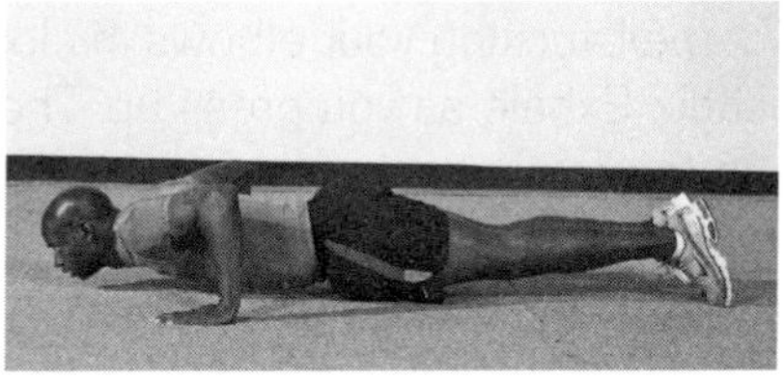

Muscle Groups Involved

Chest, triceps, deltoids, abdominals

Performance

Start on your hands and toes with your hands shoulder-width apart, your abdominals tight, and your torso in a straight line from the shoulders to the feet. Inhale as you bend your elbows and lower your nose to the floor, and exhale as you straighten your arms and press upward. Keep your head in line with your spine and look at the floor; avoid locking the elbows at the top of the movement.

Precautions

- If you experience any wrist discomfort, perform the push-up on your knuckles or on push-up bars or place hex dumbbells under your palms to keep your wrists neutral.
- Limit your range of motion to a right angle in the elbows if you have any shoulder issues.
- To prevent lower-back discomfort, keep your abdominals tight and your hips slightly raised.

Variations

- If the toe push-up is too difficult, perform this exercise on your hands and knees, or try placing your hands on an elevated bench (the incline makes it easier).
- To progress from the knee to the toe push-up, begin by lowering down while on your toes, then lower your knees at the bottom position and press up while still on your knees. Repeat by returning to your toes before lowering once again.
- Elevate your feet on a low 4- to 10-inch (10-25 cm) bench or place your knees, shins, or toes on a stability ball to increase the difficulty.
- Add a backpack or weight vest to increase the intensity.
- Perform a narrow-grip push-up with your hands close to the ribs to target the triceps.

DUMBBELL FLY

Muscle Groups Involved

Pectorals, deltoids

Performance

Lie on your back on a bench with a dumbbell in each hand and your palms facing each other directly over your chest. Keep feet flat on the floor, on the bench, or on a step to keep the spine neutral. Inhale and slowly lower your slightly bent elbows directly to the side until your hands are even with the shoulders. Keep a slight curve in the arms to protect the shoulders. Exhale and return to start.

Precautions

- Do not lower the dumbbells below shoulder level and avoid locking the elbows at the bottom position.
- Keep your spine neutral by elevating your feet with weight plates or placing your feet on a step or on the bench.

Variations

- To build core stability, perform the fly on an exercise ball, keeping your hips high and supporting your head and shoulders on the ball.
- Perform one arm at a time on a ball or bench with the legs wide for support.
- To target the upper pectorals, perform this exercise on an incline bench.

PARALLEL BAR DIP

Muscle Groups Involved

Triceps, chest, deltoids, abdominals

Performance

Use parallel bars or a machine-assisted apparatus in which you position your knees or feet on a support pad that helps you lift your body weight. Begin with your arms straight, supporting your body in a vertical position. Inhale and slowly lower your body until your elbows are at right angles; lean slightly forward to target the pectorals more directly. Exhale and straighten the arms without locking out at the top.

Precautions

- If you have had previous shoulder injuries or feel discomfort in the shoulders when doing this exercise, do not include it in your routine.
- Avoid whipping the body or legs to get the last range of motion for a repetition. Stop the exercise before using poor form.
- Focus on allowing the elbows to go straight behind you rather than out to the sides.

Variations

- Use a weight belt, dumbbell between your knees or ankles, weight vest, or backpack to add intensity once you can dip your body weight.
- To perform the bench dip, sit on a bench. Position your hands on the bench edge, just outside of your thighs, with your fingers pointing forward and wrists neutral. Start with your knees bent and your feet close to the bench; the farther your feet are from the bench and the straighter your legs, the harder the exercise becomes. Inhale and bend the elbows until they are just shy of forming a right angle; exhale and press up. Once you master bench dips, place your feet on a 10- to 12-inch (25-30 cm) box or on a second bench or add weight to your lap to increase the difficulty.

BENT-ARM PULLOVER

Muscle Groups Involved

Pectorals, latissimus dorsi, deltoids, triceps, abdominals

Performance

Lie lengthwise along a flat bench with your feet resting on the floor and your head and shoulders supported on the bench. Cup one dumbbell in both hands and lift it directly overhead. Maintain a slight elbow bend throughout the exercise. Inhale as you lower the weight down behind your head until your arms are parallel to the floor or the weight dips just below bench level. Exhale as you pull the weight up to the starting position. Keep your abdominals tight and your lower back pressed into the bench.

Precaution

If you experience any shoulder discomfort, reduce the load or hold the ends of the dumbbell so that the palms are parallel rather than overlapping in the middle.

Variation

Use an overhand grip on a barbell or an EZ bar rather than lift a single dumbbell.

TRICEPS PUSH-DOWN

Muscle Groups Involved

Triceps

Performance

Stand upright, knees slightly bent, facing a top-attachment cable stack with a narrow-grip attachment. Once you have the attachment in hand with palms parallel or facing down, keep your elbows close to the ribs and pointed to the floor as you inhale. Exhale as you straighten the elbows and press your hands toward the thighs in a smooth arc. Make this a pressing movement rather than a pulling one.

Precautions

- Keep the abdominals tight, spine neutral, and legs braced to provide a strong base of support.
- Reduce the load or use a stagger stance if you feel any discomfort in the lower back. Avoid rocking the upper body.

Variations

- Perform with a single-arm handle for a unilateral version.
- Use a rope attachment, your palms slightly turned in, to perform a rope cable push-down. Exhale and press the rope down toward the thighs, flexing the heels of the hands out to each side as you reach the bottom of the movement. Inhale as your hands return to shoulder level.

LYING DUMBBELL TRICEPS EXTENSION

Muscle Groups Involved

Triceps

Performance

Lie faceup on a flat bench with a dumbbell in each hand. Your palms should be facing each other and directly over the shoulders. Inhale and slowly lower the dumbbells to your shoulders, keeping your arms tucked in close to your head and your elbows pointing directly to the ceiling throughout the movement. Exhale and raise the dumbbells back toward the ceiling.

Precautions

- If you feel discomfort in the elbow tendons, try a different bench (incline or decline) or a lighter weight.
- If you are unable to keep a neutral spine with your feet flat on the floor, elevate your feet on the bench, on a step, or on weight plates.

Variations

- For the pronated triceps extension, turn your hands to face your feet (thereby increasing the recruitment of the triceps) as you raise your hands to the ceiling, and squeeze as you flex the heels of the hands outward.
- Perform standing with neutral spine, slightly bent knees, and arms straight overhead. Keep your elbows pointing directly up to the ceiling and close to the ears as you lower the dumbbells behind the head. Exhale and lift back to the starting point. Use one or two dumbbells or an EZ bar.

BARBELL DEADLIFT

Muscle Groups Involved

Quadriceps, hamstrings, gluteals, spinal erectors, forearms

Performance

Load a barbell with the appropriate weight and set it on the floor in front of you. Stand with your shins almost touching the bar and your feet directly under your hips. Use an overhand or a mixed (one overhand, one underhand) grip and bend down to clasp the bar. Keep the spine neutral, press the chest forward, and hold the bar directly under the shoulders. Exhale and press your feet into the floor, pulling the bar to your thighs and moving your shoulders back and up without overextending the back. Inhale as you lower the bar to the floor, following the same path you used to lift it.

Precautions

- Coordinate the pulling movement so that your legs and arms work in conjunction with one another rather than contributing sequentially to the movement.
- Maintain the normal arch in your back (as for squats). Keep your shoulder blades contracted, head raised, and eyes straight forward.
- If you experience back discomfort, lighten the load or get coaching input on your form.
- If you use a mixed grip, make sure you spend equal time with the right hand and left hand in the overhand position. If your grip fails using the overhand grip, use wrist straps so forearm and grip strength are not the limiting factors with this exercise.

Variations

- For the dumbbell deadlift, hold medium to heavy weights in each hand. Your palms should be parallel and face the outer thighs and your feet should be shoulder-width apart. Inhale and push your hips back as you lower the weights until they are at shin or floor level. As you lower, keep your weight in your heels, the dumbbells directly below your shoulders, your eyes up, your chest forward, and your back flat. Exhale and lift upward, making sure your knees do not buckle inward and your chest stays lifted. Stand upright at the top position, leading with your shoulder blades, and resist hyperextension.
- A home option is the pack deadlift: Perform the deadlift while holding a weighted backpack by the shoulder straps or the top loop and bottom gear loop.

ROMANIAN DEADLIFT

Muscle Groups Involved

Hamstrings, spinal erectors, gluteals

Performance

Stand with your feet hip-width apart and squat to pick up a loaded barbell. Use an overhand grip on the barbell, and position your forearms just outside your thighs. Exhale as you pull the bar off the floor as in a traditional deadlift and end in a vertical position. Then bend your knees slightly (approximately 20 degrees) and hinge forward at the hips. Keep your weight in your heels and stick your buttocks out. Press your chest forward, keep your head neutral and your arms directly below your shoulders, and contract your shoulder blades throughout the exercise. Maintain a neutral spine. Inhale and bend forward at the waist until you feel a maximal stretch through your hamstrings, and then exhale and return to vertical, fully upright, with your shoulders back at the top of the movement.

Precaution

If you feel this exercise in your lower back, your form may be compromised. By maintaining a neutral spine with your weight in your heels, your legs straight and knees unlocked, and your buttocks pressing back, you should feel the stress in the hamstrings and gluteals, not the lower back.

Variation

To perform the dumbbell stiff-legged deadlift, hold a heavy dumbbell in each hand and use the same form used for the Romanian deadlift but with a neutral grip (palms facing outer thighs).

ONE-LEG DEADLIFT

Muscle Groups Involved

Gluteals, quadriceps, spinal erectors, hamstrings

Performance

Stand on one foot while holding a dumbbell in one or both hands. Keep the other foot lifted but near the floor in case you need to touch it down for balance. Hinge forward at the hips with as much or as little knee bend as you wish until you can touch the dumbbell to the floor. Exhale and return upright.

Precautions

- To develop balance and facility with the exercise, keep the back foot ready to touch down to provide support.
- More flexion through the hips targets the gluteals more strongly, while more flexion through the knee targets the quadriceps. If you feel any knee discomfort, try another variation or bend more from the hip than from the knee.

Variations

- To increase the difficulty, pause at the bottom, increase the weight, or add repetitions. You can also stand on a step, weight plate, or two-by-four for added range of motion or propel yourself upward as though you were going to hop.
- For the one-arm, one-leg deadlift, hold one dumbbell in one hand, complete half the number of the desired repetitions with that hand, and then, without changing legs, complete the same number of repetitions with the other hand before repeating the sequence on the other leg. To challenge your balance, alternate each repetition (right hand, left hand, repeat).

HAMSTRING PULL-THROUGH

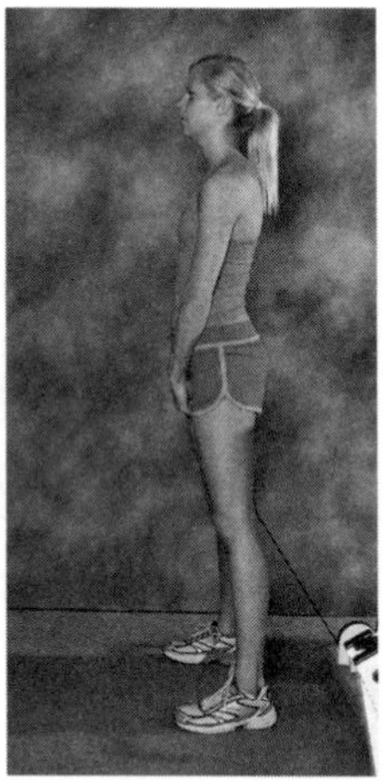

Muscle Groups Involved

Hamstrings, spinal erectors

Performance

Stand facing away from a low-attachment cable stack set up with a one- or two-handle attachment or a triceps rope. Bend forward at the hips until your torso is parallel to the floor. Maintain a neutral spine, and with both hands clasp the cable between the legs. Stand upright and squeeze the gluteals to thrust your hips forward as your shoulders and head come up and back. Pull the handle up as you exhale. Inhale as you lower the weight.

Precaution

Avoid overextending the back. If hyperextension is contraindicated for you, choose other hamstring exercises to build up your endurance and strength first.

GOOD MORNING

Muscle Groups Involved

Spinal erectors, hamstrings, gluteals

Performance

Place a barbell or safety bar at nose level in a squat rack. Grasp the bar with your hands wider than shoulder-width apart, and then step under the bar to position the middle of it low across your shoulders at the cervical spine. Step away from the safety pins and with your feet shoulder-width apart and knees slightly bent throughout the exercise, inhale as you prepare to hinge forward at the hips. Keep a neutral spine and press your buttocks backward slightly to keep your weight over the heels. Bend forward until your torso is parallel to the floor without rounding the back. Exhale as you return your torso and the barbell to the upright position.

Precautions

- Start with a very light weight in order to master form before increasing load.
- Keep the spine neutral and the shoulder blades squeezed together throughout the movement to target the gluteals and hamstrings and maintain form.
- If you experience discomfort in the neck while using a bar, hold a weight at your chest or wear a loaded backpack.
- If you lack flexibility in the hamstrings, bend forward until you feel them engage significantly but do not force the forward movement to parallel unless you are able to maintain a neutral spine.

Variations

- For the Zercher standing good morning, stand holding a lighter barbell in the crook of your arms, cross your arms, hold the weight tightly against your torso, and bend forward from the hips to complete the good morning movement.
- For the Zercher seated good morning, which is especially useful for paddling, sit in a wide straddle position on one end of a bench with the bar cradled as for the standing version or a dumbbell or weight plate held against your chest and hinge forward at the hips until you feel a maximal stretch in the inner thighs. Your elbows and the barbell, dumbbell, or weight plate will dip below the surface of the bench. Maintain a neutral spine rather than rounding forward, and exhale as you return to upright.

MACHINE LEG CURL

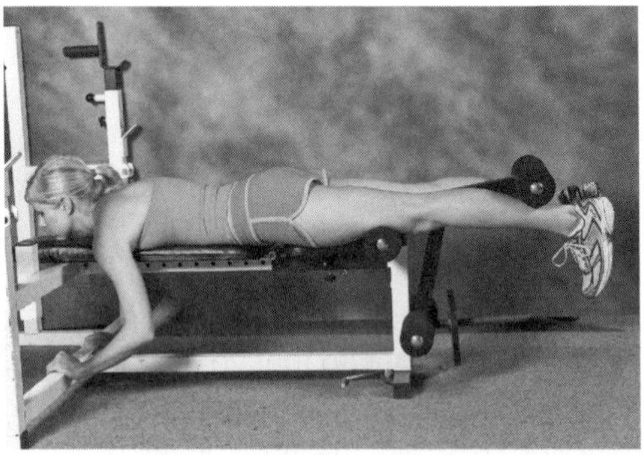

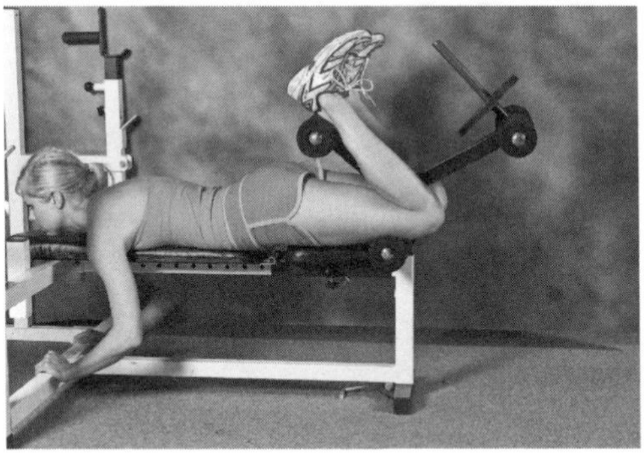

Muscle Groups Involved

Hamstrings

Performance

Lie facedown on your stomach on the leg curl machine with your ankles securely under the ankle pads or rollers. If necessary, pad your hips with a towel to provide slight support for the lower back. Exhale and contract your gluteals and hamstrings to curl your weighted ankles toward your buttocks. Inhale and slowly lower your legs to the starting position.

Precautions

- Avoid hyperextending the lower back; do not allow your hips to lift off the bench.
- To reduce the risk of a hamstring strain, begin with a light weight and use your arms only to brace, not to pull.

Variation

When working at home, you can (a) use ankle weights while lying on a flat bench or incline board, (b) lean across a ball for support and do single-limb leg curls with ankle weights, or (c) try the band leg curl by attaching a heavy resistance band (such as those by Jump Stretch) to a vertical surface (such as a table leg) and looping an end around your ankles. Stand facing the attachment and lean slightly forward. Brace yourself on the standing leg and exhale as you bend the knee and raise the foot behind you toward your buttocks.

BALL LEG CURL

Muscle Groups Involved

Hamstrings, gluteals, spinal erectors

Performance

Lie flat on your back on the floor. Keeping your ankles together, rest your heels on top of a stability ball. Exhale and lift your hips several inches off the floor so that you are in a bridge position similar to the bridge (chapter 15). From the lifted position, keep your hips high and use your feet to roll the ball in toward your buttocks. Inhale and return to start.

Precautions

- If you have a dominant leg, the ball may roll to one side or the other; have someone spot you by gently holding onto the ball while you try rolling it in.
- If your hamstrings cramp, rest your hips on the floor between each repetition until you build your strength and endurance.

Variations

- Do a one-leg ball curl by placing the foot of your working leg in the middle of the ball and holding the nonworking leg straight up in the air. Your hips may need to be lower than they are when performing the two-leg version. Keep hips squared to the ceiling to avoid twisting through the spine.

STANDING CALF RAISE

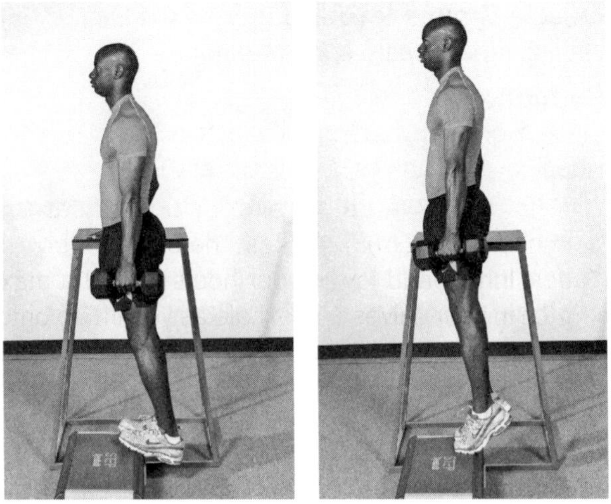

Muscle Groups Involved

Gastrocnemius, small muscles around the ankles

Performance

Stand with the balls of your feet on the edge of a sturdy stair. Allow your heels to hang off the edge. Hold onto a rail or other stable object with one hand for balance. Hold a dumbbell in the other hand or wear a loaded pack. Inhale and lower your heels as far as comfortable. Then exhale and lift onto your toes as high as possible.

Precautions

- If you feel any tightness in your calves, stretch them thoroughly instead of doing this exercise.
- If you have trouble with balance, hold onto something for support.
- Keep your legs bent very slightly at the knees, and squeeze your gluteals to feel an added stretch throughout the leg with each repetition.

Variations

- To increase the resistance, hold a dumbbell in one or both hands. If using one weight, be sure to perform the same number of repetitions with the weight in right and left hand so the calves get loaded evenly.
- To challenge your balance, perform the standing calf raise on one leg without holding onto any support. As with any unilateral exercise, begin with the nondominant or weaker side first and do only as many repetitions on the strong side as you can successfully complete on the weak side.

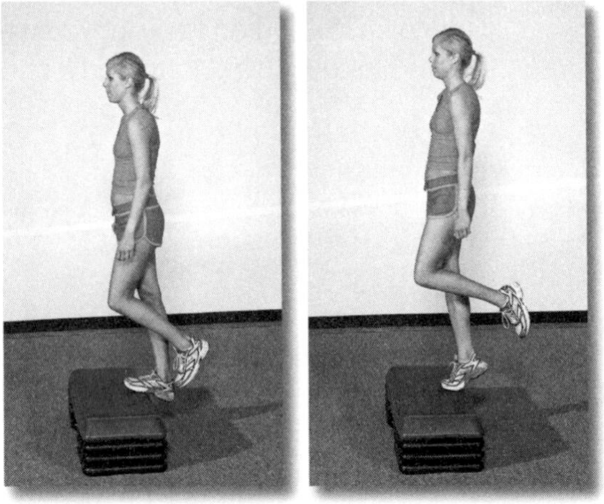

- A good home option is the pack calf raise: Perform the standing calf raise on a stair while wearing a loaded backpack.
- Other gym options include doing the leg-press calf raise with a Nautilus straight-leg calf raise machine or a Smith machine. You can also use a safety bar that allows the weight to balance on your shoulders without hand support.

SEATED CALF RAISE

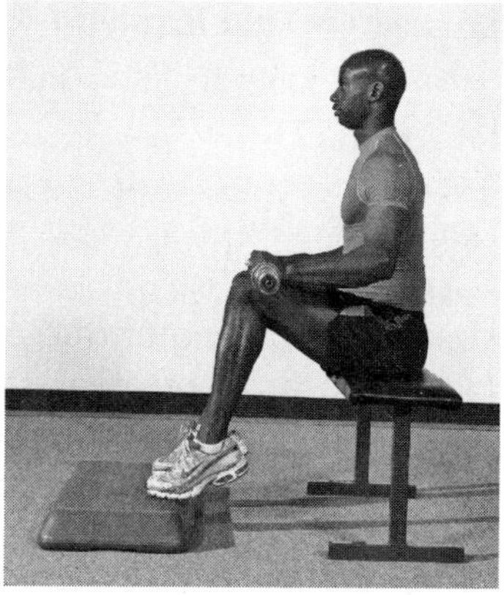

Muscle Groups Involved

Soleus, small muscles around the ankles

Performance

Load a barbell or an EZ bar with an appropriate weight and sit on the edge of a bench or chair with the balls of your feet on a sturdy step or bench that is 3 to 6 inches (8-15 cm) high. Rest the bar just above your knees. Inhale and lower your heels to feel a maximal stretch in your calves and exhale as you lift up onto the toes as high as possible. Many gyms have a seated calf raise machine that is comfortable, easy to use, and applicable to this exercise.

Precautions

- Pad the bar with a towel for comfort or wear sweatpants to protect your thighs.
- Avoid letting the bar roll too far back on the thighs or sit too close to the patellae.

Variation

If you do not have a sturdy, stable low step for your feet, do these calf raises on a thick, heavy weight plate that will not slide across the floor.

Quadriceps-Dominant Lower-Body Exercises

BARBELL BACK SQUAT

Muscle Groups Involved

Quadriceps, hamstrings, gluteals, spinal erectors

Performance

If you perform this exercise without a spotter, do so inside a squat rack with the safety pins adjusted at waist level to offer you a spot in the bottom position of the squat. Position the barbell on your shoulders below the cervical spine. Stand with your feet shoulder-width apart or slightly wider, your toes pointing out slightly, your weight in your heels, your chest forward, your spine neutral, and your elbows under the barbell. Inhale, remain tight in the abdominals, and press the knees outward from your midline and push your buttocks backward. Lower your body until your hip joints are just below your knee joints; keep your weight in your heels. Exhale and stand up to vertical, your chest up, your abdominals tight, and your back neutral.

Precautions

- Maintain a neutral spine with your shoulder blades contracted throughout, your head up, and your eyes forward.
- Coordinate the leg push with the back straightening to prevent overloading of the lower back. Straighten the legs and hips simultaneously.
- Master form before increasing weight. Consider squatting in front of a mirror to make sure your weight stays centered over both legs and your knees press outward.
- If you experience discomfort in the back, lighten the load or have a trainer check your form.

Variation

The wide barbell squat is an option for anyone with knee discomfort, as this variation allows for increased stability and emphasizes the hamstrings, gluteals, and lower back more than the quadriceps. Stand with your feet wide apart and your toes slightly turned out and squat, making sure your knees track over your middle toes. Keep your weight in your heels, and do not allow the torso to lean excessively forward. Sit back with your eyes up and your chest forward, as though you were lowering yourself into a chair. Exhale and squeeze back up into the standing position.

BARBELL FRONT SQUAT

Muscle Groups Involved

Quadriceps, hamstrings, gluteals, spinal erectors

Performance

Load a barbell in a squat rack and hold the bar far back on the shoulders in front of the body, with your elbows pointing forward. Keep the elbows high to prevent the barbell from rolling forward. Rest the bar between the thumbs and the forefingers (your hands will be snug against your neck) or use a crossed-hand grip. Keep your torso upright and your weight in your heels and inhale as you lower as far down as your strength and flexibility allow; exhale as you stand up.

Precautions

- For some athletes, upper-body strength (isometric hold in the biceps and rhomboids) will be the factor that limits how much weight can be used.
- Use roughly 60 percent of the weight you can use for a back squat, although if this variation is new to you, you should err on the side of caution until you have mastered your form.

Variation

You can perform this exercise while holding dumbbells on your shoulders. Some gyms also have special devices that make it easier to hold onto the barbell.

ONE-LEG BULGARIAN SQUAT

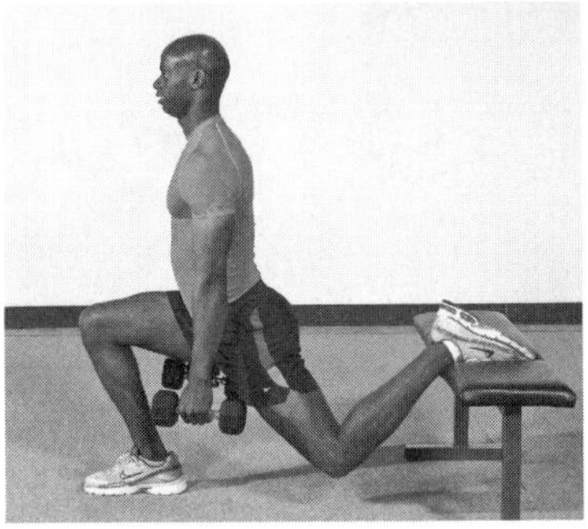

Muscle Groups Involved

Hamstrings, gluteals, quadriceps

Performance

Use a low, sturdy bench for this exercise. Hold a light dumbbell in each hand and place one leg behind you on the bench (toes or top of the foot is up to you) so that as you drop your torso toward the ground, your back knee approaches but does not touch the floor, giving you a very strong stretch in the quadriceps of the rear leg. Keep the torso vertical or slightly leaning forward.

Precautions

- If you feel challenged by balance, try this exercise first without the weight.
- If you feel discomfort in the forward leg, make sure the forward knee stays behind the shoelaces.
- If you feel discomfort in the back leg, lower the bench height or do a lunge version with the back leg on the floor. As your strength and flexibility increase, raise the step height or add weight.

BACKWARD LUNGE

Muscle Groups Involved

Quadriceps, hamstrings, gluteals

Performance

Stand upright with a dumbbell in each hand. Make sure there is plenty of space behind you. Take a step backward, ending with your forward and back knees bent 90 degrees and your torso vertical. Complete all the repetitions on one leg at a time or alternate between legs.

Precaution

If you experience knee discomfort, use a lighter weight or try a static lunge to eliminate the forward or backward movement.

Variation

Use a backpack or barbell instead of dumbbells.

DUMBBELL LUNGE

Muscle Groups Involved

Quadriceps, hamstrings, forearms, gluteals

Performance

Hold a dumbbell in each hand and stand with your feet parallel and shoulder-width apart. Take a natural stride forward with one foot. Keep your torso vertical, your shoulders directly over your hips, and lower your body until your knee is an inch above the floor. Exhale and press up through the heels to activate the gluteals. Return to standing.

Precautions

- If you feel discomfort in the forward knee, minimize the distance it moves forward over the foot.
- If you feel discomfort in the quadriceps of the back leg, shorten the range of motion or keep the back leg straighter; this exercise strongly stretches the hip flexors and quadriceps of the back leg.
- If you have trouble keeping your torso vertical, you may need to increase your flexibility. Try the static dip (see the variations section), which does not require a stride forward or back.
- If you have difficulty keeping your balance, make sure your forward stride is not too narrow; your foot should be placed in front of where the hip was when you were standing rather than in front of the other foot.

Variations

- For the barbell lunge, hold a barbell low across the back of the shoulders and then perform the lunge.
- For the static dip, hold the legs in the split (lunge) position and simply lower and raise the trunk by bending and straightening the knees.
- To perform the walking lunge, start as if performing the forward dumbbell lunge but link together 6 to 12 strides, keeping the torso vertical and continuing along a straight line such as a hallway. Trail runners, scramblers, and climbers can do the walking lunge unweighted while going uphill.

- To challenge balance and increase recruitment of the calf muscles, do the walking lunge on your tiptoes. This variation is an excellent one to do unweighted as part of a dynamic warmup routine.

LEANING LUNGE

Muscle Groups Involved

Gluteals, hamstrings, quadriceps, spinal erectors

Performance

Hold a dumbbell in each hand and position yourself as for a lunge. Take a natural stride forward. Instead of keeping your torso vertical, inhale and hinge forward at the hip. Your spine should be neutral and your chest should be down toward your thigh. Reach your hands and dumbbells down toward your toes and lower until your front knee is bent 90 degrees. Press through the heel of the forward foot to fully engage the gluteals. Exhale as you push back to vertical. Complete all repetitions on one leg before repeating to the other side.

Precautions

- Keep your hips squared forward to target the appropriate muscles.
- If you feel discomfort in the back toes, you can rotate your foot slightly to the side, though it will change the stretch in the back hip.
- If you feel discomfort in the front leg, reduce the weight, do not bend down as far, or try a different lunge variation.

Variations

- Add dumbbells, a backpack, or a barbell across your shoulders to increase the intensity as you get stronger.
- To add intensity to the gluteals, perform pulsed lunges by starting with your hands next to your toes and lifting your hands only to your midshins before returning to the bottom position.

STEP-UP

Muscle Groups Involved

Gluteals, hamstrings, quadriceps

Performance

Place a sturdy step that is 6 to 28 inches (15-71 cm) high in front of a mirror (a 12-inch, or 31-cm, step is a good place to start). The higher the step, the more range of motion you will have for this exercise. Start behind the step and place your nondominant foot on top of it. Turn your toes out 5 degrees. Keep your hips and shoulders squared forward at all times. Hold light dumbbells in each hand. Slowly lift yourself up, using the leg on the step rather than pushing off the floor with the lower leg. Inhale as you lower back to your starting position on the floor. Repeat. Progress this exercise by increasing the step height or adding dumbbells, a weight vest, a barbell, or a pack.

Precaution

If your knee is wobbly, if you feel any knee discomfort, or if the leg on the step buckles toward the midline of your body, reduce the step height, use a lighter weight, or turn your toes slightly outward.

Variations

- A home option is the pack step-up, a step-up performed with a loaded backpack.
- To perform the side step-up, stand to the side of the step and start with your feet parallel or with the foot on the step just slightly in front of the foot on the floor. Exhale to lift, inhale to lower, and be sure the leg on the step is doing the lifting—do not rebound off the floor.

LUNGE STEP-UP

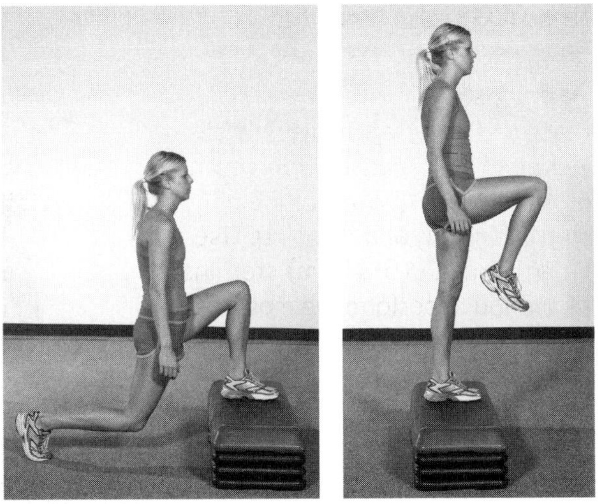

Muscle Groups Involved

Quadriceps, hamstrings, gluteals

Performance

Stand a natural stride distance away from and facing a 6- to 18-inch (15-46 cm) high step with your hands on your hips or holding dumbbells at your thighs. Stride forward with the working leg so that your entire foot lands squarely on the step. Then, in a smooth motion, lift onto the step until your torso is vertical without touching the trailing leg on the step, maintaining balance throughout the repetition. Reverse the movement, returning to the low lunge before pushing back into starting position with both feet on the floor. Repeat for the desired number of repetitions before switching legs.

Precautions

- When returning to the bottom lunge position, step softly and quietly so the muscles remain fully engaged. Do not let gravity drop you down to the floor; maintain control throughout.
- If you have trouble with balance going from the lunge to the step-up, touch the trailing leg to the step briefly until your strength and balance have improved.
- If you feel any discomfort in the knees, reduce the load or lower the step height.

Variation

Perform with a barbell across the back of your shoulders or wear a pack or weight vest.

REVERSE STEP-UP

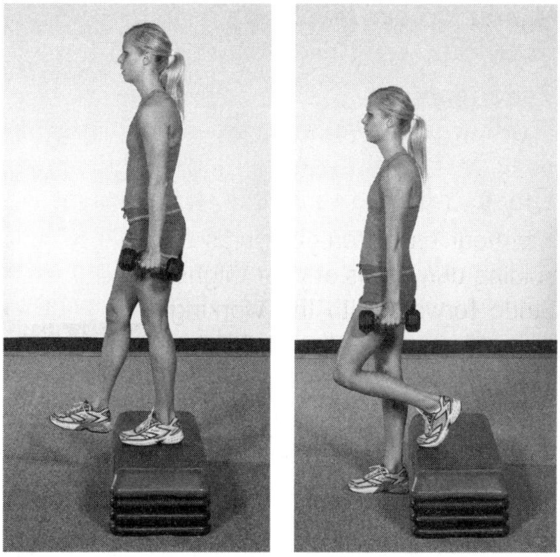

Muscle Groups Involved
Quadriceps

Performance
This is one of the most effective and specific exercises you can do to strengthen the quadriceps for downhill hiking and climbing. Use a 6- to 12-inch (15-31 cm) step that allows you to perform the movement without excessive lateral knee movement. Start on top of the step, with your toes turned out about 5 to 15 degrees and light dumbbells in each hand. Slowly step off the front end, rising up on the toes of your back foot as you do so, as though you are walking down stairs. At the bottom, reverse the movement, starting on your toes and using the leg on the bench to lift yourself back on top of the step. Maintain control on both the way down and the way up. On each repetition, make sure your knee is tracking over your middle toe rather than collapsing toward the midline of the body. Both the concentric and the eccentric phase of this exercise should last 2 to 3 seconds.

Precautions

- If you experience any discomfort while stepping, reduce the step height or the weight. Subsequent sets will feel more stable as the muscles get warmed up and the exercise becomes more familiar to you.
- Do not turn this into a one-leg squat (keeping your weight fully over the bench leg and dipping toward the floor). The movement is a downward step fully onto the floor, *not* a toe touch (the latter loads the patella more than this exercise loads it).
- Your step height for the reverse step-up should typically be a few inches lower than whatever you use for the step-up (page 275).

Variation
For greater resistance, use heavier dumbbells in each hand, a barbell low across the shoulders, a medicine ball at the chest, a resistance band looped under the step (keep one foot on the step at all times so it will not flip), or a loaded backpack.

LEG PRESS

Muscle Groups Involved

Quadriceps, hamstrings, gluteals

Performance

Position your feet forward on the machine foot plate so that your knees will form right angles at the bottom of the movement. Push the weight slightly off the machine safety stops and rotate the handles out of the way. Inhale and lower the weight by bending your knees to right angles, keeping your buttocks against the seat pad. Exhale and press the weight back up.

Precautions

- If you experience knee pain, reduce the load or try another foot position.
- If you experience lower-back discomfort, do not let your buttocks roll under at the bottom of the movement.

Variations

- Use a wider, higher foot position, pressing through your heels, to target the hamstrings and gluteals; use a lower, narrow foot position, pressing through the forefoot, to emphasize the quadriceps.
- For a unilateral variation, hold one leg off to the side as you perform this exercise. Keep your pelvis squared to avoid any torque. Start with your weaker or nondominant leg and let it determine how many repetitions you complete on your stronger side.

Appendix

Test Results Tracking Forms

Cardiovascular Assessment

For each cardiovascular test, record any changing variables (resistance, speed, ramp height, or power output) and the specified heart rates so that you can perform repeatable future tests. Before the tests, warm up at sufficient intensity to raise your heart rate to greater than 65 percent of your MHR; once you complete the tests, cool down for 5 to 10 minutes.

13-minute Aerobic Graded Ramp Test

Goal: to determine fitness level

Date and time: ________________

Mode: ______________________ Stride rate, speed, cadence: ____________

Starting Resistance: ____________ Starting (resting) heart rate: ____________

HR following 5-minute warm-up (at least 65 percent MHR):

____

Minute	Level	Resistance/speed	Heart rate
3			
6			
9			
12			
RHR 13			

Additional notes: ____

____

Sum of HR for minutes 3 + 6 + 9 + 12 + 13: ___________

Anaerobic threshold HR (if found): __________

30-Minute Aerobic Steady Field Test

Goal: to approximate anaerobic threshold

Intensity: 80-85 percent MHR

Date and time: ____________________ Target HR for duration: ____________

Mode: ________________________ Starting (resting) heart rate: ____________

HR following 5-minute warm-up (at least 65 percent MHR): ____________

Minute	Level	Resistance/speed	Heart rate
5			
10			
15			
20			
25			
30			

Additional notes: ____

____

Average HR for minutes 10 + 15 + 20 + 25 + 30: ______________________

Average HR for minutes 110 - 30: (SUM) / 5 = Approximate AT: ____________

Tabata Protocol

Goal: to increase anaerobic conditioning

Intensity: less than 95 percent MHR; reset to 0 at start of 4-minute test

Date and time: __________________ Target HR for final interval: __________

Exercise mode: __________________ Starting (resting) heart rate: __________

HR following 5- to 10-minute warm-up (at least 65 percent MHR): __________

Additional setup notes: ____

____

Highest HR: ____________________ Distance: ________________________

1-Minute Anaerobic Test

Goal: to gauge anaerobic progress

Intensity: as hard as you can go for a full minute; reset to 0 for test

Date and time:____________________

Exercise mode: __________________ Starting (resting) heart rate: __________

HR following 5-minute warm-up (at least 65 percent MHR): ____________

Working HR for seconds 55 through 65: ___________

Additional setup notes: ____

____

Highest HR: ________________Output or distance: ______________________

Strength Assessment

Allow at least 12 minutes to complete a single 5RM test and assess each of the eight strength exercises every 4 to 6 weeks. Be sure to include the three warm-ups and the prescribed rest between each. Circle tests where you fall below the recommended range as areas for immediate improvement and turn to chapters 4, 15, and 16 for suggestions on how to improve the different areas.

Date and time: ____________________

General warm-up for 5 minutes. Cardiovascular mode selected: ____________

Strength exercise: ________________________

Warm-up weight 1: Do 50 percent of 10RM to 12RM for 5 repetitions and rest 1 minute: _____

Warm-up weight 2: Do 75 percent of 10RM to 12RM for 4 repetitions and rest 1 minute: _____

Warm-up weight 3: Do 100 percent of 10RM to 12RM for 3 repetitions and rest 2 minutes: ____

Test 1: Add 10 percent for 5 repetitions. Weight/reps: ____________

Test 2: Add 5 to 10 percent for 5 repetitions. Weight/reps: ____________

Test 3 (optional): Add 5 percent for 5RM. Weight/reps: ____________

Pull-Up Perform pull-up with palms forward and hands shoulder-width apart (see page 242). Do as many as possible. Your goal is to complete 2 to 20 pull-ups. If you are unable to complete at least 5 pull-ups, then do warm-up sets on the lat pull-down or weight-assisted pull-up machine.

Date: ________________ Number: ________________

Number of pull-ups	0-1	2	10	20	>20
Rating	1	2	3	4	5

Dumbbell Overhead Press Do standing dumbbell press (see page 251). Your goal is to complete a 5RM using 25 to 70 percent of your body weight.

Date: __________________ Weight: _________ Reps performed: _________

5RM % body weight	<25%	25-49%	50%	51-70%	>70%
Rating	1	2	3	4	5

One-Arm Dumbbell Row Pull the dumbbell to your rib, keeping your torso still (see page 246). Your goal is to complete a 5RM using 25 to 60 percent of your body weight.

Date: ________________ Weight: ________ Reps performed: ________

5RM % body weight	<25%	25-39%	40%	41-60%	>60%
Rating	1	2	3	4	5

Dumbbell Bench Press Press dumbbells from your shoulders to above your chest, moving in the shape of the letter *A* (see page 253). Your goal is to complete a 5RM using 40 to 100 percent of your body weight.

Date: ________________ Weight: ________ Reps performed: ________

5RM % body weight	<40%	40-69%	70%	71-100%	>100%
Rating	1	2	3	4	5

Step-Up The leg on the step should lift the body up for each step-up; do not rebound off the floor (see page 275). Your goal is to complete 5 unweighted repetitions while using a step height that is 50 to 80 percent of your inseam.

Date: ________________ Height: ________ Reps performed: ________

5RM % inseam	<50%	50-64%	65%	66-80%	>80%
Rating	1	2	3	4	5

Barbell Deadlift Pull the barbell from the floor until you are standing upright with your shoulders back (see page 261). Your goal is to complete a 5RM using 50 to 150 percent of your body weight.

Date: ________________ Weight: ________ Reps performed: ________

5RM % body weight	<50%	50-99%	100%	101-150%	>150%
Rating	1	2	3	4	5

Medicine Ball Twist Lean back 15 degrees while holding the weight and rotate your torso from one side of your body to the other (see page 224). Your goal is to complete a 5RM (10 total, 5 on each side) using more than 15 percent of your body weight.

Date: ________________ Weight: ________ Reps performed: ________

10 rep % body weight	0	1-14%	15%	16-30%	>30%
Rating	1	2	3	4	5

Back Extension With your legs straight, extend your torso until it is parallel to the floor (see page 233). Your goal is to complete a 5RM using 20 to 60 percent of your body weight.

Date: ________________ Weight: ________ Reps performed: ________

5RM % body weight	<20%	20-39%	40%	41-60%	>60%
Rating	1	2	3	4	5

Flexibility Assessment

For each of the flexibility tests, record how close you come to the specified goal. Circle any tests that are difficult for you as areas for immediate focus and turn to chapters 2 and 14 for suggestions on how to improve those areas.

Frog Stretch Do the frog stretch (see page 217) with a dowel or pole directly overhead. Your goal is to squat with your heels flat, your feet shoulder-width apart or up to 6 inches (15 cm) wider, your buttocks touching your heels, and your arms straight and wide with the dowel directly overhead. See page 30 to interpret your results.

Hamstring Range of Motion Lie on your back with one leg straight along the floor and the other up in the air as close to your head as you can get it. Your goal is to stretch your straight, lifted leg until it is at least 90 degrees to your prone body without the other leg bending or the opposite hip rising off the floor. See page 30 to interpret your results.

Butt Kicker March in place, swinging your heels behind you to kick your butt. After 5 marches, grab one leg with the same-side hand and bring the flexed heel to your butt. Your goal is to touch the back of your thigh with your calf. Complete 5 more marches and repeat on the other side. See page 30 to interpret your results.

Lying Trunk Rotation Lie on one side, knees bent at right angles and hips stacked. Extend both arms straight out in front of the body with shoulders stacked. Your goal is to keep the bottom hip and leg on the floor while opening the top shoulder to touch the ear. See page 31 to interpret your results.

Reach Behind Back Raise your right arm overhead and drop your hand behind your head and between the shoulder blades. Reach your left hand behind your back and try to touch your fingers behind the back. Repeat the stretch, switching hands. Your goal is to overlap fingertips regardless of which hand is above and which is below. See page 31 to interpret your results.

References

Chapter 1

Hampson, D. 2002. $\dot{V}O_2$max: What is it, why is it so important, and how do you improve it? www.coolrunning.com/major/97/training/hampson.html.

Chapter 2

Friel, J. 2006. *Total heart rate training: Customize and maximize your workout using a heart rate monitor.* Berkeley, CA: Ulysses Training.

Siff, M.C. 1999. *Supertraining.* Denver, CO: Supertraining International.

Chapter 3

Tabata, I., K. Nishimura, M. Kouzaki, Y. Hirai, F. Ogita, M. Miyachi, and K. Yamamoto. 1996. Effects of moderate-intensity endurance and high-intensity intermittent training on anaerobic capacity and $\dot{V}O_2$max. *Medicine & Science in Sports & Exercise* 10:13.

Chapter 4

Ebben, W.P., and R.L. Jensen. 1998. Strength training for women: Debunking myths that block opportunity. *The Physician and Sportsmedicine* 26:5.

Haskell, W.L., I. Lee, R.R. Pate, K.E. Powell, S.N. Blair, B.A. Franklin, C.A. Maera, G.W. Heath, P.D. Thompson, and A. Bauman. 2007. Physical activity and public health: Updated recommendation for Adults from the American College of Sports Medicine and the American Heart Association. *Medicine & Science in Sports & Exercise* 39(8): 1423-34.

McArdle, W.D., F.I. Katch, and V.L. Katch. 2000. *Essentials of exercise physiology.* Philadelphia, PA: Lippincott, Williams & Wilkins.

Chapter 5

Askew, E.W. 1996. Nutritional needs in cold and high-altitude environments: Applications for military personnel in field operations. Washington, DC: National Academy Press.

Colgan, M. 1993. *Optimum sports nutrition.* New York, NY: Advanced Research Press.

Gastelu, D., and F. Hatfield. 1997. *Dynamic nutrition for maximum performance.* New York, NY: Avery Publishing Group. 283-295.

Hanson, K., and M. Hanson. 2002. *Planning an expedition to Denali.* Seminar presented at the Seattle Mountaineers in Seattle, Washington.

Harris, S.S. 1994. Exercise-related anemias. In *Medical and orthopedic issues of active and athletic women,* Agostini, Rosemary, Ed. 270-275. Philadelphia, PA: Hanley & Belfus, Inc.

Marion, J. 2007. *The cheat to lose diet.* New York, NY: Crown Publishing Group.

Price, W.A. 2008. *Nutrition and Physical Degeneration.* La Mesa, CA: Price-Pottenger Nutrition Foundation.

Chapter 6

Armstrong, L.E. 2000. *Performing in extreme environments.* Champaign, IL: Human Kinetics.

Cox, S.M., and K. Fulsaas, Eds. 2003. *Mountaineering: Freedom of the hills.* 7th ed. Seattle, WA: Mountaineers Books.

Chapter 8

Cox, S.M., and K. Fulsaas, Eds. 2003. *Mountaineering: Freedom of the hills.* 7th ed. Seattle, WA: Mountaineers Books.

Chapter 9

Bompa, T., and L. Cornacchia. 1998. *Serious strength training.* Champaign, IL: Human Kinetics.
Brookfield, J. 1995. *Mastery of hand strength.* Nevada City, CA: IronMind Enterprises, Inc.
Goddard, D., and U. Neumann. 1993. *Performance rock climbing.* Mechanicsburg, PA: Stackpole Books.
Lawrenson, D. 2008. http://www.muscleandstrength.com/articles/six-basic-rules-of-strength-training.html.

Chapter 11

Burke, Dr. E.R. 2008. Weight training adds strength to your endurance. http://www.active.com/mountainbiking/Articles/Weight_Training_Adds_Strength_to_Your_Endurance.htm.
International Mountain Biking Association. 2004. *Trail solutions: IMBA's guide to building sweet single-track.* http://www.imba.com/resources/trail_building/trail_solutions.html.

Chapter 12

Krauzer, S.M. 1995. *Kayaking: Whitewater and touring basics.* Trailside Series Guide. New York, NY: Norton.
Mattos, B. 2002. *Practical guide to kayaking and canoeing.* London: Lorenz Books.

Suggested Readings

General Outdoor Sports

Armstrong, L.E. 2000. *Performing in extreme environments.* Champaign, IL: Human Kinetics.

Cox, S.M., and K. Fulsaas, Eds. 2003. *Mountaineering: Freedom of the hills.* 7th ed. Seattle, WA: Mountaineers Books.

Sloan, J. 1999. *Staying fit over fifty: Conditioning for outdoor activities.* Seattle, WA: Mountaineers Books.

Waterman, J. 1991. *Surviving Denali: A study of accidents on Mt. McKinley 1910-1982.* Golden, CO: AAC Press.

General Training

Baechle, T.R., and R.W. Earle. 2000. *Essentials of strength training and conditioning.* 2nd ed. Champaign, IL: Human Kinetics.

Brookfield, J. 1995. *Mastery of hand strength.* Nevada City, CA: IronMind Enterprises, Inc.

Cressey, E., and M. Robertson. 2005. *Magnificent mobility: 10 Minutes to better flexibility, performance and health.* DVD. Indianapolis, IN: Robertson Training Systems, LLC.

Friel, J. 2006. *Total heart rate training: Customize and maximize your workout using a heart rate monitor.* Berkeley, CA: Ulysses Training.

Maffetone, P., and M.E. Mantell. 1996. *High performance heart: Effective training with the HRM for health, fitness and competition.* San Francisco, CA: Bicycle Books.

Siff, M.C. 1999. *Supertraining.* Denver, CO: Supertraining International.

Sleamaker, R., and R. Browning. 1996. *Serious training for endurance athletes.* Champaign, IL: Human Kinetics.

Nutrition

Agatston, A. 2003. *The South Beach diet.* Emmaus, PA: Rodale.

Brand-Miller, J. 2007. The new glucose revolution shopper's guide to GI values 2008: The authoritative source of glycemic index values for more than 1,000 foods. New York, NY: Marlow.

Colgan, M. 1993. *Optimum sports nutrition.* New York, NY: Advanced Research Press.

Eberle, S.G. 2000. *Endurance sports nutrition.* Champaign, IL: Human Kinetics.

Marion, J. 2007. *The cheat to lose diet.* New York, NY: Crown Publishing Group.

Wolcott, W.L., and T. Fahey. 2000. *The metabolic typing diet.* New York, NY: Broadway Books.

Technical Climbing

Ainslie, P.N., I.T. Campbell, K.N. Frayn, S.M. Humphreys, D.P. MacLaren, and T. Reilly. 2003. Physiological, metabolic, and performance implications of a prolonged hill walk: Influence of energy intake. *Journal of Applied Physiology* 94(3): 1075-83.

Braum, B., G.E. Butterfield, J.T. Mawson, S. Muza, B.S. Dominick, P.B. Rock, and L.G. Moore. 1997. Women at altitude: Substrate oxidation during steady-state exercise at sea level and after acclimatization to 4300 meters elevation. *Medicine & Science in Sports & Exercise* 29(5): 784.

Goddard, D., and U. Neumann. 1993. *Performance rock climbing.* Mechanicsburg, PA: Stackpole Books.

Lewis, S.P., and D. Cauthorn. 2000. *Climbing: From gym to crag.* Seattle: Mountaineers Books.

Messenger, N., W. Patterson, and D. Brook, Eds. *Science of climbing and mountaineering.* CD-ROM. 2000. Champaign, IL: Human Kinetics.

Soles, C. 2002. *Climbing: Training for peak performance.* Seattle, WA: Mountaineers Books.

Twight, M. 1999. *Extreme alpinism.* Seattle, WA: Mountaineers Books.

Trail Running

Barrios, D.S. 2003. Runner's World *complete guide to trail running.* Emmaus, PA: Rodale; New York, NY: Distributed to the book trade by St. Martin's Press.
Chase, A.W., and N. Hobbs. 2001. *The ultimate guide to trail running.* Guilford, CT: The Lyons Press.
McQuaide, M. 2001. *Trail running guide: Western Washington.* Seattle, WA: Sasquatch Books.
Poulin, K., S. Swartz., and C. Flaxel. 2002. *Trail running: From novice to master.* Seattle, WA: Mountaineers Books.

Mountain Biking

Barry, D.D., M. Barry, and S. Sovndal. 2006. *Fitness cycling.* Champaign, IL: Human Kinetics.
Friel, J. 1996. *Cyclist's training bible.* Boulder, CO: VeloPress.
Friel, J. 1998. *Triathlete's training bible.* Boulder, CO: VeloPress, 157.
Trombley, A. 2005. *Serious mountain biking.* Champaign, IL: Human Kinetics.

Paddling

Backlund, G., and P. Grey. 2004. *Easy kayaking basics: A paddling handbook for the Pacific northwest.* Madeira Park, BC. Harbour Publishing.
Glickman, J. 2003. *The kayak companion.* North Adams, MA: Storey Books.
Jacobson, C. 2007. *Basic essentials: Canoeing (Falcon guide).* Guilford, CN: Globe Pequot.

Snow Sports

Gaskill, S.E. 1998. *Fitness cross-country skiing.* Champaign, IL: Human Kinetics.
Prater, G. 2002. *Snowshoeing: From novice to master.* Seattle, WA: Mountaineers Books.
Vives, J. 1999. *Backcountry skier: Your complete guide to ski touring.* Champaign, IL: Human Kinetics.

About the Authors

Courtenay Schurman, MS, CSCS, is an avid outdoor enthusiast active in mountaineering, rock climbing, biking, strength training, rowing, and step aerobics. She is a certified strength and conditioning specialist through the National Strength and Conditioning Association. She has more than 10 years of experience training wilderness athletes, including amateur skiers, kayakers, hikers, and clients wishing to tackle Mount Everest or 100-mile trail runs. Courtenay has been a climb leader for the Seattle Mountaineers since 2003. She coordinates, develops, and teaches seminars and workshops in the Seattle area and offers outdoor conditioning consulting for clubs, groups, and individuals. She authored the chapter on alpine conditioning for the seventh edition of *Mountaineering: The Freedom of the Hills,* which has sold more than half a million copies; coauthored and coproduced *Train to Climb Mt. Rainier or Any High Peak* DVD (2003); and authored numerous magazine articles, e-books, and over 500 training pages for various wilderness sports at www.bodyresults.com. She is co-owner of Body Results, a company that specializes in outdoor strength and conditioning.

Doug Schurman, MBA, CSCS, is a competitive powerlifter and has been a certified strength and conditioning coach through the NSCA since 1998. Active in mountaineering and rock climbing, he coauthored and coproduced the *Train to Climb Mt. Rainier or Any High Peak* DVD (2003) and coauthored numerous wilderness sport articles at www.bodyresults.com. He is a qualified climb leader for rock, ice, and glacier climbs and has been a member of the Seattle Mountaineers since 1992. He is co-owner of Body Results, conducts wilderness sport fitness training seminars and workshops, and coaches wilderness athletes from around the United States to achieve their adventure sport goals.